PUSH THE

RIGHT

BUTTONS

A PRACTICAL GUIDE
TO BECOMING AND
SUCCEEDING
AS AN AUDIO ENGINEER
AND PRODUCER

BY NEIL KESTERSON

ISBN-13: 979-8-9890351-3-7

ISBN-10: 9890351-3-7

Printed in the United States of America

2 3 4 5 6 7 8 9 10

www.neilkesterson.com/book

Table of Contents

21. A Sound Education 463
  The Birth of Recording *463*
  The Soundtrack of the Prohibition *467*
  When Recording Writes the Music *469*
  The Father of Hi-Fi *476*
  Things That Go BUMP In the Night *478*
  Fantasound *480*
  The Lasting Legacy of Bell Labs *485*
  3D Audio on the Right Track *488*
  Listening to Light *491*
  Video on Vinyl and Other Turntable Transgressions *495*
  Is the Mix Tape Back in the Mix? *497*
  Analog Rules! *500*
  Get in the Groove! *502*
  Audio Letters to Home *505*
  When Old is Old Again *508*
  Wagner, Vader, and the Viking *511*
  The Rebirth of AM Radio? *513*
  Heads, Tails, Grooves, and Needles *515*
  Walla, Ripple, Plop! *517*
  2-Bits, 4-Bits, 6-Bits *520*
  The Color of Sound *524*
  Leftover Beethoven *527*
  Bong, Bong, Bong *539*
  I Might Not Can Say That Word *532*
  The Golden Years of Podcasting *535*
  Why Your Listeners Might Be Sleeping Through Your Every Word ... *538*
  The New Year '22 .... *541*
  Sound Farming *550*
  Is the Wax Cylinder the Next Big Thing? *553*
  SOFAR So Good *556*
  PSSST! *558*
  Requiem of the Bells *563*
  Pots and Pans: Cooking Up Stereo *566*
  22 Bazillion ● 2 Gazillion *569*

DEDICATION

To my parents, Walter (Owey) and Elizabeth (Libby) Kesterson. Their shared belief in how to raise a family and mutual encouragement allowed me and my sister Abbe to follow our dreams, no matter how farfetched. They were overachievers themselves, but made us feel like we were better, smarter, and would go further. They worked to instill in us the same sense of pride, achievement, and dedication they had in themselves. When I embark on something new and unfamiliar, my trepidation gives way to anticipation because I will remember my father just diving in, treating failure as just a trivial possibility. When I find myself slacking, I hear my mother nagging me to finish the job, do it right, and put a bow on it.

PREFACE

My memories of life almost always center around sound. My sister Abbe zeroes in on smells and tastes, while many others mostly recall visual details. I have many early memories, and one of the earliest is from a vacation we took to Lake Erie in Ohio when I was 3 years old in the mid-1960s. As we waited to board a ferry that would take us out to an island, there was a teenager holding a small transistor radio to his ear. It was turned up loud, and the music washed over the waiting crowd of people. The ferry's big, deep-throated engine was idling and couldn't drown out his little radio. As the breeze from the lake whipped a different direction, it carried the radio's sound with it, muffling the rock-and-roll tune. On the ride, the boat rocked back and forth on the Erie as me and my sister playfully ran from side to side with the sways, screaming as if we would be thrown overboard. I remember leaning over the side and listening to the crashing sound of the waves as they pummeled the steel hull. On that same trip, I remember hearing a muffled band, just out of sight, coming towards our barracks early one morning. We were staying at Camp Perry where my dad, a member of the National Guard, was training. When the Army band marched around the bend of the road playing a military march, it brightened up and was very loud and precise. The soldiers' boots stomped in tempo with the military tattoo. And man, were they good. My sister probably remembers everything she ate on the trip. The only food I remember eating is Rice Krispies out of the mini cereal box they came in. And yes, they did snap-crackle-and-pop that morning along with the pop-pop-pop of target practice as soldiers shot drones out of the sky and into the lake.

It wasn't until I was well into adulthood that I realized that I have cataloged much of my life into sounds. I was surrounded by unique sounds, how could I not pay attention? My dad was always singing little ditties around the house. My mom played piano and was often humming. I played the piano, trombone, and guitar. My sister had a gift for finding new music and would play it for me on the record player. Television was starting to dictate American life in the 60s, so the set was on if there was a big game, or it was movie night. When my Aunt Muriel would babysit me, she would turn up the volume of the television FULL BLAST when her soap operas were on. That was so she could be doing something in the other part of the house and not miss an argument, kiss, or murder. I usually fled to my room, but I can still remember hearing the distant announcer saying, "Like sands through the hourglass, so are the days of our lives." Dad liked to play classical music on the stereo all day on the weekends. He would sometimes put a Dvořák record on repeat and go outside for some chores. I think he liked to hear the wash of music when he walked into the house to cool off. We also had several cats and a yappit dog named Fifi. There was always some kind of sound inside our house.

Outside was even more interesting. Our little town of Ironton, Ohio was long and thin, sandwiched between the rolling Appalachian foothills and the Ohio River. Railroad tracks flanked both sides of Ironton. Across the river in Flatwoods, Kentucky were the large railroad switchyards that my grandfather worked at. The sound of distant train wheels rumbling on the tracks is like a calming sedative for me. I would often fall asleep at night hearing the train wheels rumble as the lowest earth-vibrating sounds rocked the window weights in our house back and forth like wind chimes. I now live near railroad tracks and the sound of the train moving down the tracks (there's one coming down the tracks as I write this, in fact) makes me feel relaxed just hearing it.

Ashland Oil had a riverside airstrip beside the trainyards in Flatwoods that their private jets would use. The breaking sound as they landed always sounded like a huge release of steam. We heard barges on the Ohio River as they made their way between bridges, sounding the ship's horn as they approached. We also heard lots of thuds, hisses, horns, and other factory noises from the steel mill and other factories down the river. My sister catalogued all the bad smells from there.

We lived on a one-way street that ran most of the five-mile length of the city. The firetrucks and ambulances traversed it to get to the east end of town and the hospital, so we got to hear all the different sirens. Our state senator Oakley Collins lived on our end of town, so when he was coming back from a legislative session in the state capital Columbus, he would travel the length of the town on our street, honking his horn and waving all the way home. At night, the few cars that went by were the police on patrol. The police department had five or six cruisers, and I could tell just by the sound which one was passing by our house. One cruiser had something rattling underneath, another needed a new tire, and the chief's car was a big heavy brown Dodge Monaco that purred like a tiger.

We had a Portland cement mine on one end of town near my grandma's house that would use explosives underground from time to time. We got used to the rumbles and pictures on the wall moving back and forth. There was a tragedy one day when a large fuel storage facility about a half-mile away blew up. When it happened, me and my parents were outside. The sudden and deafening blast was followed by a warm pressure wave as we watched an orange mushroom cloud ascend on the horizon. There was an earthquake one time that happened just as I was coming through the front door. I thought Mom and Dad were throwing furniture around upstairs. When I realized I was walking like a drunk from the ground moving, I ran back outside so that nothing would fall on my head. It sounded like distant thunder from Mordor all around me.

Sound has made quite the impression on me for as long as I can remember, but I didn't know I would eventually work in the sound profession. I just naturally gravitated to it because sound has been my strongest sense. It almost folds over into a few of my other senses. I've often seen colors associated with sound. In simple terms, a mellow sound is blue or green, something loud and sharp is red or yellow. I see little puffs of orange when I hear a steady putt-putt-putt of an engine, or a long bright yellow sword shape stabbing through the air from a high and loud trumpet note. These visions[1] are not distracting, they complement what I hear (I think it helps my audio production skills if I can "see" a sound before I find it). This may be why I gravitated towards being an audio engineer, to harness the vivid beauty or intense ugliness that sound can bring to

---

[1] Synesthesia is when one sense crosses into another. Most of us have some form of it. My type is somewhat common, but many experience much stronger reactions than I do.

our senses. It can affect our emotions, heal our woes, and take us places we've never been. When I finally decided to pursue a career in sound, I had no idea where to begin.

My life as a professional audio engineer and producer officially started in the mid-1980s. But to just get to that point, I went down a bumpy, uncharted, and foggy road. And it continued, even throughout my early career, to remain curvy and hilly, sometimes hitting a dead end. But I kept pushing ahead.

When I first started out on my path to becoming an audio engineer, I thought that recording music was the only way to go. I was surrounded by music growing up, I played several instruments, and the spotlight always seemed to shine on the music industry. But as it turns out, my path led me to an amazing variety of projects that I hadn't even considered. And because I have so many other interests than music, I believe this alternate path has enriched my life far beyond what I could have imagined. I've worked on soundtracks for television, film, and videos; advertising; radio; audiobooks; stage; live sporting events; games; novelties; undercover police recordings; and many other interesting endeavors. Oh, and I've recorded music along the way as well – it's in my blood. I have zero regrets about working on the "other side" of audio engineering because it's been just as rewarding, if not more interesting, than if I'd worked exclusively in music.

In my thirty-five-plus years in the business I can unequivocally say that I'm not the best engineer in the world, and I'm definitely not the worst. I've just made a decent living doing what I love and earned a little respect along the way. I'm not famous, I don't have studio gear with my name on it, I'm not in any history books or documentaries, and I'm not well known outside of my little corner of the world. So why would you listen to me about how to get into the business? Hopefully because I'm willing to share some of my experiences, good and bad, that influenced my career decisions and the way I work. Your experiences will be different from mine, but I hope you will be able to learn from my successes and failures. And yes, I had many failures along my way. Hopefully you will find your path to becoming an audio engineer a little easier than mine.

There were only a few schools to learn this craft back when I started my trek, now there are many. Most of my education is what you call "seat of the pants" or "on the job" training. I've been extremely fortunate to have had some great mentors along the way and I hope you'll think of me as yours when you're done reading this book. We'll touch on many subjects and problems you might encounter, most of which will have common sense solutions. There will be some technical instruction, but nothing that will melt your brain. There will be some business lessons, but none that will bore you to death. There will be psychology tidbits, but only ones that will help you get the most out of an artist – or sooth a difficult client. And finally, there will be some soul searching. I find that this is the most vital part of what I do, because there will be some very trying times that will make you want to give up, get worked up, or throw up.

I want you to feel good about your decision to become an audio engineer, because it's a really misunderstood profession. It's like magic or smoke-and-mirrors to most folks. People have this murky and shadowy idea of what we do. I hope to clear up some of the misconceptions, biases, and uninformed ideas of what it takes to be an audio engineer. You'll find out that it takes more than creativity; it takes determination, skill, thoughtfulness, and a little bit of luck. Now, let's pull back the curtains and reveal the tricks behind the magic.

PART I

DECIDING ON A FUTURE

1. SO, YOU WANT TO BE AN AUDIO ENGINEER

"If there is no struggle, there is no progress."

Frederick Douglass

I t's time for deep soul searching. No, this isn't a lesson in existentialism, but you do have your own free will to choose your direction. It's a plea for you to look inside yourself and honestly assess your reasons for taking a path into this world of twiddling knobs and pushing buttons. Of course, it's more than that, but a lot of people will view you as just that – a "button pusher." You may also be regarded as an "audio nerd," "gear head," "DJ," "audio dude," "audio gal," "one of the girls," "one of the boys," "You can't stand there, I need to put a light there," "You can't stand there either," or just "Hey you." And if you command a little respect, you may be called "Ears," or "sound guy/girl," or "You can't stand there," or "Hey you."

Still want to be an audio engineer? Okay, how about some more disrespect. In the video world, an audio engineer is rarely included in any mid to lower end production budget. First comes the camera (of course), the lights, the director, the producer, the talent, the grips, the location, the travel, the hotel, the craft services…the .."Oh yeah, we're gonna need someone to operate the boom. Oh wait, Chuck you can do that after you set the lights, right?" And this extends into video post-production[2] as well. Video editing software has become so powerful that sophisticated audio tools that correct common problems are included in many programs. Some video editors have a deep understanding of how to use those tools, but most only have a thin working knowledge of the

---

[2] "Pre-production" is the planning phase of a project, "production" is the actual filming or recording part, and "post-production" is the assembly and editing of the project.

intricacies of fixing audio issues and getting a passable mix.[3] But I get the feeling from time to time that some producers cross their fingers and hope that the audio will magically be glorious all the way from beginning to end without hiring an audio professional.

If you look back into television and film history before the 1970s, you rarely see the sound crew getting much credit. Most of the time it was just the sound company that got listed. Once they started to include a few names, they ended up late in the credit scroll, usually after craft services. Yes, we all have to eat before we can think about the audio. It really wasn't until Ben Burt (of *Star Wars-Indiana Jones* fame) came along that sound designers began to get top billing. And "sound designer" was coined by Burt. You have to hand it to George Lucas for recognizing everyone's contributions to his success. After all, he said – and I'm paraphrasing here –sound is half the movie.

Still want to be an audio engineer? Let's look at the decades-long stereotype (pun intended) of an audio engineer. We're pot-smoking, alcohol-fueled losers who just want to hang out in windowless studios with deadbeat musicians. We're not serious about business, we're in a nowhere job, we're just playing around all day.

I sound pretty harsh, huh? Well, I've heard every one of those assumptions, some of them to my face. I even had some of those same opinions and prejudices before I started working in a studio. I simply didn't know what to expect. My views were solely based on bad movies and TV shows, hearsay, or some of the wild stories being told about rock bands' studio exploits in the 1960s and 70s. I was also being judgmental. Funny how we humans tend to judge something or someone we know nothing about.

Even though I had those misconceptions about the audio business, I still wanted to be part of it. So, in the late 70s, I set out to find out more of what it meant to be an audio engineer. I started with my high school counselor and found some hard data about careers in the sound business. Much of this data was compiled from labor statistics by the U.S. government. It had salary ranges, job titles, growth projections, etc. Not quite as detailed as a job in

---

[3] Like my experience with video editing – I know enough to be dangerous, but can't effectively do the fine tuning without help.

construction or medicine, but I remember thinking that if this was the kind of job *not* to be taken seriously, then why was the U.S. government taking it seriously? I started to do some of my own soul searching. What if some of my assumptions were correct? I think we could pretty well pick any one of these disparaging labels put on sound engineers and find at least one that fit it perfectly. Some might even fit two or more. There might even be one person that fits them all (I think I've met him before). Part of my soul searching began with the question, "What if I encounter one of these studios that doesn't take anything seriously? What if all they want to do is lay around and do drugs and pathetically attempt to record music?" Well then that wouldn't be a place I'd want to work. I'd just have to move on.

I did in fact come across one of these places in one of my job searches. It was on a horse farm here in central Kentucky.[4] I kind of pushed my way in to an interview with the guy who happened to answer the phone. It *was* (notice the past tense *was*) a very nice place built into a former horse barn, complete with professionally installed equipment, great acoustics, and beautiful natural maple trim around all the rooms. I showed up in my coat and tie, opened the door, and was hit with a fresh blast of pot smoke. Now I'm not a prude, in fact I'm quite liberal when it comes to low-risk drugs such as pot, but I immediately thought "losers!" I was in business mode, but I kept reminding myself to keep an open mind. After all I was in *their* house, and I had requested the interview. There was one fellow on the couch noodling away on an unplugged electric guitar, his beer resting on the nearby coffee table. I remember worrying that when I got back to work it would smell like I had smoked a joint during my lunch break. The youngish owner, or whatever title was bestowed upon him, showed me around the modest studio. I noticed right away the huge mixing console in the center of the room. I don't remember the make or model anymore, but I was duly impressed. I also noticed that a previous liquid spill of some kind on its top had not been cleaned up. I was surprised

---

[4] The thoroughbred and quarter horse industries are a large part of the economy here in central Kentucky. Many horse farms are centuries-old plots of land with impossibly ornate mansions and stables. There has been a struggle for the last 50 years between developers and the industry over the land. The horse farm in my story sadly disappeared only a few years later, becoming a large upscale neighborhood with generic homes and streets.

that the console still worked. There was a layer of cigarette/funny cigarette ash over everything. There were huge stains of God-knows-what on the carpets. The studio windows looking into the performance booth were foggy from smoke. What had these pot-smoking, alcohol-fueled losers done to this beautiful place?

I immediately came out of full-time job seeker mode and went into damage control. I thought of just bolting, but I had already handed him my resume with my name and street address. I had to just politely talk with him and slowly work my way towards the door. In actuality, he was very nice and proud of his studio that Daddy Warbucks had built for him. He even played some well-produced songs recorded in his space for me. It dawned on me that he wasn't really interested in running a studio business, he just wanted to record his music with his friends. How could I think ill of him for that? I did want to give him a tongue lashing for not taking care of his gear, but it was his and he could do whatever he wanted with it. But I'm not sure Daddy was happy with it.

So, he did fit the stereotype somewhat. But in all fairness, he obviously wasn't serious about a career as an audio engineer. I was. Are you? Ask yourself what it is you want to accomplish. Do you want to be the greatest engineer ever? Do you want to own your own studio some day? Do you want to produce records and win a Grammy? Do you want to work in film and win an Oscar? Do you want to work in television and win an Emmy? Do you want to design game audio and win a G.A.N.G. Award? Do you want to work in radio and win a CLIO? Do you want to mix live music for the hottest music act in the world? Do you want to mix live stage plays and musicals and win a Tony? Do you want to design software and create the next Pro Tools? No goal is too high. And none too low either. That is if you're serious about your career. But I must buffer those aspirations a little. The reality is that there are very few of us that win those big awards. The rest of us are just living the dream and having fun.

Still want to be an audio engineer? Most of what an audio engineer does every day is solve problems, be creative, make clients happy, and go home at night with a sense of accomplishment. There are no awards for that, only rewards. How many people do you know that are truly happy in their job? I mean truly happy? Do they absolutely love what they do? Do they think about it when they're not at work? Do they want to grow and be better? Do they put pride and accomplishment before money? Are they proud to say, "I did this"? If not, then they may just be button pushers, if you know what I mean.

Happiness in your job does not come from where you work, or whom you work for. It comes from how you value yourself and your work. I have worked with people, in situations, and at places that I loathed. I admit that it sours your attitude a little, but you must always look *within* yourself when you're in these challenging moments. How can I rise above the distractions? How can I still take pride in my work? What must I prove to *myself*?

There will be times where you are the button pusher – undervalued and underpaid. My dad told me once that you aren't worth anything if you're not worth more than you're paid. What he meant was that you must be valued as a contributor rather than just a worker bee. You must prove that you're worthy of moving up and taking on more responsibility. This sage advice has helped me throughout my career. It has kept me from being a robot among other robots. There's nothing worse than having to work with a bunch of people who don't want to be there: constant negativity, continual gossip, doing the bare minimum, taking shortcuts. They are not proud of their work. They probably aren't even proud of themselves. In these situations, dare yourself to <u>do</u> better, not <u>be</u> better. Trying to <u>be</u> better than those negative nellies only lands you on their downward path. It becomes a competition about who can be less negative. Trying to be better than someone else can lead to smugness, arrogance, and pompousness. Trying to <u>do</u> better leads to a better work ethic, a better product, happier clients, happier bosses, happier you. Don't worry about the other stuff. Show up, shut up, and do your best work. The rest will come.

So, do you still want to be an audio engineer? Are you ready to ignore the snide remarks, battle the stereotype, and be proud of what you do? Are you ready to be humble, always strive to know more, and learn from criticism? Are you ready to tell yourself that you're a serious professional who actually loves your job? Are you ready to learn good business skills, be a self-promoter, and to build a career? Are you ready to be creative, solve problems, and learn new skills? If so, then let me teach you some real-world lessons that I've learned. This won't be a technical manual, although some engineering techniques will be explored. This will be a book about how to succeed as the best audio engineer and producer you can be.

2. How I Became an Audio Engineer

"Pursue your interest. As soon as somebody says you're spending too much time on something, you're on the right track."

Bob Lefsetz

Some young people know exactly what they want to do when they "grow up." I always envied them a little because I had so *many* things I wanted to do. So, I chose to explore several routes. It was this whole range of experiences and feelings and understandings that eventually coalesced into my realization that I wanted to become an audio engineer. You might even recognize some of yourself in my story. So, let me tell you about my erratic journey that led me to where I am today. Maybe you'll be able to avoid some of the potholes I encountered along the way.

Truthfully, most of my previous non-engineer experiences have guided me along the path to becoming an audio engineer, as farfetched as some of those may seem. Other experiences have helped me become a better engineer and producer. As you will find out, your path will probably be easier than mine because these days institutes of higher learning take this profession more seriously. Learning just the technical stuff will only get you so far in your job. You may not realize it now, but many of your life experiences and interests will be drawn upon as you create soundtracks, interact with artists, and build a career.

My interests have always been diverse, even since early childhood. But deep down, I always knew I wanted to do something in recording. When I was a tiny tot, I remember thinking that when every song on the radio ended, there was another band right there in the studio waiting to play the next song. When I asked Mom how they could fit everyone in there, she explained that they were just playing records. Although the magic vanished, I realized that I wanted to be the wizard behind the curtain turning the knobs.

When I started to seriously explore being an audio engineer, I was a teenager in a small town at the very southern tip of Ohio. It was 1978, and like a lot of high school seniors who were feeling the pressure to make hard decisions about their future, I honestly had no idea what I was going to do with the rest of my life. I had many interests, but none were screaming out at me – except for audio recording. But because that world seemed so distant and secret, I looked at more traditional career paths. I traveled down some very crooked and winding paths to get where I am, but I feel that my false starts and wide interests have helped me become a better producer. In a sense I have come full circle, because my mother told me, "I always, always knew you would be an audio engineer."

I was a child of the space race, and like a lot of baby boomers, I wanted to be an astronaut. This is my earliest memory of critically thinking about my career. The astronauts were squeaky-clean all-American hunks. Each mission was a triumph of mankind. How could you not want to be part of the great glossy machine called NASA that churned out hero after hero? I had a GI Joe astronaut and toy Mercury capsule.[5] I remember the two Gemini spacecraft docking. I watched Neil Armstrong walk on the moon. But it was the Apollo 13 crisis that peeled away some of that luster. I was, like the entire world, on the edge of my seat during the excruciatingly long wait for three candy cane-striped parachutes to come out of the clouds. Finally, the tiny little gumdrop-shaped spacecraft appeared and radioed Houston. I realized at that moment that space travel was really, really dangerous. That was the end of me wanting to be an astronaut.[6]

I've always loved airplanes. For one of my earliest birthdays, Mom and Dad took me to a nearby airport just so I could watch the planes take off and land. Today I go to air shows to get my thrills. Back in the 1960s and early 70s, fighter jets from a nearby

[5] Probably worth a fortune today if it had survived the "space" flights around my house.

[6] I always lied to myself that I could have become an astronaut if I really wanted to, but my poor eyesight would have grounded me.

National Guard airbase routinely broke the sound barrier over and near our town. They would create a sonic "boom" that would shake houses, break windows, and rattle nerves. My most unnerving experience with one was while our family vacationed at a nearby lake. Our cabin was nestled among the trees on the side of a hill overlooking the lake. I happened to look up to the sky and see a fighter jet zip over my head just above the tree line. I wasn't sure if I really saw it because there was dead silence. Then a split second later – KABOOM!!! That young cocky pilot had zipped the lake at the precise moment of breaking the sound barrier. That would make a lasting impression on me. But alas, fighter pilots, like astronauts, didn't wear glasses, and mine were Coke-bottle thick.

I tinkered with cars a lot and thought about being a mechanic. I always seemed to be surrounded by cool vehicles. I had a buddy who raced cars at the drag strip. Another high school friend rebuilt a 1930-something Chevy coupe from the frame up in his garage. I had a good friend who owned six cars while in high school. No lie. He parked them all in his parents' back yard. One was a 1958 Plymouth Fury (like the one in the 1983 film *Christine*). It had pushbutton transmission, no exhaust, and the front bolts on the bench seat were rusted away. When he gunned the giant V8, the front seat would swing back wildly until we were staring up at the headliner. As soon as he let off the gas, we would come crashing back down. That big throaty engine definitely made an impression on me.

Dad and I talked seriously about this profession. He had been a large vehicle mechanic's assistant during World War Two and still tinkered with cars. His dad and brother had been professional mechanics. Dad continued his military career until the 1970s in the National Guard and Army Reserves. He brought every kind of military vehicle home whenever he could – jeeps, personnel carriers, large trucks – he would have pulled a tank into the driveway if he thought he could get away with it. His day job was the city auditor[7] of my hometown Ironton, which, in a small town

---

[7] Dad got his accountants degree on the GI bill following his service in WWII When a very young me told him that I also wanted to be an accountant, he cautioned me off saying, "It's a boring job, you won't have any fun." He did though. He had an uncanny propensity for mathematics and enjoyed the big picture parts of his job, like municipal bonds, taxes, economic development, and budgets. Yawn. But as a person, he was anything but boring.

means you have access to just about anything. When the police department would get new vehicles, he would bring one home before they put on the decals and lights. We're talking about the *Adam-12* black-and-whites, right in our driveway.[8] We would sometimes try out one of those four-barrel carbureted police interceptors just outside the city limits on a curvy road. He would take me to the city garage and let me play in the old fire trucks, dump trucks, street sweepers, and the little three-wheeled meter-reader car. So of course, I was enamored with vehicles. But after asking around and looking at employment opportunities available back then, it didn't look very promising. Today is much different, as high-tech schools and certifications enable one to specialize and actually make a great living.

I dabbled in photography. Well more than dabbled, I worked as a stringer for the local daily newspaper. Again, my dad's experiences influenced me. He loved taking pictures and had a few nice cameras. His pictures proved that he was better than average and had a good eye for composition and lighting. When I showed an interest in photography beyond snapshots, my parents bought me an honest-to-goodness 35mm SLR camera – a Minolta SRT-101. It was the real deal, so it earned me a place on our school yearbook and newspaper staffs. My connections there led me to becoming a freelancer/stringer for the Ironton Tribune, the local paper with a daily circulation of about 30,000 in those days. I was too young to drive to most of my assignments. So, if no one could take me, I would ride my bike. I remember peddling up to the county courthouse or Kiwanis Club or some other lofty-sounding place on my yellow Huffy 10-speed with my camera and flash hanging around my neck. I would take a boring picture of some group that was being presented some boring award by some boring county commissioner. But I was having the time of my life. I was learning something new each day, I was being creative, I was being productive, I was being responsible, I was in the middle of news, and I was earning mad money to boot. This is one path I seriously considered more than once. Later while in college (more on that later), I was offered the position of chief photographer on this newspaper. I turned it down because I was already on the education

---

[8] Fresh *Adam-12* episodes were being aired during this time, so I was up on all the vehicle makes and models.

path and wanted to give it a chance. Working as a stringer was a great career lesson that taught me to be independent, responsible, and how to interact with others.

I've been a musician almost my entire life. I learned piano at the tender age of six from a woman who gave lessons out of her dad's house. He was nearly deaf, so he would sit in the adjacent room with the TV blasting at full volume while I attempted to play "Scaling the Wall," or some other song from the John Thompson piano book. My mother said she knew I was really interested in music when I would just tinker on the piano when I wasn't practicing my lessons.

My fascination with music continued. When I joined the grade school band at twelve-years-old, I wanted to play the drums. Sorry, we already have drummers. How about the saxophone? Sorry. How about the trumpet? Sorry. We need trombone players. I'll add that the band director was a trombonist. You know that funny trombone failure sound you hear in the cartoons? That was what I heard. Wah-wah-waaaahhhh. But I slogged on because I wanted to be in a music group. I continued to play through high school, eventually earning a pretty good college music scholarship to play the trombone.

Our little river town had cable TV in the 1960s. It was only 12 channels, but we got stations from cities miles away like Columbus and Cincinnati, Ohio and Charleston, West Virginia. The cable company reserved one of those channels for my high school's television station. That was pretty progressive for the time. It was in this little TV station that I first got exposed to production. I never took any television courses because I was so busy with band and the newspaper, but I hung out there with my friends a lot. Some of them had jobs in radio, so it was through them that I got exposed to radio broadcasting. My first time in a radio station was at WIRO-AM, which stood like a beacon on top of a hill overlooking my hometown of Ironton, Ohio.[9] Radio was a big part of everyone's life back then. My clock radio woke me up every morning to WIRO playing Ray Stevens' "In the Mood" being sung by chickens. They broadcasted

---

[9] NPR's Noah Adams also got his start in this very radio station.

our high school football games. I'd sit with my Papa on his front porch listening to Cincinnati Reds ballgames while swatting away flies. So, when I first set foot into the station, I thought I was in the Taj Mahal. After several visits to the shack on the big hill, I started to see under the layer of gloss. In truth, it was just another small-town, five-hundred-watt radio station that had old equipment, worn floors, and outdated furniture. But I loved being there because microphones, tape recorders, record players, and cables surrounded me. I was in my element.

Me at 12-years-old playing DJ in Jerry Miller's basement.

One of my best friends growing up, Jerry Miller (J.B. Miller on the radio), has become a legendary broadcaster in the tri-state region of West Virginia, Kentucky, and Ohio. He started out modestly – in his basement. Jerry's dad installed a turntable, cassette player, a crude mixer, and a microphone with a low-power

FM transmitter in it. The antenna was a small thin wire that dangled off the end. To the end of this, he attached a coax cable that ran to an old VW Bug antenna mounted on the top of the house. I could pick up Jerry's little radio station all the way over at my house a whole five blocks away. I had a "radio show" from time to time. I never knew what to say when the music ended, but Jerry did. It was in his blood. Jerry's older brother Bob was a DJ who became a staple of the Portland, Oregon airwaves. He used to pull up in his big sedan, open the trunk packed full of records, and say, "Go ahead and grab a stack of 'em." "'Em" were mostly network idents (music and voiceover or singers identifying a radio station or network), jingles, or bad country music. But I played them over and over because they were from the radio station! Jerry eventually got a job at WGNT-AM radio in Huntington, West Virginia, just down the river. Jerry was better than good. By the time we graduated high school, Jerry had bought himself a new car.

I'm not one that likes hearing my own voice, so you wouldn't have believed it if you knew me as a kid. One day Dad brought home a portable cassette recorder. About the size of a cigar box, it was one of the smallest for its time. Pop a tape in, press record and play, and talk into the handheld microphone. I was constantly shoving it into everyone's face and demanding they say something. I sang, yelled, read, and squawked into it. I recorded the cats hissing at me, the dog barking, the appliances, the outside, and the radio. It was a bit like taking a Polaroid and seeing it develop. The replay was more fascinating than the actual moment. It wasn't my voice I loved listening to, it was this incredible sound that was coming from this little box. I could make it sound different if I moved the microphone around. I even figured out a way to record layers of sounds. I would record background sounds on one tape player, rewind, start another tape deck recording, press play on the first deck, and make new sounds. Both sounds would be blended together onto the second cassette. I was layering sounds. I was in control.

During high school I became interested in guitar. My parents, who were great at nurturing our interests, bought me a decent entry-level guitar complete with lessons at the music store. I had great teachers, the last one being Dave Staton. Dave had rock-and-roll hair, a Zen-like demeanor, and could manipulate his long fingers around the frets like an octopus. One day he announced that he was leaving the music shop and giving lessons at his home to a few choice students. I was a little reluctant at first, because it had been a burden for my parents to drive me the twenty miles to Huntington every week, and his house was even farther away. But he said the magic words that would fuel my argument to my parents: "I have a recording studio in my basement."

Dave and his dad took one room of their finished basement and lined the walls with mattresses.[10] Over top of that was the obligatory wood paneling that dominated houses of the 70s. He had a Leslie amp in the corner, a bunch of microphones on stands, and a TEAC 4-channel reel-to-reel recorder. Dave taught me basic recording techniques such as loading a tape, setting levels, and overdubbing. In fact, I wrote a song and played all the parts over a two-month period. We started by laying down drums, which I had never played but always wanted to (remember grade school band?). I was so bad that I had to record one drum at a time. Thump, thump, thump, thump. Bong, bong, bong, bong. Rat-tatta-tat-tat. Splash, pause, splash, pause. Then came the bass, which wasn't too difficult, followed by the guitars. And you know I just had to use that Leslie with its motorized whirling speaker. Over top of all the other instruments were trombones. When you're working with only four tracks, you have to lay down three tracks, then mix (or bounce as it was called) those three down to the fourth track. You would erase the first three tracks, and then lay down your next few instruments. Those would be mixed with the fourth previously bounced track down into the last free track. Erase three tracks and start again. This is how the Beatles did it at first. You had to get it right from the beginning or it all went to crap, which the final product pretty much was. We counted about eighty tracks in all if I remember correctly. And eighty tracks of tape hiss. It sounded like I was on an ocean beach in a hurricane, but man was that fun. I was hooked.

The itch to record was now stronger than ever, and I needed to find out how to make a career of it. I asked my friends in radio how

---

[10] I would never recommend this as a way of soundproofing. They're flammable, might have bedbugs, and don't absorb a lot of sound.

to go about it without having to be an actual DJ and, you know...talk. Their replies were mostly shrugged shoulders. Someone pointed me towards broadcasting school, but the two disciplines of study were journalism and engineering. I was already a photojournalist by this time and not interested in broadcast journalism. I definitely didn't want to repair transmitters or build radio towers. I loved using radios and electronics, but not working on them. Besides, I was always tearing radios and tape recorders apart, only to find I couldn't put them back together. I would have to look elsewhere, but where?

As I got closer to graduation, the high school counselors were planting seeds among the upperclassmen about picking a vocation. They did aptitude tests, had military recruiters come in and give us their best pitch, and gave us pamphlets on different careers. I gave the Air Force a serious look, partly because of their excellent broadcasting reputation, and partly because of their superb bands. Had I chosen the Air Force and been a broadcaster, I don't think I could have gone wrong. I would have just traveled a different path in the same world.

One day I saw a magazine ad for The Recording Workshop in Chillicothe, Ohio. It advertised a six-week program to learn the craft of recording. It was an hour-and-a-half away, so Mom and Dad took me up to see the playground. It was amazing to walk into a real studio with quiet rooms and professional gear. They gave us a tour and explained the different programs they had. The full Monty was two or three months of intense instruction. That didn't scare me, but we had to give it some thought as a family. Although the tuition was a lot for our family, Mom and Dad were willing to pony up if it's what I wanted. And I have to say that they always supported me in whatever decision I made, even the hair-brained ones. Having parents that are behind you in your development can go a long way in your success. I just wish every kid had parents as great as mine were.

The one thing that worried me about going to The Recording Workshop was the short amount of instruction time, and then Bam! I'm out on the streets looking for a job. I tucked this option away in case I might need it. Like the Air Force option, it wasn't a bad one, only different. But I still couldn't find a school that offered in-depth instruction in recording and production.

I'm a self-declared nerd. I've always loved twiddling knobs and pushing buttons, and I admit to being a bit of a gear head. Although I'm not verse in all the different model numbers of gear, I know what I like and what works. I have especially always liked radios. My love affair with radios started with listening to WCMI radio from Ashland, Kentucky on my mom's white Zenith radio with a gold-threaded cloth grill that sat on top of the refrigerator. The rich sounds of music from that big speaker influenced my listening. Later on, my dad had a little cube-shaped Sony radio that he would put on the kitchen table and listen to Cincinnati Reds games on as he did somebody's taxes. When Joe Knuxhall was calling the plays, he would shut up and let the sounds of the ballpark paint the picture, sometimes for minutes at a time. We had a budget SounDesign stereo[11] in the living room that me and my sister would use to listen to a very different kind of FM radio back then. There were very few commercials, DJs would play whole albums uninterrupted, and there were groundbreaking comedy programs like *The National Lampoon Radio Hour*.[12] I enjoyed anything that was different than the mainstream. And so, when we could hook up the cable TV coax to the antenna input and hear distant radio stations that the cable company piped down the wire, it opened up a new world of FM radio from different markets. I was starting to see the power of radio.

When I was a teen, the CB radio (Citizens Band) craze hit America. The venerable CB radio was the star of TV shows, movies, and songs. 10-4 good buddy! Most of my friends had one, and I had several: a really nice mobile unit, an old tube base station that hummed like a barbershop quartet, and some Radio Shack walkie-talkies. Dad helped me put a big antenna on the roof, and then *Telstar* (that was my "handle" or on-air name, and a nod to my interest in space) was talking around the whole tri-state area. It was really a fun time to be into CB radio, because you heard every kind

---

[11] Our choice in rock music would almost blow up the speakers in this under-powered stereo. I built some bigger speakers for it later on that "helped" it some.
[12] 30-minutes in length. Many comedy legends got their start on this show, like Chevy Chase, John Belushi, Bill Murray, Christopher Guest, Gilda Radner, and Richard Belzer.

of conversation. People would talk for hours about one subject, sometimes politics or religion, but most of the time it was about a movie or TV show, the ballgame, or just about their CB radios. It was very similar to social media today. Sure, there were instigators, trolls, and crazy people on there like the internet today, just not as many. There were also comedians, like my friend Jimmy Herrell. Jimmy, a natural born entertainer, could fake a voice on the CB airwaves and have anyone thinking he was someone else. He could also fool you into thinking he had a better radio.

Let me set this up for you. Jimmy's uncle was an electronics nerd like me and Jimmy. He had a dedicated radio room in his house, and it was wall-to-glorious-wall with ham, shortwave, and CB radios. The centerpiece of that room was – CUE THE ANGELS – a Browning Golden Eagle radio. This was a beautifully designed vacuum tube radio that had separate transmit and receive units. When you keyed the mic (a superb Shure, by the way), the transmitter unit came alive out of standby, and the receiver muted. But the Golden Eagle had a distinctive "ping!" sound at the beginning of each transmission. The ping was really just the tail end of a short and decaying feedback from the receiver not muting quick enough as its vacuum tubes slowly went into standby. One day Jimmy called me and told me to meet him on the CB radio (even though he lived only a block away). Okay…I wondered what he wanted to tell me over a public radio frequency for all to hear instead of on the much more private telephone call we were already on. So, I turned on my radio, listened, and heard Ping!, "Flying Saucer to Telstar, come in." Was that a Browning Golden Eagle ping I just heard? I asked him if he was at his uncle's, and he said Ping!, "No, I got a Golden Eagle!" I dropped the mic and ran over to his house – that one block seemed like ten! Bursting in, I expected the Rolls Royce of radios to be bathed in a beam of heavenly light, calling me to squeeze the mic and hear that glorious Ping! But it wasn't on the counter where he usually sat when talking on the radio, his regular CB was there. "Where is it, in your basement?" I asked, still huffing from my ten-block run. He was stifling a laugh and pointed to the same old radio he'd always had. Beside it stood an empty glass and spoon. He picked up the spoon in one hand. While simultaneously keying up the mic with the other hand, he tapped the spoon on the mouth of the glass. Ping! "Breaker-breaker, Flying Saucer here." I was angry and impressed with him at the same time. This was an early lesson in manipulating the listener with ordinary household items.

Jimmy and I were in the high school band together. We had a fairly large band for a town our size.[13] There were usually about 150 players in the band every year, and we averaged ten players in the trombone section. During football season we marched with valve trombones, which resembled small baritones.[14] Three out of my four years in high school we received new marching trombones, because in those days the school systems were actually supporting the arts. We also had a band boosters club, which meant the students had to sell stuff like candy and raffle tickets. I usually wound up eating all the chocolate bars and owing the band fund. When I was a freshman, they decided to cut a record of our "Million Dollar Marching Band." One day a recording crew showed up, set up three or four microphones, and ran snakes of cables from the practice room down to their van. We played all the goodies into those mics, like our fight song, "Hold that Tiger" (we were the Tigers, after all), the alma mater, and a handful of popular songs. When I first heard the record, I couldn't believe that it was us playing. Once again, the magic of a recording had gripped me.

When I was of the age to form my music tastes, rock music was maturing and transforming. It was only about two decades old when I was a teenager in the 70s, so a lot of things had not been done yet. David Bowie, Pink Floyd, Boston, and Frank Zappa were not only cranking out great music during my formative years, they were also pushing recording technology into the stratosphere. The experimental recording techniques of the past were now coming to

---

[13] Ironton, Ohio had about 15,000 people in the late 1970s.

[14] I learned to play valve trombone early on in grade school when I broke my left arm. The band director, also a trombone player, gave me a modified slide piece that had 3 valves (like on a trumpet). The slide didn't move, so you just played the valves. Since I couldn't hold the trombone up with my left hand, I rested the bell on my left knee while I played. For those interested, a trombone has 7 positions. The valve sequence to emulate it is: Position 1=Valve Open, 2=Valve 2, 3=V1, 4=V1 & V2, 5=V2 & V3, 6=V1 & V3, 7=all 3 valves. This is the same descending order that any 3-valve instrument plays. During my whole career playing trombone, I saw both slide positions and valve combinations in my mind whenever I played.

market as mature formats. The stereo LP (long play record) was now commonplace. 8-, 16- and 24-track recorders with effective noise-reduction were cheap enough that home studios were popping up all over the place. Transistors had replaced vacuum tubes and made recording consoles, tape recorders, and microphones more compact, efficient, and cheaper (like the TEAC 4-track my guitar teacher had). The popularity of surround sound at the movie theater pushed into music as quadraphonic LPs hit the market in the 70s. Special equipment, such as a decoder and four speakers were required to play these, and one of my friends had the right setup. He was a few years older than me and was the leader of our trombone section. The band Chicago was still popular at this time, so we brass players worshipped their signature horn sound. When I first heard Chicago in quadraphonic, I thought I was going to jump out of my shoes. The horns were isolated in one speaker. We could turn down the other speakers and now hear just the horns. After we worked out the horn parts, we'd start the record with that horn channel turned down and play along with the rest of the band. We felt like we were part of Chicago. It was a lesson in learning to hear individual sounds in a clutter. If you know what something sounds like by itself, you can pick it out when it's buried down in with others.

In band, I eventually worked my way up to first chair trombone. I was really serious about music at this point, driving my parents crazy by practicing in my bedroom at all hours. It's the kind of homework that everyone in the neighborhood knows you're doing. When you're first chair, you're expected to be the leader of the section and to make sure everyone is playing his or her part. One day a man from Pikeville College came to town. I'd never heard of this college that was buried in the Appalachian Mountains way down in eastern Kentucky. Heck, I'd never even been to that part of the state. I'd never heard of the man either, but he was here recruiting for his music department. Jim Andy Caudill had light blond hair, light blond eyebrows, and bright blue vibrant eyes that were placed close together. When he fixed his eyes on you, he commanded your attention. You couldn't look away. Jim Andy was a fabulous trumpet player and had even played on the Tonight Show, so he was hot stuff. He was also a good salesman. He had us all believing that this little college would give us the opportunity of a lifetime. Several of us played a few tunes for him and then left school that day not thinking anything else about it. A few weeks later our band director, Ralph Falls, called me in to his office after band practice. Jim Andy had offered scholarships to me and a few others in the band. I remember thinking, "Me? What's so special about me?" But it was my first solid opportunity to go to college. I now had a plan – sort of.

Many of my fellow students who didn't know what they wanted to major in just went to school anyway, hoping to figure it out along the way. I almost did that. My older sister was just finishing up her degree, so the prospects of an eight-year financial drain on my parents had them pushing me to make a solid plan. I weighed the other two options in my back pocket: recording school or the Air Force. The Air Force route never really excited me. The Vietnam War and the backlash against the soldiers who returned home was still fresh in my mind. The cost of recording school was about the same amount of money that two years of college would be. It was a tough decision, but I think I made the right choice for that period in my life.

Mom offered one more option to me that I hadn't thought of – go to Nashville and try to make it. My mom, the one who went to college in her 30s while raising two kids, taught high school reading and English classes while getting a master's degree, the pro-education and literacy advocate, was steering me *away* from college. My mind was now a jumble.

I didn't know it at the time, but I wasn't mature enough to go to Nashville and hustle for a job. I'd never had a traditional job before. A paper route and freelance photographer are not your typical types of employment. I simply didn't know how to do it. I didn't know anyone there, I had little to no experience in a studio, and I had no training. It frightened me to death. Years later when I was feeling particularly blue about a job that was going sour, my mom said, "I wish you would've gone to Nashville when I told you to." I finally replied that I wasn't mature enough to. She nodded her head, "Yes, I suppose you're right about that. You weren't ready." What I needed at that time was a clear path laid out for me. I think a lot of young people this age that are trying to figure out life need to be pointed in a direction, whether they want to be or not. Once they're on a path, they can decide if it's the right one.

While weighing all my options, Mom and Dad said something that tilted the scales in favor of going to college. They told me that college was more than learning a career. There were so many other things I would be exposed to. I would learn how to write and communicate effectively, expand my knowledge of science, discover history, and experience other interests through electives. I would also make new friends, learn new social skills, and most importantly, be away from Mom and Dad while I became an adult.

So, there it all was, laid out in front of me like vacation brochures. Six weeks at recording school. Road trip to Nashville. Music program at college. Frying hamburgers at Wendy's. It was decision time.

It was a hot and muggy day when we took the exit off the highway and headed into town. My parents had driven me two hours to get here. The two-lane road wound past a few houses, a gas station or two, and a thrift store with a big picture window like the ones the fighter jets used to break with their sonic booms back home. It finally straightened out and seemed to narrow as we rolled towards the quaint downtown. A few moments later we were crossing a rusty bridge that had seen better days. I looked down at a green, sludgy, stagnant path of water that was about 50 feet wide, maybe a foot deep, and arched around this tiny town like a horseshoe. Its rank odor flooded into the cabin of the car. A river flowed here not too long ago. What had they done with it? God, what had I gotten myself into?

We climbed a steep hill on a desperately narrow street with sharp turns. Despite this road that seemed to defy physics, parked cars lined one side all the way up. They looked like precariously placed Hot Wheels that were about to fall down a staircase. The road finally straightened and leveled off in front of a clump of very scholarly-looking buildings with dry names like "Wickham Hall," "Record Memorial," and "Administration Building." From up here on the side of a hill, you could see the entire town. There was a steep set of ninety-nine steps that led down the side of the hill to the downtown. We were at the base of some buildings and the top of others. Looking up, I could see more buildings at yet higher elevations. This little college in the mountains really was "higher" education.[15]

I had arrived at Pikeville College (approximate attendance of 750) in the little Eastern Kentucky town of Pikeville, Kentucky (approximate population of 4,500) to learn music. More specifically, I was here to get a teaching degree in music. Jim Andy's piercing eyes and big smile had won me over. After check-in and a quick tour of the campus, Mom and Dad said their goodbyes and snaked back down the hill. Pikeville College, or PC as we called it, was a suitcase college. Only about thirty or forty of us stayed in our dorm rooms on the weekends. At that time, coal mining was the area's largest economic force. PC had excellent mining technology and geology programs that drew in students from the Appalachian region. It also had a solid music department with some outstanding professors.

I learned so many lessons that would impact my life and profession while at Pikeville College. It was here where I learned to really listen. Because our music department was so small, we had to participate in just about every ensemble: orchestra, jazz band, choir, pep band, etc. Being on one side of the stage and listening to the clarinets play their part before your cue comes up forces you to listen outside your range. Playing very progressive atonal music with odd meters and dissonant chords makes you tear each note down to hear where the piece is at that moment. Singing next to a fabulous tenor with perfect pitch reveals just how bad you are because the slightly out-of-tune note you're singing sourly beats against his flawless tone. Learning the real way to play a trombone, an instrument with a variable slide instead of fixed-pitch valves, allows you to make microscopic pitch adjustments. I also learned that when someone is yelling in your face, it's probably only to help you.

---

[15] The "Pikeville Cut Through" is the second largest civil engineering project in the western hemisphere, next to the Panama Canal. The U.S. Army Corps of Engineers moved 18 million cubic yards of earth while cutting a swath 1,300 feet wide, 3,700 feet long, and 523 feet deep. The project rerouted the Levisa Fork of the Big Sandy River, railroad tracks, and a highway around the flood-prone city. Since its completion, the project has undoubtedly helped Pikeville become a regional destination for tourists, students, businesses, and residents.

I was really looking forward to my very first jazz band practice. Jim Andy Caudill had the horns on risers in the cavernous auditorium in Record Memorial. As we warmed up, I still remember the velvety reverberation from the empty hall. Jim Andy passed out a few tunes scribbled out in his own hand and started the count off. We didn't make it through a few lines before he stopped us and corrected some wrong notes or rhythm from someone. Count off again. Stop again. This happened again and again. Suddenly, Jim Andy is worming through each section screaming rhythms into several of our ears, including mine. "DAH-DA-DAH-DAH-DAH!!! DA-DAH-DA-DAH-DAH-DAH!!!" If you've ever seen the 2014 movie *Whiplash*, you would immediately identify with this scene. Finally, as if surrendering, he waved his arms around, "STOP, Stop, stop." The place became dead silent, except for his decaying command reverberating off the back wall. He hung his head and peered up at us with a submissive smile. "Okay you freshman. Your eyes are all…" he made big circles around his eyes with his fingers mimicking a scared cartoon character. "I'm not yelling at you. I'm yelling at what's coming out of your horn!" From that point on, I totally relaxed and let him teach me jazz – even while yelling in my ear. I remember this experience every time I work with an overly excited director or pretentious producer. They're not yelling at *me*, they're yelling at what's coming out of the speakers.

One evening, me and a friend were digging through old records in the school's music library. On a desk sat a reel-to-reel recorder. After asking around, it seemed no one knew how to use it. Ah ha! I did, at least a little bit. I dug around and found a microphone and some tape to record onto. I started recording our jazz band rehearsals and concerts. I remember standing backstage in the concert hall, all decked out in my tuxedo, waiting to perform. With trombone in one hand, I would hit "record" and "play" on the reel-to-reel deck with the other as I walked out on stage. At intermission I would flip the tape over to side two and repeat the process. By default, I had become the designated house recording engineer. It was a step at least.

My guitar playing never stopped in college. I was playing, and even teaching guitar quite regularly. Trying to figure out a chord progression, singing over your strumming, or just simply playing lead with the radio will help you listen. I continued to listen – and learn. I was finally getting into the groove of college, and my playing was about to go to the next level. Then the hammer came down with a thud. At the end of my sophomore year, Pikeville College announced they were closing down the music department. Whoever remained would earn their degree, but no new students would be coming in. I assume that lack of funding was the main reason, but this was the beginning of the era when the arts were considered superfluous. Professors began to bolt. Students were bolting. With heavy heart I bolted back to Ohio.[16]

I took a few years off, went to night school while working a dead-end job in a K-Mart, and then returned to school full time at the University of Kentucky. Here, I was exposed to so much more than I would have been had I stayed at PC. We had about thirty trombone players, two jazz bands, orchestras, marching bands, operas, two performance halls, single-instrument professors, and dozens of practice rooms. There was only one problem: money. Because my parents had divorced and were not rolling in dough, I was putting myself through school as an out-of-state student, mostly on my own. This meant my tuition was two or three times as much as my in-state colleagues. I worked odd jobs around campus to make ends meet, at one time having four jobs plus a full class load. Something was gonna break.

And break it did. I like to think of it as my "lucky" break. I had started to realize that although I was a decent player, I wasn't good enough – correction, driven enough – to play professionally. I was also not keen on being a band director. At this time in the 1980s, Kentucky's public schools were in poor financial shape. Schools in cities would get tremendous financial support while rural schools would struggle to buy pencils. I know firsthand because I student-taught in several of these bad luck schools in Appalachia while at Pikeville College. This was quite a shock to me because, remember, I came from a high school that bought new instruments almost every year. One school I visited had a sousaphone held together with coat hangers and paper-mâché. I was not ready to be a martyr

---

[16] University of Pikeville recently restarted their music department, almost four decades later.

for music education, so I decided to start thinking seriously again about being a recording engineer.

I started taking those "electives" my parents told me about. I took some broadcasting, computer science, and astronomy classes. I talked my way into upper-level music arranging and composition classes outside my major. I was trying to learn how to listen and how to construct tonal layers. At some point, I realized I had to get some real world, on-the-job experience in a studio if I ever hoped to get a job in a recording studio. So, one day I simply walked into the college radio station and asked for a job. WUKY-FM (at the time it was WBKY) is an NPR affiliate and the oldest college FM station in America.[17] In 1984 it was housed in an old campus building from the late 1920s and had shadowy remnants of its yesteryear. A performance space that had permanent risers for a choir or band was now home to boxes, mic stands, old desks, and an impressive reel-to-reel dubbing system. The main control room had a black grand piano positioned under speakers and a broadcast clock. There was a room off to the side that had thousands of records, most of which were 78s and early LPs. Another room had a couple of record cutters the size of washing machines. It was late afternoon, and the place was still abuzz with activity.

I had made an appointment with Roger Chesser, the program director. He showed me around the station introducing me to a few people along the way. Back in his office I gave him my back-story and work history, explaining that I thought that some radio station experience would help me to become an audio engineer. We shook hands and I started my half-hour walk back home. By the time I got home, my girlfriend said that Roger had already called and wanted to meet with me again the next day. I called him right back and we set a time. The job he offered me was once-a-week, overnights on Friday. I really didn't care if I would be "emptying wastepaper baskets," as they say, I was in.

For my orientation, Roger showed me the basics of the station and gave me a few hard and fast rules: keep us on the air, learn the Emergency Broadcast System (EBS), and clear the Teletype

---

[17] NPR's Noah Adams also worked here before going on to great things. I felt like I was stalking his career to help mine.

machine every hour.[18] All I had to do was babysit a satellite show and give a station ID once an hour. My shift was 11:00 PM to 7:00 AM, which meant that Fridays were going to be *very* long days. My days usually started with an early walk to the Fine Arts Building so that I could snag a practice room before 8:00 AM. I'd practice until my classes started at 9:00 AM, get more practice sessions in throughout the day, perform in jazz band, have more classes, and try to find time to study. I also had two other jobs in research labs at UK Hospital. Those weren't mandatory that I show up at a particular time because I washed and sterilized glassware, mixed base solutions, and cleaned up lab benches. I got these jobs because my sister managed a research lab (she is the smart one!). Over time, I found that just staying up for 24 hours was the best recipe to keep from falling asleep at the radio station. Taking an evening nap just made me groggy all night. I certainly couldn't do this today, but when you're young, your body can take all kinds of abuse.

My time at WUKY was like going to Disney World every week. One thing that Roger told me was that after I gave the station ID, the studio was my playground. He encouraged me to practice recording and editing, hook up microphones, and explore the station, "Just keep us on the air." Keeping us "on the air" required me to do system checks, a few calibrations, some record keeping, and to monitor off the FM receiver. During my orientation, he handed me off to a few of the other announcers, who eagerly showed me the ropes. I got the feeling that I was filling a shift that had been begrudgingly passed around the station to the shortest straw.

They showed me how to backspin a record, which is manually cueing it up to the beginning, and then spinning it backwards a quarter-turn. This allowed the record player to quick-start and get up to speed without a wobbly sound. They showed me how to back-time music so that you can talk over the beginning instrumental

---

[18] The teletype, although a holdover from the 1960s at this radio station, was the only trusted news source for WUKY. The teletype lived in a soundproofed room between the news department and the on-air studio. The machine itself was housed inside a metal box with a hinged lid. If a particularly important bulletin came through, it would trigger a bell and a red light above the door. I always prayed we wouldn't get a bulletin on my shift so I wouldn't have to interrupt the program announcing that flying saucers have landed on the White House lawn. I was sure I would be out of breath and my voice would crack like a 12-year-old.

before the vocals come in. I learned how to switch and time network breaks, how to record air checks, and how to edit tape. Whatever I asked about, someone was willing to teach me. I would sometimes go in during the weekdays just to hang out and ask questions. The people who worked here were used to being in a teaching environment, but I think that they also wanted to let me in on the secret. They knew most people think that what we do is smoke and mirrors, voodoo, magic. I was now in the club.

If I'm really, really tired and don't want to sleep, I try to keep active. I think adrenaline kept me awake on my first Friday night at the station, though. The last thing I wanted to do was screw up and knock the station "off the air." The evening shift announcer, Hal Leet, stayed around for an extra hour to make sure I got the hang of it. One thing he showed me was a little two-position switch on the console that said "Stereo – Mono." At 11 o'clock we were broadcasting NPR News for the first five minutes of the hour. This was in mono, so I had to flip the switch form "Stereo" to "Mono." When the satellite program "Jazz After Hours with Jim Wilke" started after the news, I needed to switch it from "Mono" back to "Stereo." This seemed trivial, but Hal said that this was one of those "Roger Chesser things" that he obsessed over. He said he couldn't tell the difference, but he didn't want Roger getting all bent out of shape.[19] No problem, Roger was my boss and the one who gave me this opportunity. If he wants me to flip that little switch, then I'll flip it, by God. Alas, the next Friday night I totally forgot to flip the switch back to "Stereo" after NPR News. At 2:00 AM the studio phone rang – it was Roger all flustered, "You forgot to switch to stereo! We've been broadcasting in mono for hours!" Oops. After that I imagined Roger getting up in the middle of every Friday night to check on me. As you'll find out, that wasn't the case.

I made great use of the playground at night. I started out by wheeling in an Otari 2-track reel-to-reel to the piano in the control room. I would play backing chords on one track, and melody on the other. More than once, I would bring my guitar or trombone

---

[19] In actuality, broadcasting FM in mono reduces the static when a receiver is on the fringes of a signal. Stereo FM is not two equal channels of mono, it's a matrix made up of the base mono FM signal and a second AM signal that carries the second channel information. Roger must have felt that hearing the news clearly was more important than someone losing a signal to static drift.

and do overdubs of original music. Microphones were plentiful in that old place. I remember opening drawer upon drawer and find them stuffed with old "Elvis" mics like Shures and E/Vs. They had a nice production studio that looked out over that big room with the boxes and old desks. It was in here that I would sometimes mix down my Frankenstein music productions. There wasn't a shift, except for one particular night, that I wasn't doing some kind of recording or editing the whole time I worked there.

That night started out like most others, with me making the half-hour trek from my house to campus on foot. This time it was bitterly cold, and I was feeling more run down than usual. I should be home in my warm bed right about now. I got to the station in plenty of time, did some transmitter checks, and began my weekly task of keeping us on the air. The last thing I remember was starting a record, announcing, "You are listening to WBKY-FM 91.3, Lexington-Beattyville, Kentucky," and switching back to satellite. Now, something was nagging me. Kathump...kathump...kathump...kathump. It sounded like a drum. No, it was pounding. No, it's scratchy sounding, too. I wish it would stop. Oh, my neck hurts. Oooowwwww, my face is smashed. I woke up to find myself lying prone over the console. The record was thumping away at its end over top of Jim Wilke's jazz show. I immediately checked the console to see if we were still on the air – yes! I next checked the clock. It was after 6:00 AM. I had been asleep for five hours. No police outside, no firemen banging on the door, no Roger Chesser breathlessly shaking me awake telling me to, "flip the switch to stereo!" My little nap had gone unnoticed. I scrambled out of my chair and nearly fell over. I was dizzy beyond belief. I managed to gain my footing and started getting everything in order for the next shift announcer – who was due any minute! I groggily walked home in blowing ice, collapsed into my bed, and spent the weekend there. I had contracted the flu and had been too busy to even notice. That was the one and only time I ever slept on the job. Even though I eventually figured out that no one was listening to me overnights, I kept this job for a year-and-a-half. The simple fact that I worked at the station led to my dream job in a studio – all over a beer and fried chicken. Let me explain.

I was attending classes full-time at UK, working four jobs, was engaged to be married, and paying a hefty tuition. And adding more to this heap was that most of my music class credits from the now defunct Pikeville College music program weren't accepted at UK. I exhausted all my appeals, but because there wasn't a music school at PC anymore, there wasn't any kind of reliable reference for my appeal. I was taking all my second-year theory, history, and performance classes all over again. I will say that after being away for more than two years, they helped to shore up some basic music understanding. But life was very difficult at this time, trying to juggle all the flaming torches. I was becoming disillusioned with my current plan.

I worked in my sister's lab at UK washing glassware for most of my time at UK. One day she said a friend of a friend (isn't that how it usually goes?) worked in a recording studio, and the studio was hiring. I called him and we met at a local dive called High on Rose at the corner of…wait for it…High and Rose streets. I made my way past the bar and up the stairs to the restaurant where I found Don Nelson sitting at a table near the kitchen. He already had a pitcher of beer and couple of mugs on the table waiting. I remember immediately thinking that this was probably going to be a very relaxed meeting. At first, I was nervous a little like most of us get while in an interview. But I was more excited at the prospect of this new opportunity. As we talked about the potential job, the studio, and my experience, it never felt like a traditional interview. Don was relaxed, personable, and easy going. We ordered some fried chicken that the restaurant was known for and talked about everything under the sun. We had many mutual friends, and were probably at some of the same parties. At the end of the night, we shook hands and I asked what my chances of getting the job were. He said, "Oh you got it. You had it before you ever walked in the door?" I looked bewildered. He continued, "It's because you work in a radio station, that's good enough for me." Well, I'll be a monkey's uncle. I didn't have to take a test, fill out any forms, or sit by the phone hoping, hoping, hoping. I was a card-carrying member of the club and didn't know it. Of course, it really isn't this easy to break in, but I was batting two-for-two on lucky breaks.

That next week I went over to Don's studio he worked in, House of Commons. The company was owned by Ed Commons, a man with a rich background in theater, television, sound recording, and film cinematography. It was situated, like many production houses, in a light industrial/warehouse district on the outskirts of town. At the front door, I was greeted with walls that were covered with rough-sawn wood planks. The two-story building, which was built on a slight hill, also contained an automotive body shop and a silk-screen business. Offices were on the upper story at street level, with three garage doors and warehouses below, down the hill and around back.

The machine room at House of Commons with 16mm audio players.

The audio production area, though quaint, was located in the left front of the building. It had a workroom with desks, shelving full of records and tapes, a reel-to-reel edit station, and three large equipment racks full of 16mm magnetic film audio players. Some of the walls had that cool rough sawn wood, while the ones around the edit station and 16mm machines had this rigid soundboard that resembled stiff swirls of discarded spaghetti, and used to be found in airports and factories. A door led into the long and narrow control room. The equipment racks and shelves wrapped around the engineer's position behind a small mixing console. In front of the console was a couch. About ten steps forward was a glass window that looked into the voice-over booth. The side walls had several zigzagging sound absorbing panels jutting out that resembled teeth on a gear. Pieces of plywood with dark brown carpet on their surface were angled out from the wall. Each panel was roughly four-feet wide by eight-feet tall, with one long side resting against the original wall behind them. The other long end was angled out about one foot. This long end had a one-foot wide by eight-foot-tall piece of drywall that hid the cavity, which was filled with building insulation. Above the couch just forward of the mix position hung the speakers. It was deathly quiet, a lot quieter than the college radio station with its 1950s tiled walls and creaking steam radiators.

The mix position at House of Commons. Notice the rack with several tube-based compressors.

At the other end of the control room was another door that led into a hallway full of offices. The door to the voice-over booth was just a quick turn to the left. Through this door was a *sound lock*, which is a sealed entryway with two doors. The booth, raised up about ten inches off the floor, was through this second door. Except for the back wall that was covered with rough sawn wood, it was completely lined with sound-absorbing charcoal-colored foam. This was a "room within a room," where the little booth was built inside another room. All the framing and materials were isolated from outside vibrations. It was cozy, but two people could fit in here if they liked each other.

In the back of the building was a small suite of offices that contained the accounting area, Ed's office, and the film edit room. Across from that was cold storage for film and magnetic tape. There were a few other offices, and a very nice conference room lined with rough-sawn wood. A narrow closet beside this had a long window looking into the conference room so that film and slide projectors could run and not disturb clients watching our latest creation. There was also a huge unfinished area that was full of boxes, books, and other items best kept out of site. Below this entire floor of offices was a sound stage complete with a three-sided cyclorama (a filming background with smooth and concave inside corners that created an infinity look on film), a darkroom, and storage area for equipment. Back in those days, shooting on film was common because video was either too expensive to maintain, or the lower-cost formats were best used for news footage and corporate videos. There were so many lights, stands, flags, scrims, cables, and gels. There was a huge aluminum dolly with running boards, seats, and a large boom. This dolly and several of the huge lights had "Paramount" stamped on them. It turns out that a lot of this gear was used on the "I Love Lucy" and "Star Trek" sets.[20] Wow! I was already a Trekkie, so I was impressed.

By this point I was really stoked to work here. I was also a little intimidated. I had little to no experience and didn't know what two-thirds of this gear was. My life had been consumed with music for the last several years, so I always assumed that my work as an audio engineer would be in music. But I wasn't about to let any of those concerns stop me. This was a foot in the proverbial door. I could learn, I could adapt, I could maybe even like working in film. Who knows?

As a formality, I went through a job interview with Ed, though it was more casual than any that I'd had at a typical department store. I think Ed's main concern was if I had the desire to learn and work in the grind of production. I guess I passed muster because he was anxious to have me start right away. That would have to wait, because I had more pressing things to do first.

Here it was the month of May in 1985. I was offered my first real studio job. It was also Finals week. I also had something else on my schedule – my marriage. Because we were as poor as paupers, my fiancé Margie and I had set our marriage date in May to save a

---

[20] Indeed, they were, I saw the provenance papers from DesiLu Studios that accompanied the sales receipts for the gear. I have no idea what happened to any of this equipment, but I did blow up a big 2K light one time on a set when I accidently sent 220 volts to it instead of 110 volts. Whoops!

little on costs. Most weddings are in June when rates for everything are through the roof, so we thought we would sneak in before season. I told Don and Ed that I wouldn't be able to start until after our honeymoon which was still a few weeks away. I was ambivalent that they would fill the position, but they were very understanding and gracious. So off I went to take finals, get hitched, and bake in the Florida sun. What a whirlwind that May turned out to be.

I came back all tanned (as much as a pasty German-Scots-Irish-American can be) and ready for action. The place was hopping when I walked in. Machines were whirring, people were scurrying back and forth, and sounds could be heard coming from several rooms. They were juggling several projects as well as an awards show for the local advertising club. The awards show was a non-money maker, as most production services are donated in-kind[21] in this industry. What better way to test the young blood by having him edit the long and laborious voice-over of the award winners for this year? No problem! I had learned basic editing from the jocks at the radio station, so I was ready. Don showed me some quick tips and turned me loose.

I was given several large reels of audiotape to edit. These were the *pre*-digital, *pre*-nonlinear, *pre*-convenience days. You played the tape in real-time, waited for a mistake, marked that point on the tape with a white China marker, pulled the tape up to a splicing block, sliced that with a razor blade, rethreaded the remaining tape, pressed the *edit* and *play* buttons, fed the miscue through the pinch roller and into a waste can, stopped when the good take began, marked that point with the China marker, pulled the tape up to the edit block, sliced that mark with a razor, pulled the other end of tape up to the edit block, butted the two ends together, cut a piece of adhesive tape, laid that over the joint, pressed it down, threaded the tape back over the heads, pressed *play*, and listened. Whew! Now do this over and over again for the next several hours and you have an edited track. I learned early on that I <u>hated</u> to edit voice-over. That fact would only drive me harder for the rest of my career.

---

[21] *In-kind* means you can't claim a tax credit for services, only hard money costs. We are always donating in-kind services to organizations, individuals, and causes, even though there is no official tax break for it. You will, and should, donate much of your time to causes throughout your career. Your expertise can help a non-profit organization reach its goals, an individual attain an education, or help advance a worthy social cause.

Because I hate it so much, I became lightning fast at it. I am an excellent voice-over editor for one reason: if I am sloppy then I will have to go back and fix my mistakes, thus spending even more time doing something that I hate. I try my best to get it right the first time. You can apply this same methodology to so many tasks in your everyday work life. Never do anything – no matter how much you loathe it – half-assed. My mantra has always been to get the voice-over editing out of the way so I can move on to the fun stuff.

The House of Commons was a film production company. Just like my radio station gig, I had taken a recording job outside of music. I was surrounded by much of the same technology that a music studio would have, so I tried to extract what I knew from the music world and apply it to what I was learning about in the film world. What I found out pretty quickly is how similar they are. With music you have tones, rhythm, motion, cadence, melody, harmony, and emotion. The same can be said for film.

I continued to work and work and learn and learn over the next few years. I also tried to continue school, hold down several jobs, and make a marriage work. House of Commons had hired a full-time audio engineer named Bob Davis. Bob was an educated broadcast engineer who had built radio and television stations and was a talented recording engineer and voice-over artist. Bob became one of my mentors and good friends. I learned the basics of wiring and studio construction under Bob. His methodical approach taught me to slow down and think through large tasks before tackling them.

The school thing started to be an insurmountable financial mountain, with no end in sight. It also became clear that getting a music education degree and not pursuing that avenue was wasted time and money. Then one day Bob took another job. That left the full-time position open. Mountain of debt in one hand, promising career in the other...Hmm. Maybe we should give this studio thing a shot.

For years I regretted not having that piece of paper that said "Bachelor of Arts" on it, but I've gotten over it. To my knowledge, it never hindered my career, but a few supervisors got persnickety about it. My response, which usually shut them up, was that there wasn't a degree for what I do when I was hired. I count myself lucky because I've only worked three full-time jobs, *if* you count owning my own business as one of them. I've also worked on many broadcast, live audio, film, video, and recording crews. I taught a college audio course, I advise high school and college media programs, and I've mentored too many interns to count. I enjoy sharing my experiences and knowledge because it was shared with me time and again from my mentors. Now, let's get to work and start your path to a great career.

3. WHAT DOES AN AUDIO ENGINEER DO?

"Choose a job you love, and you will never have to work a day in your life."

Unknown

Let's start with how the U.S. Department of Labor classifies an audio engineer (2016):

`27-4014 Sound Engineering Technicians.` Operate machines and equipment to record, synchronize, mix, or reproduce music, voices, or sound effects in sporting arenas, theater productions, recording studios, or movie and video productions.

Maybe you're a little foggy on what kind of jobs there are that classify someone as an audio engineer or audio producer.[22] When I first started thinking about what an audio engineer did, I thought it was someone (usually a man, because there were and still unfortunately are very few women in this field) who sits at a mixing console and looks through a window at musicians or announcers in front of a microphone. That's how they're always posed in pictures. An engineer twisted knobs and slid faders up and down. I really just saw it as an isolated, single job. It intrigued me though, because it meant that person knew what all those knobs and sliders did. That person was also participating in something exciting and creative. I have never forgotten how I felt when I got sucked into a piece of music or radio program. And when I would look at the back of a record and skim through the credits, I started to notice that there were names other than the performers. They would credit the

---

[22] For a raw, very basic primer on what recording and engineering is, read my chapter "Engineering and Recording Concepts" on page 194.

recording engineer, the mixing engineer, the mastering engineer, the producer, and the studio. It dawned on me one day that they were being recognized for much of the creative process along with the musicians. That told me that these people were more than button pushers. They were vital to the success of that record.

Some of the names that kept popping up on the back of my albums were: Alan Parsons, Phil Ramone, Tom Dowd, Eddie Kramer, Bruce Swedien, Rudy Van Gelder, and Geoff Emerick. Of course, if you look these names up, you'll find out how they shaped the way we hear recorded music today. They were more than button pushers, they actively participated in a song's sound. Each one has many stories to tell about how they worked with an artist or producer to push the envelope and make a truly unique recording. Anybody can stick a couple of microphones in front of a drum set or piano and get a decent sound. What sets these engineers apart is they had built enough trust with the artist that they could try new or unusual techniques that would enhance the song. They had the chops and confidence to sometimes go out on a limb and risk their reputation for the sake of making a great record. That's why they're on the back of the album along with the musicians.

When I started researching audio engineering jobs in high school, I knew I wanted my name to be on the back of an album, I just wasn't sure how to get there. I was also foggy about what kind of jobs there were. Then, as now, many audio engineering jobs aren't cut and dry like some careers. In the healthcare field for example, many jobs are well defined, like respiratory therapist, nurse practitioner, orthodontist, or physical therapist. Of course, there are specialties within each job, but overall, the job title tells exactly what you do. Not so in my field. In one week, I may record and edit part of an audiobook, broadcast a radio program, go on-location and record an on-camera interview, design a television commercial soundtrack, and run live sound at a stadium. You think I'm making this up? No way, but that's a very busy week. We often spread our skills out across the table because many of my tasks and tools are similar. So, let's look at some of the jobs that you can explore. This is not an exhaustive list, and some of my descriptions may only reflect the core of what that job entails. Also, some of these jobs will go away, change, or morph with other jobs over time.

Recording Engineer. Probably the most sterile and broad type of job title there is in the field. This job requires skills to use microphones, mixers, recording devices, and software to record sound. Work environments can be anywhere, from recording studios, venues, offices, homes, broadcast outlets, or outside. The recording engineer is responsible for reliably capturing sound as a recording. The recording engineer will often be responsible for editing the recording and delivering a final product as an audio file, physical format, or part of a multi-media format such as video, game, or web content. Knowledge of microphones, acoustics, recording equipment, and audio software is required. Additional skills that are helpful are musicianship, grammar, and directing. Ability to work with clients and under tight deadlines is critical.

Sound Designer. Assemble layers of sound such as sound effects and music to create a persuasive listening experience. Many different mediums require sound design, but the most common are: films or videos, games, stage plays, musicals, radio programs, podcasts, albums, music, web sites, and live musical acts. Knowledge of microphones, recording equipment, audio software, and the final medium is required. Helpful skills include music theory, programming, theater arts, cinematography basics, and broadcast techniques. Precision sound placement, editing, manipulation, and mixing are crucial. Creative choices based on storyline and audience reaction dominate the workflow.

Mastering Engineer. Prepare, sequence, and output final programs, albums, and soundtracks into formats for distribution. Use specialized equipment and software to enhance, equalize, de-noise, control dynamics, edit, trim, or otherwise alter sections of a program, album, or soundtrack. A final cohesive sound for the entire project is desired. Specially built control rooms with accurate monitoring and signal chains are required. Knowledge of equalizers, compressors, mastering software, and different media formats is required. Helpful skills include music theory and electronics.

Live Sound Engineer. Set up, tune, align, equalize, and operate amplification equipment including microphones, mixers, direct boxes, amps, speakers, and software. Knowledge of acoustics, electronics, music, and radio / wireless theory is expected. Heavy lifting, long hours, and travel are usually associated with this career. Skills acquired as a recording engineer often parlay well into live sound engineering, and vice versa. Helpful skills include musicianship and electronics. Engineering in large arenas and venues usually requires years of experience.

Broadcast Engineer. Engineer live on-air or recording of programs, news, performances, talk shows, or other forms of entertainment. Mediums include radio, television, or internet streaming. Use microphones, mixers, playback devices, recorders, software, communication devices, signal patches, and connection devices. Knowledge of journalism standards, and broadcast principles, regulations, and methods is critical, and often necessary. Some broadcasts require travel, equipment set-up, and problem solving. Some engineers are also on-air talent and "Broadcast Technical Engineers," which is designing, building, and maintaining broadcast equipment.

Post-Production Engineer. Also known as "re-recording engineer" in the cinema world. Mix, master, and format final audio elements of dialog, sound effects, and music for cinema, film, television, game, and web videos. Most commonly associated with the film industry, this is the final phase of a film's soundtrack. Use mixers, surround sound monitoring, playback and recording devices and software. Knowledge of complex mixing consoles and software, multi-channel surround systems, film/video format standards, theater sound system standards, streaming platforms, and television format standards. Understanding of acoustics, psychoacoustics, and film/video editing are helpful.

Dialog Editor. Edit, assemble, manipulate, smooth, and blend dialog tracks for film, video, and web. Most commonly associated with the film industry. Use audio editing and restoration software, compressors, equalizers, and reverb software. Knowledge of entire film soundtrack chain is essential. The dialog editor's main goal is to match and manipulate cuts from multiple takes into a cohesive, even dialog track. Understanding of acoustics and location sound principles is helpful.

ADR Engineer / Editor. (Automatic Dialog Replacement) Replace or alter dialog in a film or video with new recordings. Noisy, clipped, missing, or changed dialog is recorded using special microphones as used on film sets. Special software and mixing consoles are utilized, usually in specially built studios. Knowledge of film soundtrack chain, location recording techniques, acoustics, and specialized software is essential.

Sound Effects Editor. Record, collect, edit, manipulate, and mix sound effects for film and video. Use microphones, mixers, compressors, equalizers, reverbs, and software to create sound effect tracks that support the visual and story elements of film. Travel, research, and experimentation is usually required. Knowledge of the film soundtrack chain is essential.

Foley Engineer. Similar to, and sometimes also working as a sound effects or ADR engineer, a Foley engineer records a Foley artist performing replacement sound effects. A Foley artist will watch a film scene while simultaneously recreating sound effects such as footsteps, grunts, body sounds, doors, and other sounds of movement. This is usually faster and more acceptable than creating effects one at a time in the editing environment. Requirements are the same as ADR and sound effects engineer.

Location Engineer. Also known as a "sound mixer" in the cinema world. Record and mix dialog and sound effects on film/video sets and locations. Use specialty microphones and mixers, portable recorders, and other film/video specialty equipment. Requires travel, knowledge of film/video techniques, mobility, some lifting, problem solving, and understanding of acoustics. Knowledge of video cameras, set lighting, acting basics, and electronics is helpful. There are subsets of this position when more than one location engineer is required. One is "boom operator," who is responsible for positioning and holding a boom pole and directional microphone over the actor/speaker. The hierarchy of audio personnel on a medium to large set is usually: A1-lead engineer and mixer; A2-assistant engineer, equipment management; A3-general assistant duties, may include boom pole operation; A4-general labor, cable placement and management, equipment loading/unloading, runner.

Game Audio Engineer. Record, edit, manipulate, design, mix, and program sound for interactive games. Use microphones, mixers, editing and mixing software, and specialized game audio creation software. Knowledge of game authoring chain is essential. Experience in film/video sound design is helpful, sometimes a requirement. This job may require extensive creation of dialog, sound effects, and music tracks.

Forensics Engineer. Analyze and enhance recordings made by law enforcement, transportation, security systems, communications, surveillance, and other sources. Recordings are usually difficult to understand or contain sounds that are critical to investigations or civil and criminal cases. Use specialized software for removing noise, enhancing audio, and analyzing waveforms. Formal training in acoustics, audio engineering, and physics are highly desirable. Courses, certificates, and degrees in audio forensics sciences are available. Many forensic engineers are employed by government agencies or companies that work under government contracts.

Restoration Engineer. Analyze, enhance, reduce noise, and master vintage or poorly recorded programs. Work with older and vintage formats such as analog tapes, records, wax cylinders, wire recordings, and outdated digital formats. Use mixers, equalizers, compressors, and specialty software. Usually not a defined job, there are companies, institutions, museums, and organizations that employ full-time restoration engineers based on the volume of work.

Loop Creator and Editor. Record, edit, mix, and program musical samples for use in music sample software and keyboards. Use microphones, mixers, compressors, equalizers, reverbs, and specialty software. Musicianship, programming experience, and music theory basics are usually necessary requirements. These jobs are usually offered by keyboard manufacturers, music software designers, and recording studios.

DJ. Originally known as "disc jockey." Playback recorded music to live crowds in dance clubs, music venues, parties, sporting events, and other functions. Use software, digital and analog playback units such as turntables, sequencers, and CD players. Use specialized software for playback and beat synchronization. Usually a part-time freelance job, many have made a successful full-time career, usually choosing their own environments and venues to work in. The DJ is also usually a musician, and some live DJ shows can be considered performances and unique musical compositions.

AV Technician. Provide sound reinforcement, playback, recording, and other services for conferences, meetings, weddings, and other events in hotels, conference centers, schools, hospitals, organizations, and other venues. Additional duties may include setting up video players, podiums, PA systems, pipe and draping, stages, lighting, and other live event technical needs. Knowledge of live sound and video projection are helpful.

Audio Design Engineer. Research, design, and develop hardware circuitry and/or software for manufacturing of audio capture or playback equipment. Use software, microphones, and mixers for research and development. Manufacturers of telephony, playback and capture devices are the most common employer. Formal training in engineering and/or computer programming are usually required.

PART II

GETTING THERE

4. Taking the First Step to Becoming an Audio Engineer

"That's one small step for [a] man, one giant leap for mankind."

Neil Armstrong

I have no magic bullet, potion, secret handshake, or incantation to instantly make you an audio engineer. But I have a crystal ball that you're welcome to peer into and see a possible future. Look deep into that ball and see yourself sitting at a mix console. Of course, there's a little fog and some dark shadows, but there you are. Now see yourself moving a microphone to the front of an orchestra. These are worthy visions and dreams to have. But the reality is you don't just become an engineer or producer overnight. You must work hard to achieve your ultimate goal, one small goal at a time. One surefire way is to start to act and think like an engineer before you become one. How? I'm going to borrow a term from the still photography and cinema world: *previsualization*.

The legendary master photographer Ansel Adams worked in a time before digital photography. He had no preview screens or histograms. He had to have complete faith in his camera, film, and most importantly his experience, before taking a photograph. Adams would *previsualize*, or "see" the final print in his mind, before ever tripping the shutter. He would select film stock, shutter speed, aperture, and any filters needed for the camera. He would also plan how he would develop the negative, what grade of paper it would be printed on, and what areas of the print might need to be dodged lighter or burned darker in the darkroom. *Then* he would snap the picture. You can apply this technique to the athlete as well. Before a drive, a golfer will first envision where the ball needs to end up, the choice of a driver, the direction of the wind, the power needed to launch the ball, and the arc of the ball's path. Then she will imagine the muscles in her body flexing, joints pivoting, as she drives the ball over the fairway. *Then* she swings. What I've described are all conceptualizations based on repeated experiences. Adams threw away countless negatives while mastering photography. The golfer has deposited the ball in the rough hundreds of times on her way to becoming an elite athlete.

The key here is that they saw the desired final result *before* they made their first move. The print may not be exactly as envisioned, or the ball may pull a little to the left, but with careful planning and going through each step one-by-one in their minds, they came close. In order for you to envision and attain your goals, you must do as Adams and the golfer did – carefully think through each step *before* you leap. It's that simple. The great basketball player Michael Jordan said, "You have to expect things of yourself before you can do them." I'm going to give you the steps in a nutshell first, and then we'll break them down in more detail later. But a word of caution: this first step may be the hardest one you take. Are you ready?

Step 1: Envision where you'll be five years from now.

You basically have three different routes to go: attend a college, go to a for-profit trade school, or jump right in and start looking for a studio job. It's best to be pragmatic and not sugar coat where your place will be on the studio totem pole in the beginning. Assuming that you don't just luck into a full-time studio job right off the bat, let's presume that you're still in high school or have little to no college experience. If you take the route of going to a four-year college, in five years you might have a piece of paper from State College and be waiting tables or selling shoes in the mall. But…you might also have a part-time job at a radio station or recording studio. This is not a bad position to be in because you're earning some dough and have a foot in the door. My first two jobs were part-time after all. If you opt for a two-year certificate program, you might be three years into an entry-level position with a hotel AV company five years from now. Or you might be selling home security systems while working evenings in a small local recording studio. If you choose to go to a for-profit trade school, then you might have to put everything on hold until you finish it.

This might give you a jump-start in your career if the school has a good reputation. None of these situations are bad. You're working and your taking steps toward your ultimate goal. None of these routes are wrong either because they're all forward steps.

Step 2: Envision where you'll be in ten years.

Okay, this one's a little harder to see. But since you've already envisioned your place in five years, this one's not as scary. At first, you're probably thinking that you should just throw darts at the wall blindfolded. But there can be a method to the madness. What do you want to do the most? Record rap music, make music for films, run sound for a rock concert, engineer radio broadcasts, or design sound for stage? There really is a direction to point your rudder if you really think about what environment you want to be in. Your path may change on your way there, but at least you have a direction to go in. I originally saw myself recording orchestras. Even though my path went a different direction, I did get to record an orchestra within ten years of getting my first studio job.

Step 3. Gather Information.

By reading this book, you could argue that you've already taken this step. Congratulations, you've started to gather knowledge. Knowledge, as they say, is power. In this case it really is, because you must have some idea of where you're going and how to get there. Don't amble around like I did, point yourself in a direction and GO! This may be visiting a school's website, talking with a professional engineer, or hanging out in a buddy's basement studio while asking a lot of questions. I have young people shadow in my studio all the time, so I'm sure there's a studio nearby that will be willing to let you stand in the corner and watch for a few days. If so, then this is your chance to find out how they got to be engineers, what pitfalls to avoid along the way, and maybe pick up some recording tips as well. You never know, they might even hire you for a gig or two. The more you learn, the more informed you'll be about the profession and how to plan your steps to a career.

Step 4. Decide on your path.

While counseling students, I often find they have only a vague idea of what steps they should take to get into this business. I try to get them to think about steps one and two so that I can advise them on what direction to go. By doing step #3, hopefully you've explored some of your possible end paths. If one of the things you want to do is to design audio circuits or write software, you will probably have to look into a post-secondary education. If you want to run a record company, you should probably look into college business courses. If you want to mix live sound for a rock band, you might look into touring with a band for a summer. No path is wrong if it leads you to where you want to go. And it's okay if you change paths. It's also okay if you don't want to go to college – it's not for everybody. People who choose college aren't necessarily smarter than you are, it's just their chosen path. People who choose to not attend college are just following their own paths as well.

Step 5: GO!

Mark Twain said, "The secret of getting ahead is getting started." Then get off your duff and get going, the world awaits. Carve your path. Make haste not waste…and all those other motivational poster phrases. Do whatever it takes to make your dream come true. Your next steps will decide your future.

In the next few chapters, I'm going to break down each of these steps and help you learn how to envision your future, gather information, and decide your path. Let's see what buttons you can push.

5. EDUCATION AND TRAINING

"An investment in knowledge pays the best interest."

Benjamin Franklin

In step 1, I asked you to envision where you'll be in five years. This may be hard, or it may be easy for you. But the key to having a concrete vision is to be pragmatic about your current situation, your prospects if you don't go the audio engineering route, and what kind of mettle you have to stick to a plan when things get challenging. If you stay the path, you'll probably be working your first real full-time audio engineering job in three to five years. But the truth is that most entry-level jobs are not glamorous. When I was teaching audio production at a local college in the early 2000s, digital audio was becoming the norm, but reel-to-reel players could still be found in small, low budget radio stations and studios. So, one day I rolled a reel-to-reel deck into the classroom and started to teach the students how to thread and play a reel tape. Some were fascinated, but one young woman was appalled and told me so. She said, "Why do we have to learn that old stuff?" I replied, "Because most of you will be working in a 500-watt daytime AM radio station in Podunk[23] when you graduate." Cold hard truth sometimes hurts. "Nuh-uh," she retorted, "they said we'd have good jobs." "They" were the college recruiters, whom I suspect didn't quite phrase this glowing guarantee the way she chose to hear it. She went on to tell the oft-repeated story of one young man who got a job at a major news broadcaster right out of this very college. I knew this graduate's real story, he was a "tape operator" on the graveyard shift. It was a foot in the door, but hey, you gotta start somewhere. From that point forward, I've been determined to bring students down to earth a little. I don't want to completely obliterate someone's dream, I just want to keep it real. If you land a job

---

[23] Population varies by how many possums are within city limits.

mixing Saturday Night Live right out of college, then either NBC is off their rockers or you're a prodigy. (Kudos to you if you get that gig, I'll be jealous.) The bottom line is, when you're trying to envision yourself in one, two, five, or ten years, keep it real, but don't ever forget your dream.

So how do other people envision the future? A little education goes a long way. This comes in many forms: structured, mentoring, experiential, research, and observational. My education in audio engineering came from a little bit of the first, structured; but most of what I learned was from the last four of these. As you'll see in this chapter, the many audio education opportunities that are available will allow you to utilize all five of these. But first, let's talk about what talents you already have.

In the sports world, there are many extremely talented athletes that never realize a long and fruitful career in professional sports. Barring a career-ending injury, many of these athletes lacked the desire, discipline, experience, or mental toughness to go to the next level. As they say, talent will only get you so far. This is so true in the production world.

You may be able to recognize an out-of-tune note in a popular recording, or do an incredible mix of your friends' bar band one night in the pub, or whip out a song by your band in three hours and have it entered into an online contest just in the nick of time. But can you repeat that performance over, and over, and over again? Do you have the discipline to learn how to hear those sour notes? Do you have the experience to know how to balance a lead singer against the wailing guitar solo? Do you have the mental toughness to shake off a bad mistake and keep working intelligently to meet the deadline?

These are not tools that most of us are born with. We must learn them from experience and the experienced. We need teachers, mentors, and a knowledge base to draw from. The teachers and mentors can recognize your strengths and help you hone them. They can recognize your weaknesses and help you eliminate them. They can share their experiences about how they also made many mistakes before they learned the correct way. When one of my students is trying something new and messes up, I always tell them "The first time is not a mistake if you didn't know the right way." I go on to tell them that this first experience was just deposited in their learning bank. The second time they make the same error only fortifies their experience. The third time is truly a mistake and they only have themselves to blame.

We need experience to learn new skills. There's an old riddle among professional photographers that goes something like, "What's the difference between an amateur photographer and a professional photographer? A professional took *waaaaayyyyy* more terrible pictures to get the good ones." I'm here to tell you that if I'm really good at something, it's because I've made a ton of mistakes to get where I'm at. I may have to rely on a little bit of natural talent when starting something new and unfamiliar, but experience is the only thing that will allow me to turn that into a skill. Repetition, repetition, repetition.

And let me add "smart" repetition. A basketball player that can't shoot free throws is usually someone that didn't put in smart and disciplined practice. Sure, he can stand on that foul line and throw the ball at the rim a hundred times in a row and then declare that he put in the time. But smart repetition is when you analyze your previous attempt for positives and negatives:

- It hit the rim, so the positive is that it went further than the last shot.
- Why? I made sure my shooting arm extended all the way to my release point.
- The negative is that it didn't arc high enough.
- Why? I didn't follow through with my fingers at the release.
- What else am I doing right? I'm putting the correct back spin on the ball.
- What else am I doing wrong? I'm not bending my knees enough before beginning the throw.

This kind of smart analyzation between every shot usually creates a high-percentage free throw shooter. We can learn from this exercise and apply it to audio engineering. The basketball players that are good at shooting free throws probably had good coaching as well. I know that when I'm struggling on a particular guitar riff, I can still hear one of my guitar teachers in my head telling me to lift my elbow and quit dragging my hand on the neck. So, you need an educator, mentor, or professional to guide you through the learning process and teach you solid, good habits. Whether this comes at a college, technical school, internship, or from just hanging around a studio, it is vital that you are receptive to learning.

I don't make that last statement lightly. There are too many people that think they can master something without help. Very few humans can actually do this, and we build monuments to them. Your job right out of the gate, and for the rest of your career, is to learn your craft. Remember the movie *Karate Kid*? Ralph Macchio wants to learn karate from Pat Morita. He's chomping at the bit to break some boards and kick some butt. Morita grabs a can of paint and a paintbrush and directs Macchio to start painting his fence. But he must only paint up and down one hand at a time. Naturally Maccio is resistant to this, but he reluctantly obliges. Next, Morita has him wax his cars with a swirling motion of each hand. Then he has Maccio sand his deck and paint his house, each with unique and repetitive motions. Macchio eventually has had enough and exclaims that he wants to learn karate, not painting and sanding and waxing. Morita quietly has Maccio go through the motions of painting, sanding, and waxing. Then Morita makes quick offensive moves that Macchio easily defends using the same up/down, side-to-side, and swirling motions that he just spent days training his hands to do. Mind blown.

As an educator and mentor, I use these same techniques with my students. I will often have them edit some audio using only menu choices. This familiarizes them with the program's capabilities, but also starts to build frustration. Their frustration comes from having to use two or three moves and clicks to accomplish something they're now familiar with. At that point I show them the shortcut. We then move on to the next frustration, or in Macchio's case, fence slat.

What should you take away from these lessons? Be humble, it will get you far. Nobody wants to help a know-it-all, but most of us are glad to help someone who's eager to learn. And please stay humble your whole career. I'm not saying that you shouldn't pat yourself on the back once in a while or take pride in a job well done. But if you're willing to step outside your bubble and accept that you can always learn more, then you're going to acquire many skills and accumulate so much knowledge that you can pay forward.

I used to teach Audio Production 101 as an adjunct professor at a nearby college, Asbury University in Wilmore, Kentucky.

Asbury's media production school is nationally recognized for turning out highly skilled broadcasters, producers, and talent. I was thrilled when I was asked to help shape the minds of young people wanting a career in production. I had been mentoring and teaching interns for about 15 years at this point, but I had never taught a structured class. I was stoked and terrified at the same time. Mom to the rescue.

My mother Libby Kesterson was a lifelong learner and educator. She didn't get to go to college until her early thirties, but from there she never looked back. She started out teaching high school English, Literature, and Speed Reading.[24] And yes, I had her for Speed Reading. At 8:00 AM. In the morning. As a teenager. Ugh. It's hard to speed read with your forehead plastered to the desk.

Mom continued to teach full time while earning her master's degree in Education. Needless to say, we hardly saw her. My dad, the ever-supporting husband, became a 1970s version of Mr. Mom. One of her most intriguing graduate courses focused on how to construct a test. She learned how to *write* tests by learning how to *take* tests. OK, that sounds funny, but Mom learned that many tests are built around multiple-choice. Using discipline and odds, she learned to successfully pass many industry accreditation tests with no knowledge of that field. For instance, she passed the written part of the bar exam on the first try because (at that time in the 1970s) it was mainly constructed around multiple-choice. How'd she do it? The secret is to pick a random choice ahead of time, like "B," and stick with it. Quickly go through the test and only answer questions you know to be correct. Mark ones that you might know but need more time with. Any questions that you have absolutely no idea what the answer is, mark the "B" choice. Now go back and spend more time on the ones you marked. If you still don't know but think the answer is between two choices, you just improved your odds, pick one quickly and move on. If a question you absolutely don't know has three or more possible choices, just mark "B." I'm not a statistician or a gambler, but she could quote her

---

[24] Mom went on to become and educator and administrator at several colleges and universities, became a grant writer, and headed up an international educational consortium of universities. At the same time, she also read several books a week, renovated a hundred-year-old three-story house, and edited books and theses. She was an overachiever!

odds for each approach and usually come out with at least 70% success. With much relief, she said that she miserably failed the MCAT exam because it was knowledge and problem solving-based. That means that most doctors are really smart and know their stuff.

And she knew her stuff. She helped me organize my lectures and classes around the syllabus without running off the rails. The syllabus is a structured road map with simple concepts laid out (kind of like the steps to your future). But to expand on each subject and teach 15 people for 3 hours seemed daunting. I remember telling her "I don't know how to teach what I know because I've forgotten how I learned it." She said I would have to be prepared to teach everything 15 ways because everyone learns differently. Kaboom! That's the last thing I wanted to be told, but I needed to hear it. In time I learned to enjoy coming up with different ways of teaching something. I made it work by using a lot of analogies students could relate to. I also learned how to construct a test that taught students while they took it, instead of having them regurgitate memorized minutia.

But the one big lesson I learned from teaching was that I found out how much I <u>didn't</u> know. I've often heard that one learns from teaching. I know what that means now. Up to this point I had been mostly getting by on talent and technique by rote. I had really only been tested once on my technical knowledge (more on that in a moment). Remember, I had no formal education in my profession; I was just adapting my desire to record with my training in music. This wasn't a bad combination, but in order to teach audio basics I had to buckle down and crack open the books. I thought I fully understood what a dB was, how a watt is measured, what mic level is, and how acoustics affect the recording. It turns out I only had a working knowledge of these terms and ideas, but I could not clearly explain them fifteen different ways.

Let me sidetrack a little bit here. What I'm about to tell you next is not bragging. It's an admission. About a half-a-dozen years before I started teaching, I was disgruntled about my employment situation and started looking for another job. One place I really wanted to work was Kentucky Educational Television, or KET as it is known by. KET is a network of several public television transmitters around the state. Its main focus is on "tele-education," so KET produces hours and hours of educational programs, much of which is distributed nationally. They also produce documentaries and series for their main public PBS channel. For years it was a model public television network, right up there with WBGH in Boston. The main facilities in Lexington are drool-worthy and include studios, equipment, and personnel usually found in major cities. But being a state-funded operation, it was hard to get hired on. The process to fill a vacancy took months and lots and lots of paperwork. When I applied, there was no impending vacancy, I just wanted to get my name in the hat in case someone retired. I was sent to Frankfort, our state capital, to take an audio engineer proficiency test. Having done career research about 15 years earlier, I had no idea a test like this even existed. The test, which had been developed by some very smart KET engineers, had a few situation-based questions that required you to solve problems. But most of the test was multiple-choice. Bingo! I knew how to take these. Though I knew roughly half of the questions with certainty, about a quarter of them were completely foreign to me. Some were trick questions about audio level measurements, others were very deep dive technical ones. I remember looking at these thinking, "I don't know anything. I might as well pack it up." So, I employed my mother's test-taking rules and picked a letter to just finish this damned test. Probably "B" for B.S. A few weeks later I nervously called the Frankfort office where I took my test to find out the results. The woman on the other end of the line shuffled some papers, and said, "Oh yes, Mr. Kesterson, congratulations," she said excitedly. "You have the highest score ever recorded on this test!" That "high" score didn't garner a bit of attention from KET, but did start me on a quest to finally learn more about the field I was working in. I couldn't B.S. my way any longer.

In the years following that test I began to get very curious about all those test questions I "aced" but knew nothing about. I started to pay more attention to metering, wiring, equipment specifications, and anything else that I didn't understand. Almost like I was back in school, I really started to drive myself hard trying to learn everything I could. But as I was going back to basics, the world was changing rapidly. It was interesting times in the audio production world in the 1990s. Analog was fading away and digital was trying to find its footing. We were using early software-based digital audio workstations (DAW) in the early 90s. Sirius and XM-radio began transmitting digital satellite audio. Our company became the first in the state to distribute commercials digitally to radio stations. It was all exciting, but also intimidating to a non-educated audio engineer. Interfacing analog and digital technologies while creating new workflows was very difficult, but the world was not going to slow down for me. I had to learn – and now! Also during this time, I was laying the foundation for starting my own business. I started to learn business fundamentals, I was developing a business plan, and I was saving money. And I was raising a child. I look back now on everything I had going on and shake my head with amazement that anything got done at all.

Back to my college teaching gig, I put my nose to the grindstone and learned how to teach what I know. Sometimes I was learning the subject myself right up until class time. It also really helped to have students challenge me with interesting questions. If I didn't know, I'd say, "I don't know, but I'll find out and we'll learn together." Was I any good? I think a class of 15 will have 15 opinions on that. But I found that those who wanted to learn did. My classes were divided into roughly 25% who were deeply interested in audio and soaked up everything; 25% who were mildly interested but learned; 25% who had to take the class for credit and just cruised by; and 25% who had no interest, didn't want to be there, and either failed or squeaked by. You need to be in that first 25% or you're wasting your time.

If you ever get the chance to teach, either a full class or one-on-one, jump on it. My time teaching opened up a new world for me and allowed my career to advance to the next level. Understanding the fundamentals of audio helps me solve problems, learn new industry standards, take on large-scale projects, build studios, and most importantly, share my knowledge with those eager to learn.

So far, I've been preaching about getting an education. Like I said earlier in this chapter, traditional secondary education is not mandatory. Nor is technical school. They can be helpful for the right student. But let's face it, the single largest barrier for most would-be students is cost. It's not cheap to go to school. And unless it's a well-established licensed profession such as in the medical field, there are no guarantees. Only you and your family can decide if additional structured education is right for you. If so, you'll need to decide the route you want to take. While not an exhaustive list, let's look at your primary options for getting an education beyond high school.

THE FULL-TIME COLLEGE ROUTE

Going to a four-year college full-time can certainly give you a well-rounded education. If you've done well in high school, you'll find college challenging but fun. You'll be able to take elective classes that interest you beyond your major. And speaking of major, unless it's a school that specifically has a recording degree, you'll have to major in a related field that might include recording arts as a minor or single class. For example, if you know that you want to be a record producer, you might want to seek out schools that offer this as a major. These types of majors include music, recording, and business classes tailored to the music production profession. These programs are usually found in, but not limited to music-rich cities such as Nashville, New York, and Los Angeles. They can also be some of the most expensive and toughest schools to get into, so be prepared to step up academically and financially. A few of my past interns have successfully gone through a few of these programs, and they found them very rewarding.

Another obvious route to becoming an audio engineer via a four-year college is to major in broadcasting. Although most programs focus on television and video, all students must take basic audio production classes. Many schools allow students to earn a degree with an emphasis on a particular field. You would leave the program with knowledge and experience in all phases of TV/radio production, which could open up your career choices. This is a prudent way to approach your future career, especially if you also enjoy video, directing, hosting, lighting, set construction, management, and other facets of production. Throughout my career, I've been called on to run live sound in stadiums, engineer live radio and television broadcasts, mix live music in bars, design sound for stage plays, grip lights on film sets, run video cameras, direct talent, and even be on camera myself. So, a little bit of experience doing all or most of these can't be bad. Hopefully you'll branch out and won't have to spend your entire career behind a console in a windowless room.

You can also major in music at a school that has a recording studio as part of their facilities. Even if they might not offer a major or minor in recording, they often have a few classes you can take that will get you in the engineer's chair. Also, many schools have an on-campus radio and/or television station that accepts work-study students, internships, or even part-time jobs. Just like my experience at WUKY-FM, the University of Kentucky's NPR radio station, the personnel at campus stations are usually receptive to teaching students one-on-one. UK now has two radio stations, the NPR station, and a student run low-wattage station that I helped get on the air years ago, yet another slice of experience I would not have been privy to had I not been open-minded about learning.

Of course, the best path in a four-year program is to get in a program specifically for the recording arts. These kinds of programs are accredited and give you a well-rounded education with a heavy emphasis on what you will need to not only fiddle with faders, but to: manage or own facilities; produce music, theater, film, or radio programs; marketing and advertising strategies; personnel management; music theory and history; writing skills; business and accounting practices; and many more skills vital to our profession. These programs usually have strong ties with record companies, recording studios, production studios, and other entertainment-related companies that provide instructors and offer internships. They also favor graduates from these schools over other job applicants. These schools are also usually found in cities with a large base of entertainment and production jobs available.

THE ASSOCIATE DEGREE ROUTE

Another great option to get a great education is with an associate degree. Though not as complete as a four-year program, it can enhance your high school education with basic core classes. Just like a four-year program, you normally choose an area of concentration for your studies. At most of these schools, you can fit classes around your work schedule. You could earn an A.D. very quickly if you earned college credit in high school and go full-time, or you can spread it out over several years if you're working a full-time job. These programs also cost a lot less than four-year programs and often offer financial aid. There are some media arts associate degree programs, with more popping up all the time. Some schools offer select classes that compile many disciplines into one.

A local community college I sometimes guest taught at has a Film Certificate program. This one semester class meets five days a week for a half-day. It takes students from concept and scripting, through shooting and editing. Many guest lecturers came in for several days at a time and worked with students on their specific discipline. There was a scriptwriter, a composer, a videographer, a lighting grip, an editor, and me. I gave a four-day crash course in location sound. One day was lecture with some hands on. The next day was mostly hands on with some Q&A at the end. The last two days were on set during a planned video shoot. At the very end of the last day, we would meet for about an hour and go over everything we learned. In my experience, most, if not all of the students were interested in video and storytelling. Some had audio experience, but I never felt that any of these students were going to go on to be full-time audio engineers. If you decide to pursue one of these programs, make sure it has elements that you can use later on in your career. I certainly wish I had taken one of these classes when I was younger, I'm sure it would have helped my production career. But I don't think I would have become a full-time filmmaker because of it.

Where to get an associate degree? Community colleges, small colleges, universities, and for-profit schools. There are pluses and minuses to each of these choices, so study your options carefully. In my opinion, your best bet would be a community college or university off-shoot program. They tend to be regulated more carefully and usually vet educators more thoroughly than others. On the other hand, there are some great for-profit programs out there that work closely with area universities to supply accredited core classes. If you go this route, it's wiser to choose a school that has a dedicated degree for audio recording and producing. These are usually found in production-rich cities with many seasoned professionals that may adjunct teach at the school.

THE CERTIFICATE OR "CERTIFICATE" ROUTE

You can bypass formal education and go with a for-profit, non-accredited school that only teaches recording and related skills. Different from community colleges, these can consist of career colleges that are regulated by state agencies tasked with making sure post-secondary private schools comply with state laws. Then there are others that don't fit into this category and are strictly private. Most of these programs ditch all the math and English classes and go right to the core. They typically offer a variety of choices:

- A full-bore two-year program teaching everything from recording, editing, and mixing audio; to music theory; digital media and video production; and basic marketing skills.
- An audio production course only, usually spread out over several weeks or months.
- An a la carte approach that lets the student cherry pick classes of interest.
- A short crash course in audio engineering, usually from two to six weeks in length.
- Advanced classes in engineering, production, management, technical, or other industry-related skill.

A mix of industry veterans, educators, and former students typically make up the staff of these programs. Some offer audio engineer certifications upon completion of a course, but beware that there is no officially recognized certification for audio engineers or producers in the United States. These certificates may be only a framed document you get when you finish the course and pay your bill. Some of the better ones may rely on high standards set by the company, a non-profit educational organization, or from long-standing industry expectations. Either way, they are only as real as the paper they're printed on. But if you go through one of these programs and feel as if you got a great education, have a greater understanding of the craft, have new confidence in yourself, and didn't get ripped off, then that's great. Let other budding engineers know about it.

The best thing to do when researching these types of schools is to talk with former students. Don't rely entirely on the school providing those contacts, ask around or research on the web. You need as many unbiased opinions as you can get about their experiences. Because a lot of these schools are unregulated, you can't really know what you're getting ahead of time. If the school has a good reputation, then explore further. But if all you find is marketing material, then tread carefully. Some of the smaller programs may be simple start-ups with great intentions but little track records. Others may be long-standing and respected schools that have great teachers and resources. I've heard from both ends of the spectrum from students on their experiences in these schools, from crowded classes with little hands on, to one-on-one instruction and post-graduation assistance. It pays to do your research.

SPECIAL CERTIFICATE CLASSES

More and more universities, colleges, government agencies, and organizations are teaming up to offer training classes for film industry crews. These can get very specialized, from makeup, gripping, camera assist, production assistance, and location audio. Many offer a certificate upon successful completion. Again, there is no official audio engineering certification, but these usually carry a little bit more weight on a resume because of the involvement of large education institutions. These classes are usually short term – maybe a day, weekend, or week. They are also very concentrated, teaching theory, technique, and etiquette. They can be very useful if you are trying to break into the film industry or add new skills to your toolbox. Taught by industry professionals and/or certified educators, they can be well organized and complete. Look for these in your area by going to web sites of state film commissions, local industry organizations, nearby colleges and universities, and national organizations such as the Audio Engineering Society (www.aes.org).

MILITARY TRAINING

Another option to consider is joining the military to receive training for broadcasting, journalism, and media relations. Each arm of the U.S. military has its own department for handling public affairs. Many of their efforts funnel into the Armed Forces Radio and Television Service (AFRTS, lovingly called "A-farts"). A short time in a military broadcasting job can jump start your engineering career while building trust with future employers. I've worked with several professionals with a AFRTS background and all had positive experiences and solid training. There are a few considerations for these jobs, however. One is that there are no guarantees you will get into your desired field. Researching opportunities is essential if you are looking at this route. The other consideration is if the military life is for you. It's a serious commitment for sure, but it can also be a positive life changing decision.

THE OBSERVATIONAL AND EXPERIENTIAL ROUTE

Remember earlier in the chapter when I said that education comes in many forms, including structured, mentoring, experiential, research, and observational? Well, this is mostly the path that I was forced to take. Getting a non-paid internship in a recording studio, broadcast station, video production company, or other media production organization can give you direct exposure to audio production. Let's get some of the real-world pros and cons to this path out of the way now.

Pro	Con
Direct contact with working professionals	Unstructured, informal, and a little bit demeaning
Some professionals may take you under their wing and mentor you	You will do all the dirty work and work long and/or late hours
You'll be around the buzz of the industry	You may be only seen as free labor
You'll be able to ask questions	It's usually a thankless job
Hard work and "face time" may lead to a job	No pay

These pros and cons are usually true, even in school-sponsored internships. Paid internships with large organizations are usually a little bit better because the organization or company has some skin in the game. Although internships are really low on the totem pole, remember how much you'll see by looking up.

THE ON-THE-JOB ROUTE

This is essentially the route I took because of the lack of formal audio education classes being offered in the late 70s and early 80s. My enthusiasm, drive, and determination landed me a part-time job in a radio station where I could learn and absorb everything audio. This is also how many of my friends got their training. It's still a viable path today, even though it's an unstructured and potentially chaotic one. What kind of audio engineering jobs would be available to someone with little to no work history in the field?

- **Hotel A/V technician.** Set up video players, podiums, PA systems, pipe and draping, stages, lighting, and other live event technical needs. There may be paid basic training opportunities with these types of jobs.

- **Hospital, school, corporation, or organization A/V technician.** This is essentially the same job as hotel A/V. There may be added responsibilities such as janitorial or maintenance. There may be overriding requirements such as IT specialist.

- **Clerical, administrative, sales, or other position.** Getting an unrelated job at a broadcasting outlet, studio, company, hospital, school, etc. where there is some kind of audio/video production going on can sometimes lead to an engineering job. Simply showing interest in production can get your foot in the door. We used to call this type of job "emptying trash cans," because of one's close proximity to the action. Making face time with the production people can sometimes give you some credibility if you decide to ask for a production job. Of course, your dedication to your "real" job will further cement your reputation and work ethic. One possible caveat to this route is that no matter how high you advance in the company, your level of respect may always be viewed as the first job you worked. At one company I worked at, my manager experienced this. He got his first job here while he was still in college. And being low man on the totem pole, he would have to set up A/V equipment in the board room. When he was elevated years later to a vice-president position, guess what – he was still called on to set up A/V equipment.

- **Create your own engineering job at a company.** This is not as far-fetched as it first sounds. If you are in a position in an organization that may require media content to be created, you may become the point person. If you're supervising a project that needs more than a PowerPoint presentation, your keen skills may sway the boss into letting you buy a microphone and some editing software. Often times, companies that are paying outside resources for media creation will try to cut costs by doing it themselves. We sometimes call these decisions "Someone with an iMac and iMovie." It's a little disparaging I admit, because it usually means that company watched me, the professional, do my job and figured they could do it cheaper themselves. Because media software is more robust than ever, they usually deliver a decent product out of the box if the content is good. But when things get complicated, the company will sometimes come back to me, the professional, with hat in hand wanting me to fix their bad mistakes. But my griping aside, sometimes these decisions by companies can jump-start a full-fledged media department. I worked for a college sports marketing company, Host Communications, Inc. for 14 years. They started with sales and marketing only, then eventually bought out a recording studio in their same building. That little studio in an office building's basement, where I started, eventually broadcast live national radio programs, serviced major ad agencies for such brands as Long John Silvers and Valvoline, and had a couple of video producers. We would eventually build the department up to two recording studios, a six-bay radio broadcast center, and two video editing suites. We produced weekly national network television shows; serviced major ad agencies and brands; broadcast local, regional, and national radio shows; and operated the NCAA Radio Network with more than 2,000 affiliates. All that from a company wanting to bring production in-house. Never say never.

- **Get paid to learn audio production.** If you work for a large company, university or college, or organization, they may offer full or partial education reimbursement. If they see the value of having you learn a new skill that you can eventually apply to your job, this may be a sweet route for you to take. You basically continue to work your current job, which may include some production, while taking night classes, special certification classes, or attending seminars and workshops. Check with your employer to see if you qualify.

- **Transition from another production job.** Maybe you are already working in media creation as a video editor, shooter, or production assistant (PA). Most video companies, or organizations with a video department, don't have separate audio facilities. The iMovie on an iMac syndrome is often at play here as well. Video editing programs are often limited in audio tools. Or, if they have decent tools built in, they are often misunderstood or underutilized. If your goal is to be an audio engineer, then you can start to work with your supervisor to get the skills necessary to, at the very least, acquire a separate audio app to have more precision and control over your soundtracks. This may lead to a full-time audio position along with the creation of an audio suite. When I was working at Host Communications, an engineer that I had hired several years before came to me one day. He admitted that he was nervous and scared to tell me that he didn't want to work in audio anymore. Our department had two video editing suites and a team of video producers that were cranking out national television shows, sports videos, and other fun projects. He had been watching what they were creating and fell in love with it. So, we came up with a plan to slowly train him in video production that would lead to an eventual full-time job as a video producer. It worked, he became a damn good producer, and I hired another engineer. It all worked out for him, the company and me. He was excited about his job; the company gained another valuable video producer; and I didn't have someone working for me that didn't have their heart in their job. I've always told my employees "This is my dream. If it's your dream too, then we'll do great things together. If it isn't then let's figure out what your dream is." It would save a lot of time and grief if employees and management were honest with each other from the get-go.

THE FREE-LANCE ROUTE

Free-lancing from the get-go will at first be similar to stepping into a job with no experience. I don't recommend trying this full-time right off the bat. Slowly work your way into recording studios, onto film sets, or into theaters. If you have a little bit of experience, you might pick up a small job here and there. This can be challenging no matter what size market you're in. A large production market like NYC, LA, Chicago will be swarming with hungry sharks with lots more experience than you, and you'll be competing for non-union jobs against non-union freelancers. On the other end of the spectrum, small markets will not have enough work to go around. This is one route that you'll be constantly scouring ads, sending emails, getting on crew lists, and sending resumes. This is more of a long play, in that it may take months or years to get any regular work. Many forces will be in play that will determine whether there are a lot of jobs open, who gets them, and how well they pay. Here are what some of those freelance jobs entail:

- **Free-lance film/video sound engineer**. Among film production crews, this is one of the most common forms of "employment." Once you work with an assistant director or shooter, you may wind up on their short list. Attending a college program for film / audio / video / broadcast / theater will also put you in touch with industry professionals that need free-lance crew. Many students work free-lance jobs during semesters and summer break.

- **Free-lance broadcast engineer**. Many medium and larger markets have opportunities to work at local sporting, entertainment, and news events that are being broadcast on TV, radio, or the web. These types of jobs are usually grunt work like laying cable, erecting sets, or other manual labor. With experience and luck, some jobs may entail setting microphones, configuring mixers, distributing communications gear, and coordinating wireless microphones. And the more you work on one crew, the chances increase of getting more responsibility. Check with all your local venues, broadcast outlets, and production companies for opportunities.

- **Free-lance live sound engineer.** Live events like sports, music, stage plays, seminars, conferences, church services, auctions, etc. usually need live sound. Live event companies will usually provide amplification equipment and lead engineers, but they often need free-lance help for laying cables, setting microphones, and even audio playback and recording. Some venues may have full-time personnel, but they often need help for large events. Popular nightclubs with their own sound system often need back-up engineers for certain nights. Check with local live event companies, concert halls, stadiums and arenas, schools, churches, and live music clubs for opportunities.

- **Free-lance music engineer**. For music jobs, live concerts and stage plays are the most common, but some studios need help with larger projects. Some of these may be remote recordings in venues for music acts or musical theater. Often these will be for orchestras, choirs, or multi-performer events. Check with local recording studios for opportunities.

- **Free-lance recording engineer.** There are also opportunities for recording speeches, oral histories, weddings, church services, lectures, depositions, meetings, and other events. Of course, local recording studios are usually called first for many of these, but they often need help. There are also local and national A/V and event companies that rely on local free-lancers to record events and meetings. Some may also require you to set-up and operate video projection equipment and perhaps own your audio equipment. Owning a small arsenal of recording equipment can definitely increase your chances of being hired freelance. You can build up equipment over time as you work more often. Carefully buying a mix of new and gently used equipment can help your bottom line. The latest and greatest gear doesn't usually get you the job, but your skill in capturing and delivering a quality product surely will. So, as you build your kit, only buy what will make you money. Contact A/V event companies, churches, university history departments, venues, schools, court reporting services, wedding videographers, and auditoriums.

So, as you can see, there are many ways to get into the business, whether by formal structured education, or just talking yourself into a job. What you do next however, will shape how well you do in your next job.

6. Building Your Foundation

"The loftier the building, the deeper must the foundation be laid."

Thomas A. Kempis

Let's take the second step towards your ultimate goal: *Envision where you'll be in ten years.* In Chapter 3, I had you look down the road a decade from now, and hopefully see yourself finally doing the kind of sound work you really want to do. Because life can take us in different directions, your initial goal may not be realized in ten years, twenty, or ever. But aiming in that direction is what will keep you on course to succeed in the industry. Remember my story of being dead set on recording music, only to wind up doing mostly film sound design and advertising? Well, I love what I do and have no regrets. But truthfully, I'd jump at the chance to record jazz groups all day long if that opportunity came along and I could make a living doing it.

I parlayed my music experience and training into succeeding at creating soundtracks for film, radio, and stage. While I was working my first real job at the film production company, I recorded music with my friends and family. I also recorded my own stuff, even selling some jingles and backing tracks along the way. These music experiences within a recording studio designed for film soundtracks and advertising just solidified my opinion that we're all in this profession together. Whether we're recording music, creating film soundtracks, making ads, talking on the radio, or mixing live music in an arena, we all basically use the same tools. We're all card-carrying members of the Benevolent Society of Button Pushers (I just made that up, but wouldn't it be a cool name for a band?). We use mixers, microphones, speakers, and our ears. I liken it to science laboratories. One lab may synthesize drugs, another may sample DNA, and yet another may research molecular biology. To the untrained eye, all these labs may look alike because there are constants in the tools they use, such as test tubes, pipettes, exhaust hoods, centrifuges, and white coats. But scientists will tell you that the difference between all labs is more in how they are used, not what they use.

I bring this up because no matter where you are working after your first jump into the job market, learn your tools. You will be able to use them in all kinds of ways you haven't imagined. If your dream is to record and produce hip-hop but you work in a public radio station, use that to your advantage. Learn to work the microphone so that it doesn't pop when you say, "Peter Piper picked a peck of pickled peppers." If you want to mix live music but are working as an AV technician in a hotel, learn to equalize the PA system so that you get maximum gain without causing feedback from the podium mic.

Here's a real-world example. When I transitioned from a small film company to a corporate media company, I handled most of the projects just fine. Host Communications was primarily a college sports marketing company, and our studios produced programming for various sports radio networks around the country. Some of these programs were live radio broadcasts from our studios with hosts, remote locations, and sound bite and music cues. I was big time intimidated. Sure, I had worked at a radio station in college, but all I had to do was pot up my mic once an hour and blurt out the station ID (and not fall asleep). This was a very different situation. When it came time to observe my first live broadcast, I watched my boss Tim Campbell move his eight arms back-and-forth from faders to cart machines in a flurry, all while cueing the announcer and hitting seventeen other buttons. At least it sure looked like that to a wide-eyed young engineer. Later, as he was breaking down every step of what he did, I had a *Karate Kid* moment. It dawned on me that live radio broadcasting was exactly like mixing a band in a bar. Let me explain.

My brother-in-law was in a rock band that I used to mix live occasionally. During this time, I had also recorded them in the first studio I worked at, so I knew all their cover songs and originals pretty well. When the guitar solo came, I knew to raise that fader and bring down this other one. When the solo is over, bring that down and raise the vocals. It was all about hitting cues and knowing where your sources are. That's exactly what live broadcast is. Hitting your cues. When it came time for me to step up and engineer my first live radio broadcast, I couldn't wait. I admit I was nervous, but not as nervous as poor Tim was. Before every broadcast Tim engineered, he would close all the office doors, turn off the office lights, illuminate the red ON AIR light, and take a deep, slightly quivering breath. It must have worked for him because he rarely let a mistake slip by. But that was not my style. When I got ready for my first solo flight, I intentionally left all the doors open and the office lights on because I didn't want anything to be dramatically different from how I worked every day. I did however ask Tim to go to his office because I needed to do this on my own. I just mixed the show like a big, long music set in a bar, letting the lead vocals shine here, a solo come out there, a drum solo over there. After the program ended Tim came in and congratulated me, all the time bewildered that I hadn't done a total lockdown and blackout.

Here's another real-world example. Flash forward about fifteen years to my first year in my own studio, Dynamix Productions. We were sandwiched in the back of a medical office building along with a video production company, biding our time until our group could find a bigger facility to move to. In order to get to my digs, visitors came through the front lobby, entered the video production company, went around and down the hallway, through the storage area, through the kitchen, and finally to our offices. If we needed to record a voice-over, we had to escort the talent back through the kitchen and storage area, up the hallway to the front of the video company, and into a little converted coat closet. It was a cozy situation to say the least. One day we got a call from MGM Studios in Los Angeles. A young actor, Dakota Fanning, was in the area filming a movie and they needed for her to come in and do ADR for a movie called *Hide and Seek*. **A**utomated **D**ialog **R**eplacement, in the simplest terms, is when a line or more of dialog needs to be replaced and is re-recorded while synchronized with the picture. The actor watches a video of the scene while performing the new dialog line. It requires special microphones, synchronized video and audio equipment, and in this case, a digital two-way connection between my studio and a studio in Los Angeles.

Stay with me on this, it will get a bit thick on technical stuff but there is a payoff. In my VO booth, I set up a short boom microphone similar to what would be used on a film set. I also put a video monitor in the booth for the actor to see the video. The LA studio sent their ADR engineer to Lexington to supervise the session. Robert (R.J.) Kiser brought a videotape of the scenes that we would be overdubbing. The studio in LA had an exact copy of this videotape so that we would all be on the same page. Now to make things a bit complicated. I needed to synchronize the videotape with my digital recording software so that when I pushed play on the video player, my audio would chase, or "slave" to the video. This was accomplished by accessing a special audio track on videotape called a *timecode* track. Timecode identifies each frame of video with a unique running clock number, like 1 hour, 3 minutes, 7 seconds, 14th frame, expressed as 01:03:07;14. This track was plugged into an input on my computer that my audio software recognized as timecode. When the videotape is at 01:03:07;14, my audio software is at exactly the same place. This way video and audio will be synchronized during recording.

Now to get even more complicated. The film's director, who was in LA, wanted to watch the video and hear the actor's performance at the same time we did. This could only be accomplished with a real-time digital connection between studios. This was the early 2000s when internet speeds were not even close to what we have today, so we relied on a digital transmission method managed by telecom companies called ISDN[25]. Today in the 2020s it's nearly dead, but some broadcasters still use it for its granite-like reliability. For this project, I needed to send the output of my mixer to one audio channel of the ISDN, and the timecode from the videotape to the other audio channel of the ISDN.[+] This way, when I pushed play on the video player, my audio program would play and record in sync. The director's video player would also play in sync and he would hear the actor's new line of dialog. Add to this the verbal communications that had to take place between me, the ADR engineer at my side, the actor in the booth, and the LA studio. They were doing their own complex communications gymnastics in LA as well.

Now the fun begins. In order to get Lexington and LA synchronized, I had to rewind the videotape to 30 seconds before

---

[25] Integrated Services Digital Network

[+] Timecode exists in two forms: VITC, Vertical Inverted Time Code, which is burned into the video along with other information; LTC, Longitudinal Time Code, which is an audio signal which sort of sounds like a dial-up modem.

the new dialog cut-in point. I then played the videotape machine (VTR) for 5 seconds to remotely cue up the VTR in LA. We call this "burst." Here was my procedure:

1. Rewind to 30 seconds before cue.
2. Stop.
3. Cue LA that burst was coming.
4. Burst for 5 seconds.
5. Stop.
6. Rewind 5 seconds.
7. Stop.
8. Wait for LA verbal cue to proceed.
9. Play VTR.
10. Verbally cue talent that tape was rolling.
11. Verbally cue LA that tape was rolling.
12. Hit record on audio software.
13. Play through scene while recording new line.
14. Stop.
15. Rewind to 30 seconds before cue.
16. Stop.
17. Cue LA that burst was coming.
18. Burst for 5 seconds.
19. Stop.
20. Rewind 5 seconds.
21. Stop.
22. Cue LA that playback was coming.
23. Play VTR for playback of previously recorded take.

This went on and on all afternoon. When I first started to do it, I was nervous, confused, and out of sorts. It was nothing like anything I had ever done, or so I thought. My training in broadcast and live music suddenly kicked in and I had another *Karate Kid* moment. I remember turning to Robert and saying, "Oh, it's just like broadcast!" I was back in my element. The rest of the day went smoothly, and it became one of those "never forget" experiences. Who would have thought that my parlayed experience of music to broadcast would parlay my broadcast experience to ADR? Fortunately, digital video is incorporated directly into audio software these days so that two studios can synchronize nearly instantly without all the bursting and cueing (and cussing).

One amusing situation occurred during that intense ADR session. In between takes while cueing and bursting, the director would be talking with the talent. The slightest pause in conversation would have the LA engineer and me quickly saying, "Burst," or "Cued," or "Locked." This was because everything was going back and forth on one shared audio line. About halfway through the session, I heard an unfamiliar voice in LA giving me cues. I didn't respond for a minute, thinking it was someone else cutting in from the machine room or something. Well, I got an earful from that voice. They had switched engineers midstream without even telling me. I was being tag teamed!

Another tool I use when engineering broadcasts or ADR sessions is my music training. While playing music, you draw on things you learned in rehearsals, like which notes to play, rhythms, tempo, and playing through mistakes. Before playing a concert, a musician warms up by playing scales, tuning the instrument, oiling valves, and playing some passages. Before every broadcast or ADR session, I "rehearse" by testing microphones, moving faders into position, checking outputs, going through cues, and tracing every signal path in case I need to change something. Warmups and rehearsals help get you into the right frame of mind for the task you're about to do. If you're an athlete, I'll bet that you go through stretches, warm-ups, and mental exercises to prepare yourself for the competition. A basketball player visiting a new arena will warm up on the new court to familiarize themselves with the floor, rims, and backdrop. Even though the court is the same size and the goals are the same height as anywhere else, it helps to draw on similar experiences when doing something new and different.

The lesson here is to use the tools you have and be willing to adapt to new situations. Skills you learn in seemingly unrelated jobs and experiences can be tapped into later when you least expect it. When I was toiling in between college studies, I took a job at the local K-Mart, a discount department store chain. It was a floor job in the home improvement department. We sold paint, wallpaper, tools, lumber, fencing, concrete, roofing, and a small assortment of other items found in larger home improvement centers. My dad was one of the reasons I took this job (and the fact that I was broke). Dad could build anything, and he did, including furniture, a screen porch, a house, and a bridge. The bridge was part of his Army National Guard engineer training in case you were wondering. He was determined to pass on these skills to his children. So just about every weekend, he would call me to the basement or backyard and declare that today he was going to teach me something new. As a teenager, that was the last thing I wanted to do (rolling eyes here). But Dad could be persistent, so I usually relented, and (head down kicking dirt) I always had fun with him. I'm glad he took this initiative, because I am an intrepid homeowner that balks at paying someone else to do something that I know I can do myself. His lessons helped me work that K-Mart job. Knowing what a 2x4 is, how to mix concrete, how to paint a wall, and how to shingle a roof were all bits of wisdom I passed on to customers. I even sketched out a plan for a backyard shed for one customer (I hope it's still standing). Working that job at K-Mart taught me much more than home improvement, however. It taught me how to deal with customers (good and very, very, bad), managers (passive and overly ambitious), and fellow employees (sympathetic and backstabbing). It also taught me how to count money (and know when someone's dipping into the till), stock and front shelves (to make a nice appearance) and drive a forklift (use the right tools for the job). And lastly, it taught me to pick your battles wisely, and have empathy for other retail workers. I apply most of those skills and lessons I learned at K-Mart almost every day:

- The customer is always right, even if he's not.
- The boss is always right, even if she's not.
- **Learn to work with fellow employees** so the job gets done. Don't fall into the trap set by disgruntled, gossipy, or backstabbing people.
- **Keep an eye on the money** (and your time, because time is money) – some people will try to steal it away from you when you're not looking.
- **Your outward appearance** will affect how customers/managers/employees see you and your company. A good-looking product display entices customers to buy it. A neat-looking employee shows you care about the company and the customer.
- **Use the correct tools** when lifting heavy loads (and projects). Don't try to do everything yourself.
- **Not every wrong is worth starting a war over**. Don't look at the outcome you desire. Look at the toll and damage the battle will create, and then decide if it's worth it.
- **Treat others the way you would want to be treated**. If someone chews you out for no reason, it's not you, don't bite

back - they're probably just having a bad day. If they have a reason to chew you out, don't bite back – be calm and take steps to fix the problem.

Like my K-Mart job, I also draw on lessons I learned as a newspaper photographer in high school and college:

- **The public can be very finicky.** With social media dominating the way people perceive each other, you need to heavily guard your public face. Stay away from anything controversial and stick with cat videos.

- **A deadline is a deadline.** Deadlines wouldn't exist if they weren't important. Although many deadlines are flexible, get your project done on time. If you get it done early, you'll look like Chief Engineer Scotty, the miracle worker on *Star Trek* who was always being pushed by Captain Kirk to fix the ship faster than what seemed possible.

- **Managing your time carefully won't leave clients frustrated.** Build buffers into your schedules in case of unforeseen events and problems. Back time your deadlines so you know when to stop one task and move on to the next one.

- **Careful planning of projects will keep you from having to stop and restart multiple times.** A road map is critical to success, even if you have to take a detour. Fewer surprises allow you to focus on giving the client the best product.

- **A front-page byline today is old news tomorrow.** Accolades are nice, but people have short memories for the good things you do. However, one misstep today will be remembered for a long time. You're really only as good as your last project with most clients, so make sure that every project is a good experience for them.

- **A bad image can sometimes be saved.** If you do have a misstep or something goes terribly wrong with a project, correct the problem right now. What you do immediately after a problem occurs will set the tone for your client's confidence in you. If it means sending your client to another studio, refunding their money, or working through the night, the client will see your dedication to fixing the problem at all costs. Fall on your sword and they will remember the fix more than the mistake.

- **Always "fess up" to your mistakes.** What do they say about dirty politicians and leaders? It's not the deed, but the cover-up that's so bad. You may lose face today, but admitting – and correcting – your mistakes will go a long way to building customer confidence.
- **Get all your facts right, then double- and triple-check them.** Before you deliver to your customer, always assume you made mistakes. Go through your project from beginning to end while checking your notes. If possible, step away for an hour or a day and recheck with a fresh mind. When you work so closely on details, you can forget that there is a forest around you.
- **You are not the story.** A reporter's objective is to be a fly on the wall and report facts, not insert themselves or their opinions into a story. Your goal should be to facilitate the goals of the business, project, and customer. You're there to help the business and customer succeed. Do that, and you too will succeed.
- **Don't barge into a darkroom without knocking.** If you do, you could ruin someone's work. Thinking only about your needs can imperil someone else's efforts, and ultimately the entire team's efforts. Being one-sided can cause problems for other people. Before doing anything drastic, check with fellow employees, your client, or your boss before proceeding.

The takeaway in all these lessons from other jobs and experiences is to always be on the lookout for ways to learn. Almost any skill from one experience can be helpful while learning a new skill. Knowing how to cut wood and swing a hammer eventually helped me as an audio engineer. How? Thanks to Dad teaching me construction skills, I was able to build my current studio. We built walls, doors, floors, windows, acoustic panels, and studio furniture. Thanks to my high school geometry teacher Mr. Jenkins, I can build studios with walls and windows skewed 6° for standing wave deflection. Thanks to Mom, my high school speed-reading teacher, I can quickly scan scripts for key words. Thanks to my music education, I can read a conductor's score while recording an orchestra. Thanks to playing solo on stage, I can empathize with nervous people that have never been behind a microphone. Everything that you are and that you've experienced is your foundation. The steps you take now will build on that for a solid future as an audio producer.

7. KNOWLEDGE IS POWER

"Knowledge is Power"

Francis Bacon

Y ou've heard the phrase "knowledge is power" over and over again. But it's true. In step three, I direct you to gather information. This could really be a turning point for you if you don't jump off the train too early. As you're researching the industry, you may be satisfied right out of the gate with a particular school or opportunity. If it's exactly what you want, then take that next step and go for it. However, I would always recommend going into it with eyes wide open. Research the crap out of that school. The glossy brochures only show the outside, what's inside?

For most of my career, I have been around thoroughbred horse racing. After all, I live in the self-professed "Horse Capital of the World," Lexington, Kentucky. It's a major industry in this part of Kentucky and affects nearly everyone that lives here. Streets, neighborhoods, and shopping centers are named after horses or horse farms. I can pet thoroughbreds along white fence lined roads just ten minutes from my doorstep. My sister was even once a co-owner of several thoroughbreds. As part of my job, I've been to many horse farms and racetracks. These are usually beautiful places to drive by, and when you get a chance to actually get inside one of these places, it can be magical. Mostly.

Our local racetrack, Keeneland, has earned a worldwide reputation as a class act. Built in the 1930s as an architectural nod to the great courses in Britain, it lies on rolling farmland just outside Lexington's beltway. Next to Keeneland is the storied Calumet Farm. Yes, the Calumet Baking Powder name originates from there, as does a record eight Kentucky Derby winners. When you drive through the old iron gates of Keeneland, you're greeted with a canopy of trees leading up to a gray stone clubhouse that faces the racetrack. Every tree, blade of grass, bird, and cloud in the sky is perfectly positioned. It's a wonderland of beauty. Go into the grandstand, and all the seats and rails are painted a regal dark green. Venture into the clubhouse lobby and feel the warmth from the massive fireplace facing cozy antique furniture. Go anywhere the public can at Keeneland, and you're knocked over with its charm and elegance. But go in the back rooms, back where the servers hurry with trays of food, runners carry racing forms to the concourse, cleaners carry a broom, and it's...nice.

I have been all over Keeneland – in the stalls, in the kitchens, inside the scoreboard, up on the roof, and in a barn. Everything under the cover is in place and orderly. I can't say that about some other racetracks I've been to. They will remain nameless, but most are pretty famous. There's one I used to work at that was elegant on the outside, and just old on the inside. Nothing terrible or unexpected, it just has the look of a place that has been well worn but well loved. But another one has spit and polish on the outside, and just spit on the inside. Whenever it's on television, they either show a really wide shot from far away, or really tight close-ups of the jockeys and horses. There's just too much dilapidation for any beauty shots.

As in racetracks and books, you can never really know what's behind that glitzy cover without looking inside. It has to be more than just a peek – it's got to be a thorough looking-over. If you're looking at a college to attend, it will pay to wander around campus and observe the activity on your own without a guide. Go to the buildings where you will take classes. Go to the administration offices. Go to the cafeteria. Go to the mundane places that are not polished up for the public. Listen to people talk. Are they generally happy, frustrated, nonchalant, bored? Unguarded conversation can be telling of the mood of a place. Look in the classrooms, bathrooms, offices, and parking lots. Are they clean, messy, organized, filthy? Look at the structure, roof, foundation, and grounds of the buildings. Are they orderly, in disrepair, being updated, outdated? What's behind the mask can pretty much tell you most of what you need to know about an institution. It won't tell you everything, for that you'll have to do some research.

Go online to the Better Business Burea (www.bbb.org) and check out that institution or private school. If they are a member of the BBB and in good standing, they will have met high standards of resolving complaints (if there are any). Even if the school is not a member, any egregious complaints lodged with the BBB will be noted here. Look closely at any complaints and resolutions to see if they are telling of a systemic problem with the school or are more a result of administration errors common to large organizations. As a general rule, the larger a company or organization, the more complaints will be registered, regardless of fault. It just goes with the territory.

Check with any associations or accreditation agencies the school lists they are a part of. Find out if there are any complaints, or even accolades, for the school. Ask the staff if there are any other resources you can research to find out more about the school you're interested in. A little personal interaction can sometimes yield more avenues of research than the internet can deliver.

And finally, contact people working directly in the field you want to get into. For instance, if you want to work in radio broadcasting, contact radio station managers and program directors for their opinion on your current path to a career. Once they know you're not asking for a job, they will usually be more than willing to share their knowledge and guidance. Don't ask them to rate a school you're interested in, they may feel trapped into giving a positive opinion when in fact, they have very little good to say about the school. Instead, let them know that you are looking into this particular school, but are interested in alternatives to achieve your goal. After your conversation, send them a handwritten thank you note in the mail. Include your email and telephone number just in case they may have an opportunity or additional information for you. By the way, please don't have a cutesy sounding email address for business. I don't know how many students and job seekers give me a personal email that sounds like a drunken weekend theme. There are plenty of free services out there to have multiple email addresses. Keep your personal and business lives separate – more on that later.

Once you've nailed down a few schools you're interested in, it's time to start thinking about your finances. If you can afford to pay outright, that's great. But most Americans need some kind of financial aid. Get with the school of your choice and talk about your options. Ask about scholarship opportunities. These are often not publicized, so ask what scholarships are available, you just might qualify for one. Some are small, but anything helps.

For-profit schools may also offer financial aid or payment options. If the school has a good track record and is what you're looking for, this may be a good option. But watch out for inflated interest rates for payment plans. It might be better to get an unsecured loan from a bank or family if the total payback amount is too high.

You could also work a job or two while going to school. I held down four part-time jobs while attending full-time. I would not recommend anyone do that though, because something will break (and did). However, for many, working while going to college is the only option. That's okay, most make it work. Make your school aware of the situation because there may be opportunities for grants, scholarships, or freelance jobs that may come along. Whatever route you take to finance your education, make a plan before you start so that you can completely focus on your schoolwork instead of worrying about the money. It may be hard to get by while in school, but keep looking to the horizon and know that one day you'll be living your dream.

If you have decided to forgo the education route and to strike out on your own, then prepare for some hardship and/or waiting. If you will not be employed while you look for a job in the audio industry, be prepared to have at least six months of living expenses. Most full-time jobs at larger companies take about two to four months to fill, so you can't be in a hurry. Free-lance work will come and go. It's really hard to predict the ebb and flow of production work year to year. So, if you are going to rely completely on free-lancing, especially if you're starting out, it's a roll of the dice. Contact production companies around your area to see how much work is available, especially over those last few years. Start your conversation with a producer or production manager in a way that doesn't sound like you're asking for an immediate job. I often get calls from people either new to town or just starting out. They are usually just getting a feel for the free-lance market while also getting their name out there. Networking is a must for free-lancers.

And speaking of networking, even if you have secured financing and are ready to go to a school for recording, it's good to get your name out there now. I'll have a section later on in the book dedicated to marketing yourself, but if you can lay a foundation when you're still in school, it will only help to speed up getting hired when you graduate. If your school takes summers off, then that's the time to work as many free-lance gigs as you can. As a general rule, film and video production increases in the warm months. Getting your name in the hat early gives you a leg up when summer starts, so start contacting production companies in the late winter.

One other thing to think about when looking at schools is to find out what, if any, placement programs a school has. Though no school can guarantee employment upon graduation, most will have some kind of program in place to increase those chances. Don't procrastinate and only start thinking about this during your last semester, this is something that you need to start your sophomore year (if you're in a four-year program). Meet with a counselor from the placement office or career center to map out a plan. You should also talk about an internship while you're there. Most accredited schools offer class credits (and some with pay) for internships with local companies. I accept interns from a multitude of colleges in the area. This can be a great experience for you and may lead to a job down the road with the company. I have had interns that I've hired either part-time or job-to-job because they had skills and promise. Larger companies routinely utilize interns as a testing ground before they hire them.

8. THE JOB SEARCH

"If opportunity doesn't knock, build a door."

Milton Berle

O K, let's take a trip into the future. You're either almost out of school or out on your own, so you should be looking for a job right now. In the chapter "What Does an Audio Engineer Do?" (page 55), I outlined all the possible job titles in this field. Each company that is hiring probably has a unique description of the job title that doesn't quite fit into the neat little label I gave it. That's fine, because every professional field blurs the lines when it comes to titles so that they fit into each company or organization's hierarchy. You can define your desired position on your resume, but you should be flexible with potential employers. You should also be flexible in what types of employment you are seeking when you first start looking. Yes, you should definitely focus on your intended target, e.g. "radio broadcast engineer" or "live sound engineer", but be willing to interview for similar positions that might either lead to a better position or offer more learning experiences for you on your way to your dream job.

For example, let's say you have set your ultimate goal on designing sound for video games. There aren't that many game sound developers compared to other types of audio production, but there are companies that are doing things that are very similar. Don't pass up a chance to interview for a theater company needing a live sound engineer. In this type of job, the performance space has usually already been set up and tuned with audio reinforcement. This job will usually require you to place mics on actors or on stage, play music and sound effects cues, and occasionally mix a musical act. You will also need to program audio cues into software, learn the cues in the script, communicate with the show director, technical and stage directors, actors, musicians, and other support personnel. You may even get to create and design sound cues for productions. You will learn a wealth of information and gain so much experience that you can use down the road doing this job. Timing, audience reactions, creativity, programming, and rapport with everyone on the set are just a few of these.

If your ultimate goal is to be a film sound designer, then your first job at a radio station could be fruitful. Though most radio stations are automated these days, some still offer live programming, such as sports and talk. "Board-oping," or operating the audio console during a live broadcast, can be a really fun gig. You have to hit cues, match levels, and manage your time very closely. This can really help your sound design timing, from knowing when something goes on too long, or finding that right moment to play a sound cue. You might also be called upon to create commercials and show opens / closes with voice-over, sound effects, and music. You will also learn to work as a team member where everyone relies on each other to make the whole machine operate.

You can see from these two examples that almost any job in the industry can lead you down your chosen path. You have to be honest with yourself – and your future employer –of your path. The expectation of any entry-level job is that it's not a forever job. The employer knows this, the employee knows this, so don't paint an unrealistically rosy picture in your interview. Often, employers needing to fill an entry-level job treat it as just that – entry-level. They expect the candidate to either work themselves up and out of that job into a better one within the company, or to bide their time until another job comes along somewhere else. What you do need to tell the employer, with your whole heart and commitment, is that you'll do your best at the job and not let the company down. In the interview for my first job at the campus radio station, I told the program director that I was wanting to gain experience in the audio recording field and that I thought a radio station was a good place to start. I didn't rosy it up by saying I wanted to be the next great NPR host, I kept it real and honest. When I landed my next job at the film production company, I told them I wanted to work in a recording studio and that recording music was my goal. Being an entry-level position, they told me that I would gain valuable experience using the same tools that other recording studios use. The street can go both ways when everyone is honest with each other.

Which leads me to a note of caution. When interviewing for an entry-level job, be weary of any promises that sound too good to be true. Sometimes an employer will promise rapid advancement, bonus potential, rah, rah, rah. Unless it's in writing and a clear-cut path is detailed, be wary of such claims. No one can predict the future, and a few employers that need to quickly fill a position may be disingenuous with their intentions. This is not the norm, so don't assume someone is trying to mislead you if they promise potential advancement. Listen carefully to them, and politely ask if there are policies already in place that detail steps to advancement, such as employment time, revenue goals, or other definable and trackable milestones. With small companies, it's nearly impossible to predict an advancement timetable, so take any promises with a grain of salt. But if the position and the company are otherwise attractive to you, just file these promises away in your "pick your battles carefully" drawer to mull over later. Your advancement within a company is largely up to you. Good jobs aren't just handed out willy-nilly. Your commitment, drive, performance, and self-marketing will really be the driving force for your climb up the company ladder. We'll touch on this later.

There are so many books, blogs, articles, and videos about how to look for a job that I will not detail all the minutia. I will, however, give you my impressions as an employer.

First impression. The number one impression a job seeker makes on me is if they do or do not know who I am and what my company does. It may sound egocentric, but it's not. It's simply a gut feeling I have as to whether a potential employee understands my business or not. If a job seeker is just blindly sending out resumes, then I don't want a drive-by employee. As an employer, I will be investing time and money in a person new to the team. I need to make sure that employee is going to absorb and use the training I will be giving them in a productive way for the company. I am giving them tools to succeed, so I want them to succeed for my company. An employer-employee relationship should be reciprocal.

When you first contact a company for employment, make sure you know:

- What the organization does
- Its mission
- Its history

- Its place in the market
- Its key players and personnel

You don't have to know minute details about its operations, those change all the time, but have an idea if, for example, they mostly produce content for Christian broadcasting. Or if they mostly record audiobooks and podcasts. Who started the company? Are they a big player in the local market, or a start-up? Not knowing some of these answers may not matter but knowing most will make a good first impression. And for heaven's sake, get your potential employer's name right. My last name is not that hard to spell or pronounce. Kes-ter-son. Kester-son. Kesterson. NOT Keeterston, Ketterman, Kettmmmm. Call the receptionist ahead of time and ask how to pronounce the name if it's a toughie.

Below is an example of a blind email I got (which I acknowledge might be phishing spam but has industry-specific slang and terms). This was the second one I got from this individual – you might say it was the "follow up." My initial and overall impression was that this person doesn't pay attention to details – that's a big red flag. For demonstration purposes I marked it up like a brutal 4th grade schoolteacher. Now you might think I'm cruel (maybe a little), but I would never share these remarks with the sender. I *might* be more tactful and help out this unwitting job seeker with their letter writing if it weren't for the first line that begins with "Unfortunately…"

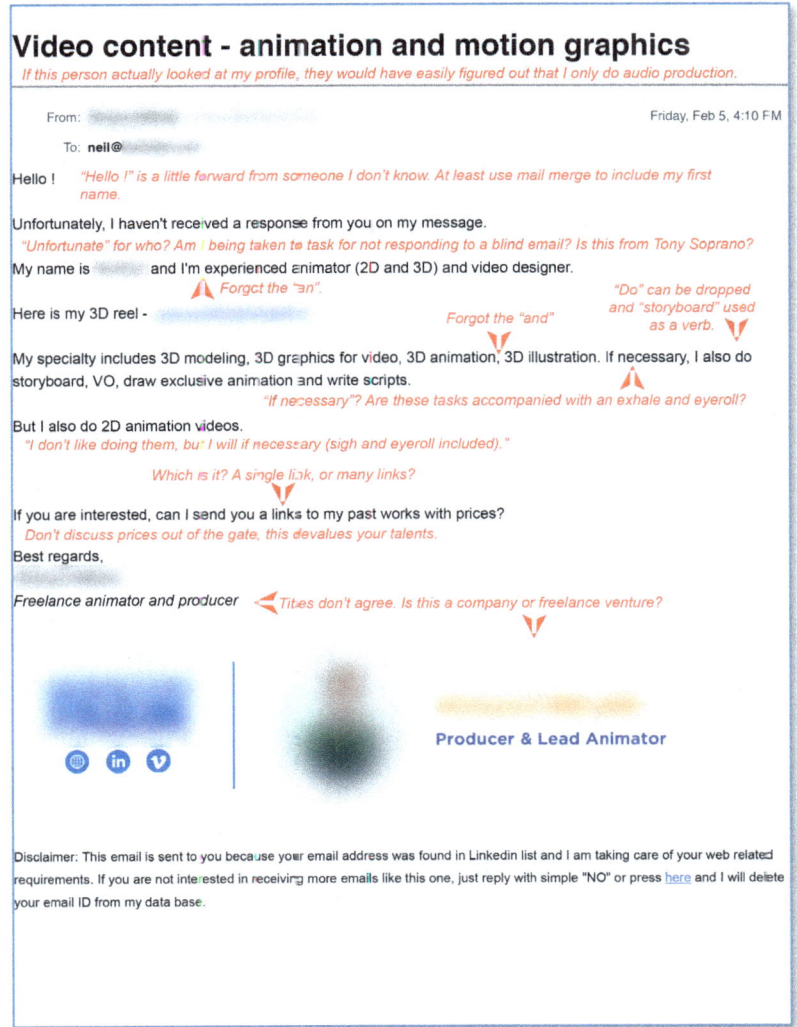

Video content - animation and motion graphics

If this person actually looked at my profile, they would have easily figured out that I only do audio production.

From: ▓▓▓▓▓▓▓▓▓▓▓▓▓▓▓▓   Friday, Feb 5, 4:10 PM

To: **neil@**▓▓▓▓▓▓

Hello !   *"Hello !" is a little forward from someone I don't know. At least use mail merge to include my first name.*

Unfortunately, I haven't received a response from you on my message.
"Unfortunate" for who? Am I being taken to task for not responding to a blind email? Is this from Tony Soprano?

My name is ▓▓▓▓▓ and I'm experienced animator (2D and 3D) and video designer.
Forget the "an".

Here is my 3D reel - ▓▓▓▓▓▓▓▓▓▓▓
Forgot the "and"

"Do" can be dropped and "storyboard" used as a verb.

My specialty includes 3D modeling, 3D graphics for video, 3D animation, 3D illustration. If necessary, I also do storyboard, VO, draw exclusive animation and write scripts.
"If necessary"? Are these tasks accompanied with an exhale and eyeroll?

But I also do 2D animation videos.
"I don't like doing them, but I will if necessary (sigh and eyeroll included)."

Which is it? A single link, or many links?

If you are interested, can I send you a links to my past works with prices?
Don't discuss prices out of the gate, this devalues your talents.

Best regards,
▓▓▓▓▓▓▓▓

Freelance animator and producer   *Titles don't agree. Is this a company or freelance venture?*

Producer & Lead Animator

Disclaimer: This email is sent to you because your email address was found in Linkedin list and I am taking care of your web related requirements. If you are not interested in receiving more emails like this one, just reply with simple "NO" or press here and I will delete your email ID from my data base.

Second impression. The next thing that tells me what potential a candidate has is how they carry themselves. Are they confident, shy, over-excited, drawn-in? I need employees that can communicate with clients and actors without ticking them off. I need to feel good that someone will not be afraid to just plow in and get the job done. I need someone that can tell me when my plan might fail and why. You need to walk into your interview with the expectation that you already have the job, and that you're here to help in any way you can. Don't be overconfident or overbearing, but having a positive attitude going in will show the employer that you have things under control.

Third impression. Dress for success. I'm not into fashion or people cow-towing to me because they want something from me. I do however believe that one must not look ragged for an interview. I had a corporate job that required me to wear a coat and tie every day. For years, I was afraid I would strangle myself if my tie got caught while rewinding reel-to-reel tape. My clients thought it was silly and a little pretentious that we had to dress to the nines when they wore business casual. Eventually the corporation relented and relaxed the dress code. My rule of thumb has always been to dress for the client or occasion. If I'm on a hot film set recording dialog, I'm wearing shorts and tennis shoes. If I'm working every day in my studio with ad agency producers, I'm wearing khakis and golf shirt or button down. If I'm going to an awards presentation, I'm putting on a suit. As an employer, I'm okay with someone coming to an interview in business casual. But showing up in cutoffs and a t-shirt is not a good start. It's not a deal breaker for me if there are many other great qualities, but it does not make for a good impression. Dress like your employer. When in doubt, wear a dress, pantsuit, or suit.

Fourth impression. Quality of career development. Experience in the field is of course important, but for entry-level positions, I'm looking more for how this individual has prepared themselves for a career. If I see some education in audio production, that's a big plus. If I see delivering pizzas while in college, that tells me that this individual is probably a hard worker. If I see they started a web site and blog for their favorite comic book hero, that tells me they are creative and have an imagination. If I see that they're in a band, that tells me they can listen very well and probably work well with others. Someone just starting out in a career feels like they're in a catch-22 scenario – they need experience to get a job but have no experience because they can't get a job. Remember in Chapter 6 (page 89) when I showed how my many previous unrelated experiences were actually foundation builders for my career? You can highlight your past experiences on your resume and in your interviews to show what value you gained from them. When I set out to build my current studio, my then-employee Dane Dickmann shared that he had done handy work and painting while in college. Because of both of our backgrounds with carpentry, electrical, and painting, we were able to successfully build the studios with a minimum of outside help. During the several months of construction, there was only one accident – I drove a Philips bit though my fingernail (I had an X on my fingernail for weeks). Unbeknownst to us, our fathers had prepared us for building recording studios.

I've taken you through what I am looking for as an employer. I would also like to share just a few tips that I've been collecting over the years to help you make a good first impression. Read what others have written about preparing for interviews to strengthen your chances.

- **Broadcast yourself.** There's no way a potential employer will know you're out there if you don't make yourself known. This means making calls, emailing companies, asking around – generally making it known that you're looking for a job as an audio engineer. Don't sit around waiting for someone to contact you out of thin air.
- **Have a short resume.** A one-pager if possible. A resume is a brochure, a ticket to get in, an elevator pitch. It's not your life story, it's a targeted introduction to what you can do. An interview is the time to go into detail. If I see a dense or long resume, I cringe. Ugh, do I have to really read this thing? I just want the headlines
- **Have more than one resume.** Your job search will take you to different types of companies. Your resume should be tailored to each company or type of company. Highlight your experiences that relate directly to that job opening or industry.
- **Don't include a "Career Objective."** I know this will make a lot of career development people angry, but I don't care what someone's "career objective" is. I bet the objective is to have a career. Yawn. I can look at experience and skills and immediately tell what someone wants to do. If you must have an introductory paragraph, then have a "Summary" and quickly explain what I'm about to read anyway.
- **Don't B.S. on your resume.** Never lie or embellish on a resume. Never. Assume that Congress will convene a special counsel and review every detail. It's just not worth it. Many people lie because they're afraid they don't have enough experience. You just need to highlight the positive things you

learned working as a dog walker instead of lying and saying you owned a kennel.

- **Have a cover letter.** An envelope with just a resume looks like it was part of an assembly line. Personalize a short letter to whom you are sending a resume to. And don't have it addressed "To whom it may concern" or to some other vague biped. I'm not "Whom," and it concerns me that someone thinks I am. Just do a quick introduction, tell me how you got my name, spell my name correctly, and give me your contact details (even though they are also on the resume). Short and sweet, I don't have a lot of time.

- **Drive to the interview location ahead of time if possible.** Don't rely on your GPS, especially if you're running late. If it's in your same town, drive over the day before at about the same time as your interview. If it's out of town, do Street View on Google Maps and trace the route from the exit to the business so you'll recognize landmarks. Assume traffic will be heavier the day of and arrive early. Sit in your car and play games on your phone to relax before you go in. Don't go in earlier than 5 or 10 minutes before your appointment. Tell yourself a joke on the way in to make yourself laugh. You should be totally relaxed because you know you're going to get this.

- **Don't wear cologne or perfume in abundance.** And don't forget to shower. You think I'm making this stuff up? I had an interview very recently where I couldn't stand to be closer than 5 or 6 feet from this individual. The best practice is to not have any odor emanating from your body.

- **Dress for success.** I think this goes without saying, but there are some interviewees that are clueless. Don't wear shorts, jeans, a t-shirt, a ballcap, anything revealing, showy, glitzy, etc. Just dress conservatively. Whether that's a suit, dress, pants suit, or business casual. You pretty much want to dress at least just above what the job will require. When in doubt wear a suit or dress/pants suit.

- **Engage your interviewer.** Be respectful, confident, and make eye contact (but don't stare at them like something from *Talking Dead*). Listen to what they are telling you about the position or company and respond with short, polite answers.

Smile when you meet them and try to maintain that smile when answering or asking questions.

- **Relax.** Going for a job interview can be a stressful situation for most of us because it's not something we do every day. It's intimidating and you feel like you're on display in a shop window on Park Avenue. Before you go into the interview, take a very long, slow breath. Hold it for five seconds, and let it out just as slowly as you took it in. Do this one more time. It's easy for me to tell you to do these things like they're second nature, so here's another tip. Pretend that you absolutely do not need this job and that you're a shoo-in for it anyway. I'm not telling you to be cocky and overconfident. But if you don't feel like you're clawing your way up an unfamiliar cliff, you'll relax a little and be more like yourself. Remember that the person interviewing you may be nervous as well because they probably don't conduct interviews every day.

- **Don't seem too eager.** You *can* be enthused with the position, company, and opportunities the job promises, however. But if you are too eager to give answers that you think they want to hear or that conflate your actual experience, the interviewer will catch on. Don't plead for the job (I've had this happen, complete with stalking and begging on their knees – ugh, very awkward). Do profess your genuine enthusiasm for the job and company.

- **Let them know how you can help the company and expand the position.** Rarely do employers want a robot employee that just fills a void on the assembly line. They want people who can think on their feet and do more than their job description. Try to approach the job as an opportunity to troubleshoot and increase the bottom line for the company. You may already have a few ideas during the interview, so share those in a general way. Don't be so detailed that they take your idea and run with it, however.

- **Don't ask about the pay.** This is a big no-no in first interviews. The intention of a first interview is to gauge whether you and the company are a good fit. Your main objectives are to sell yourself and to find out about the culture and climate of the company. Sometimes employers will either advertise the salary range or come right out and tell you. This usually happens with public funded organizations or larger corporations that operate strict budgets. Salaries are usually non-negotiable with government agencies and organizations, but a little more flexible with large companies. I will sometimes give a dollar range late in the first interview if I'm interested in the applicant. Some employers will force your hand and ask you what you will need. I'm really against this sort of tactic by companies because it diminishes the quality of the applicant and emphasizes the cost to the company – like you will always be in the "negative" column on the ledger. Big red flag. When faced with that tactless question in an interview, this is your signal to avoid getting into money negotiations too quickly. I might delay my answer by citing the need for more information about expectations, advancement opportunities (in writing), health insurance, education reimbursements, parking allowances, etc. If your interviewer demands an answer, set your bar high, but not out of reach if you are still considering working for this company. This is a classic bargaining scenario that goes back to the invention of money. The first one that mentions a dollar figure will usually be the loser: ask too much, you lose; ask too little, they win. If you did your research about the company, position, and the pay that others are getting for the same job in similar markets, you can be on more equal footing. Never base your answer on what you're making now (my salary plus 25%), or what your living expenses are (rent + utilities + groceries + gas + car payment + entertainment, etc.). It should be "What should that job pay a qualified person?". Add 20% to that for wiggle room, more if you think they're desperate to fill the position. You can also reply with a respectful answer such as, "I'd love to talk with you further about that if I'm considered to be a top candidate for the position." This is basically your signal that you're not *too* eager, you can't be pushed around easily, and that if they really want you, they must come to your table. If money is never mentioned in the interview, don't despair. Companies will often interview a bevy of candidates before whittling down the best people. This usually means they are being careful about who they select and can be a good indication about the quality of work the company performs. If you haven't heard back from them in three months, you're probably off their radar. However, I once got a job offer from a television station six months after I applied, so you never know.

- **Send a follow up personal letter after the interview.** It's always a nice gesture to send a follow up "thank you" letter to your interviewer, regardless of how the interview went. Thank them for their time and wish them success with their candidate search. Keep it short and sweet. Hand sign the salutation. Keep it all business.
- **Don't bug the company about the job.** Once the interview is over and you've sent a thank you letter, cool your jets. They have all the information they need about you, so don't pester them. If they want you to come back for a second interview, they will call. Otherwise, don't contact them again to find out if the position has been filled. If it has and you've made an impression, they may call on you in the future for another position. If you have bugged them about it, it may leave a bad impression and your resume will be filed in the round file cabinet.

If you get a callback, congratulations! You can now feel good about yourself that you have passed muster. Regardless of the outcome, pat yourself on the back and know that you're on the right track to be a professional in this field. Don't feel too sorry for yourself or get angry if you eventually don't get the job, because you were in the top rank. Let me tell you about a recent experience I had that is similar.

For fourteen years of my professional life, I worked in a company that provided broadcast radio services. My production studios were separate but interwoven into the broadcast facility. We had the capability of doing live broadcasts from our rooms and were often called upon to assist in the broadcast center, sometimes going on the road for remote broadcasts. From these experiences, I understood how a radio network operated by the time I went out on my own. This wasn't a business that I pursued when I went solo, but I continued to keep my feet in the wading pool, so to speak. I did fill-in "board op" engineering gigs with that company for several years; and I digitally connected my studio live with National Public Radio (NPR) and some of its affiliates, the BBC, and other national and international broadcasting outlets as part of my regular business. But I had no aspirations to operate a radio network.

Then one day I got a call from a former associate that now managed the PR and broadcast operations for a large national sports marketing firm. They had just won the bid for a university's marketing and broadcast rights and were looking for someone to handle all the radio broadcasts. I seriously listened, honestly voiced my concerns about my facility's ability to handle the potentially insane schedule, and tried to disinterest them. However, they were very insistent, and cited my attention to quality, which really flattered me if I'm completely honest. Long story short, I put together a five-year plan that utilized the rooms I have now and the ability to scale up as needed. I realized early on that it was something I couldn't do by myself and would have to rely on talented engineers that were already familiar with the process. It was big thinking, but I was up for the challenge. However, I wasn't kidding myself. It was a long shot that I was going to get it because the main challenger was a huge national network everybody's heard of, and they already had facilities and services in place. My friend was naturally concerned about being another hamburger in the automat's vending machine and losing control of the quality and sound of the network.

They fought really hard for my studio, but in the end, it naturally went to the big network. However, I'm told that my bid was neck-and-neck until the final minutes. The deciding factor was the offer of free satellite services, something that was impossible for me to provide for no cost. Was I disappointed? A little. But knowing that I was toe-to-toe with Goliath made me feel much better about my professional reputation. Plus, the whole exercise of putting together the proposal forced me to re-evaluate my studios and my ability to provide broadcast services. Since that proposal, we recently broadcast a live national radio show out of our studios and are now producing weekly and periodic radio programs for a local and regional NPR affiliate, partly because of the renewed confidence in myself as a radio producer.

Back to your second interview. You can be a little more relaxed now, so go in with confidence. Some employers may give you a "trial run," asking you to perform some engineering tasks or solving some technical problems. This is usually another good sign that the company really cares about who it hires, this can work in your favor. If you are faced with unfamiliar software or equipment, be honest but try to compare it with what you do know. If you don't get the job because of your lack of experience with a specific tool (*ProTools* for instance), then bone up on it before your next interview. Most employers that want an applicant to perform some tasks are mostly looking to see how you handle challenges rather than your specific knowledge with a tool.

Some second interviews will have a room full of people. This can be intimidating. Again, this can be a good sign that the company is being careful during the hiring process. These people are there for a few reasons, mostly to gather more information. Some of what they seek is to see how you handle a little pressure or adversity. Don't think of this moment as running the gauntlet. Treat it like a think tank with your future peers. You may be working with these people daily, so speak with them conversationally. Make an interesting comment about the building or neighborhood the business is in, or a picture on the office wall that has may have a fascinating feature. Stay away from personal comments, other than maybe an interesting watch someone may be wearing or last night's amazing game. And I have to say it, because you know, I've seen it happen – stay completely away from politics, religion, opinion, stereotypes, etc. Homogenize it and keep it mostly business.

From my experience as both a job seeker and an employer, experience in a particular position is not the overriding deciding factor. If you're in a second interview for a job that will involve doing things you've never done before, congratulations. They realize that you are starting out and may lack some experience (because you were completely honest on your resume and in your first interview like I told you to be). They are most likely looking for someone with the chutzpah to take the bull by the horns and grow into, and beyond, the job. When I hire part-time contractors for editing audiobooks, I'm looking for someone with some editing skills, but not necessarily on my chosen edit software. I'm also looking for someone that can make detailed creative, pacing, and technical decisions with accuracy. I'm learning new software all the time – it's part of the job – I know any decent editor will pick up the subtleties quickly. As you gain more experience in the field and seek more jobs, you will always be applying for jobs that entail more than you're doing now. That's called growth. Get used to it if you want to have a successful career.

Another little side note to pump you up. Whenever I'm faced with a huge undertaking that is unlike anything I've ever done before – like building a radio network – I keep reminding myself that I've started my own business. I may suck at certain parts of it, but I did something that not a lot of people do. I made it through the one-year, two-year, five-year, and ten-year gauntlets that statisticians like to cite as markers for business failures. The Small Business Administration states that "30% of new businesses fail during the first two years of being open, 50% during the first five years and 66% during the first 10." As of this writing I'm more than twenty years in. I treat each coming year as a challenge I haven't done before and pinch myself when I notch off another year. You should have the attitude that every new job opportunity is a welcome challenge. Your enthusiasm will show.

9. YOUR FIRST JOB

"You can't build a reputation on what you're going to do."

Henry Ford

W oohoo! You've landed your first job. Whether it's a volunteer position, or an all-out full-time salaried position, you're in the club now. To make the most of it, you need to plan your next move now. That may sound cold and calculating, but the fact is most people work at more than one place during a career. This may be your dream job out of the gate, but more than likely it's a bottom-rung position. So that means you'll eventually be moving on to (hopefully) better things. If you start thinking about your next opportunity now, you'll be ready when it's time to jump on it. During your planning process you did with my guidance in Chapter 4 (page 63), I asked you to envision where you'll be in five years. If you did this exercise 4 or 5 years ago and just completed college, I urge you to look at your five- and ten-year visions you did. Are you on track? Are you in the position you thought you'd be in? When you go through life and a career, you should always be updating your five- and ten-year visions, so now is the time to revise your goals.

The secret to moving toward those big goals is to break them down into smaller goals. Something like, "In one year I want to be able to operate all the equipment in the studio proficiently." Or "In two years I want to set up and engineer a live sound event so that I can start looking for a more challenging position in live sound engineering." An hour of time goes by one-second at a time, so occasionally glance at your career clock to see how you're doing. It's easier to make small course corrections than one large one.

Don't try to rush your growth. Just a steady hand on the rudder will get you there. If you're impatient, you may sidetrack your path. Good experience is usually gained through time spent and dedication to your job and employer. A baseball player puts in batting cage time every day so that when the bottom-of-the-ninth-and-two-on rolls around, he'll be ready to swing with confidence. Bide your time by dividing your small goals into even smaller ones. I used to set vacations as mileposts for growth. In six months before holiday, I'm going to learn this new skill. In April I'm going to learn how to synchronize these two devices properly. By Friday, I want to read two chapters in this audio how-to book. By setting small goals, victories are easier to come by. You'll start to see progress if you look back on what you've accomplished last week, month, or year. Keep a calendar or journal of your goals and mark them off as you go. Treat yourself to an ice cream when a small goal is met, and a movie when a significant goal is reached. It sounds corny, but just picture yourself at the bottom of a long set of stairs. At the top is the chest full of gold. One step at a time gets you closer to the top, but if you try to leapfrog your way up, you might slip and fall all the way back down.

Another way to reach your goals is to focus on the job at hand. You must commit 100% to your job. It may not be what you want to do the rest of your life, but you have to practice giving your all to the company. Your goal should be to go down in history as the gold standard for employees. Your company hired you to help them make money. Your job as some type of audio engineer or producer is probably not to directly make money, but you're just as important. My job at Host Communications, the sports marketing company I worked at for fourteen years, was basically fulfillment. Salespeople would go out and sell sports sponsorships to corporations. In return, that corporation would be given advertisements in the game print program, banners in the arenas, and maybe some commercials inside the game broadcasts. Our studio would provide those commercials, completely customized to the event and sponsor. We would sometimes create radio or television programs just to either sell sponsorships or fulfill a contract the salespeople offered. These programs would play during the sporting event's broadcast, or sometimes were self-contained sports shows on local or national networks. We were charged with creating effective and creative commercials for the sponsor, or programming that the sponsor wanted to be associated with. If we spent too much money and time producing something, then that would have a negative effect on the company's bottom line. But if we rammed it through the studio without care, our company would look like a cheap fly-by-night. Each employee, from the CEO down to the floor stocker, must have the company's bottom line in mind every day.

That's really easy for me to say, but in reality, it's sadly not the case everywhere. Effective communications and recognition from the top down is imperative for a company to survive. Even if you start to feel underappreciated, you must continue to maintain that 100% commitment. A company can't give out awards every week to keep you pumped up, so you must find your own ways to recognize your own good work. You could set small goals to find a cheaper supplier for data storage. Or find a new client. Or streamline a procedure that cuts down on time by 10%. Every little bit helps. And by the way, keep a tally of these small accomplishments and send a memo to your supervisor when you've met your goal. They aren't going to walk through at five o'clock and ask how much you've saved the company today, so you've got to fly your own flag. Is this kissing ass? No, it's self-marketing (I have a chapter later on just that topic). Kissing ass would be if you get coffee every day for your supervisor and congratulate them on their meaningless decisions.

Speaking of supervisors, each one deserves your respect, no matter how you feel about them. A professional will always keep the even keel, never walk the line, or talk back. Your supervisor has a much tougher job than you. They must watch the bottom line, meet deadlines, come in earlier and leave later than everyone else, keep *their* boss happy, manage all the employees and their tantrums, disagreements, deficiencies, etc. Some handle it better than others, and I've had all kinds of them. I've had the "Just take care of it" kind that don't want to manage, and therefore are of no help when things get tough; to the "You're back 5 minutes late from lunch " kind that put more stock in your warm body in a chair than how you're performing. No worries, just give the tough ones what they want to placate their egos. Fortunately, I've mostly had good to great supervisors that care as much about me as they do about the company. These are usually easy people to work for because the respect goes both ways. They respect your abilities and experience, and you respect their decisions and authority.

Which brings me to authority. Most companies are a dictatorship. Hard to swallow, but generally true. You have the head cheese at the top, the dictator, with a motto on their desk that says, "The Buck Stops Here." You have the little generals (VPs) their colonels and lieutenants (department heads), the captains (immediate supervisors), and enlisted soldiers (you). Everyone up and down the chain of command is jockeying for a better office, pay, title, etc. Anything to please the dictator at the top. You get a lot of smashed fingers and toes the lower you are on the totem pole in the more ruthless companies.

My little, tiny company is also a dictatorship by my own definition. In big business decisions I have the final say because this is my dream, my risk, and my future. I don't take these big decisions lightly, but fortunately I'm not called on to be a "dictator" on a daily basis. My everyday management style has always been driven with a "wheel" mentality. I'm the axle in the middle, surrounded by all my co-workers. They rely on themselves and the people on either side of them to turn the wheel and reach their goals. If they need help, they come to me to facilitate a fix. If I need to, I go to other facilitators in the company to get the problem fixed. I'm not afraid to hear from someone that works with me (or "for" me in the strict corporate parlance) that an idea I have won't work. Wouldn't you want someone to tell you that you're about to walk off a cliff? I don't get my ego bruised very easily because I feel like I'm always learning and trying to find a better way to get something done. If I show respect to someone in the wheel, I'll get it back, even if I'm wrong. Without all of us working *together*, the wheel won't turn. Even in your little world at the "bottom" of the totem pole, you can make this method work. If you start to work with others as if you are all in a wheel together, you'll notice that things will start to get done. You might even earn some respect along the way and get noticed for getting things done.

As you start to accomplish your small goals, keep setting more and more. After a year on the job, do a serious review of your accomplishments. Look at what goals you set a year ago and how many you met. If you achieved all of them, you're a superhero. But most of us will have met about half of them. Pat yourself on the back for completing these, because each one is a step in the right direction. Your company might have an annual review, so this is the time to bring up some of these accomplishments to your supervisor. If their review process is any good, your supervisor will have a constructive list of areas that need improvement. Add these to your own list of goals. This review is also the time to request the company's help in attaining some of your own goals. If you want more experience in a certain procedure or type of production, let them know so that they can implement a plan. Smart bosses like it when they see employees that are driven to self-improvement, it benefits the individual and the company.

PART III

ON THE JOB

10. BUSINESS HOURS

"There is no substitute for hard work."

Thomas A. Edison

To succeed in your new job, I don't think I have to mention the obvious things about showing up on time, putting in your hours, etc. But in audio production, broadcast, theater, and other types of jobs where you, the audio engineer will work, the hours can be long and unpredictable. This just comes with the territory. So, if you're a clock watcher, this profession isn't for you.

It's not unusual for me to log ten or twelve hours a day, six days a week – or more – during busy periods. It's also not unheard of for me to occasionally log 24-hours straight in the studio. It does and will happen from time to time. I don't ever recall someone telling me early on in my career that this would happen, it just did, over and over again. And I will probably pull another all-nighter before this year is out, maybe a couple. I don't like to work long hours regularly, but it's just part of the gig. Employers should let you know that you are expected to work long hours on occasion. Those that don't are either not in the profession or are hiding that fact so that you aren't scared off.

Let's look at some of the reasons why you might have to work long hours:

1. **The "S#!T rolls downhill" deadline crunch**. Somewhere up the line, someone miscalculated how long a process took. It might have been the salesperson, the producer, the writer, the traffic, the weather, or even you. The more moving parts you have, the greater the chance for error. When you're at the end of the line (and audio is usually the last phase and the last to know), the full weight of the assembly line comes down on you. Maybe you got the project late, maybe you got it in time but meeting the requirements takes longer than anyone calculated

for, or maybe you're too slow to get it done on time. You gotta phone home and tell 'em to not wait up for you.

2. **The "Lack-of-preparation" deadline crunch.** My mother used to have a sign in her office that read, "Lack of preparation on your part does not constitute an emergency on mine." Again, the more moving parts, the likelier someone drops the ball before it comes rolling down to you. We're all human, so sometimes we don't give 100% all the time. If you screw up something that makes someone else work late, apologize and buy them dinner or give them a six pack of craft brew to make up for it. But sometimes there are systemic or personnel problems that repeatedly force senseless deadline crunches. One example is advertising. There are usually tight deadlines built into the industry as a matter of course, but clients who don't understand the long train behind the locomotive usually drag their feet on approvals that cause the producer to deliver late, which in turn causes the editor to deliver late, which in turn forces you to be severely crunched on your deadline. Sometimes there is someone along the line that consistently causes the train to slow down. If you know where the problem lies and it can't be corrected with tact, we usually learn to err on the side of safety and start setting that person's deadline much sooner than needed.

3. **The "Can't quit changing things" deadline crunch.** I love George Lucas and all that he's done for storytelling and cinema. But GOOD GOD quit tweaking your Star Wars movies. The original three were just fine, that's why they're beloved and they made millions. Any old film can benefit from a digital restoration but adding scenes and backgrounds to a classic is sacrilege. In my world, we all have to deal with a producer or director that blows through soft deadlines because they just can't leave something alone. I don't know how many times I get a "locked" picture [26] and then it's changed at the last minute because someone keeps tinkering. That usually means

---

[26] A video that has its edits and timings set in stone so the graphics, special effects, and sound can be finalized. If any timings are changed afterwards, it cascades down the entire line of specialists who have to usually start that section from scratch to accommodate the changes.

I'm not leaving at 5PM, it'll be more like 5AM (while they're sleeping like a baby at home).

4. **The "Clueless" deadline crunch**. There will occasionally be the cog in the wheel that just doesn't understand the production process well enough to be calling the shots. That person may either be new to the game, was thrust into the production unexpectedly, or is totally clueless as to how much they don't really understand.

5. **The "Trying to impress the client" deadline crunch**. I really detest having to work under immense pressure and very, very late because the person driving the train wants to impress a client. They may over-promise a certain quality or standard of production in an insanely short timeframe. Or sometimes the client doesn't understand the amount of time and work that are required to produce a given product, but the salesperson is too afraid of jeopardizing that relationship by shooting straight. In the end, the client usually never knows exactly how much blood, sweat and tears went into their finished product.

6. **The "bug in the equipment" deadline crunch**. Sometimes our gear just doesn't want to cooperate. With so many cables, connections, knobs, sliders, buttons, fans, logic boards, transformers, lines of software code, memory chips, and other points of failure, something's gonna give when you least expect it. It really pays to use professional equipment, keep your computer updated, and run tests before starting a large or important project. But equipment will fail, software will crash, and power will go out at the worst time. Nothing to do but to call home and let 'em know you're gonna be late.

7. **The "Act of God (or squirrel)" deadline crunch**. The forces of nature will temporarily interrupt production occasionally. If you've protected your studio properly (back-up UPSs, earth grounding equipment, AC surge protection, etc.) then power outages, brownouts, and surges will cause minimal damage. I've had almost every kind of uncontrollable event pause production: Downed power lines from wind and car wrecks, squirrels on the transformer, ice on the transformer, sub-station overload, tornados, thunderstorms, snow and ice storms, and a really big one: flood. There's nothing you can do but wait it out or find an alternative solution to your problem.

8. **The "procrastination" deadline crunch**. And by this, I mean you. It's going to happen sooner or later: you put something off for so long that it causes you to work late. I still get myself into this pickle every now and then, but I've developed a habit where I try to get little things done early and right away. I also use my calendar and reminder app religiously to schedule the most mundane things, just to make sure they get done. I always get this great reaction from clients whenever they email me about a small job that isn't due right away, and I complete it before the hour is up. Of course, I'm trying to do high customer service, but I'm also getting it done before it slips through the proverbial crack.

9. **The "Slow is me" deadline crunch**. Sometimes, we just take too long to do something. Maybe we're learning a new process or piece of software. Maybe we're taking extra time on finessing something. Maybe we've hit a creative wall. Maybe we're just too damn slow. If others aren't waiting on you to get your part done or you're not screwing up your personal life by taking extra time on something, then go ahead and stay late to perfect your product. I try to never take a shortcut on anything, that's bad production. However, I have learned to speed up certain parts of production that are back-pocket, everyday processes. If I can figure out a faster way to do something that's mundane but necessary, then that leaves me more time for creativity and invention on the back end. Learn to use templates and presets for common tasks so that you aren't building every project from scratch. Start paperwork and plan track assignments, formats, and other project-related decisions before you begin. Always start with the fundamentals before putting the icing on the cake. Trying to jump ahead to the end will only slow you down in the long run – take my word for it.

10.   **The "Production just takes a long time" deadline crunch**. This is probably the number one reason for staying late. There's just no way around it, audio production is time consuming. In the beginning, you'll take a lot of time doing something because you're new to it. After you have a lot of experience, you take a lot of time because you want to do things right. But all of the time, you're in it for the long haul. When I was working exclusively on reel-to-reel tape, we dreamed of faster ways to get the work done because it was so time-

consuming rewinding tapes, splicing edits, mixing down, and making dubs. Now, we waste our time cleaning dialog, editing cuts, mixing down, and uploading files. It's a complicated process and it has always taken extraordinarily long stretches of time to put out a good audio product.

Another reason you might work long hours is the type of job you're doing, like location audio. Long days are synonymous with film and video production. A typical major motion picture, if shot over six weeks, averages 12-hour days. Large amounts of money are on the line, so any minute wasted costs more than an automobile. Television shows can be just as brutal with six- and seven-day weeks and long, long days. Local video productions are typically shot in one- to five-days, depending on the project. They will usually have call times very early (like 6 AM) and wrap by 6 PM or so. If it's a one-day shoot that requires moving to a lot of different locations, then it might be a 12- to 18-hour day. Each production is unique and there really isn't a rule-of-thumb on a length of day that can be applied to all. If you do take on a location audio job, just be prepared for a very long day and be happy if it ends early. Location days are grueling – one day on location seems like a week in an office job. Because it's hard on your mind and body, I have some tips on how to prepare for it:

- Get up extra early the day before the job if you can. Go to bed extra early that night (you'll probably be tired from getting up early anyway).
- Set two alarms: one by your bed, the other on the other side of the room so you'll have to get up and out of bed to turn it off. I have a wind-up clock with a really loud bell that I use for my second alarm.
- Don't party or drink alcohol the night before. Alcohol interrupts sleep patterns and you'll need your rest. Plus, you don't want to be hung over on your big day.
- If you drink coffee, just have one cup, otherwise you'll have to pee when you're on the set.
- Drink orange juice if you can, it has natural energy instead of caffeine. Even better, choose a caffeine-free drink that is fortified with vitamin B-12.

- Avoid caffeine during the day, especially the energy drinks. You want to maintain alertness throughout the day and caffeine, especially energy drinks with caffeine, will make your energy levels roller coaster.

- Avoid sugar, especially sugary drinks like cola and sugary snacks like doughnuts. Sugar will give you the same roller coaster effects that caffeine does. Sugar and caffeine combined, like a cola, only double the up and down effect.

- Eat something for breakfast that will sustain you for a while, lunch may be several hours away. I like to have something with egg in it. A breakfast burrito is also a good choice but beware of the beans! You don't want a "noisy" film set.

- Bring a power bar or other snack to fight off the hungries. Most location jobs include some kind of lunch, but it's better to be safe and bring something.

- When you do get to eat lunch, make sure to not overeat or have heavy and starchy foods. Avoid large quantities of meat as well. All of these will make you sleepy in the afternoon as your body tries to digest everything. I try to get the vegetarian selects if the lunch is catered because I can still get my protein and not feel overstuffed.

- Take your vitamins, especially some vitamin B-12. Natural energy is always better that temporary energy like sugar and caffeine.

- Drink plenty of water while on the set, but not so much that you'll be running to the bathroom every 20 minutes. If you're outside, try to drink a sports drink to replenish your electrolytes.

- While on the set, try not to yawn. Everybody will be yawning because nobody slept well the night before. That's right, even though you went to bed early, you'll probably toss and turn because you're anxious. Don't feel bad, even the director goes through this. If it's a multi-day shoot, you'll probably sleep like a log the rest of the nights.

- Wear comfortable shoes because you'll be standing and/or walking a lot.

- Wear a hat if you're outside in the sun. You don't want to get sunburned or have a heat stroke. Plus, being in the sun all day will sap your energy really fast.

- Wear extra warm gear in the winter. The colder your get, the more energy you use trying to stay warm. Dress in layers and make sure you have thick gloves, thick socks, a hat or toboggin, and a scarf. I find a toboggin works great because you can stretch it over your headphones.
- Bring a handkerchief to wipe sweat from your face. Film sets aren't as hot as they used to be now that cooler LED lights are used, but they can still get warm when the HVAC is cut off during takes. If you're working outside during the summer months, sweating is a given.
- Have fun! Don't mope about how early you had to get up or how long a scene is taking. Everybody has a job to do and is under pressure. If you relax and soak it all in, it can be a very rewarding experience. You'll also probably make a lot of new friends and contacts.

Long days in the studio can be just as taxing as location work, believe it or not. If your client is there with you, it can add to the tension even if you're getting along with each other. Remember, they're experiencing the same tension and fatigue as you are, so keeping everything light-hearted and fun can help make a long day less brutal. Here are some tips on surviving a 12-, 14-, 18-, or 24-hour day in the studio:

- Stand up every 20 minutes. Stretch your legs and back. If you can, walk around the room or go up and down a flight of stairs. By the way, you should practice this all the time, even when you're watching TV or reading at home.
- Get out of the studio for 5 minutes every hour if you can. Walk around the facility or go outside. The key is to remove yourself from the monotonous computer screen and speakers, even from other people. Studies have shown that a 5-minute walk every hour can improve mood as well as lower blood pressure and blood sugar.
- Every 4 hours take a longer break. Go on a 10 to 20-minute walk or go get some food. Play a word game on your phone. Call somebody and talk for five minutes to divert your attention. The key is to do a soft reboot of your mind and body.
- If it looks like you'll be heading into the 12th or 14th hour, do some pushups, sit-ups, jog in place, anything that's

cardio and that stretches your muscles. Sitting in a chair for a long time can cause many lingering aches and pains for days. Limbering up during your late working hours can mitigate most of the problems.

- After about 16 or 18 hours you will hit a wall. This is when you might actually drink some tea or coffee, leave for 30 minutes, and even splash cold water in your face a few times. Try to decompress your auditory senses by seeking out some silence for 30 minutes. Don't go to sleep if you still need to go several more hours. Trust me, it's better to just stay awake than to take a nap and be groggy afterwards.

- Hopefully you're done with your project and can go home after 24 hours. Even though you have done something very unnatural to your body and mind, it's amazing how much energy you sometimes have after this long in the studio. When I see an end in sight, I kind of actually get ramped up as my adrenaline starts coursing through my veins. But your body is about to do a major revolt and get back at you for putting it through this torture. You will come crashing down pretty hard about an hour after you finish. Have someone take you home or call a taxi/ride share because you are effectively drunk at this point and could pass out at a stop light, or worse, while driving. To decompress your ears, listen to light classical music, simple folk music, or some other type of music that is pure toned and unchallenging to the mind. Listening to hard rock, fast country, or anything that is highly rhythmic and hard edged will not help and will jangle your nerves, even if it's music you love. Remember that you are not your normal self at this point. You need to slowly glide down, down, down until you finally fall asleep.

- Follow the location recording pointers above when it comes to food and vitamins because treating your body correctly will help you survive these marathon sessions.

Other types of audio jobs that will require long hours at times include sporting events, broadcasts, music shows, theater plays, news coverage, conventions, and others. These are not usually everyday events, so you usually know beforehand that you will be working long hours. Sometimes there is just no way around having to put in the extra time. I can give you some actual real-world situations that I've worked long hours and lay out what we did, why we did it, and how we solved problems along the way.

THE TRIPLE CROWN
WORLDWIDE RADIO BROADCASTS

For several years, I was on the crew to broadcast the radio programs of the Triple Crown of thoroughbred racing: the Kentucky Derby, the Preakness Stakes, and the Belmont Stakes, plus a few Breeder's Cups every October. In 1999 the new entity, Premiere Radio Network, had bought the rights from ABC News Radio and kept most of the same crew that had been doing the Derby for several years. The company I worked for at the time, Host Communications, was a partner in the new network, so much of the technical and marketing responsibilities fell on us. Our company was providing on-site technical support and engineering, as well as producing the final program in our master control center in Lexington, Kentucky. We were feeding the entire broadcast to radio affiliates in the U.S. through the satellite facilities at CBS Radio Network in New York. We were also feeding the broadcast around the world through the Armed Forces Network, as well as a separate Spanish language broadcast originating from each racetrack. Whew! That's a lot of wheels moving.

My job was kind of accidental. The very first broadcast that our new network did was on my birthday at the Kentucky Derby at Churchill Downs in Louisville, Kentucky. I got a call the night before that one of the crew (from the old ABC crew) was suddenly sick and was in the hospital (thankfully he survived his illness and retired shortly after that). He was the "tape-op," and I do mean *tape* op. The network had purchased all the remote equipment that was dedicated to the Triple Crown directly from ABC, who had been broadcasting it for several years. This included all mixers, intercoms, microphones, cables, headsets, and tape recorders. Absolutely no digital equipment.

This was 1999, so although analog tape players were still around, we had moved to digital production seven years earlier. Even location film sound recorders were primarily on DAT tape by now, and radio stations were beginning to play back commercials and programs from digital cart machines, computers, and self-contained playback units with an internal hard drive. The equipment kit from ABC had two Nagra reel-to-reel recorders in the case, and nobody knew how to use them. Our chief broadcast engineer Daryl Doss, who was heading up the technical team at the Derby in Louisville, remembered that I had worked for a film company and had experience with these little gems.

What makes a Nagra so special? Well, it's a Swiss-made high-end miniature location recorder for the film industry. They started in 1951 and revolutionized the location audio industry. The small size (roughly two hardback books stacked on top of each other), outstanding build quality, reliable electronics, and superb sound made the reel-to-reel recorders a standard. One of my favorites is the extremely tiny version that was designed to be mounted on a film camera when the audio engineer couldn't get close by. You see these in old movies and throwback TV shows, sometimes being used by the FBI or police as a hidden tape recorder. The other thing that makes the Nagra special is the ability to record sync-sound audio. A hidden audio track records a constant timing frequency that is later used to control the Nagra's motors and play the recording back at exactly the same speed it was recorded at, a necessity for picture lock. Newer models also recorded timecode directly to tape. Needless to say, these were very expensive units and ABC had two of them in their kit: one for recording, and one for editing and playback. The area in the broadcast booth where the tape-op sat is usually very tight, so miniature equipment was vital.

I drove from Lexington to Louisville the next morning arriving at the track at 8 AM after a nearly sleepless night (I was very, very anxious and nervous, no doubt). I had roughly eight hours to get everything up and running for the 5:30 PM broadcast. With equipment I had never touched. With a crew whom I had never even met before today. On a program I had never heard. Broadcast around the world. Gulp.

Adding fire to the fire, I needed to record and edit interviews throughout the day for several purposes: To play sound bites during the live broadcast; to play short two-minute sound packages for the radio affiliates every hour from 11 AM until the race began; and to record interviews with trainers, owners, jockeys, track officials, and reporters for the sound packages and live program.

So, needing to have my first package[27] together before 11 AM – just three hours away! – I had to dive right in.

I hadn't edited reel-to-reel tape in years, so I was a little bit rusty. But, just like riding a bicycle, it came back pretty quickly. However, I had a major problem with my Nagras – they weren't designed for editing. Let me explain.

Photo 1.   Reel-to-reel machine. The tape feeds from left to right from the supply reel to the take-up reel. The pinch roller is the small cylinder just outside of the tape path.

When you edit tape on a standard studio player, you are usually working with a three-motor unit. There is a motor behind each of the two spools, and one that feeds the tape along the path between the spools. As a tape machine runs, the tape to be played is on the left spool, the supply reel. The tape travels along a path that goes across the playback head and between a free spinning rubber wheel (pinch roller) and a motor shaft (capstan). This action at the pinch roller and capstan feeds the tape to the take-up reel on

---

[27] A "package" is a short, self-contained news presentation that includes narration, interviews, sound bites, music, and/or natural environmental sounds. It's edited and mixed before broadcast and played later during a (usually) live broadcast. It's typically introduced by the host or anchor. You see these every night on the news.

the right. The whole time this is happening, the motor for the left supply reel is actually trying to gently run backwards against the forward pull of the pinch roller/capstan. This is so the tape supply on the left reel doesn't unravel too early and spill onto the floor or snap the tape. It's kind of like downshifting a car while going down a hill so you don't build up too much speed. Meanwhile, the take-up reel's motor on the right is gleefully pulling along the tape that is fed to it from the pinch roller.

If you need to edit a tape, by cutting out a portion, you pull the tape away from the playback head, cut it with a razor blade on a special splicing block, and feed or dump the unwanted part onto the floor. To accomplish this, place the player into "Edit" mode. This turns off the right take-up reel motor and plays the tape from the left reel, dumping off onto the floor as it rolls between the capstan and pinch roller. You stop it when you hear the end of the bad part, then cut the tape, splice that to the new part with adhesive tape, take up the slack in the tape, take the player out of "Edit" mode, and play your new creation. It's really ingenious for the time. By the way, those motors behind the reels also act as rewind and fast-forward motors.

Photo 2. The Nagra III (ca 1957), very similar to the ones I used at the Kentucky Derby.

The Nagra only has one motor (the capstan) and belts that connect to and spin the two reel platters. This is also how most cassette players are manufactured in order to cut cost. The Nagra doesn't need three motors because it is only designed to record or play back, not edit. I had forgotten that tiny bit of information when I tried my first edit at the Derby. When I cut my tape and started to pull the bad part off, it back fed the good tape while turning both reels. No matter which way I pulled, the reels would back turn against me. It was just like a Three Stooges movie where Moe is in one room pulling a wire, while Curly is in another room pulling it back. They get into a tug of war and destroy the house in the process. I was feeling like that wire, or more like a Stooge. Eventually I worked out a clunky method that I could work with, but it really slowed me down. Hats off to the engineer who did this at the Derby all those years.

During that day I had to pack up one of the recorders and a microphone and trudge over to the track president's office for some sound bites. We were located high up just to the left of Churchill Downs' famous twin spires, right on the finish line. The president's office was at the end of the grandstand, about 800 feet by the way the crow flies. When I stuck my head out of the window, I could see the entrance; it was not too far away, maybe a five-minute walk. But I had to go through the crowded press box, down the elevator, through the grandstand elbow-to-elbow with people, through the paddock full of people, through security at the offices, and up the elevators. That took a half-hour. The recording went fine, but it was another half-hour trek to get back. I just blew about 90 minutes for 90-seconds of audio.

I had to do more recording that day, going from reporter to reporter in the press box and asking for their pick of the Derby winner. These responses were edited together for a 90-second package that was played during the broadcast.

Throughout the day, various reporters hired by the network would bring me interviews recorded onto cassette tapes (it was still commonplace in those days to use them, usually recorded with professional portable decks that collectors salivate over today). Most times the reporters either had the tape logged[28] or would just

---

[28] A running text account of what is recorded with time marks. A shorter version would have just the first and last words and might look like:

tell me who the interviewee was and the topic. Either way, I had to listen to the entire interview and record pertinent parts to reel-to-reel for later use, many of which the producers were relying on me to judge what was best for broadcast. Remember, I had never heard this show before, but I did work in sports broadcasting so I had some inclination as to what might be interesting and work in the broadcast.

I would string together all these fragments of interviews, or "sound bites" to a single reel-to-reel spool, each separated by a few feet of white paper tape so that I could actually see them delineated when I looked at the wound spool. I would keep my own running log of these sound bites with: Order on tape; Person in interview; First several words and last several words for reference; Total sound bite length in time. As the broadcast neared, the main host and roaming live reporter would review the clips I had saved. As I re-ordered the clips on yet another reel-to-reel spool, they would go over to an old-fashioned typewriter in the corner and bang out a script in minutes. Then, one of them would put on a headset[29] and record their narration while I played back the sound bites "live" to tape from a second reel-to-reel deck. The final piece would be played during the broadcast as a package. Man, those guys were so good at being able to quickly write compelling stories around soundbites. It was like watching an old-time movie about a newsroom full of reporters yacking, typewriters clackity-clack-clacking, and phones constantly ringing. And it was almost like that in the booth. There was constant activity, people coming in and out constantly; and I was positioned halfway into the doorway to the engineer booth. I had to constantly bend out of the way or get off my stool to let someone by. There was no other place for my gear to go.

Meanwhile, I would start organizing all my cuts and packages that needed to be played during the one-hour broadcast. When I

01:20 – 01:56 - Murphy: "I needed to save space…why I invented that bed."
A log might also be less specific and just generally mark where on the recording someone commented on a reporter's question.

[29] A pair of headphones with a microphone extending from one earpiece. It's what a courtside announcer would wear during a basketball game, for instance. The microphones are specially selected for close proximity and have rear and side rejection of noise, such as fans screaming. They are usually of very high quality and can have excellent results in noisy environments.

was done, I would record all of these over to a back-up cassette deck with about 5 seconds of dead space between them. During the broadcast, I would simultaneously press play on both the reel-to-reel deck and cassette deck. The cassette would be muted of course, but I was ready to make the switch over to it in case the reel-to-reel tape failed.

Next, the broadcast started. The race is usually at 5:30 or 5:40 PM, so the show starts at 5:00 PM. There is a <u>host</u> (when I was working these events it was the late, great Don Chevrier, former voice of the Toronto Blue Jays), a <u>color analyst</u> (usually Hall of Fame former jockeys), an on-the-ground <u>remote reporter</u> (Fred Manfra, former voice of the Baltimore Orioles), and the <u>race call announcer</u> (I worked with several greats including NBC's Tom Durkin and ABC's Dave Johnson, instantly recognizable with his phrase, "And *down* the stretch they come!"). We had lots of time to fill, after all the race is only two minutes. There were discussions; predictions; chats with the remote reporter (engineered down on the track by the late, amazing Carl Hoyan, who worked exclusively with Howard Cosell and was friends with Bob Marley) and whoever he was interviewing down in the jockey room or paddock; and of course the packages and sound bites I had prepared and cued up on a reel-to-reel player. Our lead engineer Gary Jeffries (his credentials are *way* too long to list, but his work is all in New York City) was his usual calm, cool, and collected self in his face, but his hands would fly from faders to switches in a flurry as he would bring different sources up in the program. In addition to the host, color analyst, race caller, and reporter, he was taking my tape feed and blending several microphones planted throughout the racetrack. *And* he was communicating to everybody's headphones through an intricate intercom system. I was glad I wasn't stepping into that role in an emergency, they would have had to stop the race while I found the next fader.

By this point in my career, I was used to playing cues live on the air. It was a daily occurrence, but I was used to cart machines (those big blocky cartridges that look like 8-track tapes from the 1960s) and digital playback machines, which fire the audio immediately when pressing a *button*. The Nagra required turning knobs and flipping levers to play. Fast-forwarding, rewinding, and generally finding your cues was kind of like driving a Ferrari on ice: too much of this sent you flying there, overcorrecting that sent you sliding somewhere else. You had to just calm down, whisper sweet nothings in its ear, and use a gentle touch. Each cut I played was like high drama. That was followed with a huge sigh of relief. But there was no time to rest, I had to cue up the next cut. I really felt out of control that day because I was expecting a disaster at any minute: A splice could break; a reel could come flying off; the wrong cue would play; I could miss the cue because the player was fast-forwarding for no reason; I would have a stroke. I was about to, but my mother taught me a long time ago how to calm your mind and body when under tremendous stress: breath in and breath out in a slow and regular rhythm. As you do this, you can start to build a wall around your fears and just concentrate on the moment, the reality. I managed to stay in the reality and made it through my first worldwide broadcast. Whewwwww!

When the show was over, you could feel the tension in the room lift like we had all been lying under an elephant deciding where to plop down. Everybody was glad the hard part was over. Our producer, the late Shelby Whitfield (former voice of the Washington Senators and sports director at ABC Sports), was very demanding during the broadcast. Shelby would bark out orders in a curt and clipped style. Someone who has never worked on a high-pressure broadcast would think he was mad at everybody. On the contrary, Shelby knew he was working with the cream-of-the-crop journalists and engineers. He didn't have to sugarcoat anything – he was after perfection. Remember my story about my college jazz band teacher Jim Andy Caudill screaming in my ear as I was playing? Like Jim Andy, Shelby was just trying to get the best sounds out of everybody's horns. And like the professional that Shelby was, he was always gracious, complimentary, kind-hearted, and respectful after the broadcast. But he was never apologetic because he didn't have anything to apologize for. Once during a later broadcast when we were using digital playback, I had accidently hit the repeat button when I fired off a cue. When it was done, it played again. I thought Shelby was going to blow a lid, but he just chuckled, "Ha, we just got two for the price of one!" He knew it would never happen again, and it didn't.

After the broadcast went off the air at 6:00 PM, it was time to shut everything off and try to grab some food in the press box before the numerous jolly and inebriated reporters scarfed it all down (I heard echoes of Hunter S. Thompson's *Playboy* article "The

Kentucky Derby Is Decadent and Depraved" as I observed some really drunk people in the press box that day). We had to tear everything down, pull and pack all the wires and equipment, and haul everything to a van. It was about midnight when we finished. There was no way I could get a room for the night because Louisville swells by about 175,000 people on Derby day, so I said my goodbyes and started my hour-and-a-half drive back to Lexington.

In retrospect, I figure I probably got up at 5:00 AM and went to bed about 2:00 AM. That's 21 hours straight with literally no breaks. It's all pretty amazing to think that on Friday I was looking forward to a Kentucky tradition: watching the Kentucky Derby on television with my family. On Saturday, I was unexpectedly on the finish line at the world's most famous horse race; I was working elbow-to-elbow with some of America's top engineers, producers, and sports announcers; *and* I was pushing buttons...err, turning knobs and flipping levers...that were sending out my sound cues to millions of listeners around the world. On Sunday at 2:00 AM I was lying in bed thinking, "Now that's a way to spend a birthday!"

After that day, I became a regular on the crew and worked several broadcasts of the Derby, Preakness, and Belmont, including a couple of Breeder's Cups. When I did that emergency gig at the Derby, I had no idea the amount of work it took beforehand just to do a one-hour remote broadcast. I found out the next year when I worked all three races. Let's skip the Derby and look at my work at the Preakness in Baltimore, Maryland.

Tuesday, four days before broadcast. I took a flight from Kentucky to Baltimore. Late that afternoon, the crew, all assembled at the hotel now, went to the track to scout it out. One of our crew from Lexington had driven a van with all of our equipment from Kentucky to Baltimore because it was just too expensive to fly with (he would drive it to New York City after the race and park it in a secured lot at Belmont Racetrack, the last of our three broadcasts). We unpacked the van and loaded all the heavy cases up to the broadcast booth. Most of the way included ramps and elevators. However, the last bit had winding hallways, multiple doorways, drop-offs, a catwalk, and metal fire escape-type steps leading up the rooftop where the booth was. The booth had a strange doorway that had you stepping over the threshold, kind of like getting into a bathtub. This meant we had to muscle every case over this threshold and try not to trip on it going in and out. Most radio broadcast booths at sporting events are very unglamorous. They're usually built as an afterthought and constructed with less design and compassion than a hay barn. The old booths at the University of Kentucky's football stadium that I worked for years had no heat and no AC. You were on your own like the players on the field.

Wednesday, three days before broadcast. Our first day of preparation on-site started in the morning. I had already spent the previous week preparing sound cues and commercials, packing equipment, including one vital addition: a computer and digital playback unit. In the radio world, engineers are always looking for fuss-free ways to play cues on the air. The cart machine was a godsend in the analog tape days. As digital came along, so did digital cart machines, which mimicked the analog tape machines in operation. That's the way technology really advances, in little steps that resemble previous versions. The playback unit I took to the races was a bit different. It was a *360 Systems* Shortcut, a desktop unit with a slanted top panel that included many soft rubber-coated buttons. In the top center was a small LED screen. This displayed cue names and other information as well as a rudimentary audio waveform. There was a QWERTY keyboard, a jog wheel with control buttons above it, and traditional rewind-stop-play buttons on the right. You could program a single sound cue into each QWERTY button so that when in playback mode, just press one and the audio fires right away. *360 Systems* also made a unit called Instant Replay (The Instant Replay 3 as of this writing) that was more geared toward playback only. It had 50 virtual hotkey buttons and 10 banks.[30] This allowed 500 sounds to be loaded onto the internal hard drive. These can still be useful today because they exist outside of a computer, which can fail. You might recognize this way of organizing sounds as similar to today's *sound bank* software apps which get their inspiration from these units.

I had packed a PC with a professional sound card, an early LCD screen (big space saver), and audio editing software (*Cool Edit*, known today as *Adobe Audition*). I would ingest all the interviews into

---

[30] Each bank of 50 hot keys could be customized for different segments or shows if one wanted. For instance, Bank 1 might be "Morning Drive" with sound effects and music cues, Bank 2 "News and Weather" that had intro music and canned announcer messages, and so on.

the PC, edit them, and then transfer them a cue at a time to the Shortcut. Shelby, the old school producer, didn't trust digital yet so he had me transfer all cuts to reel-to-reel just in case. So, during broadcasts I would be ready to play the reel if necessary. Once he was sure this newfangled digital unit would work, he allowed me to use the computer as a backup (which came in handy once or twice).

Back to that Wednesday before the Preakness, the whole crew worked from 8:00 AM to about 6:00 PM just rigging microphone cables, coordinating talkback and track-to-booth communications lines, working out radio communications and wireless microphone frequencies with the track, wiring the mixer with all the feeds, establishing digital ISDN and phone lines between the track and master control, and all kinds of other logistical tasks for an event that would be transmitted worldwide. No stone was left unturned. I was busy setting up and testing my gear, establishing a workflow, and was also ingesting interviews from one of the reporters we'd hired.

Thursday, two days before broadcast. We were back at the track very early. I spent most of the day ingesting and editing more interviews. I was putting together short packages for radio stations to generate buzz around the broadcast. There was still a lot of technical work to do for the engineers, most of which was establishing noise-free audio lines from the booth to each reporting position at the track. These were typically the press box, jockey's room, the winner's circle, and maybe one other location where an owner or trainer could be interviewed live. We also established audio feeds from microphones placed in the crowd (for crowd noise), along the stretch's inside rail (to capture horse hooves), the starting gate, and the track announcer (I recorded all the races during Preakness day and edited a package together every half-hour for radio affiliates). Thursdays were typically the longest days outside of race day itself. The crew just felt we had to be 99% ready for Friday morning when the crowds picked up and the press started to fly in from all over the world. It's very hard to run cables and move equipment through hordes of people. Oh, I forgot to mention that every day we were here, the track was still racing a full schedule with the normal race day crowds.

Friday, one day before broadcast. Today brought the reporters and hosts we had hired. Gary had all the headsets wired and fed to my mixer so that I could record their voice-overs for even more and lengthier packages throughout the day. It was also a great time for Gary, Carl, and Daryl to work out any audio or microphone problems that sometimes mysteriously pop up. When you work in any of these very old facilities (Pimlico opened in 1870, and I think they still have the original toilets!), the infrastructure can induce weird audio anomalies when you least expect it. In the case of Pimlico, on race day as 125,000 people use their cell phones, and gazenteen TV and radio stations fire up their radio and video transmitters (and didn't bother to coordinate with the track's frequency czar), a whole bunch of craziness can happen all at once. We found some of these problems when testing on Friday, but Saturday had a mountain of stray RF (radio frequency) buzzes, ground hums, and even a circuit from the booth to track that went out during one of these meets. When doing remotes, your credo should be to expect the unexpected.

Saturday, Preakness Day. Like the Derby, the drinking by the infield guests started with breakfast. There are stages, music acts, beauty contests, the "Running for the Urinals" race, fights, you name it. At that time Pimlico's infield was filled mostly with college-age kids that drank from sunup to sundown. From way atop the finish line where we were, you could just hold up a pair of binoculars and randomly point them into the crowd and see something you probably would never see again in your lifetime. I guess that's why they called it "The Freakness."

All that fun aside, it was a very early day for us. We arrived around 7:00 AM if memory serves me. We were pretty well locked down at this point. All microphones and back-up microphones were in place, all the wires were run and tucked and taped down. Everybody checked all the circuits one more time, trying to make them fail so repairs could be done early. I was now ingesting and editing even more interviews. Early morning workouts might reveal a new wrinkle in predictions, or a horse might scratch and throw everybody's handicap off. It was actually pretty exciting to see news change from hour-to-hour. I was also recording interviews in our booth. A dignitary would come by and wax on about the history of the race or their role in today's second jewel of the Triple Crown. Today is usually the day when you meet the people who have their names engraved on the sides of buildings, that movies are made about, or have plaques in the Hall of Fame. I also had to pack a recorder and mic and go record the track president for a package.

I was either recording, editing, or playing audio from about 8:00 AM until the race ended. I was very tired of listening by the time the day ended.

When the race ended, and after that darn elephant decided to sit on some other poor radio crew, we packed up everything until about midnight. It's funny how it takes so long to set stuff up, but it can be broken down in a tenth of that time. Everybody must be in a hurry to go home. Culinary-wise, the track kitchens in these large racetracks are usually top notch and Pimlico is no exception. Lunch from the press box was pretty good, but there's an old tradition after the race to serve Maryland crab cakes. These are hands down the best I've ever had. I just about made myself sick eating too many. They're more crab than cake. Chunks and chunks of wonderful chunks of crab. Mmmm. Well worth it for the hard work we all put in.

Sunday, travel home. Something I always try to do when I go to a great place like Baltimore is to book my flight later in the day so I can explore the city. Since everyone else had morning flights, I took possession of the crew's rental car and headed downtown to check out the harbor. I went on board several historic ships, explored the shops, and went out to Ft. McHenry. I remember standing behind the fort's first line of defense from the British bombardment from the harbor during the War of 1812 and imagining the bombs and cannonballs whizzing into the fort's walls. You can still see the pockmarks and holes left by the very battle that inspired Francis Scott Key's poem *Star Spangled Banner*. I would later draw on the *almost* real auditory experience when designing a soundtrack for a history presentation that included that battle. It really helped me to stand where those brave soldiers did to "hear" the history. It was also educational to see some of the actual artillery that would have been fired by both sides. It was yet another life experience that I would draw on to create a soundtrack.

So, a string of long, productive days in this example of how long production might take. The other racing events I did with this team were nearly identical in length of days and amount of work. Let's break down the Baltimore trip: Tuesday was travel day, that's 8 hours. Wednesday about 10 hours. Thursday was probably 12 to 14 hours and Friday probably equaled that. Saturday was 17 to 18 hours. And Sunday was travel day, another 4 to 8 hours. That's about 70 hours over a 6-day stretch. That's just one of many reasons why production can take a long time.

LIVE SOUND FOR
THE UNIVERSITY OF KENTUCKY
FOOTBALL GAMES

For 15 years I was the live sound director at Commonwealth Stadium during UK's football games. The stadium opened in 1973 as a semi-bowl-type structure (like two parentheses) that held 58,000 Wildcat fans. In 1999, the first year I started, the stadium was expanded by closing both ends, adding 10,000 seats, and building luxury suites at one endzone. I was consulted during the planning stages on live sound requirements, programming choices, production equipment, and personnel needed to run a live sound operation. For the sound system we looked at two options: 1) A single point of sound from an endzone scoreboard; and 2) a cluster of speakers around the perimeter of the field. We concluded that for the best sound in the stadium, clusters, or "trees" of loudspeakers would be placed around the stadium to "wash" the sound down onto the crowd. This would reduce the amount of wattage needed, would deliver even sound levels to the majority of spectators, would reduce feedback from the referee microphone, and would create less noise pollution to nearby neighborhoods. The downsides to this distributed system are the complications of engineering it and the initial higher cost. They chose the first option when the budget thinned, and the new endzone structure costs went up.

I spec'd out the gear we would need in the production booth with things like CD players, tape decks, etc. I didn't really build a definitive list because the company that was installing all the big video screens had contracted a sound installation company. No problem, I'm not a live sound installation expert, so I'd rather someone else do that. I did beg for the booth to be at the opposite endzone so we could hear the loudspeakers better. But alas, we were left in the old spot at the far 35-yard line. You had to lean over the counter and stick your head out just to hear the speakers clearly. Ugh.

I followed the progress of the stadium renovation as closely as I could. I kept bugging the Sports Video department director about getting in to familiarize myself with the equipment. There had been major construction delays and setbacks during the summer, and it was now August. Football season started in early September, and I was itching to get to know the sound system. Weeks went by, and I was getting a bad feeling about this gig. The system needed to be online and functional so they could balance everything. With large venues like these, each speaker has its own amplifier and control circuit. Each speaker's output, tone, and relative direction and angle of "spray" can be controlled mechanically (physically moving the speaker up or down, or side to side), and electrically (by manipulating loudness, equalization, and phase via computer control). This is a very methodical, laborious, exacting, and time-consuming process. An engineer will sit in the stands with a calibration microphone and laptop computer (or iPad these days) while test tones are played through the system. The laptop has control software that allows the engineer to remotely alter each speaker's characteristics. Other engineers throughout the stadium will make mechanical adjustments as necessary. The engineer with the laptop will move from section to section balancing the system while attempting to make the program listenable for all 68,000 fans (an impossible but worthy goal).

When I showed up on Thursday before the first game, there was a mixing console on the counter, a rack full of playback and other equipment, and about a thousand wires with no connectors spread out all over the room. I think they had one or two wired into the console, but everything else was undone. I was really starting to sweat about doing this gig. I had never been to a Kentucky football game, let alone been in the stadium before this year. Add to that the fact that we were an all-new crew that had never worked together as a unit before. What did I get myself into?

Friday was scheduled as a preparation day. All the videographers, editors, video switchers, grip crew, runners, and the sound crew were assembled for the first time. I had hired a friend to board op because he had done extensive live sound work, including the Astrodome in Houston, TX. Curt Mathies was also a radio veteran and guru and could advise on music cues and other details.[31] Our live audio team also had a field audio engineer, Mike

---

[31] Sadly, Curt passed away in 2021 after a long illness while I was writing this book. Curt was a self-described "radio savant" and consulted in the creation of

Pickett, who handled all microphones on the field such as the referee, the cheerleaders, the trumpeter (the Kentucky Derby's "Call to the Post" is played before kickoff), the national anthem singer, and any other live sound coming from field level.

The university had also hired a production truck that housed a video master control, replay control room, and an audio room. The audio engineer in the truck was Roger Tremaine, a KET (Kentucky Educational Television) Network veteran. Roger was responsible for any audio that originated from master control, such as a video element that was played back over the stadium's video screens. He was also responsible for all crew intercoms which included master control, replay, camera operators, production assistants, statistician, cheerleader director, band director, and live audio (me). I'm sure I'm leaving someone out, but it was an intricate network that ran all around the stadium to dozens of points. It was a job I had to learn (as an emergency backup) but never had to do, thank God.

As our production meeting wrapped, we all took our places for equipment setups and a complete pre-game program run through. The problem was, our audio production room was still being wired. They were playing tones or music or something through the system that day. Well at least it was turned on. We were unable to even operate the console because they still didn't have it ready. Our hands were tied, so Curt and I walked around the stadium just listening to the sound system. It sounded pretty thin from what I remember. Maybe the subwoofers weren't on yet. That was essentially a whole day wasted.

Game day = sweat day. Septembers in Kentucky are usually like Augusts in Kentucky – hot. I vividly remember how sweltering that day was in 1999 (94° F) and how nervous I was. It was also ungodly hot in the booth we were in: no HVAC, hot equipment, lots of people elbow-to-elbow, and loud box fans blowing right on us. Here I was once again this same year (I did my first harrowing Kentucky Derby just four months earlier), stepping into an unfamiliar situation and having to learn everything as it came flying at me. We arrived at the stadium five hours before game time, which is pretty typical for these kinds of events. On a normal

---

two of NPR's most beloved radio shows, "This American Life," and "Splendid Table."

football day (and this first day was far from normal), we work on getting the system up as quickly as possible and in test mode. If something goes wrong, you theoretically have several hours to fix it or come up with an alternate plan. In 15 years of doing this gig, that extra time has paid off more than once.

When we walked into the booth, we were presented with fewer wires strewn out all over the room. The console at least had most of the cables plugged in, so I felt a little better. However, everything was hands off because one of the installation engineers was working over the board making adjustments. After quizzing him about the status of everything, he could confirm that *most* of the audio sources were up and working. The main announcer microphone and the music playback gear was functional. I don't remember what wasn't, but I remember it was something major like the video master control audio from tape. To give the guy some space, we walked around the stadium and listened to the PA system. At least it had some bass in it today, so there's one positive thing.

We were due to start "the show" two hours before kickoff. At first, we would mostly play music over the PA system for the players to work out to. As time progressed towards kickoff, the show would pick up intensity. When the fans came through the gates one hour before kickoff, it really picked up. The really big show started 30 minutes before kickoff and was a scripted and timed program that had many cues, including live and pre-taped video, live announcer, music, cheerleaders, the marching band, singers, and fireworks. It's really impressive to be behind the scenes and see something like this pulled off in real time. But today I was just trying to make it through my first live football gig without having a meltdown.

Speaking of meltdowns, the installation engineer was still soldering wires for our board 30 minutes before kickoff![32] I don't remember a more harried or tense moment in my career as this one. Our booth was so crowded, most of us were toe-to-toe. The big windows were open, 70,000 fans were screaming, the band was

---

[32] In all fairness, I have to give kudos to the sound installation team for working through some unimaginable hard times. They were initially behind because of stadium construction delays. Then in the week of the first football game their owner died. They all took a few days to go back home to grieve and attend the funeral. We did not have this information until the next week, so we all felt bad for being upset with them. It's another instance of being patient when you do not know the big picture.

playing right at us, everyone in the booth was talking very, very loudly into headsets, and a nearby box fan was set on HIGH and blowing 94° air right onto me. The installation engineer, holding a dangerously hot smoking soldering iron, was wedged sideways between me and a producer as he leaned over the console and affixed a connector to an audio feed that we really, really needed, and soon. He quickly plugged it in, yelled, "Got it!" and – I'm not making this up – Curt raised the fader just in the nick of time.

Every fader that Curt raised that day was like revealing what was behind Door Number 3 or Door Number 1. We had no idea of what the audio levels would be, or if anything would be there at all. The referee mic was, and always will be, the diciest part of a live football game. The referee wears a lavalier microphone (like TV newscasters wear) at chest level on their jerseys.[33] It's omnidirectional, which means it's listening for sound from all directions: upwards toward the mouth, down toward the feet, and out in front. The body mostly blocks it from picking up sounds from behind the ref. Couple that with a single point sound system, crowd noise bleeding into the mic, and unpredictable environmental problems like wind, heat, and humidity. Once the referee turns on his mic, it picks up his microphone being fed through the PA speakers. Instant feedback can occur when a mic is turned toward a live speaker. Even though live sound installers try to direct speakers away from the football field to reduce referee mic feedback, there is still enough sound leakage that can easily cause issues.

There are other factors that cause problems, like the delay caused by the processors in the PA system, the natural half-second delay from the speaker to the microphone, and the bowl shape of the stadium which swirls the PA sound around. Engineers overcome a lot of these problems by "ringing out" the system beforehand, that is finding the frequencies that immediately cause feedback and reducing those with narrow-band notch filters. The frequencies that ring and the amount of feedback can change

---

[33] NFL referees use ear-mounted mics on a short thin boom that place the mic capsule near the mouth, which greatly reduces feedback. The SEC Referees Association would never approve these types of microphones the entire time I worked the games because they already wore one for inter-referee communications. For fun, watch a college game on a Saturday and then an NFL game the next day. Listen to the difference in quality of the ref announcements.

dramatically from game to game, and even from quarter to quarter due to changing weather and crowd size. But the most common change is from where the referee is standing, because he moves around the field. We overcame most of this by using a digital processor that looks for feedback as it starts, and then notches out those offending frequencies. It really doesn't work very well in real time, so we would spend a lot of time before each game ringing out all those feedback frequencies as best we could. We could make small adjustments during the game, but they were usually very minor.

The entire time I was doing these games, the quality of the referee mic was the hottest topic. The administration demanded it to be louder, but with all those potential problems I outlined, it was a gamble every time it was used. There was another major problem in these early days of the renovated stadium however, and that was the underpowered PA system. Unlike your home stereo that you usually listen to at a low level, live amplifiers are designed to be operated at 90% or higher capacity. That means you turn them up to 10 and adjust the input accordingly. There is a rule-of-thumb in live amplification that you need one watt of power for each person in the audience. The stadium held about 70,000 fans, and the PA system was just above 40,000 watts. You do the math, and you can see what problems we had that first year. In spite of the lower power however, we had tons of ref mic feedback problems. Most of this was because the single point PA system was bleeding too much onto the grass field. The referee would be in a feedback zone almost everywhere he stood. There were places along the field that were worse or better than others. I can remember holding my binoculars up and yelling to Curt, "He's on the 10-yard line, get ready for feedback," or "Ref's on the 35, it should be okay." It's like a cat and mouse game, wondering how much feedback there really will be on the 10-yard line that day.

As I said, the ref mic was always a point of contention. So much so that one day a university muckity-muck marched up to me and chewed me out at full volume for how bad it sounded, right in front of the whole crew. Now I can take a chewing out just about any time, but this was completely tactless and unprofessional by doing it in front of my peers. My guess is *he* was chewed out and had to blow off some steam, and I happened to be in his path. After he walked out of the booth, everyone was completely stunned and wondered aloud what got stuck in his craw. I don't remember what the specific problem was that day, but I recall an equipment change or failure that caused it to operate differently than usual. Plus, Kentucky lost the game that Saturday, so everybody was in a foul mood. I won't make excuses because it was on my watch, but his way of dealing with the problem caused me to lose all of my respect for him that day. I never treated him but with professional courtesy after that, but he never regained any of my respect or friendship.

When I went home ten hours later after that first disaster of a day, my body was all sticky from sweat and my ears whined and hissed. My nerves were shot, I barely slept, and my gut was messed up for days. That day was probably the worst of my professional career. Even though it seemed as if I had been thrown into a firepit four months earlier at the Kentucky Derby, I could at least count on my equipment working. But on this day, I felt completely out of control because I couldn't trust a single solder point, wire, fader, or speaker. I was sure there would be an epic failure at any point. I held it together in the end, but I was determined to not let that job eat me alive. I needed to take control, so I did.

I contacted the director that hired me and asked for access to the booth during the week so that I could familiarize myself with the console and other equipment that I would be operating. Of course, he liked that idea and gave me carte blanche to the stadium. I muddled through that season mostly learning by the seat of my pants, but I still needed to understand where, how, and why all the audio feeds traveled around the facility. When summer came, I spent an entire day tracing every audio cable in Commonwealth Stadium. I crawled behind every rack, climbed to each speaker and amp in the scoreboard, eyeballed every concourse and luxury box speaker, and located every connection at the football field and media parking lot junction boxes. This idea of tracing every cable was not new to me, it's what I've always done so that I can become familiar with a new studio. If I don't know what a button does when pushed, or how a signal goes from A to B, then I don't feel in control. I did that at all the race tracks I worked at, I've done it in every studio I've worked, and I've even done it at radio stations I've worked at. You should (with permission) get behind every rack and under every counter to understand the routing system of a studio. If software controls a portion of the routing, dig down into the details with the facility engineer so that no stone is left unturned.

You don't need to be an expert, but you should have a healthy understanding of the bones of the system.

During my time in that job, the stadium went through several renovations. The audio system was upgraded a few times, and each time it leapfrogged the old system. UK now has an appropriately powered system, a fantastic referee mic sound (probably the best in the SEC, thank you very much[34]), and a bitchin' large footprint Yamaha digital console. From almost no control with that first system to one of envy when I left, I rode that horse from a M*A*S*H-style PA system when I was first brought in, to a highly complex digitally controlled MADI sound system.

As the seasons went on, our crew developed a routine for every game so that we could find problems before they occur. Our typical crew had the following personnel:

Audio Director – Responsible for preparation and execution of any audio in the facility that is amplified or routed to media, performers, and university personnel. This excludes the coaching staff and players. During the event, the director gives cues to the board op and field audio engineer for music, announcers, and live performers.

Board Operator – Mixes audio sources and sends to all speakers and audio circuits around the stadium. Has creative and technical input for music, announcers, and performers when necessary.

Field Audio engineer – Prepares and maintains microphones used on the sidelines and field of play including referee wireless kit, emcee wireless handheld microphones, and any on-field performers that need amplification. Is the eyes and ears for the team in the booth and advises of any feedback or other audio problems.

---

[34] Whenever I watch an away college football game on TV and the referee mic feeds back really bad, I get a sympathetic gut pain for the live engineers at that stadium because I know exactly what they're going through. Some uninformed muckity-muck just might march in there after the game and tattoo a new cussword on them.

Master Control audio engineer – Is stationed with video master control and sends audio content from video programs to the live board console. Sends audio to camera operators. Sets up and maintains communications between master control, live audio booth, program director, cheerleader director, and band director.

We were also supported by several university experts charged with maintaining the scoreboard and facility video, audio, and lighting controls and equipment. In all there were about eight people dedicated to audio in the stadium.

Now I'd like to detail a typical day at the stadium so that you can see how we spent our time getting ready for a live event. Today's game has a 1:00 PM kickoff.

8:00 AM. Arrive at the stadium with coffee in hand. We would meet at video master control and yuck it up with everybody and find out if there were any problems to know about. The master control audio engineer would have his equipment running test tones to all his outputs. The videographers would be rolling camera cases to all points in the stadium, and the video control crew would be loading all their video files and checking connections. The master control audio engineer would begin running and testing intercom cables around the stadium, which usually ate up an hour or more. The rest of us (director, board op, and field audio) would head to the booth in the press box.

8:30 AM. If the console wasn't already turned on by the stadium electrical engineers, we would fire up all booth equipment (See a picture of the console on page 366). The PA amplifiers in the scoreboard would already be on because the stadium crew got here extra early. They would have tested every amp and speaker the day before. Occasionally they would be replacing a failed component the morning of. Whenever you turn on a big system like this, you ALWAYS check to make sure nobody is in the scoreboard tower at that time, because the most innocent "pop" from the console turning on could deafen someone up there. Remember, it's 70,000 watts you're pushing through those speakers. Also, ALWAYS have the output faders all the way down to OFF before turning on any console.[35] The field engineer would collect all the wireless microphones and start testing them. He would make sure that he had several batteries available for the game because those transmitters go through batteries, especially when it's cold. The board op would test all audio connections in "cue" mode at this point before playing anything over the main system. If there is a problem, we want to know now so we don't blow an amp or speaker.

9:00 AM. After testing all lines in cue mode, we once again make sure no one is up in the scoreboard where the speakers are. We then start pumping music very softly to all the places in the stadium that are amplified. This will warm up the amplifiers and gently break in the speakers, especially during cold mornings. Our console directs and redirects so many sources to so many destinations, that it can be mind boggling. Of course, we have the main PA system, but there is also a separate system for the concourse and gates where fans enter and buy food. There are restrooms, luxury boxes, and meeting rooms that require audio. All the TVs distributed throughout the stadium have matching audio from the PA. Our console also routes audio from the live radio network to video recorders and luxury boxes. We also provide a feed of PA audio and a talkback mic to the video screen closed-captioner. There is a whole audio assist radio system that uses wireless headphones to help guests with a hearing handicap. If there is a singer, group of singers, or instrumental soloist that will be performing on the field, there is a separate audio system that provides a no delay foldback of the PA system to their in-ear monitors. We also do multiple feeds of different audio sources back down to the video control room.

9:30 AM. We start testing all incoming audio sources. We test the referee and handheld wireless mics in the booth before the field engineer goes down to the sidelines. We have incoming audio feeds from the UK Radio Network booth, sometimes a television network, the video master control, a crowd mic, a local radio station that carries the UK Radio Network program, the main PA

---

[35] All the faders on our console were motorized. Before shutting off power, we would load a scene programmed into our board that set all faders and volume controls to zero. That way when you booted up, that last scene would load with all faders already at zero. You would then go on to load the regular saved scene for the gig.

announcer's headset, and an emergency backup announcer mic. The university's sports marketing department, which assembles and directs the program, has several audio sources coming to us including an Instant Replay I mentioned earlier in the racetrack section. There is a DJ located next to us who plays beats at various points before and during the game. We have a backup CD player because the cheerleaders or band may have a last-minute track that needs to be played during a routine on the field. The present console has 48 main input channels so I'm probably leaving a few sources out. I would walk down to the home and visiting radio crew booths and let them know we would be testing the referee mic around 10:00 AM. If a television network was broadcasting the game, I would track down their audio engineer and warn them as well. The referee mic signal would be split and routed to two separate inputs on our console. One would be a "dry" and direct line from the receiver. This would be distributed to the media such as the press box and live radio and television. The other fader would be routed to the feedback reduction equipment and looped back to our console. We did this because a microphone that has been "rung out" to reduce feedback usually sounds great through the speakers, but thin and tinny in your headphones.

10:00 AM. We can now start testing the referee and other field mics at full volume. UK has an agreement with nearby neighborhoods (including mine because I live just blocks away from the stadium) that the sound system would not play before 10:00 AM. The field engineer will first do some quick on-field tests of the main referee mic system. He will then walk to several places on the field to test feedback possibilities. The feedback reducer gear was computer controlled. It had "scenes" or settings that we stored and recalled. We would often recall the previous game's settings to see if any adjustments needed to be made, which was usually the case. If major changes needed to be made, we would erase most of the filters, but keep a base of about 10 of the most common frequencies that would feed back. The field engineer would then go to the most troublesome place on the field, count to ten, and then be silent while keeping the mic open and hot. The board op would slowly raise the fader until feedback started to happen. The automatic feedback control would sense it and start to notch out those frequencies. We would keep pushing it louder and louder to find the maximum we could get out of it at that point. He would then move other positions while we continued to ring out the system. This can be a very frustrating experience because as the engineer moves to another place, the feedback changes. As the temperature rises in the morning, the feedback changes. I would often put in some manual frequencies notches that I could adjust later during the game if feedback was still a problem.

Once we got the ref mic sounding decent, the field engineer would switch to an identical backup system. This was a complete duplicate kit including mic, transmitter, cables, and belt switch. Although the backup is the same brand and model, it always sounded just different enough that we made sure it didn't have too much feedback if we had to rapidly change it during a game. The engineer would now move on to field test all the other wireless and hard-wired mics. Our main goal was to get as much gain as possible before feedback. If there was unwanted feedback, we would equalize that channel some or try maneuvering the mic away from the speakers. We also tested the DJ feed from the field at this time. During pregame the DJ would position himself near the cheerleaders and players warming up.

There is one major thing to remember if you find yourself in the situation of ringing out a live sound system in a large stadium or arena: An empty space will sound very different than one with people. Bodies absorb sound, and therefore sound will bounce around more in an empty space. There will likely be problems with high frequency feedback in an empty space that will mostly disappear when the space is full. However, with a stadium full of 70,000 screaming sound-absorbing bodies, the PA system will inevitably get raised in volume during crowd swells, thus creating more potential for feedback. To mitigate this, we found that if our engineers could have no feedback with the fader at 100% during testing in an empty stadium, then we would likely have little to no problems during a game. A general rule of thumb when setting up and using live microphones during a live sporting event, is to have the mic's fader at about 70% (or ¾ of the way up) most of the time. This way you still have 30% more fader to use when the crowd cheers (or boos) loudly. Why 70%? Most of the time a mic will be active when the crowd is idle, so you need that extra headroom for when the crowd swells. And because you rang out the system beforehand with no feedback at 100% fader level, your chances of feeding back at 100% fader level during the game is diminished.

It's calibrations like this beforehand that take away much of the guess work.

11:00 AM. Lunch. We would start some softly playing hip hop or other modern music playing through the system before the gates opened in one hour. This is also buffer time in case something has to be repaired or reconfigured. I've missed many lunches because of some issue or another, so I was always grateful for this time when I needed it. Lunch is also a breather from the job, because the last half of your day is about to become ten times more intense and stressful.

12:00. One hour before kickoff. Gates have opened now, and the sound-absorbing sacs of fluid and bones start filling up the stadium while talking loudly over the music. This is also when we start to raise the music level just a little bit more. As more bodies fill the seats, we inch up the volume a little more. We are trying to gradually build excitement. The football players are now warming up on the field, so the music usually has more beats and bottom end. At this point we are also re-checking all mics, both in the booth and on the field. The field engineer has gone to the referee locker room to wire up the ref. He will come out about 20 minutes before kickoff and do a mic check with us. We do this in a cue channel[36] most of the time, but some referees want to hear their voice over the main PA system.

Another thing we are doing at this point is going over the script for the pre-game and in-game program. Everybody on the video, audio, cheerleading, band, and marketing teams have a master script with every possible entertainment event charted out that will happen at specific moments in time. Some people, like the in-game live PA announcer, will have an additional script with announcements. The director of the whole "show" is on a master intercom headset that communicates to all sub-directors (like the video director or the band director – I'm standing right beside this person, so I don't need a headset link to hear them). Each event is listed by minutes before kick-off. For instance, at 2:00, or two hours before kickoff, we start warm-up music over the PA system. At 1:00,

---

[36] Sometimes called "AUX" or auxiliary. A separate side circuit for each channel that can be routed to a control room speaker or headphones. We use them to check audio sources before we raise the fader and send to program. Very useful in live sound and broadcast.

or one hour before kickoff, we play the "air raid" siren to alert the tailgaters in the parking lot to pack up their brews and food and head to their seats. This goes on right up until kickoff. So that we can follow along easily, we mark all audio cues with different colored highlighters for quick view. Good directors will preface all their verbal cues with who it is directed at, such as, "Stand by video for cue 7. In three, two, one, roll video." If they only said, "Stand by, and roll!" then about 10 of us would be wondering who was supposed to roll (and yes, I've worked with a few noobie directors that I had to tactfully explain how to make things go smoother). So, I got used to only listening for the word "Audio." That's a whole lot easier than trying to constantly sift through the cacophony of multiple people giving cues in the booth.

And speaking of who's in the booth? In ours we had:

- The scoreboard operator
- The scoreboard operator's assistant and spotter (relaying hand signals from on-field referees and line judges)
- The live PA announcer
- Two spotters for the PA announcer (giving player numbers, yard line, down number, etc.)
- Program director (gives cues to video, audio, band, and cheerleaders)
- Video banner control engineer (switches stats, advertisements, announcements, etc. to all in-stadium banners and parts of the scoreboard that contains ads.)
- Video and sound sizzle engineer (for quick music cuts and energy videos such as "Third Down Make Noise"). The sound from this unit is hard wired to the sound console and usually stays active the whole time so we don't miss a cue. The board op may fade out audio from this so that the PA announcer can be heard.
- Production assistants (usually two or three floating in and out of the room doing errands)
- Live sound director (me)
- Live sound board op (sometimes me when relieving the regular engineer)
- DJ (not in the booth the entire time, depending on program)
- University electrical engineers and sound/video equipment specialists (usually two or three who are regularly checking

conditions and data from scoreboard, concourse, and luxury box video and sound equipment. One engineer is designated as the emergency sound system switcher in case of total power failure (such as during a storm). If the fans need to be evacuated, there is a totally separate and electrically independent sound system that the live PA announcer can make important emergency announcements over.

That's a lot of people with a lot to say to each other. We are also using a walkie-talkie with the field engineer and talk back with the control room audio engineer. It can get quite loud in the production booth, especially with the windows open and 70,000 fans screaming. In these situations, it's crucial to just focus on your job and listen to your product. Communicate with others as efficiently as possible so you don't wear out your voice or distract someone else from their job.

11:30 AM. Pre-game program begins. The real fun starts 30 minutes before kickoff. Most fans are either in their seats or carting back $50 worth of hotdogs and popcorn. The buzz is really loud now, so we play a succession of hype videos as the band is assembling on the sidelines. The PA announcer is reading announcements in between videos and music is being played to fill any gaps while waiting for the next cue. There is constant sound going on, either from our PA speakers or the cheerleaders and band on the field. The band will play "My Old Kentucky Home" and "The Star-Spangled Banner." A lone trumpeter will play "Call to the Post" over a field microphone just before a super hype video with incredibly loud and pumping music plays. The PA announcer is reading the names of the starting players very dramatically to build the hype even more. And just like that, the smoke machines start up outside Kentucky's locker room while the music is still pumping. And BANG! BANG! BANG! BANG! BANG! The fireworks go off filling the field with smoke as the team runs onto the field through a gauntlet of cheerleaders and band members. A brawny cheerleader yells as loud as humanly possible over a handheld wireless mic, "It's football time in the Blue Graaaaaaaassss!" The sizzle engineer starts a very beaty cut of music that builds until the moment the ball is kicked off, followed by a quick wildcat growl sound effect.

12:00 PM. Game action. The second after the first play from the kickoff is over, it's almost eerily quiet. Sometimes my ears are still ringing from the fireworks, but the crowd level peaked at about 120 dbSPL during the loudest moment, now it's back down to about 80 dbSPL. That's quite a range. We can kind of relax now, because the only thing going over the PA system until a time out is PA announcer Carl Nathe's golden voice telling everyone who just got tackled, by whom, what down it is, and how many yards to go. We might have a quick music cue or video with sound to pump up the crowd, but it's pretty easy cruising unless the referee needs to open his mic. That's when we jump to attention because we could have any type of problem:

- Feedback. No matter how much we test before the game, there are so many anomalies that can alter and affect the sound in the stadium. We just stay ready with our hand on the fader.
- Bad wiring. The refs are essentially athletes wearing electronic equipment, so a broken wire or switch could happen at any moment. They are really rough on the kits.
- Fallen mic. Occasionally a ref will accidently rip the mic off their jersey and not realize it. If this happens, then the mic is dangling when they turn on their mic. We don't know this until we raise the fader and get a faraway voice and some feedback. The field engineer will run out during the first time out and fix it. That's why refs still use hand signals.
- Open switch. Sometimes, either by equipment fault or referee fault, his mic is left open after announcing. If this happens, we just have to ride the fader, that is raise and lower it manually when he needs it. The field engineer will run out during the next time out and either fix it or inform the ref that it is open. We've been caught off guard on more than one occasion. During one contentious rivalry game, all the refs met at the 50-yard line after a penalty. Unbeknownst to me, the ref had left his switch on. I couldn't immediately tell because the crowd was still booing (Kentucky football fans *always* think the refs are out to call bad plays against them). Then I hear something like, "These goddamn boys just want to fight..." I jerked the fader down, but it was too late, everybody heard it. I just had to shrug and have the field engineer run out to the ref. A few other times the ref has blown his whistle while his mic is still hot. This is intensely loud! If a ref ever forgets to close his mic just once, from that point on until the game ends we ride his fader – just in case.

- <u>Rain or sweat soaked mic.</u> A mic will sound dull and sometimes crackly when it gets wet. If it happens early enough, we will have the ref change the mic out if he has time. Otherwise, you just have a dull-sounding referee that you have to ride gain on very carefully.

12:45 PM. First Quarter time out. Between the 1st & 2nd and the 3rd & 4th quarters, and long media time outs, the live program usually features an emcee in the endzone introducing former players, another sports team at the university, members of the community, or a goofy fan contest. Fortunately, the emcee is at the far end of the field with the back of the mic pointing towards the speakers. We usually have very little feedback problems.

1:30 PM. Halftime / Pee break. Halftime is usually fifteen minutes unless it's homecoming or senior day with extended activities. The band has an announcer that will come up to the booth and call their program on the PA announcer's microphone. This gives the main announcer a nice break to eat something and relax his voice. It also gives us a chance to unwind. After the band plays, there is usually just music playing and a few announcements until the start of action again. When the referees come back out onto the field, the field audio engineer will change the battery in the wireless transmitter and recheck the microphone and cables. We would have the referee do a mic check and listen in our cue speaker.

1:45 PM. Third Quarter. Me and the board op usually swap out for a quarter so he can get a break. He might walk around the stadium and listen for any problems. He will take a walkie-talkie along so he can relay what he hears.

2:45 PM. Fourth Quarter. The game starts really slowing down about now for some reason. I don't know if it's because everyone is tired or the teams take more timeouts, but the energy just kind of gets sucked out of the stadium. We've played all our commercial obligations, there are no more sideline guests, some fans on the losing side are starting to file out. Unless the game is close and a comeback is possible, we're really just waiting for this day to be over. Sometimes there are overtimes, and over two calendar days, I was part of one of the longest college football games in history. On November 1, 2003, SEC rival Arkansas Razorbacks came to town. Kickoff was at 8:00 PM. By the time the game ended the next day at 12:01 AM, both teams had played seven overtime periods, scored 86 overtime points, and played 4 hours and 56 minutes. Kentucky lost that game on a fumble, and Arkansas had played in three of the longest games in college football in just two years. I was at that game only ten hours, but it sure felt like twenty. The overtimes were like *Groundhog Day*, the same thing over and over and over again.

3:45 PM. Post-game. We can't pack it up and go just yet. We have direct audio feeds coming from the UK press room and the visiting team's locker room in the bowels of the stadium that get fed over the PA system and television monitors. We usually just feed the Kentucky coach, but sometimes the opposing coach is more interesting or available until our coach shows up. We have an audio engineer that goes down to the main press room and tests the microphone for us. We leave this up in our cue speaker until the coach arrives. After the press conference, we pack up and leave. The university electrical engineers will slowly shut down the entire video, sound, and lighting system over the next hours. They will usually put in 12 to 15-hours on game day.

4:15 – 5:00 PM. Postmortem and wrap up. The main audio engineers will usually meet and discuss any problems we might have had, or just talk about the next game and what might be different. We sometimes use this time to make sound system adjustments and save presets to make the next game go a little easier. I might also talk with the director about any needs we have or even receive feedback on our product. We don't always have perfect days, so it's best to listen to how other people heard the program and system so you can make corrections for the next game. We usually joke (with some truth to this) that we know we've done a good job when nobody says anything about the audio.

A typical football gameday engineering job is eight to nine hours. That's pretty doable, and assuming there were no major problems, a fairly stress-free day. It's still tiring because you're around A LOT of people, are bombarded with A LOT of sound, and have to be on your toes 100% of the time. But it's also very rewarding for several reasons. You get to apply your craft and see immediate results; you get to take part in something newsworthy; you get paid to watch a game; and you are usually around top notch professionals that are enjoying the day as much as you are. Once you get past the initial learning curve of doing a gig like this, you can have a lot of fun doing live sports.

ALLTECH'S
"CELEBRATION OF SONG"
CONCERT SERIES

Every Christmas season, a worldwide corporation in a nearby small town sponsors a huge celebration of seasonal music featuring The University of Kentucky's Opera program. It features choirs, soloists, musical groups and a chamber orchestra. It's presented live to an audience while being videotaped for later broadcast and streaming. The audio recording is later broadcast on radio as well.

Alltech is somewhat of a sleeper corporation among the public because they research, develop, and manufacture products for the agriculture industry like feed supplements, seed control, foods, and other ingredients that focus on natural sustainability. The company was founded by an Irish scientist, Dr. Pearse Lyons, who was branching out from his brewing and distilling roots of his family business by focusing on animal nutrition challenges. The late Dr. Lyons and his wife Dierdre enjoy vocal music, and thus came up with the idea of sponsoring UK's budding opera program with scholarships and community performances. One of those is the annual "Celebration of Song."

Alltech had been one of my clients when they contacted me in the early 2000s about recording the program for them to use with the video program. They had been relying on a direct audio feed off the console from the live sound engineer for a few years but were dissatisfied with the results. Any recorded mix from a live board will not sound good for several reasons. One is that the engineer is mixing for what's coming out of the speakers in the auditorium full of people. Sounds are balanced differently based on the amount of absorption from people, and the reverberations from the walls and ceiling. Plus, just like the referee mic at the UK Football games that we split into two feeds (one for radio, the other for the PA), the frequencies will be adjusted for live sound rather than recorded sound. You can hear this directly by listening to recordings of live concerts when someone has tapped off the live sound board. Try searching for Grateful Dead live recordings[37] and single out the "tape feeds" or "soundboard" versions and you'll hear what I mean.

The concerts took place in what today is called "The Square," but was originally called "Victorian Square," right in the heart of downtown Lexington. In the mid-1980s a development group took a city block of 16 Victorian buildings built a hundred years earlier and melded them into an indoor mini mall. In the very center is a three-story covered atrium with skylights. This area was originally a small alley that trucks used for "delivery in the rear." I lived a few blocks away from here before they renovated it and remember going to stores on this block. Many were in disrepair, so this project breathed new life into an area that was literally on the chopping block.

Our concert was taking place in this atrium that had a brick wall and two stories of tiered seating at the back, a brick wall on the left, a two-story seating area on the right, and stairs and balconies in the front. For our purposes, it looks like a big L. The chamber orchestra sat on the ground floor while soloists and small ensembles were scattered around the different stairways and balconies overlooking the floor. With the audience also seated and standing along the balconies, it was very similar to theatre-in-the-round with performers and listeners meshed together. It was very unconventional, meaning it was not the traditional stage facing the audience. Herein laid the main challenge.

Wide shot of The Square before set construction.

---

[37] https://archive.org/details/GratefulDead is a great site with thousands and thousands of Grateful Dead recordings.

If it were a typical orchestra with singers, I would just place two or three mics out front and use spot mics on soloists. But everybody was scattered around and some even facing each other. There would be many challenges trying to place performers into a stereo field. And I use the term "field," because this is one of the first decisions you make when starting a recording or mixing project – what is the width of your final product? The most common is stereo, but today we also choose mono and surround depending on the final audience of the recording. When you're planning on where to place sounds in your final mix, you should carefully think through the location of every sound source. In the early days of stereo records, they hadn't quite figured out the ideal listener experience, so they relied a little too much on gimmicky placement. For instance, many rock and jazz recordings of the late 1950s and early 1960s might place the drums and bass in the left channel, the guitar and piano in the right, and the singer in the middle. This sounded very different to listeners that were used to mono sound.[38] I believe the thinking might have been to recreate the sound of the band on stage. However, most night club audiences might have been back from the stage and heard most of it as a single sound point, or more monaural. As stereo hi-fis were sold, the recording space started to spread between the channels a little better. Listen to Rudy Van Gelder's Blue Note jazz recordings from the mid-1960s and you will hear the instruments more spread across the stereo field, including room reverberation that carries from one channel to the other. As the decade progressed into the 70s, so did the stereo field. Rock recordings started to put the listener almost inside the band with guitars wrapped around a listener's head and guitar solos flying from one ear to the next. This immersion-type stereo field still dominates pop music today and artists can get very creative in the stereo dimension.

---

[38] Some were also direct transfers of 3-track safety recordings made when radio stations only wanted mono pressings. The 3-track was dubbed to stereo later, usually only as an afterthought. In addition, most early mixing consoles didn't have a variable pan control, just channel assignment switches of left-center-right with no variation or combination possible.

On the floor of the atrium stage facing the orchestra position.

The following diagram is from our technical notes for the 2015 concert. Note where "Audio Control" was located that year. Our main challenges were: Where do we put the microphones and how do we fit them into the stereo field? Let me give you a breakdown of the typical performers and where they were in the atrium. It varies from year to year but follows the same basic format.

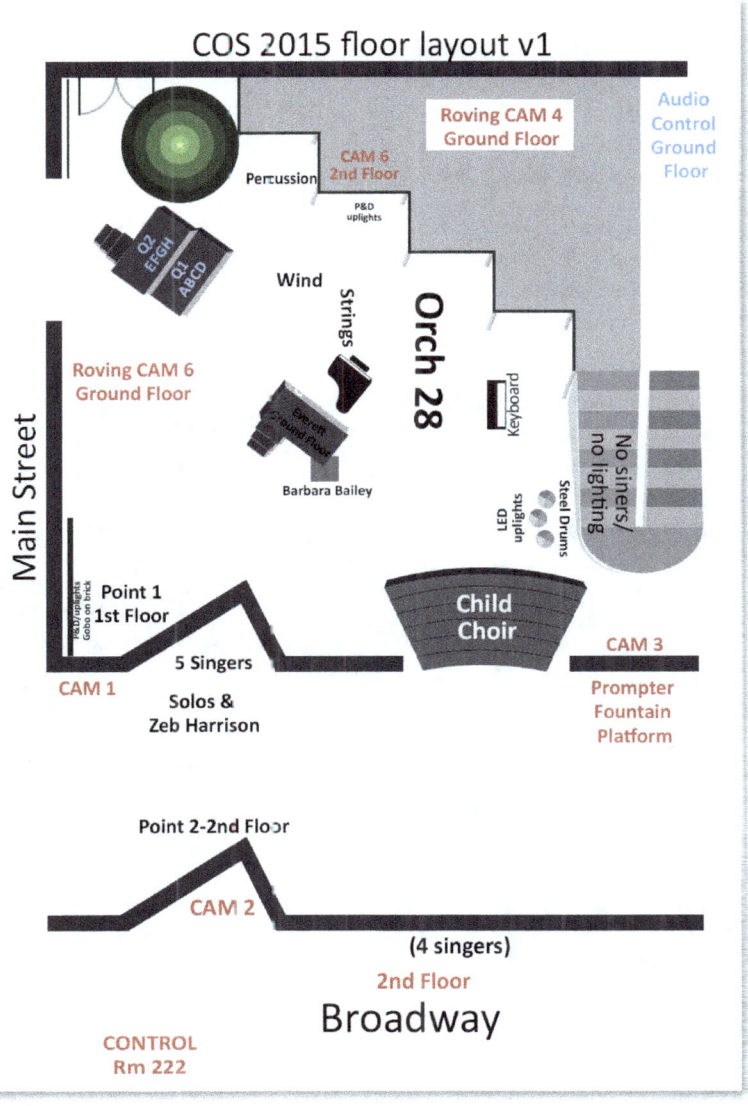

Technical notes from the 2015 concert.

Chamber orchestra. A group of about 20-30 players from the local Lexington Philharmonic Orchestra. They include string, brass and percussion sections as well as a harp, pianist, and keyboardist. The orchestra accompanies the singers on about two-thirds of the songs. They sit on the bottom main floor facing the main crowd and balconies.

Pianist. The pianist, who also will accompany small groups and even have a solo during the show, is placed to the extreme left of the orchestra towards the front next to the T-shaped singer's stage described in the next section.

Looking down onto the curved stairs facing the orchestra.

UK Opera School students. About 30 vocalists will perform, but all together only during the big finale. There are several specialty groups of duos, trios, quartets, and larger. All different musical styles are played, and some include rhythm or stringed instrumental accompaniments within the group. There are soloists as well, and some are accompanied by singers in various points in the space, such as on a balcony or stairstep. There is usually a quartet or octet on a T-shaped stage just to the left of the orchestra facing out the same direction that the orchestra does (it is slightly different in the photos but in the same location). The conductor is on the long end of the T facing the singers and orchestra.

UK Opera School faculty and graduates. There are one or two faculty members that will perform solos, usually from a small riser located on a left balcony overlooking and facing the orchestra. There will also be a graduate that has gone on to be famous and perform in operas around the world. The school has truly become one of the top opera programs in the nation. I went to UK's School of Music in the 1980s before they developed this program. The School of Music back then was pretty solid, so it doesn't surprise me that one of their programs would gain international fame.

Guest choir. Sometimes there is a children's or youth choir that will perform. They are usually placed on a set of wide arcing steps facing and leading down to the orchestra (see photos).

Guest instrumental group. Sometimes there is an instrumental group such as a jazz brass band, Calypso band, or a hand bell choir. The school always manages to find an interesting and talented group. They are placed at varying places such as in the wings facing the orchestra or on the next level up on a balcony facing the orchestra (on the far right in the technical notes page).

Show Emcee. There is always a local celebrity or news anchor that hosts the show and presents each song. This person is wearing a wireless lavalier that is amplified to the crowd. They will be reading a teleprompter located just off stage.

Conductor. UK Opera School Chair Dr. Everette McCorvey conducts the orchestra, sings one song to lead off the night, and reads a script about the performers and program at some point. Everette has also tirelessly authored and choreographed the show from beginning to end. There is a wireless lavalier on Everette.

So, there you have it, anywhere from 60 to 80 performers on stage at various times during this 75-minute show. In recent years we have increased that to two shows an hour apart. We record both shows and pick the best performances from each, which is usually the bulk of the second show. These happen a few weeks before Christmas on a Sunday. Weather doesn't seem to affect attendance because it always seems packed.

Here is a general description of the technical staff placement throughout The Square. The program is recorded and then later edited for television and streaming, but it will also be switched live for monitors spread throughout the building. Each camera has a built-in recorder, and the video director is recording the switched video feed along with a live audio mix from me. The video editor will later insert specific camera footage if he wants a different angle from what was switched.

Camera crew. There are six to eight cameras placed at various points to capture wide, medium, and closeup shots. They are strategically placed and choreographed so that one live camera hopefully doesn't catch another camera operator in the background. One of these cameras, the master, has a direct feed from my live mix for sync reference. The other cameras record live audio from their camera-mounted mics.

Grip crew. The local audio-video company that supplies all the lights, cameras, stages, television monitors, and pipe and draping has several grips on standby during the programs. They have been setting up the equipment throughout the week. They are on hand for rehearsals the day before the concert to practice camera techniques and check lighting. After the last performance, they can pack up the trucks and be rolling in less than two hours. Impressive.

Video specialist. There is a video guru in the master control room that sets up all camera links, video recorders, switchers, and monitors. He tweaks and color balances all the video and makes sure everything is flowing during the recording. His job is so far above my head that I would only be guessing at what else he does.

Video director. Chad Robinson is the director of video services at Alltech and is directing the recording and switching of the show. He will later edit the show together into a one-hour broadcast version.

Floor director. This person is also the concert master who is responsible for moving the groups into position and cueing the emcee and director.

Production assistants and crew management. There are many assistants from both Alltech and the audio-video company, as well as UK Opera and the orchestra. There are also various managers in the background making sure each crew member gets what they need.

Live audio crew. The live sound has a director, who is also usually the sound mixer. He has an assistant audio engineer that works alongside him during the show. There is also another assistant that maintains and places all the wireless lavs on the emcee, director, and all soloists.

Audio recording crew. This is us. There's me, a second audio engineer, and a production assistant. We have two mixing boards, one for tracking each mic to a recorder, and one to provide a live mix to the video recording. The assistant helps set up and tear down equipment the day of the show, as well as move microphones around during the show.

The Stereo Field

Our first decision to make was, *where in the space is the listener?* We decided that we wanted the listener to feel as if they are standing in front of the orchestra. All performances, regardless of where they physically were, would be mixed as if they were in the orchestra position. The sound field would be stereo because that's the delivery spec[39] as well as the most common way to listen to music. This concert would be presented on television, the web, and radio. The video would not necessarily emphasize the "in-the-round" experience. Cutaways, close-ups, and other shots would disorient the viewer if we tried to match the sound field to every shot. Consistency is the key when designing a sound field. For instance, when you're placing sound in a film drama, you mostly try to stick the important sound elements, like dialog, in the center channel. Environmental sounds and music can come from the other channels. Sometimes moving a character to another place in the field can be effective. A sound effect can even be a character: A threatening helicopter flying from the back of the sound field to the front where the main characters are; or the looming stomp of a

---

[39] Most projects are given guidelines for audio specifications from the start, like, "Stereo interleaved, 48KHz, 24-bit." Broadcast television networks have a very complex set of specifications that usually specify 12 or more tracks of audio that include stems (submixes of some tracks) like dialog, soundbites, sound effects only, music only, etc.

monster coming from behind. But putting the main element anywhere other than center channel, in our case a singer that we see, can be confusing.

The orchestra, the backbone of the concert, was recorded in stereo with "spot" microphones in places throughout the ensemble. Some years we experimented with three microphones in front of the orchestra utilizing a left-center-right spread, but when they reduced the number of players and narrowed the width of the orchestra, we scaled back to a stereo pair. Although this created several problems with the players jam-packed together, we found two microphones sufficient to capture a full sound. If there's one thing I've learned from recording large ensembles and choirs, it's to use as few mics as possible. We got the best sound we could with two Neumann U-87 cardioid large condenser microphones raised overhead and spaced roughly ten feet apart. Their pickup pattern is pretty widespread, which was good because we didn't have much room to pull the mics back from the front of the orchestra. We rose them a little higher than normal and angled them down about 45 degrees. The piano was right under the left one which created many problems at first, but moving the left mic towards center a little reduced it and still gave us a good stereo picture of the orchestra.

Our orchestra spot mics were intended to be used in the final studio mix if I needed to pull some individual instruments out. If I did use any, I panned them in the sound field to match where they were on the floor. I usually put one spot on the brass section, two on the percussion, one on the string bass, one on the harp, and one on the piano. These have proven to be very useful in the final mix to bring out these instruments' detail.

To minimize confusion, we placed most singers in mono and into the center channel. The few exceptions were small choirs and the occasional quartet. Any instrumental soloist was placed in mono. The emcee and Dr. McCorvey were in the center channel. The keyboards were in the center channel during accompaniments but were panned slightly to the right during orchestra passages to match where they were heard in the orchestra stereo mics. The piano was treated the same way but panned mostly to the left to match its place on the floor.

If there was an ensemble, such as a brass band, hand bell choir, steel drum band, etc., we would mic them in stereo because they were usually isolated performances apart from the orchestra. If there was a choir on the arched steps facing the orchestra, which we would mic in stereo, each performance's placement in the stereo field can be unique. Remembering that this is on video and we have to match what we see, the left mic needs to match left, and vice versa. If the orchestra is accompanying them, it can cause problems if you don't swap the orchestra left-right configuration during your mix. If you look at the pictures of the floor of The Square, you can see how tightly packed everyone is. The piano is on the left if you're facing the orchestra. But turn 180-degrees around to face the choir and it is to your right. Flipping the orchestra's stereo orientation during this performance can solve the problem of stereo confusion. It's not always perfect, but most issues are solved by carefully thinking through what the viewer is seeing and should be hearing.

The Timing

When we placed all those spot microphones around the orchestra, we created the potential for phasing because of the distance between the stereo mics and the closely placed spot mics. It takes sound 1.125 milliseconds to travel one foot. If all the microphones in this large space were open at the same time, the ones farthest from the main microphones would be early in the recording if we are using the center of the room as reference. The farther away they are, the more phase problems, i.e., muddiness, you can have. For instance, the mic over the tympani drums, which were about 25 feet from the front of the orchestra, was about 28 milliseconds (25 ft. x 1.125 ms) *too early* as recorded. That's because a tympani hit takes time to travel from the back of the room to the front mics, but would be instantaneous in the close mic. In an extreme circumstance you would hear one beat of the drum twice in the recording (the close mic first, then the front mics). In reality, it's slightly out of phase and sounds dull. We solved most of these problems by timing them from a center point of the room.

We chose a place on the floor that was in the center of the performance: right in front of the arched steps. We got all the mics placed where we wanted them first. When the room was somewhat empty of people, we turned on the recorder so that all the mics were recording simultaneously. An assistant stood in front of the arched steps and faced the orchestra. With a film slate, he clapped it very loudly so that all microphones would hear the sharp crack. He did this several times while rotating around 360-degrees just to make sure we got it on all tracks. Later in the recording studio, I moved each separate audio track left or right so that the visual of the slate spike on each waveform lined up vertically with each other. I chose one location, in this case the orchestra stereo mics, as the waveform I aligned all the others to. It's amazing how much fatter and concise your mix can sound once you do this. If you try this, do an A-B comparison of before and after to make sure you're not actually making it worse. Some channels may benefit from leaving them delayed.

The other bit of timing we had to deal with was to synchronize the video and audio together at the start of the concert. Because our audio was a separate recording than the video, we needed to make sure they could be easily synced up later. As in old-style "double system" film production, we trained a main video camera on an assistant holding a film slate in front of one of our microphones. He slated it a few times, that is he snapped the hinged top of his slate board down sharply while the video camera *and* our audio recorders captured it. The editor later lined up the frame where the slate was snapped with the sharp snap sound on the audio track. We can match time code between cameras and audio, but this is a fail-safe method when you're running so many independent recorders (6 cameras and 2 audio recorders). Something very important to remember when slating recordings like this: Don't stop and start recording on any audio device or camera until the program is done – this will break sync. Everyone will have to stop and restart with another slate, or the editor will have to manually realign the recordings in post.

The Recording Setup

I usually scout the location a few days before setup just to refamiliarize myself with the stage. The past several years has allowed us to have a separate room off to the side to record the concert. The first ten or so concerts had us located either above the orchestra on the second floor, or behind the brass section on the main floor in the back. Neither of those locations was ideal because the wall of sound hitting you from the instruments drowned out anything you were trying to hear in your headphones. I did try various heavy-duty headphones designed to block out sound, but nothing can stop a soundwave from a tuba ten feet away. The bad part about mixing in a windowless room is not seeing the live action. However, I do have a video monitor from the switcher so I can see most of what's going on. Most of the time I'm familiar enough with the program and music to just wing it.

During the week prior to the Sunday concerts, I pull out all my remote recording equipment such as consoles, recorders, and cables. Since I only use my 32-channel mixer a few times a year,[40] I turn it on and burn it in for a few days to make sure everything is working correctly. I go through all my cables and snakes (a multi-channel cable that may contain 8, 16, 24, or more mic cables) with a line tester. I pack as much of the remote gear and cables as I can. Some stuff will have to be packed after close of business on Friday because I'm still using them during my everyday sessions. In total, we take about two pickup-truck loads of equipment to the concert recording.

On the Friday before the concert, we take the consoles, multi-track recorder, mic stands, cables, tables, power supplies, and most accessories down to The Square. Me and an assistant run all the snakes from pre-determined points on the stage back to the control room. We lay a 32-channel snake from near the center of the orchestra (near the Christmas tree in the photos) and place it just under the T-shaped singer stage. From here we fan out two or three additional 8-channel snakes to the far left and right wings of the stage. One snake will take feeds from the upper-level balconies, the other will take feeds from the live mix console (more detail on that later) and back-of-the-stage instruments that we are miking. We won't wire up any microphones on this day because we don't exactly know where each performer will be placed. Those decisions will be made during Saturday's rehearsals. We run the microphone male plug ends of the big snake all the way back from the stage to the control room, snaking it around behind curtains, through

---

[40] My recording gear changes from time to time, and I now use a digital mixer with recording functions built in. We typically mirror the digital outputs via analog cables to another stand-alone multi-track recorder as a safety back-up. This way if there is a computer burp in the digital recorder, we have an uninterrupted safety recording that ran through analog circuits.

rubber walkway channels, along walls, up over doorways, through an opening cut out of the wall, under and around all the video recording equipment, and finally to our main console.

In the control room, we set up tables and put our mixing consoles on them. We connect all the plugs from the big stage snake into the 32-track console (only using the first 24 channels because the last 8 channels on the snake are usually used for monitor return channels). We set all the channel inputs to microphone level, turn on the 48V phantom power, and plug in an XLR line tester that kind of looks like a loose mic connector. This nifty little tester has a built-in circuit with a red LED on the tip that lights up when it detects 48V. It outputs a 1 KHz sine wave at microphone level (about -60 dB) back down the line. If it's plugged into channel 1 on the big box that's at the stage end of the snake, then I should see and hear that tone on channel 1 of my console. I adjust it until it's at 0dB on my console and then move on to channel 2, and so on. We go all the way through every channel this way.

We have also run a ¼" to ¼" 24-channel snake between each console channel's direct outputs to a 24-channel recorder.[41] When we are testing the snake with the 1KHz tone, I also see it come up on the meter for each respective recording channel. When we actually record the concert, each channel will be tracked one-to-one and raw. That means channel 1 on the console is recorded with no fluctuations or mixing to channel 1 of the recorder. I will mix all of the channels together later in the studio on my DAW.[42]

We also have a separate 16-channel mixing board that is used to do a quick live mix to video. We create a sub-mix on the main 32-channel console and feed over yet another ¼" to ¼" snake to the 16-channel board. I'll detail how we do that later, but it's essential to know that the 32-channel board is working dual-purpose: To track individual microphones to a 24-channel hard disk recorder without level variation; and to create a submix of groups of those 24 microphones that feed to the separate 16-

---

[41] I track my main channels to a 24-channel hard disk recorder. It's proven pretty failsafe and is easy to just pull the files off its hard drive and port to my DAW.

[42] Digital Audio Workstation. The core of most studios today that uses software on a computer to mix audio within the program. DAWs include equalization, compression, and other means of controlling the sound replacing traditional pieces of hardware in a studio.

channel console. The 32-channel mixer is known as an "in-line" console. It's an older model analog board that was designed for analog and digital tape and hard disk recording. Each mic/line input channel doubles as tape returns. For instance, you would record microphone 1 onto track 1 of the recorder. Then you switch channel 1 from "mic/line" to "tape." Now channel 1 will hear playback from track 1 of the recorder. You can now record mic 2 on channel 2 of the recorder while playing back channel 1 off tape. It's an economical way to squeeze a lot of functions into a smaller footprint.

The 32-channel console also has group bus outputs. A group bus allows you to do mini-mixes of channels down to outputs separate from the main stereo outs. This particular console has eight group outputs. It also has several auxiliary outputs (AUX) for each channel that we utilize. We split up certain instruments and types of performers assigning them to group and AUX busses that travel over the snake to the 16-channel board. On the 16-channel board, I can do a quick live mix while still having some control over the balance of the orchestra against the vocals and other instruments.

Our basic feed to groups and AUXs looked like this:

- **Group 1 & 2**: Orchestra (stereo)
- **Group 3**: Additional orchestra instruments (mono)
- **Group 4**: Keyboard and piano
- **Group 5 & 6**: Vocal and instrumental ensembles (stereo)
- **Group 7**: Singers (mono)
- **Group 8**: Dr. McCorvey lav mic (mono)
- **AUX 1**: Emcee lav mic (mono)

This might change from year to year depending on the program, but this gives me control over levels when I'm mixing down live. For the orchestra, we don't send every single mic down Groups 1 & 2, usually just the stereo pair out in front that captures the essence of the performance. As you can see in this actual spreadsheet below from a concert, we predetermined where each microphone would be plugged into the 32-channel console, what group output it would be sent to, and even where on the snake cables the mics were located. This changed slightly every year, but it gave us a road map to start with, so we weren't scratching our heads the morning of. Planning out complex recording scenarios (and even small ones) makes your life a whole lot easier.

Microphone	Position	Channel	Pan	Feed to Live Mix	Cable Sub	Cable Run	Mic Stand
U87	Orchestra L	1	L	1	8-sub 1-1	50'	Atlas Rollaround
A-T 4050	Orch Mid Cntr	2	C	1,2	8-sub 1-2	50'	Atlas (no wheels)
U87	Orchestra R	3	R	2	8-sub 1-3	50'	Atlas Rollaround
SM7	Upright Bass	4	C	3	8-sub 1-4	25'	Tabletop Stand
AT Shotgun	Harp	5	C	3	8-sub 1-5	25'	Shorty K&M Boom
Heil Pro	Piano	6	C	4	8-sub 1-6	25'	floor stand w/boom
Keyboard Direct	Keyboards	7	C	4	Direct in	25' 1/4" - M-XLR	
Senn MD421	Zeb Brass Band C	8	C	5,6	8-sub 2-1		folding stand or clamp
Shure VP-88	Zeb Brass Band L	9	C	5,6	8-sub 2-2	25' 5-pin with split	Folding stand or ovhd clamp
Shure VP-88	Zeb Brass Band R	10	-	-	8-sub 2-3		
A-T 4030	Steel Band L	11	L	5	8-sub 2-4	50'	folding stand
A-T 4047	Steel Band R	12	R	6	8-sub 2-5	50'	folding stand
KM184 with t-bar	Children Choir L	13	R	5	8-sub 2-6	25'	Floor Stand
KM184 with t-bar	Children Choir R	14	L	6	8-sub 2-7	25'	
KM184	Quartet (1st Flr) and soloists spot mic	15			8-sub 2-8	100'	clamp onto Cox stand
Singers Feed	Singers	16	C	7	Cox Line Direct	1/4"-1/4" snake	
M/C direct	Everette	17	C	8	Cox Line Direct	1/4"-1/4" snake	
Senn wireless *	Barbara Bailey	18	C	Aux 1	Direct in (or Cox)		
SM57	Steel Band xtra	19			XLR direct	25'	as needed or avail
SM57	Steel Band xtra	20			XLR direct	25'	as needed or avail
		22					
	Crowd L	23	L	7	Direct XLR	Direct XLR	Direct XLR
	Crowd R	24	R	8	Direct XLR	100' XLR	clamp w/t-bar
MXL 2001							
SM58				**To Live Mix**	**Live mix inputs**	**To R-4 Recorder**	
SM58				1-2 Orchestra	1-2 Orchestra	--> 1-2	
A-T 8035 super-cardioid				3 Addt'l orch	3 Addt'l orch	--> 1-2	
				4 Keys	4 Keys	--> 1-2	
* if possible ifnot get direct from Curtis				5-6 Ensembles	5-6 Ensembles	--> 1-2	
				7 singers	7 Singers	--> 3	
				8 Everette	8 Everette	--> 4	
				Aux 1 M/C	9 M/C	--> 4	

Microphone and channel assignment prepared before concert. Each is subject to change, however we stuck to most of it.

On my 16-channel mixer, I would pretty much mirror the group bus sends, assigning groups 1 & 2 to inputs 1 & 2, and so on. I would then assign and pan each channel to the stereo output. Now to get really confusing for you, I would also have a 4-bus group output on this mixer that I would output my mix to. I was feeding these 4 outputs to a 4-channel digital recorder (called "R-4" on the spreadsheet sample) that I used as backup. I would mix all the instruments in stereo to Groups 1 & 2, all the singers in mono to Group 3, and the emcee and Dr. McCorvey to Group 4. That way, in case all else fails, I would have a 4-track backup to mix for the broadcast versions.

So, here's what we're recording for each concert:

- 24-channels of microphones directly to a 24-channel hard disk to mix later in studio.

- 4 channels of sub-mixes to a 4-channel digital recorder as back-up.
- 2 channels of stereo mix to video recorder as live mix and as back-up.

So, we essentially have 2 backups. In my three-plus decades of recording, I can tell you this may not even be enough. I've had all the bad things happen to me – that's why I back up everything, and then back up again. In this concert series alone, I have lost the 24-track version twice, one of those times I had the 4-channel backup, the other time I only had one mono live mix. I'm very superstitious about having multiple backup options now.

The Nitty Gritty

When you do an event such as "The Celebration of Song" over and over again, a few things can happen. You get can get complacent, or you can get things right. The last concert we did, all of us looked around at each other afterward in disbelief. Chad, the director, said, "Is it just me, or is this getting easier and easier to do?" That's an almost scary statement, because the last thing you want to happen is to get so complacent that you get caught off guard. But we have developed routines over the years that make the setups go smoother. The equipment we use is not wildly different from year to year. The crew is essentially the same. The musical program follows the same basic formula every time. I still do double and triple checks before every recording and set deadlines to get phases of the setup done. Here is a breakdown of a typical setup, recording, and teardown of one of these concerts.

Two weeks before the concert. We usually have phone meetings and exchange many emails between all the team members of the various companies that are involved. My main planning is done with the director and the live sound company. This entire concert is also amplified over speaker monitors placed throughout The Square. The correct description for what a live sound engineer does is <u>sound reinforcement</u>. Correctly done, they add to the sound already being generated by the performers. Every instrument doesn't need to be amplified if the audience is hearing it clearly. The live sound engineer will fill in gaps with balanced sound from microphones. The sound company that we've worked with the entire time, CC Sound Services, shares the signals from several of their microphones with us. Because there can be as many as 20 vocalists singing simultaneously from different parts of the atrium, it's impractical for me to stick microphones on every single person. I will get with Curtis Cox of CC Sound ahead of time and let him know which signals I'll need from him. He will be doing a choreographed mix of multiple wireless lavs, handheld mics, and several mics on stands during the concert, so it's easier for me to just take submixes from him. He can preprogram these separate submixes from his console and feed five or six AUX lines. I will usually take the following submixes and direct outputs from him:

- All singers on wireless lavaliers
- All singers on hard-wired mics
- Quartet on stage
- Live instrument performer
- Emcee lav
- Dr. McCorvey lav

One week before the concert. As I mentioned before, I will thoroughly test all the equipment and cables. I'll pack what I can for my first trip down to The Square on Friday. I may go down on Wednesday or Thursday while the A/V company is setting up staging just to check on logistical items such as our control room, power, furniture, etc.

Friday. *Two days before the concert.* I'll spend the morning creating a spreadsheet of mic inputs, submixes, etc. This is a work in progress and will change between now and Sunday. I'll also finish packing equipment that will go to The Square later today. In the afternoon, me and an assistant will take a truckload down and run snakes, set up furniture, and set up and test all cables, mixers, and recorders. The goal is to have everything functional so that most of what we have to set up on Sunday morning are stands and microphones. When I get back to the office later that afternoon, I pack the rest of the gear to be used. Unless we run into a major problem, I usually get home at a decent hour today.

Saturday. *One day before the concert.* I may go down to afternoon rehearsals if I need to see and hear something that is different this year. But I'm really waiting for the director and music department to work out the final program. Chad will create spread sheets that evening after rehearsals and send to the team. I'm usually up late customizing my version with color coded cues and track assignments. This would ideally be ready a week ago, but as they say, that's show business.

Sunday. *The day of the concert.* Me, my second engineer, and an assistant meet at the office at about 8:00 AM and pack the truck. We usually are loaded in The Square by 8:30. We start to sort out all the containers and start to unpack cases. Our goal is to be ready for a quick logistical meeting at 9:00 AM. Meanwhile I power up all the consoles and recorders and start testing them.

9:00 – 11:00 AM. *8 ½ hours before the first concert.* We meet in the center of the floor to lay out where each stand and microphone will go. I've sketched this out beforehand with channel numbers and snake designations (see spreadsheet above for an example). The second and the assistant start setting stands and mics and start running cables. This can take a while because of the long and arduous routes some of the cables must take in order to be out of the way. Meanwhile, I start working out details with the director and live sound company. I run outputs to the video recorder, and unpack other gear. There are so many little details to do in these first few hours because we have set a goal to have all mics on and ready to test by 11:00. We try to set hard deadlines when setting up these concerts because there is always an issue to work out in the minutes leading up to the recording.

11:00 AM – 12:00 PM. *6 ½ hours before the first concert, 5 hours before rehearsal.* We test all mics carefully and reconfigure them as necessary. We usually do our film slate sync recording during this time. If I can get direct feeds of CC Music's submixes during this time, I'll patch from their console to mine via one of the snakes. We'll test those lines to make sure there is no distortion or noise.

12:00 – 1:00 PM. *5 ½ hours before the first concert, 4 hours before rehearsal.* Lunch time. We use this time to unwind and talk about anything that needs attention. I've sometimes skipped lunch because I have to run back to the office to get something we forgot to pack, but not often.

1:00 PM. *4 ½ hours before the first concert, 3 hours before rehearsal.* When we come back into the atrium, people are starting to fill up the space. These are usually the singers who have come for early rehearsals. Many have to be fitted for costumes and go to makeup.

The live sound team will be placing wireless lavs on them during this time so they can test the mics during rehearsal. If we were still trying to wire and place microphones, all of us would be tripping over each other, so it's always good to get the basic foundational tasks out of the way early. My second engineer will be tracking the recording to 24-track, so he takes this time to familiarize himself with the console and cue sheet. The assistant will start taping down loose cables and double-checking mic stands to make sure they are sandbagged and not about to tip over.

3:30 PM. *2 hours before the first concert, ½ hour before rehearsal.* The orchestra starts to filter in after an early afternoon performance somewhere else. They are all very busy this time of year, especially on weekends. They are tuning up, so this gives us a chance to listen to all the mics. It's not a true test, but it helps us to find any buzzes or problems now. I'll walk out to every mic and check to make sure they are tight and not ready to tip over onto someone. We've got some heavy duty stands out there that could cause some real injury if they were to fall. Meanwhile the second engineer is touching base with the harp and string bass players to set the spot mics we have on them. The assistant is moving unused cases, cables, etc. to a storage room out of the way.

4:00 PM. *Rehearsal. 1 ½ hours before the concert.* The orchestra and singers will go through an abbreviated rehearsal to learn cues and transitions. This is when we find out if we have the mics placed right. We're also hearing the submixes from the live console, so if there are any problems, they will probably pop up now. As of this moment, there's nothing major that you can change. You're committed to where the mics are, what channels are recording, and how things will sound. We use this time to decompress and just listen to the rehearsal. We'll find where each trim and fader need to be, mark up the cue sheet with notes, and practice mixing. After the rehearsal, someone might go get some coffee for everyone.

5:00 PM. *½ hour before the concert.* I go to each mic stand once again and tighten everything down because an orchestra player may have bumped into a stand. I check every cable that's been taped down so that no one can trip on it. No matter how many years I've done this, there always seems to be some small problem that pops up about now. It's always something different, but you can almost count on something throwing off your timing at the last minute. You have to navigate your way around the crowd filling up the atrium, or through the tangle of seats and cables, or back behind a console. I have kept my cases with repair tools, patch cables, and other accessories close by so I can quickly dig in and find the magic cure.

5:25 PM. *5 minutes before the concert.* We roll all cameras, video recorders, and audio recorders. My assistant goes out to the center of the atrium and gives a few slates for the cameras to zoom in on. I check and double-check that my recorders are actually rolling and registering audio on the meters.

5:30 – 6:15 PM. The stage director counts in the emcee, she starts reading from the teleprompter, and this show has begun. Me and my second are in complete concentration now; he is soloing (listening exclusively to) each channel while checking the 24-track recorder's meters; I'm mixing his submixes into a stereo program. I'm also moving my headphone plug over to the 4-channel backup recorder and checking each track. I do this several times during the recording because failure is a possibility at all times. It's a little hard for me to mix because the video director has my audio feed to him playing loudly on speakers within this makeshift control room. But this is way better than being planted behind a brass section. As a song nears its end, I'm checking my cue sheet to see what faders need to be raised or lowered for the next song. I know I usually have to bring up the emcee to introduce the next performance. I may remind the second to change a group submix assignment when we have an unusual cue. Because the 32-channel board only has 8 group outputs, we sometimes have to switch one input assignment with another when there is an extra performer. This usually doesn't affect the 24-channel recording because it's tracking every mic. We breathe a sigh of relief when the show is over.

Tech Tip

"Soloing" a channel means listening to the input before the fader. Sometimes called PFL (Pre Fade Listen), each channel has a button that when pressed, interrupts the main mix from playing over the monitors, and routes that channel's input to the monitors. It does not affect your mix, submixes, AUX sends, or direct sends. It's merely a passive monitor switch.

6:15 – 6:55 PM. *45 minutes until the second concert*. Intermission for us. they started to put two shows on the card a few years ago because of its popularity. We usually have a bigger audience for the 7:00 show as people are downtown shopping or ice skating across the street. This down time is also a chance to fix any problems and go over the cue sheet again. As before the first concert, I go out and recheck all the mic stands and cables. A few times I've found that a boom arm has fallen, or a mic has slipped. As careful as we all are, there are so many moving parts that anything can happen.

6:55 PM. *5 minutes until the second concert*. We roll all the recorders and slate our second chance to get things right.

7:00 – 8: 15 PM. Concert #2 begins. It's usually a better performance for all involved. The orchestra knows their cues now, the singers fixed their mistakes, and we fixed ours. The editor will usually use this second concert as a base when editing.

8:15 – 8:30 PM. There's not much we can do at this point to tear down the microphones because everyone is milling about and hugging each other. I start shutting down the recorders and consoles and pull all the cable plugs from them. I start packing all the small items and pull the hard disks from the recorder chassis. I immediately put these in a protective case and store in the same place as my briefcase and coat. These drives are like gold, and they will ride up front with me in the truck on the way back.

8:30 – 10:00 PM. We pack up all gear and take it back to the offices. I'll unpack it on Monday as I'm transferring the audio files from the 24-channel recorder's hard disks to my DAW. Unless it's a quick turnaround, I will not want to mix the concerts on Monday, I need a day's break.

Tuesday. I spend most of the day on Tuesday editing, cleaning, and mixing the two concerts. This might blend over into Wednesday if I have some really challenging passages. I won't get into all that I do to whip them into shape, but hopefully we've got some clean recordings that will require minimal editing and cleanup. I will deliver the mixes of the two concerts to the video editor. Each of them will start exactly with the film slate clap so he can easily line it up. After he edits it all together into a one-hour program, he lets me know which performances he plucked out of concert #1 to replace in the main performance of concert #2. I edit these into my concert #2 and remaster for the local public radio station.

It's hard to gauge exactly how many hours I put into the whole endeavor, but let's try. There's about 8 hours of pre-production like emails, phone calls, meetings, and drawing up spreadsheets and layouts. There's about 4 hours of testing and packing equipment and 5 hours of setting up on the first day. There's 14 hours the day of the concert, and 6 – 8 hours mixing the final concerts. That's about 31 hours for me, 5 hours for an assistant on Friday, and 14 hours x 2 for a second engineer and assistant. That's a grand total of <u>64</u> labor hours for a one-hour broadcast. That sounds about right to me.

Was this a hard gig to do given the long hours? Yes and no. When I first started doing the concerts, I typically ran on little to no sleep because I was worried about all the chainsaws I was juggling. Even though I had recorded orchestras, I had recorded choirs, heck I had even recorded them together, the space we were in was something I hadn't had to deal with before. Add to that the furious pace of the show, the number of microphones and direct feeds I would be dealing with, and the tremendous amount of time needed to set up and test all the equipment, and I was pretty nervous. I was also kind of giddy because I was in my element – recording music.

I don't know what I can say that will make your first concert recording of this scale go any easier, but I will give it a shot. The first thing you *shouldn't* do is panic. You *should* be focused and committed to getting it right. Identify the main goal of the project and stay with that in your planning. If that goal is to capture a performance for later mixing, then focus on making sure the recording is rock solid. Start simple and only add pieces to the puzzle one-at-a-time when all other goals have been met. For instance, when recording an orchestra, two mics placed out front in a stereo pattern will do the job nicely. Only add extra microphones to solve problems, not because someone online in a discussion group said it would sound awesome. If you have soloists, try to use as few mics as possible by thinking about where they will be singing: In different spots or will they all come to one spot? And above all, know your gear. If you need to rent equipment for the gig, learn everything you can about all of its functions well before the recording date. I won't rent if it's not absolutely necessary for a few reasons. One is that I may not have time to learn all the ins and outs, especially if it's new technology. The second reason I try to avoid rental is potential equipment failure. I don't know how easy or rough a piece of gear has been treated before it came to me. Any good rental house will check equipment before it goes out, but there is no way to catch every little potential fault.

SHOOTING THE DOCUMENTARY LINCOLN IN ILLINOIS: 1830-1860

Abe Lincoln (Joe Woodard) served as Postmaster in New Salem, Illinois, as seen in this still shot from the documentary.

I've worked on several historical documentaries for a local attorney and historian Kent Masterson Brown. Kent has become a nationally known Civil War historian and author. He's appeared on PBS, NPR, been the guest speaker at many major Civil War history conferences and was even on the board of directors for Gettysburg National Military Park. During research on his books and documentaries, he has managed to unearth previously unknown or long-forgotten facts, manuscripts and journals, paintings, and artifacts. During the decades that we've worked together, I've been on hallowed ground, seen and touched unbelievable historical artifacts, met some of the most interesting people in the world, and learned a thing or two about history.

A few years ago, we did a documentary on Thomas Lincoln, Abraham Lincoln's father. It detailed his time in Kentucky and the legal battles he endured to get back land that was swindled from him. Kent believes that Abraham's exposure to the legal system from such a young age may have led to his interest in the law. In 2018, Kent had the script and funding ready to tackle Abraham Lincoln's formative years in Illinois, 1830-1860. Not much has been told of this era, most books and documentaries seem to focus on the Civil War years. But as we learned while making the documentary, his foundation of ideals and purpose were chiseled in Illinois.

Kent's documentaries are usually a mix of on-camera and studio narration; many historical pictures, paintings, and documents; plus several historical reenactments. For *Lincoln in Illinois*, Kent and his producers planned a two-day on-location production in and around Springfield, Illinois. Because Lincoln's life and accomplishments were so rich, telling his entire story would be too large of a task. Kent decided to concentrate on Lincoln's building blocks of his law education and practice which led to his arguments against slavery. Most of the filming locations would be in the city of Springfield where Lincoln had law offices and was a legislator in the Illinois State House. Another of the filming locations would be at a reconstructed log cabin village called "Lincoln's New Salem," where he was first employed and learned the basics of law.

Most of our shots would include actors portraying Lincoln, Steven Douglas, and several other key figures in Lincoln's life. We would also use extras, many of whom were associated with the local historical society. Period costumes would be used, and surprisingly an actual suit belonging to a judge would be worn by the actor portraying him. For shots in the interior of the Old State Capitol, which has been restored to its original splendor, we were able to block out tourists during filming. Lincoln's law offices were closed to the public the day we shot there. We also filmed outside of the Lincoln family home while there were no tourists or signs of modernity in the backgrounds. And while shooting at Lincoln's New Salem, tourists were diverted around locations while filming. We had great cooperation with local historic site operators those days, which isn't always the case at these types of places.

As you can see from the itinerary below, our shoot schedule was highly ambitious. In fact, we call these tightly scheduled days "Run and Gun," much like filming fast-paced news stories.

"In the Declaration All Men Are Created Equal:" Abraham Lincoln in Illinois, 1830 to 1860

("*Abraham Lincoln in Illinois*")

FILM SESSIONS ITINERARIES

FRIDAY, September 21, 2018:

7:30 a.m.   State garage opens at Old State Capitol

7:30 a.m. to   Arrive at Old State Capitol
House Chamber
8:00 a.m.

8:15 a.m. to   House Chamber: Film scene of
October 1854 speech of
8:45 a.m.   Stephen A. Douglas in support
of the Kansas-Nebraska Act.

8:45 a.m. to   House Chamber: Film scene of
October 1854 speech of
9:15 a.m.   Abraham Lincoln in response tc
Stephen A. Douglas's speech.

9:15 a.m. to   House Chamber: Film scene of
Abraham Lincoln's June 26,
9:45 a.m.   1857 speech.

9:45 a.m. to   House Chamber: Film scene of
Lincoln's "House Divided"
10:15 a.m.   speech in June 1858.

10:15 a.m. to   Senate Chamber: Film scene of
Abraham Lincoln's Cooper
10:45 a.m.   Union speech.

10:45 a.m. to   On the landing of the steps,
in the hallway and in the

11:15 a.m.   House and Senate Chambers:
                        Film scenes of Abraham Lincoln
                        and Stephen A. Douglas –
                        separately - conversing with
                        other political officials.

11:15 a.m. to   State Library: Film scenes of
Abraham Lincoln studying the
11:30 a.m.   debates of the Kansas-Nebraska
Act, the Constitution, etc.
                        State Law Library: Film scene
of Abraham Lincoln arriving
                    at J. T. Stuart's Law Office
                to borrow books.

11:30 p.m. to   Supreme Court Chamber, main
hallway on first floor and
11:45 p.m.   room off of Supreme Court
Chamber: Film portraits of
                        Orville Browning, Stephen T.
Logan, and Stephen A. Douglas.

12:00 noon to   U.S. Courtroom: Film scene of
Lincoln, as counsel, during a
12:30 p.m.   trial with Judge David Davis
presiding. Film State Capitol
                        from window of courtroom.

12:30 p.m. to   Lincoln Law Office: Film scene
of Lincoln working in his 12:45 p.m.
    law office with two of his boys; film
scene of Lincoln
                        Reading Newspaper and scene of
                    Lincoln writing a letter.
                        Film State Capitol from window
                of law office.

1:00 p.m.   Depart Springfield for
Lincoln's New Salem State Park.

1:30 p.m.   Arrive at Lincoln's New Salem
and proceed to restaurant.

1:30 p.m. to   LUNCH
2:30 p.m.

2:30 p.m.   Proceed to site of Lincoln-
Douglas Debate.

2:30 p.m. to   Site of Lincoln-Douglas
Debate: Film scene of Lincoln-
3:00 p.m.   Douglas Debate.

3:00 p.m.   Proceed back to park and road
to Offutt's grocery and
                         Clary's store.

3:15 p.m. to   Road to Offut's grocery and
Clary's store: Film scene of
3:45 p.m.   Abraham Lincoln, David Davis,
                         and two other lawyers riding
                         on horseback to circuit court.

3:45 p.m. to   On main road in New Salem:
Film scene of Lincoln, on
4:15 p.m.   horseback, leaving New Salem
                         with townspeople hugging him,
                         wishing him well, and waving
                         as he rides away. Film scene
                         of Lincoln, on horseback,
                         leaving for the legislature.
                         Film scene of Lincoln, on
                         foot, arriving in New Salem.

4:15 p.m.   Depart Lincoln's New Salem and
return to Springfield.

4:45 p.m. to   Lincoln Home at Eighth and
Jackson Streets: Film scenes of
5:30 p.m.   Lincoln walking along the
                         sidewalk to his house,
                         stumbling. Film scenes of
                         house.

5:30 p.m.   End filming for the day.

SATURDAY, September 22, 2018:

9:00 a.m.   Arrive at Lincoln's New Salem.

9:15 a.m. to   Jack Kelso House: Film Kelso
House and scene of Lincoln
9:30 a.m.   speaking with Kelso about
Shakespeare and Robert Burns.

9:30 a.m. to   Second Lincoln-Berry Store:
Film Lincoln-Berry Store and
9:45 a.m.   scene of Lincoln as a store
clerk with a group of men,
                   Laughing and telling stories.

9:45 a.m. to   Second Lincoln-Berry Store:
Film scene of Lincoln as
10:15 a.m.   postmaster reading newspapers
and handing mail to
                   residents.

10:15 a.m. to   In front of Rutledge Tavern:
Film Rutledge Tavern and scene
10:45 a.m.   of Lincoln giving first
                   political speech. Film scene
                   of Lincoln talking with a
                   group of people.

10:45 a.m. to   Rutledge Tavern Bedroom: Film
scene of the death of Ann
11:15 a.m.   Rutledge with Lincoln seated
at her bedside.

11:15 a.m. to   Rutledge Tavern Main Room:
Film scene of Lincoln giving his
11:45 a.m.   first speech at the Debate
Society.

11:45 a.m. to   Rutledge Tavern Main Room:
Film scene of Lincoln meeting
12:15 p.m.   with Mentor Graham at a table
talking about Grammar book
                   and lessons. Film scene of
Lincoln talking to Graham about
                   surveying book and lessons.
            Film scene of Lincoln reading
                   law books.

12:15 p.m. to   LUNCH
1:00 p.m.

1:00 a.m. to   Field behind Lincoln-Berry
Store: Film scene cf Lincoln
1:15 a.m.   walking through fields to
visit Ann Rutledge.

1:15 a.m. to   Along main road in New Salem:
Film scene of Lincoln
1:30 p.m.   walking hand-in-hand with Ann
Rutledge.

1:.30 p.m. to   Lawn behind First Lincoln-
Berry Store: Film Lincoln-Berry
1:45 p.m.   Store and scene of Lincoln
drilling a group of citizen
                    militia soldiers.

1:45 p.m. to   In field behind Robert
Johnston Cabin: Film scene of 2:00 p.m.
      Lincoln surveying with chainman and
marker.

2:00 p.m. to   Main road in New Salem: Film
scene of Lincoln walking along
2:15 p.m.   with air of confidence.

2:15 p.m. to   Offutt Grocery: Film Offutt
Grocery and scene of Denton
2:30 p.m.   Offutt talking to residents of
New Salem about Lincoln.

2:30 p.m. to   Clary's Store: Film Clary's
Store and scene of Lincoln
2:45 p.m.   wrestling with Jack Armstrong.

2:45 p.m. to   Film general view of New
Salem, the Kelso and Johnson
4:00 p.m.   Cabins, Carding Mill, First
and Second Berry-Lincoln
                    Stores, Clary Store, Offutt
         Grocery, Rutledge Tavern, Grist
                    Mill: Film Grist Mill and
         Sangamon River.

4:00 p.m.   Depart New Salem.

Fortunately, these were relatively short days, but you had to be on your toes in order to get everything done. This required two audio engineers and careful planning. We first identified the most complicated scenes that would require extensive set-up and built our plan around those. One of the most complicated ones was right out of the gate on Friday morning in the House Chamber. We were filming a series of speeches by Lincoln and Douglas in front of a crowd of people. We decided to put wireless lavs on the two principal actors, hide a boom microphone at the podium position, and fly a stereo (Shure VP-88 Mid-Side) microphone over the crowd on a high stand. (see **Tech Tip** below) Each shot moved around a little, and there were two cameras. We made the decision to feed split-track stereo audio from the mixer directly to the principal camera when we were only recording two channels. If a scene required more than two channels, we would record to a portable digital multi-track recorder and slate each take (like we did during the orchestra recordings I previously outlined). If we had recorded everything to multi-track, then the video editor's workload would have been increased dramatically from synching up all the audio files.

Tech Tip

Using a Mid-Side, or MS, microphone is a unique way of playing with the stereo field during the mix instead of trying to determine how wide of an image you want during recording. In the most basic description, the microphone has three capsules: a center directional cardioid (the "mid"), and two side-facing directional capsules (the "sides"). The mid is recorded on the left channel, the sides are recorded together as mono on the right channel. Because these two side capsules are electrically out-of-phase with each other, they can be decoded into two separate left and right channels later in post. When mixing, you utilize three faders to control stereo width: left (the left "side") panned hard to the left; center (the "mid") panned straight up to center; and right (the right "side") panned hard to the right. The higher you raise the left and right "sides," the wider the stereo image. The other advantage of recording in MS is compatibility with mono. If someone hears it in mono only, then the sides cancel each other out while the mid capsule is still heard.

Split track stereo is really two-channel audio. The left channel records one microphone (such as a lav) and the right channel records a separate microphone (such as a boom). In the old days, it might also mean elements that are separated, such as mono voice-over on the left, and mono music on the right.

Note: mid-side also refers to a type of equalization where the sides and middle of a stereo image can be adjusted separately. This is not to be confused with the mid-side microphone or technique.

Another tactic we planned was to have one microphone dedicated to the Lincoln actor so he would always sound the same from scene to scene, shot to shot. We had two other lav microphones at our disposal and chose to dedicate one of those to the Douglas character as well. The 3rd microphone floated between minor characters. One way we managed to juggle the compressed schedule was to move that 3rd lav from minor character to minor character ahead of time while a scene was being filmed. I would be recording Scene A for instance, while the other audio engineer would be fitting the 3rd microphone to an actor prepping for Scene B.

For boom microphones,[43] I had a three-piece set made by Audio-Technica. Boom microphones are condensers, which means they need that 48V phantom power. Each boom microphone is a different length (short, medium, and long) but sound almost identical to each other in tone and quality. The only differences are how far they need to be from a source. A general rule of thumb is to match a boom microphone's length to the place you're recording. For instance, if I'm outside or in a very large room or auditorium, I would use the <u>long</u> boom. If I'm in a medium room

---

[43] A "boom" or "shotgun" microphone is a hyper-directional microphone designed to be held at a distance from a sound source, usually the human voice. It sounds different, and more natural, than a lavalier microphone placed on the body. Human conversation usually takes place about 5 feet from each other, and a boom captures the voice and the some of the space the person is in.

or studio I use the medium boom. If we're filming a sit-down interview with a tight head shot, I will put a short boom overhead. The amount of side air vents on the microphone capsule will determine how much a boom will reduce reverb and other noises coming from the sides. Outside or in a large room, there are many more side noises, so more side-reduction is needed. If I use a long boom in a small and tight space however, it will actually be too boxy and live sounding. The medium length boom, and also the most common, is very versatile in most situations and is my first go-to boom mic. The shortest boom is really reserved for those close and tight situations.

One other advantage to selecting different lengths of a boom is the working distance form the subject. A long boom works great for working about 10-15 feet away from someone talking outside. I've also used one to record distant sound effects like horse races and cars speeding down the road. The medium shotgun works great from about 3-10 feet away in a relatively dry room. If a room is very reverberant, such as the House Chamber in the Old State Capitol, a long boom actually reduces the reverb better, no matter the distance from the subject. A short boom works great from about 1 to 5 feet. Any further away and it loses its directionality and sounds distant.

In addition to reverb and side noise, another thing to keep in mind when selecting and using boom mics is how close you bring them to a subject. It might seem natural to bring a long boom in to about a foot from someone talking, but it can distort and sound really boomy. It was designed to be used at a distance while also picking up some of the room or space it is in. A medium boom is a popular choice for voice-over artists because it can actually be used at about 5-10 inches away from the mouth. Though be careful, because using medium booms for voice-overs can sound harsh if overdriven. Another caveat is the tight working space required for the talent – any movement beyond a few inches can make the sound dramatically fall off in volume. A short boom is great for voice-overs if a large diaphragm condenser is not available. They are also great for recording small and quiet sound effects such as watches, bugs, and soft movement noises.

I've taken you through three real situations that will stretch you thin and test your stamina. I love my job so much, that I don't always notice the long hours until it's all over. I just soldier through, hoping I can perform well at the most crucial times I'm needed. Keep in mind that you're usually working with people who are going through the same level of intensity as you are, so it helps to not complain about the situation. You also don't want to remind everyone how tired they are, that will just foul things up. There's a common feeling with everyone on these long hauls to not let down your crew mates. It's akin to being on a sports team during a championship game, or in a military unit on the battlefield. Everyone's trying their best to perform and make the production successful. During times like these, many of us form strong bonds and earn or gain the respect of each other. A job that requires intense concentration for an extended time usually hardens you to the prospect of other long production days, because you know you came out of the other end of this one alive.

11. PROFESSIONAL GROWTH

"It's not what you achieve, it's what you overcome. That's what defines your career."

Carlton Fisk

O nce you've graduated school and started your first job, learning isn't over, it's just begun. In fact, your next 20, 30, 40, or more years in your profession should be one of growth and learning. If doctors "practice" medicine and are always willing to learn new procedures, why shouldn't we keep learning as well? I still am after more than 35 years. Sure, I have to learn new software or a different procedure from time to time. I'm talking about improving our core knowledge of the craft. I keep reading industry publications, watch how-to videos, and even try to understand other sciences and industries that directly affect my job.

Keep your finger on the pulse

For instance, the tech industry is transitioning bit by bit to artificial intelligence (AI). It's already in our craft, but it's in its infancy. With the rapid speed of advancements in computer technology, it will begin to take over quicker than you think. I hope it doesn't replace us humans − I don't think it ever can − but I welcome it being a partner in production. If my goal is to create a compelling soundtrack for a documentary but I'm hung up on bad location sound, AI could quickly fix that part so that I can move on to the creative part quicker. If I could have predictive microphone levels during the recording of a concert that would save my recording from being unusable, then I would use it in a heartbeat. That's why I like to stay on top of where this emerging technology is.

I also like to keep a finger on the pulse of video. I couldn't name the latest model of 4K, 5K, 6K, or 14K camera, but I need to know what state that industry is at right now. For more than a decade while the audio world was basking in every new development in CPUs and hard drives, video was still using magnetic tape. Once the computer industry developed cost-effective digital storage for the massive amounts of data that video production gobbled up, video has embraced it fully. You now have tech companies like Apple that are actually pushing out systems to accommodate video production needs, instead of the other way around.

Read a book

Invest in audio production books. I have several shelves of useful audio books in my office. I will still look in those first if I'm trying to solve a critical problem because I think I've chosen books that can help me in the long term. I do quick research on the internet like everyone else, but you can't beat a book for a trusted source. Some of them helped me early in my career and are now useful for my students. Others are still way over my head because I haven't had to spend much time on that particular subject, but still need to occasionally reference it. There are technical books, like how to build a studio. There are reference books, like engineering principles and terms. There are books on techniques, like how to master recordings. And there are concept books, like how five top engineers mix a song. I even have books on technical writing, marketing, bookkeeping, and other ancillary subjects related to business. And I also have "The First Book of Sound" I found at a used bookstore that some children that came to my studio have actually looked at with interest. You should build a library of your own, you never know when a book will come in handy. Maybe you'll keep mine on your shelf for a while. I'd be honored.

Watch a video

Watching YouTube instructional videos can be addicting, so I won't discourage something I do regularly. You can actually learn a lot about audio production by watching how other people approach it. Some of the best-looking videos are the product videos produced by a manufacturer, but they aren't always informative enough. It's worth digging deeper and find some actual user reviews. Take these with a grain of salt because they may be skewed one way or another but try to absorb the useful parts. Sometimes a manufacturer will have a knowledgebase that includes how-to videos. These are usually more instructive and helpful.

For general knowledge on studios and production, invest in an instructional series. One of the best series I've seen is the Alan Parsons hosted *Art & Science of Sound Recording*.[44] Parsons takes you through the entire process of choosing and setting up equipment, setting up a console, recording into software, applying effects, mixing, and mastering. You get to see a real song being created from the ground up, warts and all. When I watched the series with a student, I kept remarking, "Huh, I didn't know that." It's never too late to learn something new.

Watch as many documentaries as you can on recording music, producer bios, historic studios – basically anything that's not fiction about the recording industry. The BBC, ITV, Sky Arts, and VH1/VH1 Classic aired a series called "Classic Albums" that breaks down the recording of a seminal album. There is a Roku channel called SoundWorks Collection that dives deep into movie soundtrack creation. There is an astounding documentary called "Tom Dowd & the Language of Music" that every engineer, producer, musician, and music lover should watch. Dowd put his fingerprint on so much in our world you wouldn't believe it. I could probably list two dozen documentaries about our industry, but you should explore what interests you first, and then branch out. But first watch the Tom Dowd documentary!

Take a class

If a college (online or nearby) offers classes in advanced production, it might be worth it to take a class. You could also take a class about screen writing or acting so that you can communicate with your peers more easily. I took an Avid video editing class and got Avid certified so that I could better understand that side of things. It really helped out when I edited my documentary, by the way. There are also many crash courses (at a school or online) in specific areas of production that can be helpful. We have a one-

---

[44] www.artandscienceofsound.com

week certified grip course here in Kentucky that helps people new to field production learn lighting. This increases their chances of getting hired for a studio or field production. There are always quick courses like these available, so start by looking at traditional places like universities and community colleges first. Try to find one that's certified to ensure that it is a legit class.

Join an organization

When you join an industry organization, you immediately have access to journals, papers, recordings, and other material that can keep you educated. I've gotten the most out of AES (Audio Engineering Society).[45] They have journals and articles going back decades. Every month I get an email with links to the journal, white papers, meeting notes, job offers, and many other useful information. This society is for people making recordings, making equipment and software, and those researching audio and its effect on people. It's a truly diverse and thoughtful organization that sets standards for manufacturing and recording. They have a few local/regional chapters that offer meetups and mini seminars. There is also a student division.

Another worthwhile organization is NAB (National Association of Broadcasters).[46] For audio and video professionals, manufacturers, and software engineers, the crossover of disciplines is beneficial. They also set broadcasting and manufacturing standards. They have an epic convention every year in Las Vegas where many new products are released.

A few others worth mentioning are AMP (Association of Music Producers) and SPARS (Society of Professional Audio Recording Studios). There are also a number of music, writing, education, and business organizations with ties to recording and production.

---

[45] www.aes.org
[46] www.nab.org

Go to a seminar

Whenever I attend an AES conference, I'm blown away with the opportunities to learn. In fact, there are too many to choose from. AES (and other conventions and seminars) usually offer 1-2 hour seminars designed to educate attendees. Some of these are "how-tos", others are white paper presentations on new designs, procedures, or studies. I try to pick the ones that I feel are the most important, and then buy recordings of the ones I couldn't attend. I always learn so much in each one that my head is spinning at the end of each day there. Fortunately, these seminars are buffered with trips to the convention floor to see the latest gear or software while bumping shoulders with famous producers and artists. I also try to take a guided tour of an area studio while I'm there. It can be a fabulously rewarding and educational experience for you. You should try to attend one as often as you can.

Go to college

This is always an option. At some point you may feel that a college undergraduate degree, master's degree, or a doctorate is the right path to advance your career in audio. Go for it! If you've reached this conclusion, then you are at that point of knowing what you need and want to go to the next level. Why? You may be wanting to pivot your career from production to teaching, from engineering to producing, or looking to start your own business after taking business courses. More education can be great if you do it smartly. It's a huge investment of time and money, so be sure to talk to other graduates of the program you're interested in to find out how much impact that degree had on their career.

12. MARKETING YOURSELF

"If people like you, they will listen to you. But if they trust you, they'll do business with you."

Zig Ziglar

I was once told that it will take ten years in your career to make a name for yourself. That seems about right to me in my experience. It could happen a lot sooner for some, but I believe that the single most important thing that will make you stand out is trust. Trust is only earned, and that takes time.

Why make a name for yourself? If you want to advance in your career, get better projects, and work with more established professionals, you need to market yourself. I know it sounds kind of slimy to think of self-promotion, but if you do it carefully, it will pay big dividends down the road. If you do your job and keep your nose clean, your name will eventually be associated with trust. But you need to do a few things to push your name out there. The first thing you need is a plan.

Put your name out front

You have probably already marketed yourself somewhat within the company you work for, and that's good for a promotion or two. But outside of your company, people may not know who you are at first. If you are working for a reputable company, your association alone with them is a step forward. Use this to your advantage. For instance, when you call a producer, supplier, or client, identify yourself. As in, "Hi, this is Jane Doe from XYZ Company" instead of, "Hi, I'm calling from XYZ Company." It sounds simple, but I get anonymous calls all the time. You can also add your position to add more credibility. "Hi, this is Jane Doe and I'm a producer with XYZ Company."

The same goes for emails and letters. Who are you, what do you do, and where do you work? Your boss will appreciate the extra effort as well. If your name starts to be recognized outside the company as a trusted professional, then your boss will stand a little taller and tell his colleagues, "She works for me!" If you work for yourself, you might be tempted to say your company name first, but in personal communications YOU are more important. The company name can be promoted through traditional marketing and advertising methods.

Even if you intend to work for XYZ Company for the rest of your life, it still behooves you to market yourself. It may lead to interesting side jobs like teaching, running the sound at a summer theatre or your church, or writing articles or a blog. It all starts with getting your name out there.

Avoid shameless self-promotion

Plastering your name all over the internet for "likes" and views is not only hard, but also transparent. If you don't have anything to offer, it will fizzle out very soon. When our studio used to actually make physical copies of programs (reel-to-reel tapes or CDs), I would pop my business card into each box.[47] I didn't know who would see it, but it was like my personal signature on each product. It served a few purposes, the first of which was to have my contact info available in case something was wrong with the recording. The second was to have my business card laying on a desk somewhere, my name and company hovering around people that mattered.

When you go to meetings, conventions, luncheons, or work on location, take a stack of business cards and hand out liberally. Don't stand at the front door and push them into people's hands, give them to someone after a long conversation. Write your cell phone number on it if it's an especially important contact. When they see that handwritten note, they will usually remember meeting you.

And speaking of handwritten notes, I always include a written thank you when I send out a DVD of my documentary, a stack of CDs, or even when I sell a piece of used equipment on eBay. It's a

---

[47] Today, have a thorough email signature when you send audio material out. Make sure your name, company, contact info, and website are plainly visible.

personal touch and a reminder that business is all about relationships. My motto has always been to treat everyone the same. That $5 client today may be a $5,000 client next year. That has literally happened several times for me. Treat everybody with dignity and in a personal way, and your life will be richer (in more than one way).

Volunteer

Another way to get your name out there is by volunteering. I volunteer at a nearby high school that has a wonderful "village" of disciplines. They integrate core classes like English, math, and physics into media arts, law & justice, medical, and engineering. For instance, the media arts students may produce a learning video for the medical students while the engineering students are working on green energy for the building. I once worked with the physics teacher on acoustics ahead of time so that the students understood how sound waves work when I gave my lecture. I don't market my name to these students, but I do pass on my experiences to my colleagues and clients thus adding to my arsenal of trust.

Blog or YouTube

You could write a blog or make a YouTube video about audio. Just sharing your knowledge and helping people solve problems makes you a pro in the eyes of the reader or viewer. Choose a very specific topic and use real world words and advice. Throwing out technical jargon to non-pros will only make you look brash and pompous. I write a monthly newsletter for my clients (I have included several of my favorites in this book in the chapter "A Sound Education" on page 461) that is intended to be an easy read while being informative. I try to strip down the technical jargon and make it interesting for all readers. While this newsletter may not bring me a whole bunch of new clients, it does help keep my current ones.

And that reminds me that one of your most important jobs is to keep your clients. Losing only one to something that you screwed up can cascade into years of rebuilding trust. Your self-marketing includes current clients, not just potential ones. One of my biggest surprises was when I found out that a long-time client was only aware of the one tiny service that I did for them. They had no idea that I did all this other stuff at my shop. That's when I realized that I needed to start a newsletter and do more self-promotion.

Join the theater

Produce soundtracks for your local theater troupe. Sure, it's free of charge, but guess what? You get your name in the program. If you're lucky you'll get a free ad in the program as well. And your potential clients are the ones that will be in the audience. If you look at demographics of people who attend live theater, they are in the upper middle class of income, own businesses or are in management, and are community influencers. These are the eyeballs you want on your name. It's simple. Get your name in front of those who count. If you sell trucks, then you want your name in front of truck pull fans. If you restore furniture, then you want your name in front of antique fair shoppers.

Get credit

Get your name in the credits of programs. Much of this is out of your hands, but it's always rewarding to get your name in an end credit roll. It may not be seen by many, but it's out there forever. Better yet, if your name comes in at the beginning of a program, it carries more weight. This is all up to the producer/director, so please don't jockey for a credit. They have enough people to please, and you may rub them the wrong way if you ask. Be gracious if they do ask how you want to be in the credits and be quietly understanding if you aren't in the credit roll. You'll get the next one. If the production is commercially available, you'll get personal, company, or a combination credit. If the production is for public television, you'll only get personal credit. If it's a marketing video, you'll likely get no credit. Don't sob, just accept it and move on.

If you work on a film, TV show, or documentary that will get · released to the public, jump over to IMDB.com and register. You may have to pay a fee, but it's worth it for assistant producers to easily give you an IMDB credit. If you're not on there, they're not going to create an account for you because they have hundreds of names to enter. I learned this the hard way when I worked on several Disney features and shows. I was wondering why they gave me credit in the roll but not on IMDB. Oops. Go register now.

Get free press

These days, many companies pay to have their product featured on the news. This "sponsored content" is often disguised as real news, and it is really getting out of hand. Companies that do it aren't really counting on the news audience to buy their product right away, they're really amassing video segments from those news shows to market their product as "legit" because X-number of news outlets covered it. Please don't go this route. Free press is always better.

How do you get it? Send out press releases about a program you worked on, a unique service you provide, an award you won, or something else that will pique the interest of a features reporter. When I produced my documentary "The Beat of a Different Drummer: The Story of America's Last All-Female Military Band," I sent press releases to all of the news outlets I could think of. I did get a few meaningful interviews from that. When actor Steve Zahn (who resides nearby) was coming in to do ADR for the movie "War for the Planet of the Apes," I contacted our local arts reporter about it. The story revolved around Kentucky's film tax incentive and how local businesses like mine are important to its existence. There were many pictures of my studio at work, and a video interview with Steve in our studio. It was great coverage that I couldn't have paid any amount of money to have. We were also featured in the same newspaper just after I started my business about 15 years earlier for the same reason – we were working directly with Hollywood film studios right here in little old Lexington, Kentucky. Those two articles really added to my trust bank.

Social media

Manage a social media account that gives quick tips or how-to blurbs. These can be tips on how to get a good sound while recording a guitar in your apartment, to how to comp vocals on XYZ software. But they must be short and to the point. Try to focus on things that haven't been done countless times. And you must post with regular frequency. Posting something here and there will not build a following. When I do a marketing campaign like this, I plan every post out for months in advance. Take advantage of timed posts so that you don't have to hurry and think up a post every week.

And speaking of social media, clean up your act. Your professional life WILL cross over into your private life, and social media is a huge magnet for that. Anything you say online will bleed over into your work life, and vice-versa. Be very careful what you post online, it will come back and haunt you. If you have had a lot of posts that you regret, consider deleting your account and starting anew. I know it's easier said than done, but sometimes it's the only way to get a fresh start. From this day forward, carefully cull your posts. Wait 30 minutes before posting. Have a friend read one before you post to make sure it's not too sensitive. Stay away from politics. Period. Post positive things. Don't comment on anything that may reveal a bias. Don't get into fights online. Be smart.

Give yourself a stage name

If you intend to work as an independent producer, engineer, or DJ, consider a stage name. It is a little like a company name (in fact you should probably register it as a D.B.A. with your state and eventually trademark it). This can put a little separation between your personal and work lives. If you already have a stage name as a musician, consider parlaying this over to your producing gigs. However, if you're seeking employment with a company, a stage name does not fly. Definitely have it on your resume if you've had significant success and notoriety under the name.

Teach

I've covered my teaching experiences, but you can get so much out of guiding students in the right direction. You learn so much about yourself and profession that you wonder why you didn't do it earlier. Being a teacher usually adds instant credibility and trust to your name. If you don't abuse the privileges it provides it can lead to many other opportunities. Because I taught a one-week location audio crash course at a local community college, I became friends and a collaborator with one of the students that produces online content about video production. We filmed a couple of audio production series and gear reviews that are still being watched by thousands of viewers years later. Teaching can also help you hone your own craft and message. Having to explain something that you've known for so long that you don't remember how you learned it will make you a better communicator. And the best part? Seeing that "aha" moment on a student's face.

Be a judge

When I got my first job in a studio, as you might remember, I edited the voice-over (on tape!) for an awards show. That was the Addy Awards for the Lexington chapter of the American Advertising Federation. I've since been involved with the production of most of their live shows for the last 30 years. I usually get recognition one way or another in the program. A few years ago I was totally surprised when they presented me with a Lifetime Achievement Award at the ceremony. And the person who gave it to me was Ed Commons himself, my first real mentor. He received one himself the next year. It was through my connections with the ad club that I've had a chance to judge a few competitions including the New York Film Festival and the Telly Awards. These are very rewarding and humbling experiences because you get to see the best of the best. I sometimes find myself in a jaw-dropping stance while I watch and listen to these masterpieces. I always learn a lot from these competitions, mostly that I need to up my game. By participating in industry organizations, you can solidify your reputation as a professional. And you just might learn some new things while you're helping out.

Get in a think tank

Sometimes opportunities come along to be a part of something special, like a committee, think tank, or consortium in your industry. This can be a great time to meet other influencers and professionals that you may not have had the opportunity to meet otherwise. I was asked to serve on a Kentucky state panel for film production that was trying to define and enhance current available production services. The legislature was kicking around a change to the film tax incentive that would provide significant tax breaks to movie studios that chose to film in Kentucky. All segments of the film world were represented: lighting, stages, make-up, craft services, cinematography, post-production, education, and audio (me). We made great progress, and a film certificate program was actually born out of those meetings. I will be helping students in that class in the near future. Another fantastic opportunity arose out of those meetings for me. I was asked to serve a two-year term on the state film commission. Both of these openings came about from working on a documentary soundtrack for a client. One of his executive producers also did voice-over work. I hired him for a few jobs, and he got to know me and learn of my background. I had built trust with him. Out of the blue, he got hired to run the state office for film production, and one thing led to another. Although there's no money exchanging hands, I'd call this a $5 to $5 million jump. You just never know where your next opportunity will come from.

13. STUDIO AND FILM SET ETIQUETTE

"Etiquette means behaving yourself a little better than is absolutely essential."

Will Cuppy

The film set pyramid

A company can sometimes be described as a dictatorship, with a general, lieutenants, and soldiers. A film set can too. You have the director, assistant director (AD), the producer and assistants (PAs), the director of photography (DP), and so on down the line like a pyramid. This is actually an efficient system when everybody is on the same page. Problems arise when someone either abuses their power or ignores the hierarchy.

Let's look at a well-run film's pyramid (This also pertains in a broader sense to any video, remote, broadcast, concert, play, or any other larger-scale production). At the top isn't the director, or the producer, or the film studio. It's the film. Everybody is on the set to serve the best outcome for the film, the story, the message. The director can never lose vision of the big picture, and the director needs everyone on the set to run like a well-oiled machine. Using the machine metaphor, the director shouldn't have to worry if the gas tank is full, the engine is running smoothly, the wheels are turning, and that the steering works. The director has the enormous responsibility to steer the massive machine to its ultimate destination without crashing and burning. No one else has that job. Everyone else should be concerned about their part of the machine: the engine has oil, the air filter is clean, the tires are full, and the bolts are tightened.

Photo 3.   A film set can be complicated, even smaller ones like this one with University of Kentucky Men's Basketball Coach John Calipari.

Continuing on down the line of major parts, or departments, in this big machine is the assistant director. The AD is like the central computer running the entire operation: keeping everything running on time, telling each major engine part when to operate, putting out small fires, reporting any major problems, and keeping the director from being distracted by small and incidental issues. The AD is arguably the most important person on the set, because without someone keeping order and enabling the smooth flow of operations, the machine would choke on its own exhaust and die a quick death. The best ADs I've worked for will bark orders loudly (so that everyone can hear), live and die by the clock, and release the tension with an occasional joke when the scene is over. Just like my jazz band director yelling at what was coming out my horn, the AD is only trying to keep things rolling along. Don't take anything they might yell at you personally. Help them do their job by doing yours. Only talk to the AD when you have a major problem that will affect the scene, such as equipment failure or another calamity. Smaller problems can be handled by the AD's assistants, a PA, or a grip.

The producer probably has the largest and longest-running job of everyone. She's been working on the film since its inception, finding financing, writers, a director, places to film, casting, lighting companies, camera crews, sound crews, and on and on. She's there during most filming while also securing and scheduling crews and actors for the next film location. She's there during editing and post-production and has a hand in where the film will play. The producer and her PAs seem to never stay in one place for very long, often zipping here and there with a phone on one ear and getting updates from someone tagging along in the other ear. Help the producer and PAs by doing your job.

The director of photography is there to realize the vision of the director (and the film). The DP will choose what cameras, lenses, sensors (or film stock), lighting, etc. in order to create mood and enhance the viewer's experience. The DP also solves major lighting issues, backgrounds, and other problems that will affect the overall look of the film. The DP may or may not run a camera on set. The DP must not only capture the director's vision on the set but give the film editor good material to edit with. Help the DP do their job by doing yours. Leave them alone.

The gaffer is the lighting director who helps the DP create a correctly lit scene. It's an enormous and intricate job that is as complicated as building a bridge of matchsticks over a canyon. Lighting a film set with actors that move through the scene is vastly different than a still photograph. As the actor moves from point A to point B, the lighting must (if intended) be even throughout. Each light added to a set creates a multitude of problems, such as hot spots, flares, dropouts, etc. For audio, getting a boom mic into a scene where the actors are (and will be) is almost as difficult. Because there are multiple lights set up, not creating a shadow from your boom pole is an achievement. Almost every set I've worked on has this problem. Most gaffers are as accommodating as they can be, but lighting rules. If they need to put a light where you've staked a claim, tough luck. Find another place and don't cast a shadow. On larger sets, don't bug the gaffer. Go to the best boy (second in command) and try to work out where you can put the boom. If it becomes an unsolvable problem, the best boy will talk with the gaffer, who might go to the AD for another solution. Let them decide whether to move the lighting, mask the shadow or boom mic in post, or get rid of the boom. With today's great lavalier mics and powerful digital video editing tools, there's usually an equitable solution. I will sometimes talk directly with the AD when a compromise may affect post-production so that they can notate that this scene has slightly different sound.

The key grip is in charge of all the rigging on a set, such as stands, reflectors, flags, dolly tracks, vehicles, etc. They work with the gaffer and DP. My interactions with grips are usually for a C-stand for my boom, a power outlet, or just to ask where I can stage (stow away) my equipment cases. I may ask a grip if a light or flag stand can move slightly so that I can get a boom in the scene. Grips are usually the most lively and humorous people on the set. They seem to be having the most fun, maybe because their job is like solving a giant puzzle. I try to stay out of their way and let them set up before I even move my gear onto a set. A grip will often help you carve out a place to roll your equipment cart onto the set. They are continually looking at every leg of every stand to make sure it's not a trip hazard or has moved. They're surveying any overhead lights or equipment to make sure it's safe. They are the ones actually building that bridge of matchsticks over the canyon. Let them do their job, and they will help you do yours.

Get to know the people in costume and make-up, because you will more than likely be planting a lav mic on an actor. They're usually one of the first people I make contact with when I arrive. I introduce myself and work out a plan on when and how to plant the mic. I ask to see costumes to find out if they are noisy, skimpy, bulky, or have some other characteristic that will make my job a little harder (it's rarely easy to hide a mic *and* have it noise-free). I also try to find out about the actor(s) if I don't already know them. I want to know about their temperance, their acting style, if they move a lot during their scene (which would affect how I place a mic and transmitter), etc. If you will have to spend time hiding a mic into a costume, it's good to know early on so that you can fit into your set-up schedule.

The actor(s) are as much a part of the machine as a grip, a PA, the director, or the boom operator. When I see an actor arrive on set for costume and makeup, I make a beeline to them and introduce myself. They haven't gone into their prep phase yet, so now is a good chance to explain who you are and what kind of mics you'll be using. I let them know that I'll be placing my lav mic about 15 minutes before the first dry run (I don't always have this luxury, sometimes I can't meet them and place the mic until they walk on stage). When I place the mic, I try to have someone from costume help me make sure there are no wires, creases, or bulges showing. This is a time that you can't be squirmy about touching someone.

I tell the actor exactly how I am placing the equipment and ask their permission before starting, and before any action that may be personally invasive (I will also sometimes give the microphone to the costume department to place the microphone on the actor if it will be very invasive). Be sure to warm your hands in your pockets before sticking your hand down someone's shirt. Some people wear latex gloves, most don't. I also explain to the talent that I may be coming up to them between takes to adjust a wire or something. A good time to do this is when the makeup artist swoops in to dab a cheek or dry a forehead. Going up too often though will throw the actor out of rhythm, so try to set the mic and wire correctly beforehand. One other major thing to remember: Don't approach an actor if they are rehearsing, resting, meditating, etc. All actors have different methods of preparation, and you sticking your big head in their space will only choke the engine. Remember, we're all serving the film.

And last but not least, the sound department. Whether you're the A1 or the A4 (see page 59 for location engineer descriptions), you have a responsibility to do the job you're assigned to. Stay on task and try to anticipate problems before they happen. This is like when my cousin's husband learned to fly an airplane for his job. She was nervous about going on a trip with him, but he told her there was nothing to worry about, flying is safe. It wasn't flying she was nervous about, it was landing. She was remembering that he had once told her that landing an airplane is really just a controlled crash. Whoops! Wrong thing to say, but he couldn't be more right. Location audio is like this. I'm just anticipating the next problem, hoping that I've got all my backup plans in place. At the end of a successful day, I just let out a sigh and think, "Well, not too many problems today. It was a good day."

The recording studio pyramid

The studio hierarchy is similar to a film set, but usually the person in charge is the one with the checkbook. Sometimes there's an honest to goodness director present who calls the shots and makes all final decisions. On most projects, I work with producers who are usually doubling as the director, so I yield to them on all important decisions. Sometimes a director/producer will allow you, the engineer, to direct a performer. You'll quickly find out what your boundaries are, but producers generally trust engineers with more delicate performer interactions.

If you are recording a band, ensemble, or other multi-person project, quickly establish who will be making the final decision before you start. I've been in some really messy music projects that ran off the rails because no band member could agree on the mix – make the guitar louder, make the drums louder, make the vocals louder... Discuss the need for a hierarchy with all members, establish who the producer is, and make sure all agree to the rules. If they can't, walk away, the hassle isn't worth it.

Sometimes one of the performers will attempt to hijack a session. While it's important to entertain all creative ideas, always refer back to the producer for the final decision before the project collapses. If a performer is leaning on everyone to go in a different direction, hear them out and put it on the table for a group discussion. Try to find out why the performer is trying to wrest control of the session: They may have been feeling pressured to perform outside their comfort level, their ideas may have been easily dismissed in the past, or they may simply like being in control. Whatever the reason, don't jump to conclusions, don't blow them off, listen to their ideas, and if necessary, remind them that the producer has final say.

Working on union sets

Many larger cities have strong unions for actors and crews. If a film company goes into a non-union place to film, chances are that most of the key personnel are in a union, so union rules follow them. It's in these cases when you may get hired as a non-union worker on a union set. You must follow all the rules as if you are in the union, including work and break times, reporting, etc. But the biggy is to only do your job. Don't move a light stand, a cable, a ladder, a camera, or otherwise fiddle with someone's gear. Don't tell a grip that there's a shadow, don't tell an actor how to read a line, don't look through a lens without asking. Don't, don't, don't. This is actually a good rule to follow on any set. How would you like it if someone adjusted your mic levels when you weren't looking? You'd be pretty upset. The only time you should ever interfere with any equipment is if you see imminent danger, such as a light about to fall, a tripping hazard, or some other risk that could lead to injury or death.

Follow the chain of command

I mentioned this in one way or another already, but it's incredibly important to not take matters into your own hands. If you've directed a short film before, ran camera for a commercial, or even acted in the past, you might have the urge to intervene and help the actor find their line or swivel a light around a little to fix a glare. This is violating the chain of command and disrupting the set. If I see a way to help an actor deliver a line that the director is struggling with, I might quietly call the AD over and whisper the suggestion to them. This would be a very rare and unique situation, and I would only do this if I already had a rapport with the AD. Otherwise I would come off as a know-it-all troublemaker and never work for them again. It's really best to just keep quiet and do your job.

Be on time and be ready

I gave you tips on page 131 about prepping for a long day on a set. Follow those for the best chance of a successful day. Also arrive early, or at the latest, on time. If you've never been to the location allow extra time for traffic, parking, and just finding where to roll equipment to. I'd rather arrive early and have extra time to double-check my equipment, catch up on email, and talk with any friends I might know. I hate showing up even the slightest bit late. I get rushed and I feel like everybody is staring at me. When it's time to film, be there and be ready before the actor steps onto the stage.

Don't stare at the actor

Photo 4.   Me working with football player James McNeil at Michigan University's
Michigan Stadium. Notice how I'm out of the talent's line of sight.

This one may sound funny, but never be in the line of sight of an actor when they're performing. Or if you are, look away or position yourself sideways. This can distract some actors and only delay the film if they blow a take. If I'm in this situation, I try to peek at them on a monitor or with my peripheral vision only to make sure a mic isn't showing or to troubleshoot any clothing noises. Another thing is to not move, walk, turn your head, etc. while the actor is performing, even if you're not in their line of sight. It's another unneeded distraction. Not all actors are bothered by movement, but it's best to play it safe and be like a statue. This rule also applies to working in a recording studio. The less distractions for the performer, the better.

Communicate clearly

When it's time to roll video and you're running sound, the AD will usually call out "Roll camera, roll sound!" Your response when your recorder is rolling (or if you're recording directly to camera and everything is working) should be, "SPEED!" This is an old term from the early days of film that indicated that the motor in the disc or film optical recorder was "up to full speed" and recording. The camera operator will also respond with, "SPEED" for the same reason. If something is wrong with your equipment or you're not ready, then don't yell "SPEED." Stop production and fix the problem. Better to correct the problem now than to suffer the wrath of a director that found out later in post-production that you screwed up the sound and didn't say anything.

Everybody F#@%$ up

Don't think it's the end of the world when you make a mistake. There's not a day that goes by on a set when someone doesn't mess something up. Remember, it's a controlled crash. Let me tell you a story about a film set I was on where I thought my mistake was the end of the world. I was hired to run sound for a documentary-style television program on a big network. It was a union set in my hometown of Lexington, which meant I was non-union, but still had to abide by union rules. This made me and my non-union compatriots very nervous that we were going to screw something up and look like dumb hicks.[48] We were interviewing subjects in a classroom with a medium-sized crew. I was off to one side of the room recording separately (it was being shot on 35mm film) with a boom and lav. Before we rolled the first shot, I yelled my obligatory, "Everybody quiet, cell phones off please."

As we're rolling along, I felt something vibrating on my side. I had my headphones on and was only hearing the mics on the set, nothing in my immediate environment. I soon realized that me, the audio engineer that barked orders to turn off cell phones…had left my cell phone on. Fortunately, my phone was on vibrate. Being

---

[48] Kentucky is plagued with comedians and the national press portraying us as dumb hicks and dirt-poor hillbillies. It's an unfair stereotype, as I'm sure most of those lofting those stink bombs at us have never even been here. But we still deal with it to this day. I once got a call at work from a Los Angeles number on the caller ID. When I picked up and said, "Dynamix Productions, this is Neil," the voice at the other end exclaimed with delight, "Oh, I love a Kentucky accent!" I was silent and taken aback for a few seconds. I almost said, "I'm from Ohio, you have the wrong number."

afraid that it would bleed into the recording, I hit what I thought was the "mute' button.[49] Nope, it was the speakerphone. About 10 seconds later I thought I heard my name. Having no sense of where the sound was coming from because I was wearing headphones, I yanked them off and heard my sister saying, "Neil? Neil? Are you there? Hellooooo…" Horrified, I hit the <u>real</u> mute button and swallowed my pride. A few people were looking around wondering what the sound was, but I'm confident it didn't make it into the recording because I was about 20 feet away. Besides, the interviewee flubbed something up right after that and restarted.

Then about 10 minutes later, the camera operator went to refocus and knocked the matte box off the front of the camera, ruining the take. Then about 10 minutes after that someone knocked something over during a take. Then a bit later something else happened. The lesson is, everybody makes mistakes, so chill out. It's like playing live music or performing in a stage play. You make a mistake, forget about it, and move on. You can't get back that moment in time.

Give a final report

At the end of day on the set, go to the AD and give a final report on how your part of the machine performed, good and bad. Don't sugarcoat anything, explain any problems you encountered, what kind of problems the editor may encounter, and offer any solutions for the next time. Find out who gets the audio files and notes you recorded and follow that up promptly. Everyone should be relaxed by now, so go cut up with your friends (if they're not working loading equipment out), make small talk with the actor, give your business cards out to new acquaintances, and say goodbye. Hopefully you landed the plane without any tires blowing out or pieces falling off the wings. Pat yourself on the back and go home and relax. Nice job.

---

[49] This was pre-smartphone days. I had a very nice Nextel flip phone on a belt clip. Nextel phones were really bad about inserting a rhythmic static sound in recordings when they rang or buzzed. Most phones don't do this anymore because of network advancements.

14. Working with Clients

"People will forget what you said. They will forget what you did. But they will never forget how you made them feel."

Maya Angelou

hether you work for yourself or work for a company, the client is king.[50] Give the client what they want, always. The client is always right, even if they aren't. These are pretty steadfast rules throughout the world in all industries. Some people can violate these rules and get away with it (like *Seinfeld*'s soup Nazi), but most of us have to serve the client unconditionally. And serving the client can be an enormous minefield.

The client is king

First, let's talk about why the client is king. In basic and unapologetic terms, the client writes the check. Whether it's a company owner, representative, or even a non-profit organization that you're working pro bono for, the client needs you to fulfill a purpose and it's your job to see that it is fulfilled to their satisfaction. It's really that simple. But it can get a little sticky on who the real client is.

Sometimes your client is in the middle of you and their client. They view their client, the person who hired them, as king. A good example of this is when an ad agency comes to you to produce a commercial. Now there are three layers of royalty, so to speak. If you hire a narrator to read the spot, you've added yet another layer of fealty. I'm expecting the narrator to deliver what I want, and I

---

[50] I'm using old industry slang here with no intention of gender disparity. For the purposes of this book, it's easier to define "king" as a non-gender noun referring to hierarchy. Please don't take offense.

want that to be what the ad agency wants, which, you guessed it, is hopefully what the top dog wants. The top dog also has a client, and in this case it's the consumer. And in all this, none of us have (hopefully) lost sight of the ultimate king we serve – the commercial. If everything has clicked properly along the multiple layers and curvy path that the message has taken to get to the listener's ears, and someone buys the product, then it's a success. Everybody has fulfilled their obligation to their client, and that leads us to my next rule.

Give the client what they want, always

If I walk into a paint store to get a can of fuchsia paint mixed, I expect it to be fuchsia when I paint my wall, not violet. I would be pretty upset if I went back to the store and the manager told me that they gave me violet because fuchsia was no longer in style. I don't care about what's in or out of style, I wanted fuchsia. Would you ever patronize that paint store again?

Sometimes there's a fine line between what a client wants, and what they *should* want. But you have to tread very carefully here because a) the client is king, and b) you don't know the big picture. Sometimes it seems that a client is misguided, misinformed, behind the times, naïve, or simply wrong about something. Your first inclination may be to correct them or to just go ahead and change something before talking with them about it. You must soul search to find out if your objections are legitimate or biased. Going back to the paint store analogy, that manager assumed that I came into that particular store because I wanted to buy the latest and hottest colors in home design. That manager didn't bother to ask me about my project, or even suggest a different color. The manager didn't have the big picture. Suppose I was matching the color of a previously painted wall, or I was renovating a historic home back to the original 1910 colors, or that my 8-year-old daughter picked the color for her room.

This sounds like a made-up scenario, but I base it on actual events. I once worked with a man who had moved to town after retirement from a much larger city. He'd had a long career in broadcast and had managed a television station for many of those years. He was a very talented narrator and had been involved in all aspects of production over the years. The first few sessions we did together were great. After a little bit of time, he began to change the script slightly, but would always go back and read what was written when asked. After several months he began to pick scripts apart and rewrite significant portions. Naturally this was concerning for me, and above all, embarrassing to my client. After a few of these episodes I talked with him about it in private and he reassured me it wouldn't happen again. But, not long after our talk I heard through the grapevine that he had refused to read a script as written and had berated the client about their writing style. His name was now mud. Having been in management for most of his career, was it hard for him to give up control? I'm only guessing, but whatever was going on – mental health crisis, retirement regrets, or inflated ego – I couldn't risk hiring him again. And as far as I know, no one else in town could either. What I do know is that he forgot to give the client what they wanted.

The client is always right, even when they aren't

Sometimes, a client just doesn't know what's good for them. I've delivered a few projects over the years that really missed the mark. Sometimes a client can get stuck on an idea and never waver from it, even if they've been told over and over again that it's detrimental. If you know the entire back story and have advised them on alternatives that have more impact, but they still want to move forward with their ill-advised idea, then just do it. It's out of your hands. You did your due diligence and tried to help them.

Most of what I run into that could be changed for the better is in the script. Overused phrases, bad grammar, poor targeting, and wrong syntax drive me crazy. For instance, I sometimes get a commercial that starts out, "Located in downtown Anytown across from Wally's Department Store, Acme Hardware has all your tool needs." First, don't start out with the location, and for Pete's sake don't mention the competition. The tired phrase "for all your BLANK needs" wasn't even effective the first time it was used. "Excuse me, I need a crane. Do you have that? No? Your commercial said you had all my tool needs." Sometimes these scripts are so far from being saved that you just have to record it and give them what they want. Hopefully they'll eventually figure out why everyone is going to Wally's for all their tool needs.

I've had clients bring in a family member or employee to read a script, sometimes because they're frugal, but often times they don't know how to hire a professional voice-over artist. When you immediately figure out that the family member is really terrible, it's difficult to discuss this with your client at that moment. I do my best to coax a usable read out of the talent by feeding them a line at a time if I have to. I read the line with the inflection we're looking for, and hopefully they mimic me closely. I then edit everything together later to make a complete voice track. This is a less than perfect solution, but if the client is happy, then mission accomplished.

Music choice is a huge sticking point with clients. I subscribe to several production music libraries that allow me to license backing tracks to my clients. Using real-life music in most productions is a no-no, unless the client has cleared the rights to use it. An example would be a national TV spot that uses a Rolling Stones song underneath. They have paid a 5- or 6-figure dollar amount to use that. I can find a similar sounding song in my library and only charge a few hundred dollars. If a client wants to use a pop song and doesn't have clearance, this is one of the few times you can refuse to give them what they want. If the Rolling Stones sue your client, you better bet you'll be named in the same lawsuit.

As far as what music is being used in a production, I try to steer the client towards something that supports the mood and message. Too many clients get stuck on a particular song before they even hear it with voice-over. If the entire production relies on that song, then that's one thing. But I can sometimes find something that has more impact and doesn't pull the listener away from the message. Too many people that get stuck on a particular song are listening to what's underneath the message (the music) and not the message itself. They sometimes say, "I love that song!" If the listener is paying attention to the song rather than the message, then that's a big fail. I try to relay this advice but when it doesn't penetrate their brain, I just surrender.

Sometimes you know a client's tastes and know they'll never venture out of their comfort zone. When they try, they usually get cold feet and run back. This happened one time with a client that wanted to try new music for their retail client. They had always used fluffy non-descript music, but this commercial was geared towards teens. She wanted to find a cut of music that sounded like a popular hip-hop song. I asked if she was sure she wanted to go that direction, and she assured me she did. I picked out two amazingly similar songs from my library and played the first one for her. "No...that's not really what I was thinking about." Exacerbated, I played the hip-hop song for reference, then my cut. "Can we try something else?" I pulled up the second sound-alike and played it. "No, that's not working." At this point I knew exactly what she wanted. I pulled out the fluffy cut she'd used on just about every prior spot for the store. "That's it!"

The five Ws

To help you give the client what they want and to keep from making too many assumptions, get as many facts straight as you can up front. One of the first things I always do when starting a new project is to ask what I was taught in journalism: Who, what, where, when, and why.

Who is the audience? Are they retirees, children 12 and under, men 25-45, jet ski enthusiasts, jazz lovers? Find out exactly who will be listening to the final product. If it's a commercial, it's usually been researched to death and will be precisely targeted. If it's music, it will be a wider range, but is still important to know who will listen. By knowing who is listening, you can not only make production choices, but will understand your client's needs better.

What is being sold or produced. Is it a new hair gel, an audiobook, a cover album of rock songs with bagpipes, a background soundtrack for a play? Knowing this will dictate the language of your production choices. You might pick some fun and quirky music for a commercial about the hair gel or design the background sounds for a play in a way that don't interfere with speech on stage.

Where will the production play? Radio, TV, YouTube, an auditorium, a toy bear, on a parade float during Macy's Thanksgiving Day Parade? Knowing this will put everything in context for you so that you not only properly mix the elements for the venue but understand why your client has made certain choices.

When will the client need a final product? In advertising it's usually right now. Audiobooks and albums usually have a drop date that can't be moved. Most projects for hire have short time frames, so be ready to have a tight deadline. Knowing this will help you understand some of the choices your client has made on content. They may have been rushed to cobble together something because their client drug their feet on getting them critical information. You really can't know all the details of what went into the preparation of the project before it came to you. I frequently record projects with hastily prepared scripts because my client is juggling flaming torches and live kittens every day.

Why is this project being done? To sell a new kind of paint, introduce bagpipe music to rockers, put on a radical new play at the summer festival, or introduce the college basketball team's starting lineup at the arena? Knowing the motivation behind a project will solidify your understanding of what your client wants.

The Big Picture

Once you've answered all the five W questions, you'll have a better idea of the scope of the project and be able to steer the machine in the right direction and help the client get exactly what they want. But what if you notice something that the client might want to change? How do you tactfully tell them? Hold on and evaluate your position in this. You may *think* you understand everything, but in reality, you don't know the big picture. You don't know the whole history of why the client made the decisions they did. You need to tactfully educate yourself further.

Ask them with an inquiring mind, "I think I understand the concept of the project, but could you go into more detail about how you came up the idea?" Or "I think I see what you're going for, but for clarification, is this similar to the XYZ ad on television?" If I don't understand everything 100%, I'll ask something like, "I don't understand this sentence, is this industry jargon? What exactly is a wobbulator?"

Industry jargon is a huge mass of confusion when recording narration. Central Kentucky has a high density of thoroughbred horse farms that breed, sell, and race horses. The choice of terminology when giving a horse's genealogy and racing record for instance, can really mess with your brain:

Four Dances is out of Big Mahmy, a half-sister to three black-type horses, including 4-time stakes winner, Tinsle Town. Her second dam, Hereigo, a daughter of Champion Two-Year-Old Hereiam, is half-sister to two-year-old stakes winner Iwashere, and to the dam of stakes winner Whyamihere and to currently active stakes winner Jamjam's Reserve, who, like Big Mahmy, is by a son of Themoreyouknow.

I'm not making this up, this is real copy (names have been changed to protect the innocent) that is very informative for a potential thoroughbred buyer or breeder. When I first started to record scripts like this years ago I was completely lost. I just hit "record" and took notes. Eventually I got brave enough to ask questions, like "what is 'black-type'?"[51] You must understand, or at least get the gist of what's being said or relayed to the listener.

Medical and science terminology is especially confusing to me, as I nearly flunked all my biology and chemistry classes. I don't have a mind for the sciences (only a love), but if you look at some of the big words carefully, you can usually break them down into conjoined Latin words. This sometimes helps you understand what the script is talking about. Finding a narrator that can read medical and science terminology and sound like they know what they're talking about is difficult. Most find that if they replace the unknown word with a nonsense word when rehearsing, the flow of the sentence is improved. You can use this approach to help the narrator find their footing. For instance, if the script is talking about a scientific procedure, replace the difficult noun with "apple" and the tool with "knife." For pronunciation, have the client repeat it slowly, noting how many syllables there are, and which one gets the emphasis. Practice the word a syllable at a time. When you can say it, you can then help the narrator say it. Have the narrator rehearse that part of the sentence over and over again, gaining speed on each pass so that it comes out without effort.

---

[51] In case you're wondering, racebet.com defines black-type as "The horse has won (or has been placed in) a Group or Listed encounter. Once the horse has won one of these races, their form (written in either a form book or a sales catalogue) will be printed in bold black ink and in capitals."

Sometimes industry jargon really butchers the English language. One corporation I was working for was generating training content for salespeople. The scripts kept referring to how many of their products were installed on the "premise." The premise of what? The <u>premise</u> that if they buy the product then it will be on their <u>premises</u>? There seemed to be a clear misuse or misunderstanding of the word "premise" happening here on my premises. I couldn't keep silent any longer, so I tactfully asked the client, "Can you clear something up for me so that I understand the message more clearly? The copy says, 'on the premise.' Shouldn't that be 'premises?'" She, a writer herself, just sighed and said, "That's how they say it. I know it's wrong, but it's been in use for years so I'm afraid to change it. They're just so entrenched in saying it that way." Ohhh…kaaaaay. Who knows how it got started, maybe it was a case of the emperor's new clothes. I jokingly egged on the writer to correct it and slowly reintroduce grammar back into the corporate language. No such luck.

When there is blatant misuse of grammar in a script, sometimes it's intentional, and sometimes it's just a mistake. There are tactful ways of bringing this up. Often times the narrator will point out the mistake after reading through a couple of times. She might say something like, "I'm so used to saying that phrase differently. Can I try it that way and see if you like it?" Or I might just be a little more forward and say, "Is this a typo, or am I misinterpreting the meaning here?" You can't forget that everybody in the studio is working as a team for the project, so it's not productive to finger point, or even be submissive and silent. If something just seems off, bring it up at some point before it's too late to fix. The client can always say no.

I should note that radio and television scripts are often written with intentionally incorrect grammar to compress time or get a point across. The most common intentional aberrations are sentence fragments. Copywriters try to make spoken word scripts sound like conversation, and in our everyday lives we rarely concentrate on correct grammar (except my mother who was an English teacher and writer). It also helps when time is tight, and every extra word needs to go. Sometimes sentences are way too long. If a narrator is having trouble making it through a sentence without gasping for air, it may be time for an edit. I first try to find places for the narrator to breath by pointing out commas and phrases that I can tighten up later in edit. And sometimes I gingerly ask the client, "Can we break this sentence up into two or more sentences to help our narrator?" This approach usually does the trick to get the copy to sound better and be more effective.

Something else you must keep an eye on is mixed tense in sentences or paragraphs. This is an easily made mistake by anyone, so most copywriters welcome the correction if it comes up when recording. Other errors like having a preposition at the end of a sentence or repeated text can also be delicately pointed out. Alliteration problems may not reveal themselves until the narrator reads the copy for the first time. The worst are Ss and Ts, like "Trust truss structures…" or "Frankfort's streets since then…" The narrator must slow down for these passages, or you can suggest restructuring the sentence to avoid the problem.

Sometimes the "error" is intentional. One commercial I worked on had an obvious grammatical error in otherwise stellar copy. The narrator had rehearsed the lines a day early but was confused on that "error." The spot was for TV, but we didn't have a video for reference, or even video instructions written on the copy. We didn't have all the facts, or "the big picture." He said something about it, and we agreed to ask the client about it after reading through it a few times. When the session started, the client carefully went through the script line-by-line explaining what would be going on in the video. When he got to the line in question, he pointed out the obvious grammatical error and explained how it playfully tied into the brand name and story arc. It was actually a brilliant piece of writing once we both understood the concept and had the big picture. Our tension broke when the narrator laughed and told the client, "We were really sweating about how to tell you that you used a word wrong!"

When you're faced with just plain bad copy writing, music composition, narration, musicianship, etc., you sometimes have to just roll with it and get the best product you can. I sometimes find a saving grace when working on bad commercials when the script is too long. I can then offer my editing expertise to reduce the wording (while hopefully making it better) in order to fit the copy into the tight time limits. It's my chance to dispose of tired phrases like, "For all your xxx needs," or "Located across from XYZ megastore." I can also strip out unneeded sentences so that the focus is simple and to the point. All of this is done carefully however, because sometimes the client is "married" to every word. I just ask what phrases or words must stay in. Most everything else is fair game once that is established.

Sometimes the client freely asks you for advice on making something better. Instead of looking on this as a free-for-all to change up the project, see it as a great opportunity to work as a team and create something special. Remember, the client wants something that is effective and true to their original vision. Your role is to help them realize that vision, not completely tear it down and create a new one. Look at each piece of the puzzle and try to figure out what works and what doesn't. Come up with solutions together while giving them that bucket of fuchsia paint.

Money

It's important to talk money right up front, especially with new clients. A fair question to ask during your initial conversation is, "What's your budget?" This will give you an idea of how much time to book, what to pay an artist or narrator, and what other services you might have to hire. The client usually wants to spend as little as possible for your services. You want to make as much on this project as possible. This struggle is older than money itself, but you don't necessarily want to haggle right out of the gate. You'll need to find out as much information as possible before you commit to a firm price.

Asking the five Ws is a start. If this project will be played on national TV, then you know that the client probably has a fairly large budget. If it's a locally targeted Pandora spot, then not so much. If a musician is looking to record an entire album, then you've got to determine the skill level of each musician, the complexity of the music, and the distribution expectations of the producer. In projects that I do on a regular basis, I can usually ballpark a price using a rule-of-thumb estimate of time. For instance, if I'm working on a TV show that has a narrator, simple interviews, music, a few sound effects, and some simple historic recreations, I estimate about three-quarters of an hour for each finished minute of program. That's about 30-35 hours for a 44-minute show. If it's a reality-based show with many different locations, people, and quick-cut music, I'll start at 1 hour per finished minute and go up from there once I see some footage and editing examples. If a potential client pushes me for a top-of-my-head estimate early on, I will usually only give a range, from the rule-of-thumb to 150% as a soft ceiling.

One dead giveaway to a low budget project is if a client asks about your hourly rate right up front. It doesn't mean you should dismiss them immediately. But in my experience, 95 out of 100 of these clients can't afford you. It doesn't mean that they're useless or not worthy of your time, it simply means that they're shopping. I've been graciously called frugal, so I don't want to overpay for anything. I usually answer their question right away, then ask them what type of project they're working on. I can sometimes direct them to a more cost-effective studio in town, or even offer some ready tips on how to reduce their cost while getting something of quality. I sometimes even book them for a short session so that they get exactly – and a little more than– what they will pay for. I've found that some budget studios tend to watch the clock more than their clients do, hoping to squeeze every little penny out of them. If I find a low-budget project interesting, I will sometimes offer a flat rate to the client based on how much time it might take if all the gears are oiled and operating efficiently. That way they're not afraid that if they go one minute over, they'll have to cough up another C-note. I tell them to not worry about time, let's create something together that they can be proud of.

I took on a small rap project for a gentleman one time that reaped huge rewards for everyone involved. A farmer in a neighboring county wanted to buy studio time for his teenage son. The farmer was straight out of central casting with the plaid shirt, blue jeans, and Kentucky drawl. His son was hip, fashionable, and could have been in a fashion magazine. But there was a true bond between the two of them. The farmer said, "I don't understand any of his music or what he does, but his friends tell me he's pretty good. I just want him to have experience in a real studio and see if he likes it." We agreed on a flat fee and I called in Dustin Jones, an engineer that sometimes works for me, to record him. Dustin is a classically trained musician who is also a hip-hop artist and DJ. The two instantly connected. Dustin did so much to help the young man find his footing and navigate the studio. As Dustin mixed down the songs, he explained everything he was doing so that the artist could use those techniques himself in the future. Afterwards Dustin told me that the young man was actually pretty good and had potential. A few months later the farmer booked another session with us. Dustin was floored by how much the artist had improved. I listened to his songs and I could clearly hear the improvements. You can sometimes get so much more out of a low-budget project than originally meets the eye.

I also have to relate a low budget project that gladly didn't happen. A man called up and, you guessed it, asked how much we charged for an hour of studio time. I told him our rate and asked about the project, trying to 1) gauge if I wanted to work on it, and 2) how many hours it might take so I can give him a quote. He said he was playing guitar and singing, and he didn't need anything fancy since he just needed to record about 20 songs for a demo. He then asked about how much time I thought it would take. I quickly did the math and told him to budget for 3-4 hours, but that we could get through them quicker if there weren't too many restarts. He started to immediately get belligerent, telling me that he can do them all in an hour because he knows them really well. Okay, great then. I was trying to remember the last time I recorded music where someone <u>didn't</u> make a mistake and did a retake. I couldn't. I explained that I would need a little time to set up and test the mics, and then there was time needed to edit and mix down the songs, no matter how fast we recorded them. This was when he really blew his top. He started raging about how many hours he's spent in recording studios, that he knows how the process works, and he can do everything in an hour. At this point I knew there was no way I was going to let this creep walk through my front door, so I asked him why he wanted to know how long it would take if he had so much experience? I also pointed out that with his "experience" he should know that it takes time to record and mix down music. I also said that I was probably underestimating the time because I'd never heard him play and wasn't sure if he could play all the songs without making a mistake. Click. Good riddance.

Budgets

This is probably a good time to talk about budgets and the many misconceptions we have about them. If you make a household budget, then you know approximately what you will spend each month provided you bring in the same amount of money. You then try to set aside any leftover wages for savings, your rainy-day fund, and some pleasure spending. Only you understand how flexible or inflexible your budget is. Your neighbor doesn't, your boss doesn't, and I don't. So, when a client comes to you with a budget that at first may seem small, remember that you don't know the big picture. I often see people assume that a large corporation can afford any kind of big budget production without knowing all the details. It's wrong to think that your client, often a small cog in the giant wheel of a goliath company, can just tap into the millions of dollars in its coffers. Being a business owner and having worked in a corporation, I can give you some examples of how we budgeted our spending. You then might see that budgets are a real thing.

Every company, big and small, relies on money coming in from sales. They plan, speculate, prognosticate, and almost incantate the next period's revenues. Revenue estimates are usually made for every upcoming week, month, quarter, year, five years, and sometimes the next decade. Without some idea of what might come in, a company can't plan on what will go out. If more money comes in than goes out, then you've turned a profit for that year, congratulations. If the reverse happens, which happens more than you think, then (trombone sound again) wah-wah-waaaah. Putting aside all the write-offs, loopholes, and other ways of reducing taxes, most companies strive to make a profit. That's why we go into business. But most large corporations operate on a very thin margin, especially during times of growth. That sounds contradictory, but if a company does very well for a few years and sees the potential to really kick it into high gear, they will invest in more capital to grow the company. On the outside, people see them opening new stores, building more factories, or adding more employees. But all this costs money. During those growth periods, things are actually pretty lean inside the company.

Without each division making a budget and working to not overspend it, then the overall company will not grow as hoped. Each dollar wasted hurts everybody in the company. This may sound like an idealistic view, but it really is true in the grand scheme of things. Within each division, each department must work within their budget, and each team within each department must follow theirs, and so forth. I can tell you from experience that when your department goes way over budget, there are usually repercussions.

If part of the overbudget includes unexpected revenue opportunities that more than covered the expenses, then it's usually forgiven. But I've seen people reassigned and even laid off because of grossly blown budgets. It's just like the big machine that the director must steer. Every little piece of machinery must follow the big plan to succeed.

In the tiny corner of the corporation I worked for, I had to watch every expense because I only had so much money to spend. I had fixed expenses like salary, utilities, and rent, but I also had to anticipate office supplies, equipment maintenance and repair, and other expenditures that are part of an operation. I would also include money for new equipment, training, and other items that could be hacked if we were having a really bad year. If I needed more money for a project that I budgeted for, I had to prepare an ROI (return on investment) report and back that up with examples of similar successful investments along with potential risks. It was a real learning experience that paid dividends when I started my business. I think I got pretty good at calculating ROIs. I was always conservative with my numbers in case something like a flood came along.[52] One investment I had been begging management for was to upgrade an analog control room with a DAW. This was the early 1990s and digital audio was just gaining ground, so I knew the enthusiasm for our other studio, which was all digital, was overwhelming. Management didn't really understand what we did, and they probably thought we just wanted new toys to play with. I demonstrated our need through hard data and conservatively estimated that the investment would pay for itself in two years.[53] It paid for itself in two months. I really understood my part of the business and kept a grip on all the expenses. But I was only willing to intentionally go over-budget if it meant a great business opportunity.

On the revenue side, whenever I made an annual budget, I knew how much money was coming in from contracts and repeat

[52] One actually did when I worked for this company. Our studio was in an office building's basement. A hundred-year rain came along and filled our studio with four feet of water. We scrambled to save what we could and were up and operating a week later (on higher ground). Seven months later we had two brand new studios.

[53] This is what an ROI is for, to determine when you make your money back on an investment.

events. But I couldn't count on anything else. Customers come and go, and one who spent $50K last year may only spend $10K the next year. These are variables out of your control that are hard to budget for, so during that budget year I had to watch how the numbers were doing every week and month. You can look at what came in last year during the same period to get a picture of what next year might be like, but there are no guarantees. To know if I need to spend or cut my current expense budget, I try to look at what's coming my way for at least three months down the road. If I'm uneasy about that, I will hold off spending on certain things until things pick up. (This free time is a great opportunity to up your marketing and go hustle some new business).

Having been on that side of things, I understand that when a Walmart, or General Electric, or Sony Pictures walks in the door, they aren't carrying a blank check for me. That person is responsible for their tiny corner of a very big entity. I also know that if someone pulls up in a Rolls-Royce, I am not going to salivate over the possibility of getting rich off them. You can't take a client at face value this way. This is not to say that you'll get paid their full budget. They're trying to save money like any good businessperson. But, like I outline below, you can't bend and let them lowball you on price. Just understand that your client has a framework they must work in, and it's your job to fit their dreams inside of it, all within budget.

With every project, no matter the cost, you must deliver 100% to the customer without fail. Somehow though, the low- to no-budget jobs just seem to take up more time than they should. It seems, but I'm only generalizing here, that the low-budget clients are actually more demanding than the big budget ones are. This can be true, but it's not the norm, we just remember the horror stories better. I've done my fair share of jobs for next-to-nothing, and there's one thing I've learned. Be up front with your client about what they're getting, what they're saving, and that this is a one-and-doner. By the way, this doesn't apply to pro bono and charity work, which is done for the greater cause.

For people with little to spend, I will clearly state what I'm willing to give them, and what it would normally cost. If it is a spec spot[54] or program for a contract, I will only do a reduced rate if the client promises to use me exclusively for the entire production cycle. If it's a spec for a product or service that has yet to be released, I politely decline the request to reduce my rate. I've done a number of these for low or no cost, and most don't pan out. My motto is, if you're <u>not</u> going to pay me to work on something that <u>will</u> pay you, then that's not a fair business proposal. I've been offered a percentage of revenues, a promise to use me exclusively for marketing if the product is successful, blah, blah, blah. I would only consider something like this if I actually knew what the product was, believed in it, and was able to look at their financials. The latter would never happen by the way.

If you are just starting out and wanting to get a foot in the door, then go ahead and take a chance on something like this if you feel good about the people involved. But tread very carefully. Whip up a two-way non-disclosure agreement with them that states they must never divulge your financial deal with them outside of their company, and that this is a one-time offer. If you don't, then you run the risk of them blabbing to everyone how cheap you are, and then everyone expects the get the same great deal. You must look at each offer like this and decide what you get out of it. Are you being taken advantage of, or can you contribute something important that will lead to success of the venture?

One type of deal I have made a few times is for independent filmmakers. If the project is really interesting and challenging, and I think the film has a shot at winning a competition or larger audience, I will drastically reduce my price in exchange for clips of the film to use when I teach audio production. I try to avoid projects with tight deadlines, because I will only be working on it while I'm not busy with regular customers. I also stipulate that the filmmaker cannot divulge our financial deal. In exchange, I try to use the production itself as a learning tool for interns. After the film is done, I will be able to use clips to teach the process to other interns, classroom instruction, and online demonstrations. I always credit the filmmaker and watermark the clips. It's always been a fair deal for everyone involved, and I'm happy to say that all of the films have done very well.

---

[54] A commercial or presentation demo done on "spec," or the speculation that you will get the big job or contract.

Sometimes a very large project with a very large budget falls into your lap. With these you've got to be very careful to not undervalue your time while ensuring the client is getting a great value. With very high-profile projects, extra effort and time are expected, and you should bill accordingly. For instance, a big-name artist coming into your studio will expect everything to work right out of the gate, and you must put in the extra effort to test everything and have the mics ready ahead of time. You might also want to triple check the product before it goes out the door, which takes more time than usual. You have to build in time for revisions, especially when there are several layers between you and the top dog in the client chain. You also need to budget in the "unknown unknowns," [55] or requests, incidents, and other events that will take up more time and money to handle. These are sometimes called "overages," and a budget can be wrecked if they aren't accounted for up front. How much? 20% is a good starting place.

When a large ad agency or record company comes in your place, expect to give up your personal life for the duration of the project. They have a team of people on their end that are working around the clock on the project. There will be so many changes along the way (and there were already many before it hit your desk) that you won't recognize the final product. When a lot of cooks are in the kitchen, it will get very messy. Whenever we worked on internal videos at my former corporation, we always knew there would be a host of revisions. We would label the very first iteration "Version 1." As it progressed through each layer of management, there would be more changes. These first few layers were always the worst because you had a lot of ladder climbers that just had to make some kind of change so that they could exercise some power. As it climbed higher and higher up the chain, the changes got smaller and smaller. But it was also less and less like the original concept as it ascended. It was frustrating when it would sometimes get killed off when it got to the very top. All that work for nothing.

If a medium to large project comes in your door and you sense that there will be a large number of changes then draw up a contract. The usual language includes specific details about what

---

[55] As the late former Secretary of Defense Donald Rumsfeld said in response to a question about the lack of evidence of Iraq's weapons of mass destruction in February 2002.

product the client will receive, when, and how many changes they can make before being billed extra. This way, they're forced to make sure everything is as close to right before they come in for the first session. There's no hard and fast rule about how many revisions can be made because each industry and project is different. But you can always count on several revisions in corporate-based productions, so bill up front accordingly. If it's a small project for a large entity, I will send an estimate with extra time added for changes. That way there's not a surprising invoice if they do a lot of revisions.

For established clients, I usually go a little easy on billing for revisions if they're minor and infrequent. I will usually have to charge them if I have to bring a narrator back in to re-read something, but if it's a quick fix for me I will just do it. If you have a client that habitually revises projects, make sure you keep detailed notes and bill accordingly, you don't want to dig yourself into a hole and give away your time. Once you do it all for nothing, they will expect it every time.

You might also have a client that rushes in at the last minute and expects you to pull a rabbit out of your hat. Great if you can, but here's another instance where you keep detailed records and bill for it. If I work over 12 hours in a day, I bill 1.5 times my hourly rate. After 15 hours, 2 times my normal rate. After 24 hours (God help me if I have to), 4 times my hourly rate. Weekends are at 1.5 times my normal rate with the same overtimes (multiplied by the 1.5 times weekend rate). If I come in on a holiday? 2 times my normal rate. Be totally up front about your prices before you begin or venture into overtime. It's their right to know and to not get a shocking bill. If they hem and haw about the overtime prices, help them find another studio. They usually come around when I suggest that.

Putting out fires

In my experience, rush jobs usually happen because of time management, or lack thereof. Like my mother's sign in her office that said, "Lack of preparation on your part does not constitute an emergency on mine," I have been on the emergency end so many times. I was asked one time what I did for a living, and I jokingly said, "I put out fires." She responded with delight, "Oh you're a fireman!" Dang, I blew that one. But I do feel like I'm in a dry field of scrub brush running over to douse one fire, only to have two more ignite behind me.

I have a theory about why a lot of projects come to me "on fire" and last-minute. I don't think some people employ "back timing." That is, counting backwards from the deadline and estimating how long each phase will take (see page 128). I think they have the delivery date in their head, and then at the last minute realize they haven't booked a recording session. When I'm working on a project, I always count backwards to know when to stop one phase and begin the next. For instance, if I know it will take about an hour to mix down, check, and upload a final mix, I stop the next to last phase an hour before deadline. Each phase I do in a project focuses on the most important tasks at first, then the next most important, ending with the little nips and tucks. Hopefully I have time to do all the smaller tasks before delivery. On most medium to large projects however, a lot of little "wish list" tasks don't get done. We have a saying in the industry: You never really finish a project, you just run out of time.

You can practice back timing in your everyday life. If you have a meeting to go to across town, calculate how long you think it will take to get there – let's say 20 minutes with average traffic. Increase that by 20%, and then leave the office 25 minutes ahead of the meeting time. That gives you a cushion in case you hit heavy traffic or wait for a school bus to unload. In any project, you should build in cushion for the "known unknowns,"[56] the likely delays for one reason or another that always occur. If you have extra time because things are going smoothly, then use that gift to do some wish list tasks.

When that three-alarm fire comes in your door, immediately do some backtiming on each phase, paying critical attention to the last phase. You must stop everything and move on to it when the time comes, no matter what. The first phase is the next most important. Your decisions early on will affect the last phase, so make sure you try to make the most intelligent choices based on time management of the project. If you have any doubts about anything in the first phase, tackle them head-on when they come

---

[56] Sorry, another Donald Rumsfeld reference.

up, don't wait until the very end. I had a client that used to drive me mad with changes after I'd wrapped everything up. He would delicately say something like, "I was wondering if we shouldn't change that one word in the script." I would politely ask what the context for the change was and try to reason if it was necessary. After several of these sessions, I had to gingerly explain that making these changes up front was easier for everyone and avoided duplication of effort.

The problem client

You can't go through a career without at least one run-in with a truly bad client. Unfortunately, I've had several, but I've been able to navigate around total disasters. They seem to come out of nowhere when you least expect it, so having a standard response will help you get your footing until you figure out what the real issue is. When you're confronted with someone behaving badly, first put on your "the customer is always right" hat. Try to appease them within reason. Try to find out exactly what the problem is and what their expectations are. Did they communicate those expectations clearly to you when the project started? Hopefully you've documented (or saved an email chain) all your communications with them.

Try to see the problem from their point of view, but don't try to guess what they're thinking. Any idea how well we humans can read other people's minds? We can't! We frequently misread other people's actions and emotions, especially in stressful situations, and draw incorrect conclusions based on *our* experiences and emotions. Your client's state of mind in this heated moment is not your current state of mind, so to you they might seem unhinged, crazy, or unreasonable. The late comedian George Carlin once said, "Have you ever noticed that anybody driving slower than you is an idiot, and anyone going faster than you is a maniac?" Like I discussed in The Big Picture section (page 234), you don't know what the real story is. Maybe they had a really bad experience at the last studio they were at. Maybe they have an impacted molar that's making them irritable. Maybe they're going through a divorce. Maybe they didn't get any sleep last night. You must think about all these variables <u>before</u> you react in a way that you'll later regret.

My policy has always been "Complete customer satisfaction." If they're not happy, I will reduce or negate the bill. Even if that customer never comes back, it's worth having the problem taken care of instead of festering like roadkill. I had one woman bring in a recording that needed the noise reduced and the conversation enhanced. It was already poorly recorded and lacked a lot of frequency detail to enhance. She said that another service in town had tried to enhance it and left me a recording of their version. I told her I'd try what I could, but the cards were stacked against us getting anything much better. I worked and worked on it, far longer than for what I had agreed to charge her. My version was different, maybe slightly better than the other attempt, but not better in the important places she wanted to hear. Before I start working on any project like this, I always have my client agree to pay me for my time once I begin, even if I inform them ahead of time that I may not be able to give them what they're expecting. She had agreed to this and paid me when I handed her the finished recording. On her way back home, she played it on her car stereo. Not five minutes later I get an email that someone has left a negative review on my Google page. She basically threw me under the bus and stated that I was non-professional. What? I was nothing but courteous and explained that I couldn't do much better than the first attempt. After quelling my spike in blood pressure, I called her and asked her directly, "Excuse me, why did you instantly leave a negative review without giving me the chance to correct the problem or refund your money?" She was silent, like she'd been caught with her hand in the cookie jar. She fumbled for words as she admitted that she had left a hair trigger review. I reminded her about our agreement and that I had held up my end of it, but I was willing to refund her money so that she had complete satisfaction. Another five minutes later she revised her review to five stars. I'm not one that desires "likes" or 5-star reviews, but unreasonable negative reviews will hurt my business far more than glowing positives ones will help.

Another instance of a client behaving badly actually altered the way I handle these types of situations. An older retired producer that I'd had some contact in years past hired our studio to produce a very prestigious national radio series. It had a major title sponsor and was written very well. We recorded the narration and put music behind each episode. There were some hiccups along the way before I delivered the masters, but I figured that because this guy had probably become such a good producer by being picky, I could learn from him. After he took the master recordings home and listened to them, he came back and said that the music levels were too loud. Music levels are a common complaint in the first go-around in projects, so I had him come into the studio and listen while I did a sample mix. When he okayed those levels, I noted my fader settings for later mixing. After sending a new set of masters to him, the music was now too low. Okay. I reasoned that perhaps he's listening on inferior equipment, so I split the difference to see if this version works. But he came back into the offices a few days later, still not satisfied. I was now beginning to question my abilities as an audio engineer at this point because of the respect I had for this man. He immediately started tearing into me in front of the whole staff: I was the worse engineer he's ever worked with; I couldn't mix my way out of a paper bag; and on and on. This was unusual for someone that I had known as mild mannered. He then started attacking me personally. I won't get into what he said.

That was when I motioned him into my office, closed the door, and dressed him down. I was very frank with him about how we couldn't seem to satisfy him, that we had in fact given him exactly what he asked for every time, but then he would change what he wanted. I then told him that I didn't appreciate him personally attacking me, and that he didn't know me well enough to call me those kinds of disparaging words. Finally, red faced, he barked that he was going right up to the owner of the company and report me. "3rd floor and make a left out of the elevator" I told him. A few days went by. Then weeks. I just *knew* the owner was going to call me up to his 3rd-floor office and dress *me* down. He never did. A year later I found out that this wild-eyed, foul-mouthed producer was fighting Alzheimer's disease. I had already forgiven him shortly after the incident because I knew I wasn't any of those terrible things he called me.[57] But I then immediately felt for him and his family for what they were going through. I reclaimed my fond memories I had of him before his tirade, dismissing the incident as an unfortunate medical condition. Our family would later experience that same dreaded disease firsthand.

---

[57] Forgiveness is one of the most powerful self-healing tools you can use to enrich your life and shed destructive thoughts and burdens. I highly recommend it.

From then on, I have always told my employees and students that if a client verbally berates, abuses, or harasses them as individuals, they should not respond at first. If that doesn't work, calmly ask the client to leave the premises. If they continue with their harassment and you don't feel physically threatened, take the client behind closed doors. Ask them why they are being so unreasonable. If they still persist, tell them off if you must, call them whatever you want, and then tell them to get the hell out of there. I don't want that client to ever step foot on the premises again, no matter the cost.

Personal verbal attacks on my employees are off-limits to anyone. An unruly customer that is just complaining about a service should be defused quickly by calmly discussing the problem and trying to find an equitable solution. I've been huffed at and yelled at for mistakes before. I really don't take those personally, and neither should you. But you should never let a personal attack or harassment get out of control. If you fear for your safety, walk away and call a supervisor or the police. Most temperamental clients are just venting their frustration in your general direction. Just smile and speak in a soft, uncondescending voice as you try to work out a solution. If you're having no luck, get someone else on your team to talk with the client.

Retaining clients

You should always be working to keep the clients you already have. Getting new clients is hard, but I think keeping them is even harder. You must prove to that new client that you can deliver at or above their expectations. If they come back, then you must prove yourself again and again. I still feel this way about clients I've had for decades. I want to be indispensable to their success. I hope they tell their colleagues about me, because word-of-mouth marketing is so much easier than targeted marketing. I'm also trying to reinvent myself over time so that I grow along with my clients.

Following all the rules at the beginning of this chapter will get you started on the path to keeping clients, but you must also go the extra mile for them. You want your client to walk away thinking that they got a lot more for their money than they anticipated. Most of my clients think about their budget, but they're most interested in creating an effective product. If I go out of my way to find a special music cut, custom record a sound effect, or orchestrate a complicated audition session, a client will remember. If you're not willing to give this extra effort, they will pick up on that and assume you aren't interested in their success. Imagine that you're at a restaurant and your server just slaps down your plates and doesn't check on how you're doing from time to time. You'd feel like chopped liver, wouldn't you? You want your client to feel like they're your favorite one, because they are. No client of yours should get more favorable treatment over another. Each one is your best customer.

You goal is to be top-of-mind when your customer needs audio production. How? Stay in contact with them. Calling them occasionally to remind them you're still on the planet is one way, but I find that a little pushy. If you call, have a solid reason. Maybe they were in the news recently for an award or recognition. Perhaps they had a career milestone or were promoted. These are great reasons to keep in touch. But make your call short and to the point because your customer is more than likely busy and in the middle of a project.

You could also email your client a congratulatory message. This is less obtrusive and an acceptable way to keep in touch. Another email tactic is a periodic newsletter. A newsletter shows clients that you're an active professional engaged in your business. I've found success with a monthly email and social posting that features a main article on audio history, current technology, or other fascinating audio-related subject in our everyday lives that people may not be familiar with. I try to keep it in layman's terms with a hint of technical terms when necessary. The same newsletter contains updates on all the projects I've been working on and any other message I want my customers to know about. I also use it as a tool to gain new customers by posting on social media sites where my potential customers are. In addition, I occasionally send email announcements of special events or studio news. I try not to flood my clients' inboxes and I give them a choice to opt out of the newsletters.

You should also go to industry events and seminars in your town. For instance, our local chapter of the American Advertising Federation has functions that many of my clients attend. It's a great time to talk shop and catch up. Check around your area for events that creative professionals attend, they can be goldmines for you to connect.

When you're out on a remote recording or live event, be sure to carry business cards with you. You may run into a client who's with other potential clients you haven't met. At almost every big job outside of the office I find myself handing out a few business cards to new acquaintances. Business cards have not gone out of fashion, by the way. This tiny, printed card stock will hang around a lot longer than an email in an inbox or a social media post. It may lay on a desk for a few weeks and be seen by other potential clients. I also find myself giving my business card to current clients. If it's someone who I've only communicated via email or phone, when I finally meet them in person, they're getting a business card.

Take a client to lunch one day. It's another great way to renew your relationship and remind them that they're your favorite client. Just call them up and tell them that it's been a while since you've seen them and would like to have lunch with them. Make it easy for them by proposing a few places near their office. If you have something in particular to pitch, be up front about it when you first call them. Nobody likes to be ambushed with a business proposition while trying to eat spaghetti. During lunch keep the business talk light and let them open the door to more conversation. I usually try to find out how they're doing personally because I am truly interested. Most of my clients are very intelligent, interesting, funny, and enjoy life. I know my life has been enriched tremendously by friendships I've built through business. This lunch may or may not immediately produce a new job, it's not usually meant to, but it does solidify this important business relationship. Follow up later that day or the next with a friendly thank you email. I often send along a tidbit of information about something we talked about during lunch.

Volunteer to help your client produce a project for a non-profit. We're often asked to help non-profit organizations produce videos or other type of programs that raise capital or awareness. Working alongside a client on these can solidify a business relationship, and even expand it. Your client may have only used you for one type of production and be unaware that you also perform many other services. I worked on a non-profit project once that led to a major partnership that is still going on twenty years later. You never know who you'll meet or what seed will be planted when helping a non-profit organization meet its goals.

When you've been in the industry as long as I have, you find yourself reintroducing yourself to your clients over and over again. This happens when a company turns over its staff several times. I've seen whole creative teams replaced with young fresh blood that don't know me from a hole in the ground. I have to scramble and re-pitch my services to the new kids on the block, hoping they don't see me as a dinosaur. And sometimes I may be, but because I'm always trying to improve myself, I eventually catch up. Times may change, but one thing hasn't. Your clients want to create something that sells. When I'm reintroducing myself, I detail the projects our two companies have worked on together. I point out the latest wiz-bang tools I have, show examples of the latest work I've done that may be similar to what they're creating, and expound on the quality of production my studios can offer. Above all, I show them that I've been dedicated to the success of their company over the long haul. I've found that as energetic and gifted a lot of these new creatives are, they can be appreciative of a seasoned professional to lean on when orchestrating their new projects. I in turn am appreciative of their brand-new approach to the age-old quest to sway a consumer to buy their product.

Do a little housekeeping

Always keep your house in order. The first thing a client sees when they come to your studio should not be clutter. If they see a mess, then they immediately think that you can't either finish a job, or do it right. It's true, I know you've probably experienced this. I took an old clock to a repair shop one time. When I walked in, I was immediately struck with how many clock parts and boxes were stacked up all over the place. Although the small guest area had neatly arranged clocks for sale, the rest of the place was a disaster. He had a great reputation for accuracy, but I just had an uneasy feeling about leaving a family heirloom here. The next time I came into his shop was more than a year later to pick up my clock. What was supposed to be three months had turned into eighteen filled with promise after promise. The clock worked great, but there is a joke somewhere in there about how a clock maker measures time.[58]

It's so easy to keep your studio looking neat by picking up clutter every day. Here's an old housekeeping trick passed down through my family. Every night before you go to bed, take ten minutes to pick up any stray books, dishes, clothes, etc. that are scattered around from that day. Put away loose items, cookware, or anything else. If bills or letters need sorting, put them in a stack for the next day. Straighten tables, chairs, pillows, curtains, and throw rugs. The key is to not let things get so messy that it will be a major operation to clean up. My mother's advice was to always keep my house clean enough that if unexpected company visits, I wouldn't be embarrassed. By taking ten minutes every day, you won't be embarrassed either.

To help with first impressions of your studio:

- Put away or make semi-organized stacks of papers. Having projects in-progress will always generate a little clutter, so keep it organized.
- Use desk organizers for items that can't go in drawers.
- Have a central area (preferably out of sight of clients) for storing paperwork or media for in-progress and upcoming projects.
- Hide as many wires as possible. Run along baseboards and bind multiple wires with nylon cable ties. Place black panels or cloth over wiring or backs of equipment to hide any cable chaos.
- Keep empty chairs pushed into desks.
- Keep trash cans less than half full, empty if possible.
- Dust, vacuum, and mop often. Keep small battery operated vacuums and disposable mop wipes handy.
- Keep bathrooms and kitchens clean. For quick daily cleaning, use rubber gloves and moist disinfectant wipes.
- Keep window and door glass panes clean.
- Use entry mats and rugs for dirty shoes.
- Store extra microphones, cables, etc. out of sight.

---

[58] To top it off, when he called to say my clock was ready, we agreed to meet at a specific time. While I was parking, he called me five minutes *before* our appointment wondering where I was.

When recording on location, always dress appropriately. Don't wear clothing with offensive or controversial messages. If possible, put company logo stickers on your equipment cases. Cases get beat up, but retire extremely ratty ones. Clean up after yourself at day's end by tossing cups, wrappers, papers, spent batteries, used gaffer tape, etc.

15. WORKING WITH PRODUCERS AND DIRECTORS

"Alone we can do so little; together we can do so much."

Helen Keller

T his chapter will teach you how to communicate with the people who are turning the gears of a production. It helps to know the difference between a producer and director, and the sub-rankings of each.

The "producer" title can be confusing when other words are planted in front of it. There are different levels of producers with varying degrees of responsibility, involvement, and clout. For instance, an *Executive Producer* (EP) can be someone who funds the project themselves, secures funding from others, and/or makes a major commitment of time, materials, real estate, personnel, or other tangible assets needed to complete the production. A studio head, investor, or even the leading actor can be an EP. Generally, their reason for joining the production is to 1) (hopefully) make money, 2) support or advance an agenda, idea, or cause, 3) support the arts, and 4) participate in a production. In short, the EP basically has final say on the biggest decisions.

The *Producer* is someone who organizes every little detail of a project, pulls together the money and personnel to make it work, and oversees the production until the end. The producer knows the big picture, no pun intended, of the production. The producer manages the overall budget, hires the director, production companies, and distributor. Like we talked about in the chapter on studio and film set etiquette (see page 219), the producer has probably the largest responsibility in a production. The entire project is on the line for this person, and they are making the decisions that can sink the ship or steer clear of the iceberg.

There are a multitude of other types of producers. You should do a web search for specific titles because they change over time as a result of guild and union agreements, media format advances, and evolution of industry-speak. Some of the most common you will run into are:

Line Producer, who is mostly responsible for the micro-details of budget management of payroll, insurance, contracts, etc.

Unit Production Manager, who aids both the director and production team with budgetary management of principle photography.

Creative Producer, who focuses on aligning the director and creative teams together.

Assistant Producer, who may assist any one of the above producers with smaller tasks while communicating with other departments during production.

Audio Producer, who oversees either the audio portion of a visual project like film or theater, or an audio-only project such as a radio spot or program, podcast, album, etc. This person organizes and schedules production personnel, artists, studio time, and possibly distribution. An audio producer may also be the audio engineer, director, talent, and/or the script writer. For me, this combines the business side of recording with the creative side. It can be very rewarding to pull together all the elements of a project, produce the final version, and hear it played to audiences.

Smaller productions will usually not have this many producers and one person will do the jobs of many. On any production however, the producer or EP may also be the *Director*. We talked ad nauseum about the director in the chapter on studio and film set etiquette (see page 219), but keep in mind they have control of the rutter and are steering the ship. Their word is gospel, and they won't change their mind without a completely convincing argument.

In my everyday studio world, productions aren't usually divided up between so many people with titles. The reality is that the person who is making the creative decisions can be the writer, producer, director, talent – all, or a combination of these. Local video productions may divide the responsibilities up a little more to ensure a smooth production. Either way, determine who has what responsibility before engaging that person during production.

In most productions, a producer, assistant producer, or production company will contact you for audio work. Whether it's studio or remote/location, the first inquiries will be about your availability and capabilities. A producer is also interested in cost, so that's usually a question that comes up later.

A little sidebar here. If cost is the first question someone asks when they call, it's usually a red flag for me. Even if I can do the job for the budget they have, this may be a foreboding of a less-than-enjoyable experience, with every minute of your time scrutinized and late- or no-payment. I generally sidestep the question for a moment and try to find out how complicated (or simple) the production might be because billing for complicated projects can be.. errr…complicated. Therefore, I can not only give them my hourly rate, but a completed production estimate. One example might go like this:

Phone rings, "Dynamix Productions, this is Neil."

Caller: "Uh, yeah. How much are you an hour?"

Because I have different rates for different services, I ask, "What type of project are you wanting to do?"

Now this next answer is the most frequent one I get, "I'm wanting to record some music."

They may or may not go into detail at this point. If not, I ask, "What type? Rap, hip-hop, singer-songwriter?" For my studio, which specializes in narration and sound-for-picture, producing music is not an everyday thing. Like I tell everyone who asks, I got into the recording business to record music and ended up doing everything else. So, if a caller wants to record a group, I refer them to someone else because I don't have a big studio or in-house instruments. I would love to, but in my local market music recording is a slim-profit endeavor. I also don't feel comfortable recording rap or hip-hop because I don't listen to a lot of it. I appreciate it and even love some of it, but I don't feel I could give good direction and produce something cutting edge for them.

Note: I have done it several times, but it's usually for acquaintances, an existing client, or for fun. I will usually refer them to a couple of excellent private studios that I trust will treat them right. If it's a singer-songwriter, then I explain my studio size and experience to them before quoting my rate. I do record simple singers with guitars or keyboards occasionally and enjoy it. I learned the ropes by recording myself singing with guitar, so I can quickly get the sound they want.

Another example of handling the money question up front might sound like this.

Phone rings, "Dynamix Productions, this is Neil."

Caller: "Hi, I'm looking for a studio to record a commercial. How much is it?"

This is a wildly open-ended question. Is it for radio, TV, web? Do you have a narrator already? Where will it play, etc. I will ask these general questions to determine how much I think it might cost. Someone that would ask this type of question has probably never paid for broadcast advertising before. Maybe they've only done print advertising, or maybe they've been given free production once when they bought a block of time to run radio or TV spots. You really don't know until you have a conversation with them and get more information. At this stage, and with potential clients that are new to recording, I usually give them a price range with many options. When I quote that really high number of the estimate, I usually follow it up with a qualifier like, "This is just an estimate. That highest number is in case there's extra time spent because of problems or numerous changes. I would keep that number in mind as the ceiling, that way you're not too shocked if we do have to charge that. Most of your type of projects fall somewhere in the middle." Seasoned producers know this and appreciate the price range estimate, but novices at audio production can sometimes have severe sticker shock. But you have to be honest with them up front on their highest potential cost, or else you'll have trouble on the back end when the bill needs to be paid.

And speaking of getting paid, this is a very funny business when it comes to that. The rule of thumb is to collect 50% up front for large projects whenever you can. This mostly applies to new clients who haven't established credit with your company. It's not unreasonable to ask for this, as I'm sure that most of you have pre-paid fully for an airline flight, hotel, or other service. If a new client bulks at this, especially one that you've never heard of, move on because that is another big red flag for possible trouble down the road. For well-established clients, I usually just bill them unless I will incur significant up-front costs. In those instances, I pre-bill them for those costs. When you do start billing good clients instead of collecting upon project completion, you must have enough in your bank account to operate for a few months afterwards. That's because billing cycles can delay you getting paid right away. If I bill a client on May the 2nd, they might not bill *their* client until May 31st if their policy is to invoice monthly. Then, they may wait until they get paid (maybe in a month), and another month may pass before they pay you. So, you may not see a check until three months later, or even longer. Meanwhile you've gone ahead and paid any talent or delivery fees for that project because for individual artists or small operations, waiting 60 days or longer for payment is irksome and may cause much consternation with a vital source you can't afford to piss off. For corporations, ad agencies, medical services, governments, and other large and slothly organizations, a 60-to-120-day cycle is not uncommon. If you do regular work for that client, you'll probably never notice the delay after a while because you'll be starting a new job when the check from 5 jobs ago arrives that day in the mail.[59] Nobody said running a business is easy.

Back to our producer calling you about possible work. I always try to ask as many questions as possible before committing to doing the job and quoting a price. Short one-hour narration sessions are no-brainers,[60] but anything that involves long hours, travel, talent,

---

[59] When working directly for political campaigns, don't release any materials until the bill is paid in full. I've been burned one too many times by "trusting" a candidate. If, however it's through a trusted source like an advertising agency that's established credit with you, go ahead and bill if they ask. I've only had trouble collecting from an ad agency once in decades, and I cut off all political advertising with them after that.

[60] Well, almost. If the narrator is a professional, and the script is already written and has a word count (a narrator usually reads 125-160 words per minute), then I do a rule of thumb on the time needed. I take everything into account such as mistakes, small rewrites, editing, and mastering and estimate the total time. Non-professionals reading a script may take 1.5 times as long. Not having a script written yet throws a big wrench into an estimate, so I usually take the client's

or other unique services require thinking through the project. I'm often checking my schedule to see if I can move an upcoming session to make room for this new one. If so, then I check to see if I have the right capabilities for the production. This is where you need to be completely honest with yourself and the producer. If you have no idea how to do what they're asking, tell the producer that you've never done that kind of work. If it's very similar to something else you've done, assess the differences and ask the producer if your other experience is close enough to make them comfortable. If so, then study up on that new technique before you start the work. If you absolutely don't know how to do something and you fib about it, you're setting yourself up for immense failure. That's why I always stress that being honest is the best approach.

Remember my experience recording ADR for the film *Hide and Seek* (see page 91)? That was my very first ADR production using a digital audio workstation (DAW). I was honest with the producer who called telling them that my business was new, my gear was new, but that I did have film looping experience. I had also gone through the exercise of simulating an ADR session in my new studio a few months before when another potential client expressed interest in booking us. In my previous job, I had little opportunity for that type of work (though we did a ton of productions where we locked video tape to our DAW). But my first real job at a film company (see page 47) taught me how to do old-fashioned film looping. The actor watched a film, yes real sprocketed film, while re-voicing the dialog. We recorded it in-synch onto synchronized reel-to-reel tape. It was later transferred to sprocketed magnetic audio film stock, and then the good takes were aligned to picture on a film edit bay. It was really old school, but it solidified my knowledge of film/video synchronization. For *Hide and Seek*, I had performed all the tasks separately, just not altogether. But, having confidence in myself that I could do it, and looking forward to gaining a new experience, I took on the project.

Now that you're sure you'll take the new job, talk money with the producer. Give your best off-the-head estimate if they need something quick, but we try to always send an official estimate on our letterhead. I find it hard to remember dollar specifics, so having

estimated finished-work time and double it for estimation purposes (if they think it will be 5 minutes, it will probably be 10, for instance).

it in writing keeps you from making billing errors (possibly undercharging and losing money!). I line everything out so that 1) the client sees everything they asked for with costs, and 2) a record of what we discussed because it's hard to remember every detail. I'll go over payment terms at this time just to make sure there are no misunderstandings.

If you are retained for the job, make sure you've booked a little extra time before and after the first recording session because there's usually a little meet-and-greet and discussion before work actually begins. Padding your session times keeps me from being jammed and backed up from a previous appointment. You do not want to rush your first session with a new client. I also pad the backend of an appointment because I really don't know how fast or slow a new client works. I don't want to be pushing them out the door because I have another session starting. It's not always possible to book your schedule this way, but with experience you'll find there is an art to constructing a studio schedule. If you make enough room for your client's first recording session with you, hopefully they'll find it a relaxing, uncomplicated, and positive experience.

There are many other details to discuss with the producer before the project begins, such as the deadline, technical details, delivery specifications, etc. I always immediately reply to any emails or texts they might send, no matter how mundane.[61] This shows you're listening and aware of any new details or changes. During a session or remote recording, I'll ask any questions I might have as soon as possible. If you're on a film set, wait until the entire scene is done shooting if it's not urgent. During a recording session, I might delay recording the next take if my question might be vital to what we're working on at that moment. Don't be shy or think your question will sound stupid or naïve, it's better to raise the question now than to have something go wrong later because you didn't ask. Believe me, I've asked what I thought were some really dumb questions before but have never been chastised for it. I've

---

[61] And even the late-night ones, especially if everyone is a few time zones away from each other. The last decade has increased the gray line between the workday and personal time when it comes to business communications. Now, everyone has a smartphone or tablet that notifies the user when an email or text comes in. There's almost no way to hide from business during your free time, almost as if you're on call 24/7.

even gotten responses like, "Glad you asked about that, let me fill you in." I've even circumvented some errors the client didn't see beforehand and saved them from some expensive and deadline-busting revisions by asking "stupid" questions. They'll appreciate the input because at this point in the production you're a collaborator with them. They may even start to trust you and rely on you more because they see that you're engaged with their project and want to see it done right. Bottom line: you're more than a button pusher, you're a team member.

During production, especially long and drawn-out ones and/or ones with a tight deadline, keep the producer updated. Keep them in the email chain, even if you're contacting someone else on the team (like the video editor or voice talent). Whenever I start a new phase of a project, such as mixing down a television show, I update everyone involved on my ETA for getting the final assets[62] to them. I'd rather be a little annoying with a few extra emails than have them wondering, "I wonder when that audio guy is going to get us our stuff?" Stay in the loop.

Let's move on to working with a director. Sometimes the producer and director are the same person, so it may help to treat their double role in two different ways. First get the production details out of the way with their producer half, then talk creativity with the director's half. Talking with a director requires you to forget about what buttons to push, what format you're using, or what the deadline is. You must get into the head of the viewer/listener to see how they will interpret the project. It's your job to get on the same plane as the director, to synchronize your understanding with their creative vision. A good director will give you some background on how the project came to be, why it was written in a certain way, and their choice of actors, music, or any other element that drives the narrative. When talking with a director, it's not important to know *how* the project is done, but *why*. This is often lost on some audio engineers I've worked with. They seemed too focused on the tools they were using instead of what the tools were creating.

---

[62] In the production world, especially video or film, assets are any element of the final product. Video, audio, closed captioning, etc. are all separate assets.

Someone once came to me and said they wanted to record a tuning fork choir. My jaw almost dropped because I'd never heard of such a thing. My first thought was not *how*, but *why*? I wasn't thinking it was silly, I was genuinely interested. This person had no real experience in a studio setting (but she did have on-camera experience), so I adapted my language and questions to her as if she were the director (which she ultimately was). Her idea was to record a relaxation technique that she regularly did with her clients (she was an unlicensed therapist) so that they could practice at home on their own. Tuning fork healing is a form of sound therapy that uses precisely pitched tuning forks that target specific parts of the body. It's been compared to acupuncture as a method of healing. While trying to figure out how to record eight people with tuning forks, the utmost thought in my head was that I was recording a performance. I can't get in the way or insert an obtrusive piece of technology that might interfere with the players. So, I set up an omnidirectional microphone in the middle of the studio and had the players stand in a circle around it. As they rehearsed, I moved some people closer or farther from the microphone to balance their volumes to each other. The therapist was one of the players, so I made sure everyone could see her as she directed using body gestures. I tried to be as calm as the therapist when rehearsing and recording the players, because she exuded calmness herself. I felt I was on the same plane as the director.[63] Overall, it was a thrilling experience for me. The buildup of sympathetic vibrations and overtones from the forks was completely surprising. I must admit that I was very relaxed after the session. Who knows, maybe it does work.

Tech Tip

Omnidirectional is a microphone pickup pattern that hears all sounds equally in all directions – up, down, and all sides. There are slight frequency variations in certain directions because of the physical structure of the microphone, but not enough to worry about in most situations. Using this pattern gives a recording a very

---

[63] I could have said I was "in tune" with the director, but that would be too corny.

open sound, but also introduces much more ambient background sound, which is desirable in some circumstances.

Another way to connect to a director is to look at any visual components of a project. One project brought to me was a radio project that accompanied a television, web, and billboard advertising campaign. The director brough in a storyboard for the television and nearly finalized artwork for the print and billboards.

Tech Tip

A storyboard is a vital part of any video or film project. It's very similar to a graphic novel where each part of a scene is roughly drawn out with narration and/or descriptors included with each frame. It's a guide for the director, videographer, narrator, and any other production personnel. The more detail there is, the easier it is to create. Some larger-budget projects have animated storyboards, which are similar to a cartoon with temporary voices and music underneath.

The storyboard is always immensely helpful, but in this case the colors of the print part of the campaign steered me in the right direction for the music. The colors were muted purple and teal, and the font was relaxed and gentle. Even the wording was well thought out and inviting. I don't remember specifically who the spots were for (probably healthcare), but the audience didn't need it shoved down their throats. We picked simple, but positive music that went well with the voice-over. Just seeing a script, or even a black-and-white storyboard would not have been enough to influence my creative approach. The colors directed me in the end. A little experiment for you is to think of a brand and their color. Next, think of their sound. Here are few:

Target (Red - bold and daring)

IBM, HP, Samsung, Intel (Blue - subdued, yet technological)

Mercedes-Benz (Silver – elegance, sophistication)

McDonalds (Orange/Yellow – cheerful, happy)

You can almost write their music by associating what the company does with the color of their logo. I hear fun horns and electric guitar for Target, the synthesizer "Bom-bom-bom-bommm" for Intel, a string quartet for Mercedes, and a bouncy whistling tune for McDonalds. Sure, most are cliché choices, but you have to start somewhere when you're building something from the ground up. The director might have even selected a few tunes to use as a reference. You can also make creative choices for narrators and their delivery[64] by seeing all the other elements. If you're recording music, seeing marketing material or previously produced works can help how you record certain vocalists or instruments. It can also help with the final "sound" an album might have.

If you're recording a voice-over, singer, player, or other single performer — and there is a director in the room (or on Skype, phone, etc.) — it's vital to stay out of the way. This is more for the performer's sake than the director's. The expression "too many cooks in the kitchen" is apropos here because having more than one person giving directions can be confusing. I usually only chime in if I hear something technical that I need to correct, like having the performer move back to prevent popping Ps. Or I might insert a helpful hint if the talent is having trouble understanding what the director wants. I only do this after asking permission from the director. Your job is to capture the performance, and if you do something to impede the performer(s) then you're not doing your job. If you have a suggestion on trying something different, discuss it with the director <u>after</u> they've captured what they want. Like I preached in the studio and film set etiquette chapter (see page 219), the director knows the big picture and has an awesome responsibility to pull everything together into one cohesive production.

Tech Tip

A Plosive, or loud thunderous sound that a "P" can make in a microphone, can wreck a recording if not dealt with. Bad ones sound like a thump or explosion. A foam windscreen or a gauze-

---

[64] A narrator's "delivery" is a subjective opinion about how they read the script. They might read softly, fast, whispery, boisterous, etc.

like windscreen in front of the mic can help, but having a vocalist back up or turn their mouth slightly away (sideways or down) from mic's center will re-direct the air stream. Put your hand in front of your mouth and say words starting with B, H, P, and T and you'll feel the rush of air. Exhales and loud singing or yelling will also set off alarms.

Sometimes you'll have to deal with a director's ego or temper. Unfortunately, anyone up and down the production chain can have a big ego and a course temper. It's best to keep everything professional and even keeled when confronted with these types of behavior. After all, who's the client? The project. If I have to put up with an egotistical director that really knows their stuff, then that's okay. At the end of the workday, I get to go home and get away from all the drama. I was on a set one time where the director, whom I had great respect for, was yelling at everyone, including me. I'm okay with high-intensity productions where it's required – everybody's on edge in those (like the Triple Crown Radio Network broadcast, see page 143). And, like my college jazz band teacher yelling in my ear (see page 41), I'm even okay with someone barking orders at me so that I will perform better. But this director was running on fumes from lack of sleep and was melting down in front of the clients. I was loudly called stupid for whatever I did or didn't do. I feared that the clients would see this as a weakness of the crew and lose trust in us. I quietly pulled the director into a room just off the set, and in a calm and even tone I told him of my objections to his antics in front of the clients and how we could all appear as unprofessional. I asked him to tell me what he needs in a normal voice. I also said he could blow up at me all day if he wanted, just so long as it was out of earshot of the clients. He agreed, was apologetic (which wasn't what I was seeking), and we got along famously after that.

At some point in your career, you'll find yourself directing recordings and performances, so we're going to reverse roles and put the director's hat on. Picture yourself as Cecil D. DeMille, sitting in a director's chair, sporting a beret with a big fat cigar in one hand and a megaphone in the other. Got it? And...ACTION!

That's a fun and cartoonish vision, but being a director is a really, really hard job, and the more you understand how to do it, the more you'll be able to relate to and communicate with other directors. To me, the closest profession to being a director is being a teacher. In a classroom, you may have 30 students that you're trying to explain something to. There isn't just one universal way to explain something so that everyone will easily understand, you sometimes need to find 30 different explanations. Directing is very similar. You're hoping that the performer will quickly be on the same plane as you and understand what you are trying to get from them.

The most important thing to remember about directing is that it's all about collaboration. It's a two-way street between the director and performer, and everybody's goal is to be true to the message, music, script, film, etc. Most actors and musicians already have an idea how they're going to perform something. Hopefully they've researched and practiced their part before coming to the studio, but you still must manage the performance so that it fits into the overall production. Your vision is what's important, so your goal is to get the performance you need. Sometimes an actor/performer has a different and better idea, so as a director you need to explore all alternatives you never thought of. One of the best pieces of advice I ever heard was "Trust the actor." This applies to any performer, but they are there for a purpose. They aren't nice cutlery at a dinner table, they're the main course. Let them perform what comes out naturally and then make any adjustments from there. Hopefully you've talked with them beforehand and expressed your vision of the project. This way, they can explore and hone their performance on their own, instead of being forced to come up with something on the fly.

Most accomplished actors will tell you that the way to a good performance is to know the truth. Who is the character, and what is the real truth behind their words and actions? As a director, you need to spell this out to them in basic terms. I might say, "This man has been working hard all day in a job that he hates. It's raining cats and dogs when he drives home, and his wipers are shot. He steps out of the car into a deep puddle and finds out he has a hole in his shoe. He really can't wait to just sit down and crack open a nice cold bottle of XYZ Beer and watch the game." I then let the actor explore the emotion behind the voice. For a musician, I might have them imagine there is a very excited crowd of 3,000 people packed into a night club just to hear you play solo guitar. It's really about painting a picture for the performer so that their performance sounds natural instead of forced. You can really tell when someone records a narration for a commercial and they sound like they don't want to be there. They haven't been motivated enough to just let go and play the part.

Even novices can be motivated enough to turn in a convincing performance. I try to keep them interested by not giving *too* much direction. If you paint the picture before they even try to read a line or sing a note, you'll usually get the most usable takes in the first couple of tries. Give them a simple overview of what they will be saying, who will be listening, and how you want them to deliver their lines. I might tell them something like, "This is a TV commercial for a baby seat that has a really high safety record. This will play during shows that women will mostly watch, so we're selling to new moms. Read it in a caring and positive way because you're a mom that owns one of these and really likes it. And don't forget to smile when you're reading."[65] This will yield the best results early because these instructions, and more importantly the emotion, is still fresh in their mind. They aren't thinking about plosives or loudness or timing, they're just happy to talk about a safe car seat. Once you start making technical adjustments, like "read softer here," or "slow down when you read the web site," you risk losing the feeling and emotion the narrator had early on. You can give them these kinds of instructions, but wait until you have a couple of really good takes in the can before you get out the scalpel. For corrections or "pickups," I will usually have a novice re-read the spot or paragraph again, even if I'm only going to pull a word or two out of the take to edit into my master take. This way you have all the words recorded in multiple ways, and they read "into" and "through" the passage that needed corrected. For instance, if it's a short phrase you need re-read, having them start right on that phrase will explode out of their mouth and not sound natural. By starting much earlier, then they have a running start and will get into the flow of the narration before they get to the part you need

---

[65] The physical act of smiling while talking changes the sound of the voice. Most people can tell if someone is smiling or not in blind tests. Smiling sounds positive, happy, and confident to a listener.

fixed. I've found these methods also work well with musicians that are new to recording.

The bottom line for directing is to paint a simple picture, don't get in the way of the performance, and don't give too much instruction, especially in the beginning. Professional performers can handle a lot of detailed instructions, but I've found it best that they first nail the emotion and delivery before you delve into minute adjustments and corrections. A professional will be able to give you anywhere from 5 to 10 deliveries that are all varied and solid, a novice only one or two. A professional will be able to grind out 20-30 takes with the same delivery while making small adjustments here and there, a novice only five or six. A professional will be able to pick up a line in the middle of a performance and match what they did five takes ago, a novice none to once. A professional will understand your finite tweaks to their performance and usually deliver what you want, a novice will tire quickly and start to tense up. A professional will go home after spending an hour working on a 30-second script and feel good about the day, a novice may feel worthless and have genuine vitriol for you after spending 30 minutes on the same script.

One of the best exercises I've found that will improve your directing skills, especially when directing novices, is to go on the other side of the glass. Go sit in the talent chair and try something you've never done before, such as a voice-over. Have someone with some experience direct you in several different varieties of deliveries. Try to speed up the read, try to slow it down, make word changes, etc. Have them throw everything including the kitchen sink at you and experience how disorienting it is to try to control your voice in ways you never have. I know that I've wondered why it's so hard for someone to just do something simple we're asking of them – until I had to be the talent.

People unaccustomed to the studio environment will tense up when they get behind a microphone. We call it the "root canal" seat. Most people would rather be in a dentist's chair than behind a microphone. In fact, just to relax them when they first sit down, I sometimes joke that there isn't a dentist's drill in the microphone. But they can also get nervous because they feel like they're in a fishbowl – everybody staring at them through the glass studio window and listening to every sound they make. Then when they put on the headphones, they hear their voice (Oh God, do I sound like that?) and their own breaths (I can hear my nose whistle!). I hear it all, and it's my job to relax them.

I usually just chuckle along with their nervous jokes and let them get everything out, because the more they talk, the faster they get used to their new environment and the sound of their voice. I then try and talk them off the edge of the cliff by asking them questions about their family, job, etc., things that they're familiar with. This way they start to bring the familiar into the unfamiliar space they're in right now. I don't have this problem with everyone, but it's good to have a few of these tools in your back pocket when you do encounter nervous people. It's also good to know that when someone is nervous, time speeds up for them. They will read, sing, or play too fast. Their throats are tight, their heart rate is up, their blood pressure is higher, and they may be taking quick, shallow breaths. All these symptoms of nervousness lead to a quicker pace, perhaps singing out of key, frequent breaths, and compromised attention. Let them become comfortable with the new surroundings, offer them water, leave the studio door open at first to keep the oxygen levels up (they are exhaling more CO_2 early on from nervousness), and just have a calm and relaxing conversation with them.

When you do start to get to work, have the talent do a warm-up read or performance. Tell them it's just a test so you can set some levels, but <u>be sure to start recording</u>, this may be the keeper take. Afterwards, ask them if their headphones are loud enough. Are the too loud? Do they need some water? Can they see the script okay? This banter is an intentional buffer period to cushion the upcoming tension of recording the first take (really the second one because you rolled on that warm-up, right?). Now slate the first *real* take. This may or may not be better than the warm-up, but this lets them know that it's business now. If it's a script you're recording (or even a singing performance), work through a few takes that go from beginning to end. Then, do a take where the talent reads each sentence or phrase two or three times until you get something good. You might wind up using some or all of these when you edit, so make sure you get at least one good take of each line or phrase. After that, tell them that you have everything you need and it was great.

At this point, most people will usually relax because the pressure's off. Sometimes their shoulders fall and they let out a big breath. You've got them right where you want them now and they don't even know it. Next, say something like, "Oh, but just for poops and grins, can you just go ahead and run through the whole thing from top to bottom one more time just to make sure we didn't miss something." In their mind, they've read each line one-by-one and done the hard part, so this time should be a piece-of-cake. In fact, you could ask them if there is another way they would like to try, just for fun. You've just given them license to turn the amp up and rip out a solo. To them, it's kind of like the school dance scene in *Back to the Future* when Marty McFly lets loose and shreds an Eddie Van Halen guitar solo. This last take will usually flow more smoothly and be more earnest and thoughtful. In more times than you think, it will be money.

Afterwards, be sure to compliment them on their performance, and remind them that you know how intimidating a studio can be at first (because you've tried the exercise of getting behind the mic yourself). Remember that even if their performance was bad or stilted, they stepped up to the task and made it through a nerve-racking experience that not many people go through. Hopefully, especially if they go out on a high note, they will remember their studio experience as a good one, not one that's worse than a root canal.

16. WORKING WITH TALENT

"Performing is very much like cooking: putting it all together,
raising the temperature."

David Tudor

I closed out the previous chapter with how to direct novice talent, or in industry lingo, "non-talent." Working with professional talent, or at least those with experience or training, can also be a challenge. Even if you're a professional narrator, singer, player, speaker, or something else that requires you to perform in front of a microphone, it takes a different set of skills to be in the engineer's chair and get the best performance possible from talent. If you've already worked a lot behind a microphone, you'll have a unique perspective when you're helping others achieve a great performance. But if you're like me, with limited time on mic, knowing a little 'talent speak" will speed up the journey.

My first experiences behind a microphone started as a teenager when I would record myself practicing trombone or guitar. As I told in an earlier story, I also recorded music in my guitar teacher's basement recording studio. But those times were different from recording something substantial and with meaning. As it happens, my jokes with a client landed me a job behind the mic one time.

I goof around a lot with different character voices from TV shows, cartoons, people I know, etc. I'm not any good, but I just enjoy those lighter moments. One of the cartoon characters I do very badly is Shaggy from the cartoon *Scooby Doo*. Well one day, a client was working on a radio commercial for a cell phone company and remembered me barking out Shaggy's "Ruh-roh" when I would mess something up in the studio. His script was based on a typical scene from the 1960s TV show *Lassie*, where Timmy (the young boy in the show) falls down a well. Of course, the dog Lassie is super smart and runs back to the parents to tell them, but guess what? Dogs can t talk. Oh, but they can if there is an audio engineer that can grunt out words like a dog. Since this was a bit I could do fairly easily (though badly in my mind), we recorded my grunts of simple one-word answers to Timmy's parents' frantic questions. In the end, the client decided to not run the spots, and I'm sure it was because of my terrible attempt at being a dog. But surprisingly, the ad, and my performance, won a Tall ADDY[66] Award! A "Tall" ADDY is for concepts that were fully produced but never made it to the public. Wouldn't you know it, an award for goofing off.

My other times behind a microphone include sounds for foley, group wallas, reading scratch tracks, the occasional character in a radio spot, and podcast and radio interviews. I am not a professional narrator by any stretch of the imagination, but I can say that I have learned to take direction (and I need a lot) and have some idea what a narrator or performer is thinking when recording. I think my experience behind a mic, though scant, helps me to cut to the chase when working with professional talent to get a good performance.

Tech Tip

"Walla" is the sound effect of a group of people mumbling, laughing, talking, etc. that fills dead space under a scene. Think of a courtroom scene where the defendant on the stand says something controversial and the courtroom's spectators gasp and talk amongst themselves. Or a scene where someone walks into a cocktail party and everyone is drinking, giggling, talking to each other, but you can't quite make out what anyone is saying.

A scratch track is a sample voice-over (or a sing-along reference when recording basic rhythm tracks for a song) for any project that requires timed edits to be made to the words of the script. These are very common to video projects where timings, phrases, and words need be heard with the video. Adjustments to the script or video can be made at this time before the final voice-over is recorded, rather than having to re-record expensive revisions. The person reading the scratch track must read at the anticipated final pace for this to work correctly.

---

[66] American Advertising Federation's (AAF) award competition for local chapters that advance to regional and national competition.

The Ego

But first, let's talk about the most important part of a professional narrator, singer, or performance: the ego. Oxford Languages describes ego as "a person's sense of self-esteem or self-importance." Everyone has an ego, it's the measure of one's ego that gets all the attention: big ego, no ego, egotistical, etc. In order for someone to perform, one usually needs a bit more of an ego than someone who doesn't. Almost any accomplished performer will readily admit to this. One must have confidence that their performance will not only be good, but better than what the average person can do. It's healthy to have a little bit of self-esteem, it's what gets us through life.

What often gets bad press is when a performer's ego bleeds over into everyday life. A great performance on stage does not necessarily mean a great performance while grocery shopping, or walking the dog, or going to a party. But humans are often victims of inflating their own self-importance, which then leads to bad labels. An example would be the movie star that cuts to the front of the line in a coffee shop, or the football star that drives their new Ferrari 100 mph on the freeway, or the rock star that trashes their hotel room.

Fortunately, most of the performers I work with aren't like this. I do count on them having a little bit of "performer's ego" because I want them to have the confidence to get the job done. When a non-talent person gets behind the microphone, they will usually lack self-confidence in their first try. But a professional will itch to get in the studio so that they can perform. Many get a "high" from performing, even for a dinky local radio spot. As a musician, I get this feeling as well because I enjoy the experience of playing. When I'm performing, I'm not thinking, "Wow, I'm going to knock their socks off with this solo." I'm usually in the moment, enjoying myself making music and sharing it with the audience. Most of the pros you will work with have this same kind of ego, and that's good.

Watch any sports game and you'll see a player's ego come out when they score. An athlete with a healthy ego will high-five teammates, while an athlete with an unhealthy ego will taunt the poor fool they just dunked on. As a director/engineer, it's your job to nurture a performer's healthy ego. Congratulate them when they do something well. If they flub up, encourage them to work out the issue so they can score. Some need more encouragement than others, but everybody likes a thumbs up for an accomplishment.

Let's look at how to handle those with a larger-than-life ego. Many times, a performer that walks in the door with a big ego (attitude) at least has a foundation for having that inflated ego – they're actually good at what they do. They've maybe received many awards, been swarmed by fans at airports, and travel with a posse. I think many fall into this trap because it's really hard to see themselves from the outside of their bubble of daily life. Stardom may not have been something they sought, but they're probably quite happy with it now that they have it. When they come into your studio with an attitude, you just have to deal with it.

The key to working with someone with a big ego is to focus on the working relationship. If they're a big movie star, they probably made it because they worked very, very hard to hone their skill. You might have to stroke their ego from time-to-time during the session ("Wow, that was fantastic." "You nailed it, you're a pro."), but try to sound sincere. Try not to overdo it because most of us can easily detect B.S. For most of the recording session however, you should be able to just enjoy working with a professional. You're a professional too, so if you keep it business-like, you'll usually get some respect back. I've worked with many egotistical professionals that were ace-in-the-hole performers, so my "working" relationship with them was fantastic. Would I like to invite them over to my house for drinks? No. But I don't do that with most of clients anyway, even the ones I love.

Working with a professional, especially an accomplished one, can be intimidating. It's okay to be a little nervous, but remember the old saying: *They put their pants on just like everyone else.* In the previous chapter on working with producers and directors (see page 269), I said that someone once told me to "Trust the actor." This is so true with an experienced performer. You should just stay out of the way when they're doing their thing, only interjecting something when you can truly help. These are usually technical tips, such as "You popped your P on that line," or "Move a little back from the mic, please." When doing ADR   (dialog replacement, see page 58), I might comment if the performance was in sync with the old dialog. But I mostly just make sure that I'm recording everything properly. I kind of look at it this way: I've painted a lot of walls. I've owned houses, worked handyman jobs when I was young and broke, and maintained my sister's rental property for a while. I've gone through tanker trucks of paint and consider myself a decent painter. If I showed up to paint someone's living room because they wanted a professional to paint it, I think I would be majorly distracted if the homeowner told me how to hold the roller, which way to roll, how to cut in the woodwork, or how to clean my brushes. In fact, I'd probably get a little bit snippy with them after a while. So, when a real pro is behind the mic, let them paint the walls their way. You might have to point out a missed spot or a drip after they're done, but the walls will probably look terrific because you let them just paint.

Here's a real-world example of letting a performer find their own way. I have worked a considerable amount with the famous actor William Shatner, who is best known for his role as Captain James T. Kirk in the *Star Trek* franchise. For five years I recorded his voice-over for a CBS television show called *Rescue 911*. This was a weekly show that recreated tense situations that were called into 911 emergency centers around the country. Shatner, who was also a producer on the show, was directed via phone from Los Angeles when he was in my studio here in Central Kentucky (Shatner is an avid equestrian and owns a horse farm near Lexington, Kentucky).

If there's one thing I learned about Shatner's working method, it's that he will almost always find the right read by himself. He's one of the best self-directing voice-over actors I've ever worked with. He would start off by reading a line, such as "A call came in at 4:32 AM." He would then re-read it several more times, each with different intensity and timing. Finally, he would land on the perfect one, and then move on to the next line. You could watch his actor gears turning as he found the truth in the line. Fast-forward a decade or so later when I was working on a short film for The Kentucky Horse Park's visitor center, an equestrian park and museum here in Lexington. The film *Rein of Nobility* traces the heritage of man's interactions with the horse through time. Shatner was asked to do the voice-over because of his close ties to Kentucky and the equestrian community.

He came into the studio with script in hand and took a look at a rough edit of the film. The only direction I gave him was to describe the kind of music that would be under his narration. He read through the entire script once, sometimes restarting on a few sentences. I made some notes of places that I thought needed some different emphasis. He read through a second time, this time more smoothly and, as if reading my mind, giving different reads in most of those areas that needed something different. The third time through was pure magic. He nailed the remaining areas I had noted but gave everything some extra juice that only an experienced voice actor and a horse lover could give. There was no direction I, or anybody else in the room, could have given that would have yielded the same results. I think if I had directed him in any way, it would have interrupted his train of thought and produced a more mechanical read.

There are outtake reels all over the internet of William Shatner berating some poor director that tried to get him to read something another way. They're hilarious but quite intimidating to hear. I wasn't there during any of them, but I suspect he was just toying with them. I think if you hire someone of the caliber of William Shatner, you're not hiring someone that will ape your instructions, but someone that will bring their style of voice acting to the project. Asking them to step out of that style that they've worked so hard to perfect is only asking for trouble, especially if the direction is uninformed or naive. In all the times I worked with him I never witnessed him teeing off on any director, probably because everybody understood that they were getting exactly who they hired – William Shatner.

Another example of letting the actor find their way is a session I had with Sam Shepard, the late playwright and actor. Sam Shepard also lived on a farm in Central Kentucky, so he was often in my studio for ADR and voice-overs. On this particular job, he was doing some voice-over for a new cell phone company (actually a merger between two regional carriers). Surprisingly, it was his first commercial voice-over he had ever done. He was a little flustered because he had only received the scripts the night before, which in the commercial world is pretty timely! But for a stage and screen actor, it's the last minute. I understood his concern, as it was not his usual way of preparing for a performance. When he came in, he watched the TV spots that had scratch tracks and music so he could get an idea of what the final commercials would look and sound like. The director was in a New York studio that was connected via ISDN (see page 92). Before Sam read a single line, they discussed the script for nearly 45 minutes. When the time came to record, he sat there for about 30 seconds of silence, then began. It was quite soft, but very emotive. I had recorded him several times before, so I knew that I had to raise the trim (See **Tech Tip** below) on the mic channel a little more to capture his whispering tones. He continued, as if describing the inner thoughts of someone walking through a very cinematic cityscape, fantastical lights arcing through the sky, cell phones magically beaming visible data clouds to other cell phones around the world. I shivered and got chill bumps 30 seconds later. And this was a cell phone spot. Of course, the director tried "directing" him after that. I was thinking, "This is friggin' Sam Shepard, and he just handed you the performance of the year. WHY?" They debated a little bit over word usage here and there, but Sam was able to give the same performance a few more times before moving on to the next spot. I know that I would never have been able to get that kind of performance out of someone with his experience if I had tried to mold and shape it from the beginning, it would have turned out sounding very mechanical. In fact, I could have never envisioned the performance he gave. Trust the actor.

Tech Tip

On an analog input channel of a mixer (even digital boards), the first control that an analog signal hits in the audio chain is the "trim." This is a course adjustment of the signal before it goes to other parts of the input channel, like equalization, pan, and the fader. Any analog microphone or analog line source will go through a trim pot ("pot" is a nickname for potentiometer, a variable resistor). Some mixers have one trim for both types of input sources (line and mic). Confusingly, these would range from about 0 to -60 dB, or very low signal (mics) to very loud (line).

These examples are of actors that are asked to perform voice-overs. I have a great example of working with a revered professional narrator. The late Peter Thomas was best known for being the voice of *Nova* (PBS) and *Forensic Files* (TruTV/TLC). Peter, the child of British parents, was born in Florida. His father was a minister and his mother was a schoolteacher. Peter said that throughout his childhood they stressed education and memorization. Every Sunday the family would all read bible passages aloud. Peter's father instructed him to keep a picture in his mind of what the passage was about when he was reading. If it was Heaven, he would picture one of those bucolic paintings in a bible. If it was a horse, he would keep that picture of a horse in his thoughts. This is a technique I still use when directing talent (and especially non-talent).

I was lucky that a local producer hired him for several projects. Most of these were in Peter's later years, but even when he was in his 70s and 80s, he sounded young. Like all professional narrators, Peter could reproduce a given style at any moment. For one particularly complicated project (a 2-hour documentary), we had him in a studio four different times over several months. I would play him a section where there was a change, and then he would reproduce it with exactly the same tone. It was remarkable how he knew exactly where to put his inflections and timbre, months later. Peter was very directable, but like all professionals, we would let him read a few paragraphs to see if it was what the client was looking for. I didn't like to interrupt him if I heard a mistake, because I knew I could later go back and do a pick-up. And many times he would want to re-read everything again with a different approach, usually besting his previous takes once he fully understood the project's message. This is another reason why you give professionals the space they need to find the delivery on their own – they'll usually pick the right colors to paint your room.

Tech Tip

When recording narration (or music), a pick-up is when you have the artist go back into the script and re-read a sentence, phrase, or word (or play a phrase or measure again). You would then insert edit this new take into an existing take. It helps to play back that section to the talent so that they can match the tone and delivery.

If you're working with unfamiliar actors or narrators, it's often a good idea to ask them how you can better communicate with them. This can happen before, during, and/or after the session, but it's a great way to establish a rapport with someone you might work with again. One local actor I often work with prefers that I interrupt him when I hear a mistake if we're recording audiobooks. He'd rather go back to the start of a sentence while it's fresh in his mind than to try and recreate it later during a pickup. Other actors may not want to be interrupted during a take, so it's good practice to neutralize any frustrations by asking them their preference before starting into a long recording project. Professional narrators aren't too picky as a rule because they've worked with all types of directors and producers and are usually quick to adapt.

You can also learn from actors and narrators about their craft by asking them for advice on how to better direct and communicate others. Most will freely help you understand the business from their side of the glass. Because I'm not an actor or narrator, I can only scratch the surface of understanding what they're thinking when performing, so any tips I can learn from them will only make me a better director.

One example of what you can ask is how an actor successfully transitioned from stage to studio. You will often be working with actors who only know how to project their voice on stage, so they may find it difficult to speak intimately into a studio microphone. Another example is asking an accomplished studio musician how they can play with the energy of a live performance in a dry and lonely recording studio. Many first-time studio musicians have only played live and may hold back their performance when they're wearing headphones and standing still in front of a microphone. When I ask these pros for advice, I usually explain that first, I want to have a better understanding of how they work. I then tell them that I want to be able to help other people in their profession, especially newcomers, in the studio (or on stage, the film set, etc.). The more you know, the more you can help performers reach their highest level.

The Famous and Not-So-Famous

I want to touch on how to deal with celebrities. Whether it's a local politician or athlete, or an internationally famous actor or musician, you will more than likely get to work with someone of notoriety. The recording, live sound, and broadcast business is a tool for businesses, organizations, entertainers, and others to push their message or product out to the public. Unlike a grocery store, which is for everyone, a recording studio is a magnet for movers and shakers. It's sort of like a limousine service which helps people get from point A to B in style. If you think of yourself as a limo driver – taking gentle turns and avoiding potholes while helping your passenger get to their destination – then you'll be a success. What you can't do is act like a fanboy/fangirl and ask for an autograph. This immediately kicks you out of the professional zone and knocks you several steps down the respect ladder.

When meeting a celebrity that you really admire, you are allowed to tell them how much you admire and enjoy their work/play/music. You are not allowed to ask them juicy questions about their life or ask them to spill the beans about a yet-to-be-released movie or album. Do not take a picture of them or post on social media during the session.[67] You can ask for a photo afterwards if they seem amenable. Even though it's assumed you'll be posting it to the world to see, show them the courtesy of asking permission to publish that photo on the internet.[68] You are allowed to ask them about their day or their experience in your city. You can even talk about a common interest, such as horse racing or art, but stay away from politics and religion, even if it's the POTUS or the Pope. This person is a working professional and is in your studio because you're a working professional. In fact, it's your job to give them a professional place to work while protecting them from fans and curiosity seekers.

Professional Tip

Many high-profile projects require you to sign a non-disclosure agreement (NDA) that prohibits you from divulging any information about the project until its public release. This includes photos, social media, etc. This is serious business and can land you in hot water, even if you tell your family about it in some instances. Many producers can't risk any information leaking out that might result in industrial sabotage or spying. I am still under a few NDAs

---

[67] See Professional Tip

[68] Or better yet don't bother them with those details, ask the producer or publicist. They are the ones who know all the legal fine print even if the celebrity may not have objections.

at the time of this writing that I would just love to tell the world about, but can't.

Here's a real-world "fan" experience that happened to me. Whenever we were recording William Shatner for *Rescue 911*, we made it a rule to never let anybody in the building know that he was coming. Only until about 15 minutes before his appointment would I inform the front desk attendant to expect him. I couldn't risk having his professional life interrupted by autograph seekers because it might have affected his performance (though I'm guessing that someone of his experience is used to it). I also practiced this same rule when other celebrities of note would come to my studio.

One day his publicist called me to let us know that a reporter and photographer from *People* magazine would be following him around during our next recording session. They were working on a story about his life as an equestrian, his life in Kentucky, and how he managed to have success in both the show ring and on screen. We were thrilled to help and looked forward to the publicity. When the article published a few months later, our studio was mentioned in the first sentence. Wow, we thought, that's great PR. Little did we know what was about to hit us.

Fans of Shatner began directing all their fan mail to our business. We would have to periodically pack up boxes of letters and send to Shatner's agent in Los Angeles. Our poor receptionist was fielding dozens of calls for Shatner fans each day for several weeks. They continued for months afterwards. The creepy ones came too, some to the studio itself. They wanted to talk with Shatner personally. "Well, he doesn't work here." Some wouldn't take no for an answer. One woman would persistently camp out on the front steps and deposit love letters at the front desk. We were eventually able to track down where she was staying (in a halfway house for mental health patients) and get her additional help. The fan letters eventually trickled to a stop years later. I really started to feel for some of these famous people and how much they must deal with. We had only experienced a sliver of what fame can bring.

When working with a celebrity, remember that they are people first, professionals next, and stars last. There is no denying that most of them live in a different world than we do, so finding some common ground for conversation can be challenging sometimes. But I find most celebrities to be genuine and real, almost all of them treat me with respect, and are very easy to talk to. People in the spotlight are real humans out of the spotlight.

I'm not intending to name drop here, but let me give some instances of those that I have had some great casual conversations with: Former Arkansas Governor and presidential candidate Mike Huckabee (He told me he had political and broadcasting experience, as if I didn't know who he was. He was very disarming.); Playwright/actor Sam Shepard (He thumbed through a Rolling Stones photo book I had in the studio while remarking that he was present when some of the photos were taken. I also taught him how to use an iPhone.); Actor William Shatner (So many good conversations with him. I also once took a half hour walk with him to a nearby park.); Actor Malcom McDowell (who is so down to earth, even though he got texts from Bernadette Peters when we were talking. Our shared experiences with William Shatner also came up – who knew I had something in common with a star?); Actor Kevin Pollack (who is so funny in real life and has such a dry wit. I amazed him by having him talk into a paper plate to simulate his character wearing a mask.); SNL alum and comedian Chris Redd (a very humble man. I also watched him write funny lyrics and recorded him rapping them for two SNL digital shorts – I was rolling in the floor laughing.); Actor Steve Zahn (who has been in my studio frequently over the last dozen years, we've since become good friends. In Kentucky, he's just a local farm owner who happens to be an actor.).

There are so many more great times I've had with people who could have been snippy and demanding because of their status. I've had only a handful of negative experiences with famous people. I've actually had more less-than-pleasant experiences with regular Janes and Joes. I guess the humble meter is pointing towards the celebrities on this one.

The studio business also attracts those that want to be famous. A very tiny fraction of these are people with mental health issues who see your studio as a beacon, but most are people who just want to get a foot in the door. I help when I can, but unless they have the budget and I have the time, I can't go out of my way for everyone who calls and wants to be a star. The most common request I get is from someone who has been told they have a great voice and should be recording commercials. My first question is always, "Do YOU want to record commercials? Are you passionate about learning how to? Are you willing to put in all the hard work?" If I get a lukewarm response, then I assume they think that all there is to it is to stand in front of a microphone and press a magic button to become a professional. I go through the regular routine of outlining all the training and repetition that goes into becoming a professional narrator. I also point out that having a great set of pipes (industry lingo for a deep voice) does not guarantee success. In fact, most successful narrators don't have that deep voice like James Earl Jones. Most are average sounding but have a great persuasive and believable delivery. That's where the money is.

I also get requests from musicians and song writers, but I just forward them to other studios in town that specialize in music. A business like mine can't really thrust a person into fame if that person doesn't have talent and is willing to put in the hard work to get there. I'm not even in the business of advancing someone's career, I've got enough to worry about with my own! That's what talent agencies are for. I have had several children into the studio to record demos for movie, TV, and Broadway auditions. Some of them were actually pretty good (and one I knew made it and is still headlining on Broadway years later), but one unfortunate story I was part of is a cautionary tale.

We were producing a project that required several children to come in and play some small voice acting parts that were a couple of minutes each, but required basic acting skills. You can get a real mixed bag when it comes to child actors, but at least these kids had some experience on the local stage. And, just like I thought, some were great, most were good, and a few were just okay. The kid I'm talking about in this story was part of the latter. I think some of his performance was muted by his shyness, and some from lack of experience. When I'm working with kids, I try to make it a fun experience. I don't want any negativity in my studio during the session, so that anyone with shaky nerves can relax a little when they see that we're not all serious-like. I liked this kid and got the impression that he was probably in the theater for a new experience. Maybe his friends were in it, maybe his parents nudged him into it, I don't know. My daughter kind of accidently fell into several theater classes in school before realizing she didn't like it, so maybe this was the case here.

Well, we finished the project and this kid's part worked out okay. Not to sound harsh here, but it only worked because his lines were surrounded by better performances that masked his mediocre one. His mother contacted me and wanted a copy of the project, which is very common for proud parents. A month later, she had uprooted her son, left her husband, and was in Los Angeles carting him around to any audition she could get him in. She thought he was going to be a star (maybe he is, I don't remember his name), but I really think she was looking for an excuse to escape her marriage. It's so sad when the children are used as tools in failed relationships.

Tips on getting the best performance from your talent

<u>Space and time</u>. Give your talent the space and time they need to get the maximum performance. Some actors and narrators need a few moments of silence before they begin reading, others just jump right in. Some like the lights dimmed a little for mood. Some people stand while reading or performing, others sit. Some bring their own headphones, some take them off during a take. Everybody is different, so *you* must be flexible to *their* style. If you are, they will relax and be able to channel their energy towards creating a performance.

<u>Be prepared</u>. Talent (and your client as well) will feel confident if they see that you're prepared when they walk in the door. Have your DAW and backup recorders set and ready to go, test all your microphones and headphones, have bottled water in the studio, have the script or sheet music ready and on their music stand, and have any pre-existing audio or video cued up and ready. If there is anything that makes talent nervous, it's you bumbling around because you are either unprepared or don't know what you're doing. This will cause tension throughout the studio and compromise their performance. Know your tools, understand the project, and exude confidence when talent is behind the microphone.

<u>You do the walking, let them do the talking</u>. When your performer is behind the microphone, bring them more water or the

revised script. If their mic needs adjusted, jump up and do it for them. Keeping the talent behind the mic while you run back and forth is by design. When someone does any physical thing like walking, it takes several minutes for the body and mind to settle back down to the somewhat idle state they were in. By doing the physical things for them, you can get back to recording much more quickly instead of waiting for their heart rate to drop back down. This avoids breathy takes, extra and unneeded breaths, sweaty hands, stomach noises from jostling around, and other bodily noises that bust otherwise good takes.

H_20. Keep your performer well stocked with water. Only give a vocal performer room temperature water because cold water can instantly constrict their vocal cords. Avoid other liquids like soft drinks, coffee, tea, alcohol, and juices. These will gum up their mouth and throat with sugar. Caffeine and alcohol will constrict the vocal cords and affect the performance when the effects kick in. If a performer is having throat problems like phlegm or coughing, give them hot herbal tea (without sugar and caffeine!) or hot water with a squirt of lemon juice[69] or slice of lemon or lime (again no sugar). And after they take a drink, pause 10 seconds or so before recording. There is usually a gurgle in their upper throat as the air works its way up the esophagus.

An apple a day. Red apples are a great lubricant for dry mouth. If you're doing a lot of recording of vocal performances, keep a fruit bowl with red apples handy. Offer to slice them up for the performer if you hear a lot of mouth clicks and sticky-sounding phrases. Suggest they only eat the fruity part and not the skin (which can stick in their teeth and throat).

No lipstick. Many performers are wise to not wear lipstick or lip balms into the studio, but some forget. This is a recipe for clicks and scratchy phrasing that is difficult to filter out. Break the bad news that they need to wipe it off.

No jewelry. Any dangling jewelry can ruin a good take. Earrings, bracelets, necklaces, and other floppy pieces of jewelry

---

[69] This is not an endorsement, but the brand *Italia Gardens* that's found in supermarkets is the closest to tasting like fresh squeezed lemon and lime that I've tried.

must be removed. Sometimes big rings can cause problems if it hits the music stand when turning a page.

Cotton clothing please. Believe it or not, clothing noises from arm movements and other body expressions can ruin a good take. Rustles and scuffs are one of the most difficult sounds to get out of a recording, no matter what magic a piece of software can offer. If someone will be in the studio repeatedly (like reading an audiobook), have them bring a soft short-sleeve cotton tee shirt that they can change into every day. If this isn't possible, have them remove any outer clothing like a jacket or sweater before recording. If clothing is still making distracting sounds, have the talent sit still and hold their elbows out from their body as a reminder to not gesture. If someone is wearing a cap, be aware that the bill may hit the microphone or pop filter. Have them turn it around backwards or take it off to avoid busted takes.

More of me. If you have the ability, let the talent control their own headphone level. This can be as simple as an inline passive box with a volume knob that feeds their headphones, or as complicated as a multi-performer foldback system. Hint: the simpler the better. There are devices, such as from Rolls, that have a separate control for the mic and foldback levels. The unit taps off the microphone signal and blends it with whatever else you're feeding into their cans, like background music or talkback.

Pick me up. If you're doing pickups for narration or singing, have the performer start performing the previous half or whole sentence. For instance, if we are picking up the phrase "All the rewards points earned by our card holders can be redeemed for gift cards." Have them read the previous half sentence. This smooths the transition. It would sound something like, "...more than 24 million locations worldwide. All the rewards points earned..." This can also work for just restarting a long sentence or paragraph. Doing this accomplishes a few goals. First, it warms the voice up a little. Second, it keeps the voice from lurching on the first words you need ("All the rewards"). Instead, any lurching is done on "more than 24." The third thing it accomplishes is to put the narrator back into the frame of mind they were in when they originally read the passage. For a music performance, do a "punch in" (insert recording) at the place that needs re-recording, but start playing back the previous verse about 10 or 15 seconds before the punch-in point. Have them play or sing along with the old recording so that the new punch-in has the right flow and energy.

Tech Tip

A *punch-in* is a place in a recording that you insert a fragment of a new performance. For instance, let's say a whole song is recorded but the singer wants to re-cut the second verse. You would set <u>in</u> and <u>out</u> points on your DAW where you want to re-record. That would be the start (<u>in</u> point) of verse two and end (<u>out</u> point) of verse two. Most DAWs have a special recording mode that automatically pre-rolls before the <u>in</u> point (that 10 or 15 seconds I was talking about). When it reaches the <u>in</u> point, it automatically records to any tracks that are armed for recording. It will stop recording at the <u>end</u> point, or when you hit STOP. Most DAWs let you keep all the old takes and decide later which ones to use.

<u>Warm me up</u>. Like reading part of the previous sentence during pickups, a narrator can also pre-read something before the actual script. This might be a simple "Three, two, one..." It can also be a phrase that will help them get into a certain mindset. For instance, the script might start out with "Show everybody how much of a Tigers fan you are with a Tigers credit card from XYZ Bank." The talent might get pepped up by saying, "You are the biggest Tigers fan in the land. Show everybody how much of a..." You can edit out the first adlibbed sentence and just start with "Show everybody..." This works as well with novice readers as with seasoned professionals. It can also help singers get into a certain attitude if they tell themselves aloud that they're this kind of so-and-so, or say the first words of the chorus. Anything that helps the mind connect with the mouth from the onset will yield a better performance.

<u>Pitch perfect</u>. Stage actors are sometimes trained to find the natural pitch of their voice, and then deliver most of their lines a half-step up from that. This can also work with voice acting and narration. Professional singers will usually know the natural key of their voice, but it's a novel concept for non-singers. You can try this yourself: start saying lah-lah-lah aloud. Relax as you're saying it over and over, and let your voice fall into the most comfortable

pitch. There should be no strain as you fall into an almost singing tone. Now, hold that note and find it on a piano or other instrument. Or if none is available, record it and use software (such as an audio file statistics command in a DAW, or a tuning app on your smartphone) to find the key. Next, make your voice go up a half step (such as from a C to a C#). This is your narration or voice acting key. Note how your throat feels when you sing a sustained note in this new key. You might feel a slight strain, but with practice you'll be able to land on that note easily. Why all this lah-lah-lah-ing for your natural pitch? When a voice actor/narrator wants to make emphasis, they will either pitch their voice up or down. There are usually more musical notes, or steps, above the natural pitch than below. It's easier to pitch up (like a question) than to pitch down (like a somber phrase). By finding a pitch a half step above the natural one, you can cheat when you have to hit those low tones because you've gained a half step. It really does work, and if a talent is having trouble hitting those low notes/tones, teach them this trick.

Pitch not perfect. Sometimes a narrator/voice actor will try to force their voice too low, leaving no room for emphasis. You'd think it were only male narrators trying to sound like Darth Vader, but many females do it too. I usually point out their tone and ask them to start out pitched up higher. If they insist on staying in that range, then try to get them to push more breath through the phrasing so that the voice doesn't crack or fizzle out at the ends of phrases.

Soft serve. Sometimes the talent isn't loud enough. In this case ask them to read or sing louder. If they are still holding back, it might be their headphone level. Lower it by about 20-30% so that they have to talk louder and project to hear themselves. The opposite can happen as well. A very loud person can blow your mic out, so after you've trimmed down the gain and perhaps moved the microphone back, you can try slightly increasing their headphone level. This sometimes works, but if it doesn't, you'll just have to either go with what you get or put in the extra work and help them to tone down their volume. You can often trace the origins of why they are loud speakers down to their experience, such as on stage, sports, workplace, or hearing difficulties.

Say cheese. In the chapter on working with producers and directors (see page 270), I pointed out that smiling changes the embouchure of the mouth so they we "hear" the smile. If you're working on a script (or a song) that needs a little brightness, have the talent smile. Even if it's too much during the first take, it will imprint that tone in the reader's mind. Unless they're directed otherwise, they will reference this tone in the following takes. It's harder to pull somebody's energy back than to try to forcefully pull it up.

<u>Sisyphean effort</u> King Sisyphus of Greek mythology was punished for eternity and forced to continually roll a large boulder all the way up a hill, only to have it roll back down. This is what I feel like sometimes when trying to get talent to give me more energy, urging a voice actor to put more juice into a character, or getting a singer to belt it out. I find it easier to have the talent go overboard with their delivery. I'd rather pull the energy back than push it up. I usually tell them to overdo it so much that they want to puke. We can then pick out what we liked about the over-the-top performance and build on that. When they've already hit the top (the pukey performance), then they know what their limits are. An analogy you can use with them is that they're seeing how high they can rev the engine before hitting the racetrack. This also works well when trying to read or sing very quickly. Many advertising scripts have too many words for the allowed length. It's not unusual to have a script time out at 35 or 40 seconds when it needs to be 30 seconds. I have the talent read it over a few times, each time quicker. I then have them read it at breakneck speed. We then back off this pace a tick to get the fastest, discernable read possible before we consider cutting words out.

<u>Not slow enough</u>. Sometimes we need to slow performances way down. Either there aren't enough words, the talent is too hyped, or the tempo is slower than they are accustomed to. I try to help them find a tempo to perform at, even if it's a narrator reading words. I also try to have them read punctuation, such as commas and periods. Too often people see the words on a page, know what's coming up, and speed right through natural pauses. If you get them to read punctuation but still can't get their tempo down, tell them that if they think they're going too slow, they're not going slow enough. Have them turn the script over and try to read the script from memory. This will force them to slow down and think about the words and what they mean. After they've taken a few stabs at it this way, turn the page back over and try again. Your

main goal is to get their mind and mouth to feel what it's like to say the words at that slower tempo, like a full dress rehearsal before the big event. For musicians, those that play a lot of live gigs may feel compelled to play too fast in the studio. The bright lights and energetic crowd will often hype a band up and increase the tempo. If this continues to be a problem (and they're not playing to a click track), have them play the song at half-speed to break the fast tempo, then go for a normal take. You never know, they might like the half-speed version better!

Push, push, push. Another irksome thing narrators and singers might do is fade away at the end of a sentence or phrase. This is especially true with narrators because they are reading ahead with their eyes (musicians do this too, so this also applies to them). When they approach the end of a sentence, they are already looking ahead to the start of the next one, thinking about how to deliver it. They will often trail off at the end of the sentence, losing volume, losing air, and even speeding it up. I will point this out by joking that the poor end of the sentence isn't getting any love. One way to help them to read a sentence ending correctly is to insert a pause or breath before the last few words. You can always tighten it up in edit later, but it usually makes them instantly aware of the fault and will usually be less of a problem after that. For singers, it might be a case of breath control, or lack thereof. Look at their phrasing and where they are taking breaths. Work out a breath scheme with them and have them mark the music where they need to breathe. As an exercise, have them hold out the very last note until the downbeat of the next measure, even if it's not musically correct. Again, get them used to doing it correctly so that it is imprinted on the mind.

Breathe in, breathe out. Breath control is a huge issue for most singers and narrators starting out. I even see breath control issues in seasoned professionals. When I played trombone in music school, there was so much emphasis on where to breathe when playing, that I would catch myself holding and timing my breaths as I was walking to class. We had to work out measure by measure where we were going to breathe. One bad breath in the middle of a phrase can ruin a song, so I didn't want to be the one that stopped the show. Many professional narrators and musicians know exactly where they're going to breathe because they've gone through the script or sheet music ahead of time and put in breath marks (usually

' for a quick breath and | for a big breath). These are usually at natural phrases or groups of words, or in music after several measures or during a rest. You don't want your performer running out of breath before the end of a phrase, so help them by going through breath points with them (some may be new to this). *How* to breathe is a whole chapter, but taking a big deep breath like you're about to blow out birthday candles is not the right way. Neither is a shallow lapdog-type breath. Singers, wind instrumentalists, actors, and narrators learn to expand their throat and diaphragm to quickly inhale a large quantity of air, kind of like a giant gaping sinkhole suddenly opening up and swallowing cars in a parking lot. They then slow down the exhalation by exerting reverse pressure on the diaphragm so that a steady and constant flow of air passes over their tongue and out the mouth. They keep their upper pallet in the mouth loose, being sure to not clamp down (clamping down on the upper pallet will make you sound like Jerry Lewis in a comedy). It's similar to slowly letting air out of a balloon so that it squeaks in a perfect musical tone. If you're working with an open-minded singer or narrator who is willing to learn, you can introduce them to this technique so that they can practice it on their own. It won't happen overnight though, it's a skill that requires practice.

Perfect practice makes perfect. That was the phrase my music teachers always preferred over the "practice makes perfect" version. Don't practice at 90% and hope that it will be perfect in the performance. Get it right before you step onto stage. If your talent is having trouble with a passage, have them work it out word by word, or even syllable by syllable. I will actually practice it with them myself. When I can say it perfectly, then I can show them the steps I took to get it right. If a narrator is reading a particularly tough script that has a lot of unfamiliar jargon or hard to pronounce technical words, I will repeat the hard phrase over and over again, feeling how my tongue and mouth feel when doing it slowly. I then gradually speed up until it's smooth. If it's a particularly tough word, I'll count the syllables. As I rehearse that word, I count the syllables off on my fingers and note which ones get emphasis. I then relate this to the talent and let them work through it.

A little alliteration in the narration. Alliteration is when the same syllable or sound is repeated in an adjacent or nearby word.

"Sally's sassafras smells sweet." has the Ss packed together. Try reading that aloud quickly and make each word succinct and separate. It's very difficult. Alliteration is often overlooked by script writers if they haven't read the words aloud or written much for narration. If the script can be changed, I petition for this with the director/producer. If it's an audiobook or other script that can't be altered, then we must leave the words as they are and just work out the phrase in the recording session.

A little music please. Some voice-over artists want music in their headphones when they read. This is a perfectly acceptable and common practice. It can really help them get the right feel and delivery in most cases. It doesn't have to be the same music that will be in the final mix, but it should have the same feel as the final cut. You can also get a particularly unique read from someone by playing off-the-wall music into their cans as they perform, such as *Superman* music if you want a "heroic" read, or *Loony Tunes* music if you want a comical tone. Don't be afraid to be creative and go for something out of left field if you think it will drive the read to a different and wonderful place. Be sure that the music you're feeding into the headphones isn't so loud that it bleeds into the recording, and make sure that the music itself doesn't get recorded onto the same audio track as the voice. For music performers, a different mix of the instruments may help them find the beat or key a lot easier.

Put a singer in their place. When a singer (and even an instrumentalist) is cutting their part, throw a little reverb into their headphones. It doesn't have to be a lot, or even the same type of reverb that will be in the final mix, but it usually keeps them from sounding so dry to themselves when they are performing. Be sure that the reverb ONLY goes to their headphones and doesn't get mixed into the actual recording. You can add that later when you mix.

Reading lines. If your voice actor is recording solo, but they are reading parts that will be cut to other actor reads, jump in and read the other actor parts to them. For instance, the script has Tom and Jerry having a conversation. Your talent is playing Jerry, you will read Tom's line, then Jerry will respond. This gives the actor something to play against instead of a cold, dead read of just their lines. It's helpful if you try to put a little emotion into Tom's lines so your actor can react properly. You don't have to try and win an Oscar, but you should give it some genuine effort.

Not reading lines. If a voice actor or narrator is having trouble reading a script or part to the director's wishes, try to avoid reading the line to them. I try every which but Sunday to avoid reading it the way we want to hear it because I feel that the actor/narrator must find their way to it on their own. Try explaining the feeling or emotion behind it, detail any phrasing or pausing, or give them a reference to a situation or other character. One of the few exceptions is if they're mispronouncing something or are putting the wrong emphasis on a syllable of a word. Only when you've exhausted every effort should you attempt a line read. If that time comes, I usually ask, "Do you mind if I read it in the style we're looking for?" Some actors will get a little snooty about a line read, but your main reason for avoiding it all together is for the part to come out organically, not to spare their feelings. If the actor arrives at the correct read on their own, then it can be repeated with ease if there are additional takes. Sometimes an actor either has a mental block, or is incapable of reaching that level of acting, the script is bad, or the direction is unclear. I usually point the finger at my own directing skills and strive to find yet another way to help them understand the script before reading a line to an actor.

Changing lines. Of the thousands of sessions I've recorded, there is only a small percentage of times that we <u>haven't</u> changed the script or wording in some way. Even the best script writer in the world can't anticipate how nuanced the words on a page will be once they're read aloud. We mainly write for the eyes. The eyes scan ahead, scan back to a previous phrase, leap back ahead, and move all over the page. Human speech, however, flows in one direction. The cadence of speech is vastly different from the cadence of printed text. We often speak in incomplete sentences. Our listeners can usually infer our meaning quickly, even before we've finished speaking a thought. Our eyes read text at about 200-250 words per minute. We speak at about 125-175 words per minute. There's a lot of wasted time listening to someone complete a sentence when we might know how it ends. With that in mind, we can often reparse and trim a script down to fewer words without losing the meaning. If the script is part of a video, sometimes what's on screen can explain a concept better than words. The narrator can often add some emotion or intonation in their voice that can take the place of several descriptive words. So, when you're working on a script (or song melody) that is not fitting in the time you need, consider cutting it down. I'll at least get a few good takes with the script as is, but then I'll confer with the director/producer on trimming the copy down. You will occasionally run into a writer that doesn't want a single word changed, but most are very amenable to editing the script because as they say, less is more. An adage I often refer to is "No one will ever know what was taken out, only what was left in." When editing scripts for clarity, we might also change text if a writer has repeated a word or phrase too often, made an unclear reference, or there is a phrase or reference that might not be correct. You'll have to approach any director/producer/writer carefully at first, because as I've preached on and on about, you don't know the big picture. An unintimidating approach I often use is something like, "Can I make a suggestion on a copy change that might help?" They can always say no.

Changing Places. If you have two performers reading a script, playing character parts, or even recording music, have them switch roles to get some interesting results. Let's say we have two voice actors performing at the same time. Go ahead and get as many takes as possible so that it sounds as close to perfect as you can get. Next, have them switch roles (if appropriate). They've heard the other actor work their lines in the first iteration, now they intimately know both characters instead of just one. They will often have better timing, reactions, and a smoother and more natural delivery on the switcheroo version. This can also work with musicians. It may sound kooky, but have musicians switch instruments or singers trade parts. This may not be the final take, but it will often lead to more cohesion in the music once players experience a song from the other side of the fence.

17. WORKING FOR YOURSELF

"Self-employed means you work 12 hours a day for yourself so you don't have to work 8 hours a day for someone else."

Oliver Markus Malloy

Striking out on your own and starting a business is a dream many have. But it's not for the faint of heart. Outside of parenting, it's the hardest job I've ever had. It's also the most rewarding job I've ever had. And it is a J-O-B. It's also an investment – in yourself. I was talking to a group of college undergraduates about my industry, and one eager student asked if running my own business was making me rich. I laughed and said, "I'm only getting rich off the experiences." That was something most of them didn't want to hear. I went on, "Don't get into business to get rich, do it as an investment." If you happen to get rich, then kudos to you. But the reality is you're scraping by one day and rolling in dough the next. It will then cycle back around, over and over again. Sounds like a rollercoaster, doesn't it? It can be at times. But I can't imagine doing this any other way. Why did I go into business? A little bit for the earning potential not found while working for someone else, but mostly for the freedom to walk my own path and work on projects that I was interested in.

When I started to seriously think about going out on my own, I was reacting more to roadblocks in my career path than the money part. My first pangs of entrepreneurship came while I was in my 30s. I had been working in the audio production industry for nearly ten years and started to feel constrained by the company I was working for. I felt that our department needed to branch out in a few different directions in order to grow. I could see other studios taking bold steps in marketing and offering advanced services that took advantage of the relatively new digital production tools. However, management didn't understand what we did and turned down every request to grow. We were "smoke and mirrors" and were the "creative" kind. That didn't mesh well with no-

nonsense bean counters and golf-playing salespeople. At least that's the way I saw it from the bottom of the totem pole.

There was a grain of truth to my naïve observations of managers that were responsible for keeping a big company afloat. Audio engineers were outliers in a sea of practical workers. Everybody understood accounting, sales, and printing presses, but pushing buttons and making sound was very foreign. But we were part of a symbiotic relationship with other departments: They sold corporate sponsorships,[70] and the printing, broadcast, and audio/visual divisions fulfilled the contracts with magazines, game programs, sports radio broadcasts, television shows, and commercials among other things.

When I took over the audio production studios, our division was losing money. Management wasn't concerned because we were a fulfillment department. Working for outside clients wasn't frowned upon, but it was discouraged if it interfered with contract work. Fair enough. Just before I took over, the studios were one of the area's best kept secrets because they didn't market themselves. One company kept bugging the studio manager to record at the facility because of the great engineers and gear. He finally relented and began producing commercials for a regional restaurant chain. When they started to expand one of their spin-offs nationally, they produced all their marketing and advertising at the studio for several years. That company eventually moved the corporate offices – and the production work – to New York City. Today, Long John Silvers has more than 600 locations and 10,000 employees. Our studios went on to regularly produce advertising campaigns for various national brands such as Fazoli's, Po' Folks, Valvoline, Valvoline Instant Oil Change, SuperAmerica, and others during my time managing them. At the peak of our production, we had increased our revenue 4,400% since I took over, of which 66% was from outside clients. We were a self-sustaining department that could theoretically lose all internal business and still make a profit. Then management began

---

[70] One major client was the NCAA. Our company coined the phrase "An official corporate sponsor of..." for the NCAA basketball, baseball, and football championships. This sales tactic also filtered down to individual university sports programs that we managed the rights to.

company-wide layoffs, including my department. That's when I decided it was time to go.

I had been planning my exit well before this point. I had seen the company going in several different directions for a while, many of them dead ends, which is not good for a business. I had started to talk with a fellow worker about starting our own company together. Though it didn't get off the ground, both of us learned a lot about starting a business when we took advantage of classes and mentoring offered by the SBA (Small Business Administration), and SCORE (Service Corps of Retired Executives).[71] I can't recommend either of these sources enough. I had much more clarity about running a business after my experiences with the SBA and SCORE. My next attempt was a few years after this false start, and it also didn't work out when one of the potential partners withdrew after some family events tied up their finances. But I learned a lot during this rehearsal as well, which was how to write a business plan. Or rather how *not* to write one.

All the books will tell you that you need to write a business plan before going into business. If you were hoping I would tell you it wasn't necessary, then my apologies. I think it's vital. It forces you to think about every detail, good and bad, and to work yourself out of potential problems. I'm not going to bore you with tiny details about how to write a business plan, but I can offer some observations and things I learned while writing mine.

The first thing I learned from my initial attempt was that I was focusing too much on how the new business would look and market itself, instead of how it would survive from day to day. I was weak on the financial picture because I didn't know how to run a company, I knew how to run a department. The financial big picture of a company was cloudy and murky to me. The late Jack Welch, former CEO of General Electric, summed up one of the most important things I eventually learned about running a business: "Cash is king." It's one thing to have thousands of dollars in invoices due, it's another to have thousands of dollars in the bank. When preparing for my new business, I had to figure out how I would be paid and how I would pay my bills. If there was more

---

[71] http://www.sba.gov and http://www.score.org

cash going out than coming in, then I would have a big problem. So, I buckled down to write my next business plan.

I read a lot of books and talked with several people about how to accurately forecast sales and expenses. I had already been doing this as a department manager. But in my microcosm of a budget, I was tallying up existing contracts and year-over-year client growth patterns to predict revenue. My expenses were related to my department, not overall expenses an entire company must absorb like taxes, fees, rents, and other cash drainers that don't go away no matter how much or little cash you're bringing in.

Another thing I learned from studying how other people successfully started from ground up, is to be honest and practical with yourself about the finances. Don't sugar-coat the numbers and fool yourself into thinking everything will be rosy the first week, or month, or year.[72] I would be leaving a business that was already top shelf. I had to prepare as if my clients would not follow me to my new digs. I had to think my way around generating new business while continuing to pay out expenses. So, I turned a negative into a positive. Since my current company did not want to branch out, I saw that untapped business as mine for the taking. There was my first paycheck.

And speaking of paychecks, don't expect to earn any for the first six months. I might even double that time to a year if you're completely tapping a new market. Before you hang your own shingle, save up all you can, pay off anything you owe, and live on ramen and spaghetti for as long as you can. If you have the mindset that any money that comes into the business for the first six months (or whatever timeline is reasonable) is a re-investment, then it will be easier to swallow the sudden loss of income. You must have cash in the bank ahead of when any bills are due. A good rule of thumb for a small business is to have enough cash on hand for three months of expenses, that way you can ride the ups and downs of business and cash flow. But this isn't always practical, especially in the first few years of a new business.

---

[72] The Small Business Association says that of new businesses, "From 1994-2018, an average of 67.6% of new employer establishments survived at least two years. During the same period, the five-year survival rate was 48.8%, the ten-year survival rate was 33.6%, and the fifteen-year survival rate was 25.7%."

Unlike a full-time job with a steady paycheck, there is never a constant flow of money into your checking account when you're in business. There are always overdue invoices or unexpected expenses that threaten to stop the gears from turning. If you plan in advance, and perhaps pre-qualify for short-term bridge loans, you can borrow to manage expenses during slow times. It's not always a smooth ride, but if you're regularly working for clients and understand the cycles of your industry, you can ride it out until cash starts flowing again. In my neck of the woods, the "J" months (January, June, and July) are usually the slowest. These are also months that come around holidays, vacations, and cold or hot weather. In the winter, once kiddos get back in school and it starts to thaw, I'm back to cranking out projects. In the summer, August brings prep for school, football, basketball, corporate 4th quarters,[73] political season, and several holidays. By knowing these cycles, you can anticipate when business may pick up or slow down. During the J months, I often do studio upgrades, planning, vacations, or other things that allow me to pause and take a breath before jumping back onto the treadmill. We aren't machines, so look on those slow times as time to reset, instead of it being a catastrophe.

I also try to forecast at least three months ahead for a short-term picture of cash flow. I know my "monthly nut," that is a rough dollar figure of overhead and expenses that you <u>have</u> to pay each month, regardless of whether or not any cash is coming in. Sometimes my finger hovers over the panic button if I see more going out than coming in. This is when I start to take immediate action to either cut expenses (never easy), delay payments (never good), cut my paycheck (never say never), or rustle up some new business (always good!). I like to first start talking with clients about anything that might be coming up in the near future. Even just simple contact with someone may jog their brain into thinking about your studio and a project they might have in the hopper. I've also fired up some quick email/social campaigns to target some new business. I've visited music stores to hang up flyers for mastering and mixing services. I try to get a pulse of the market and where things are going.

---

[73] Many corporations, institutions, and associations begin their fiscal years on October 1, ending on September 30. Many scramble at the last minute to spend leftover dollars in their budgets so they will get the same of more to spend the next year.

As you can see, being in business for yourself is a major gut check. Are you able to handle the ups and downs? Commit yourself to a hundred bosses (your clients) instead of just one? Be willing to mop the floors, take out the trash, and do the accounting paperwork? Always be available 24/7? Sacrifice some of your personal life to make it work? As long as you know what you're getting yourself into, go for it. It's also like a very large puzzle you have to solve – every day. What worked today may change tomorrow. There are many events that you can't control, so you must be ready to change how you work very quickly. Companies that are nimble are usually successful.

Recently, we were going through our list of services and charges in preparation for a rate increase (a necessary evil). I was surprised how many services we no longer perform that were common just ten years ago. Of course, my basic services still exist, but if I were still hanging my hat on some of the more obsolete ones, I would no longer be in business. One example of being flexible was during the financial crisis of 2008. I immediately saw a complete drop off of discretionary spending, like music recording, documentaries, and analog tape and record digitizing. We also saw declines in some advertising and marketing, with the exception of larger companies. They decided to go full throttle. They knew that in order to capture enough business to make it through the rough period, they might also capture business away from the smaller fish that weren't marketing themselves. I've heard many times that when business slows, don't cut the advertising budget –double down on it.

During the crisis, our business shifted mainly to corporate marketing and e-learning projects. We produced no documentaries, once a staple, for almost three years. Nobody recorded audiobooks. Nobody called about recording music. Nobody dropped off any family cassettes to be restored. No one was spending money they didn't need to spend. I let our business follow the lead and invested my efforts into securing even more corporate and e-learning projects. I replaced all the lost discretionary income with even more marketing and advertising income. The funny thing is, my business grew like crazy during the crisis. I was even able to build new recording studios right in the middle of it all. Then, two-and-a-half years into the crisis, I got the most wonderful phone call: "How much is it to record a song?"

I remember jumping for joy and telling several people, "The economy is coming back!" A lot of them didn't believe me, but I've always maintained that our industry seems to see the future of the economy in small drips months before the rest of the world. It took official reports and polls another six months to start reporting favorable data. Documentaries started to roll in, audiobooks started to flow, and grandmas started bringing in old reel-to-reels to be restored. And to my surprise, clients didn't go away. I guess my advice from all this is don't resist being flexible in your business. You can't force your services on people, let them show you what they want to spend their money on.

When you're writing your business plan and trying to figure out the financials, assume that your revenue will gradually increase over time. The two most important spreadsheets to build are the first year in business (month-to-month), and the fifth year of business (annually). Bankers want to see how you will fare the first year, and where you plan to take your business in five years. I was very conservative with my numbers by showing little to no income the first three months. Remember, you'll be trying to get new clients, build your studios, etc., so be realistic about the honeymoon period. You'll also need to break down your annual revenue in percentages in your text portion of your plan, such as: 30% music, 30% advertising, 20% corporate, 10% audiobooks, 10% other. These should be realistic percentages based on what's in your market and what segments you'll be marketing your business to. If you plan on growing one or more portions, reflect that in your numbers and text. Bankers want to see market segments and that you plan to capture and grow certain markets. Year #5's client base should not look exactly like year #1's if you're growing your business.

Realize that once you're in business, you'll have a lot of plates spinning. You want to grow your business. You'll also want to keep what business you have. You'll lose customers. You'll get some surprise business. You'll also be leaking money like a sieve.

Figure out where that money will be going and how slow you can make it leave the grasp of your sweaty hands. Do you really need to start with five desks and twenty chairs? Not if you don't have any clients. Start out modestly and add office essentials and gear as you need it. Try to delay taking a paycheck for as long as you can. Try to only hire contract workers at first, and then think about moving them to part-time or salary after a few years in business.[74]

On the income side, figure that you'll be getting paid 60 days after your job, not right away. You'll need to factor in invoiced jobs, cash customers, and credit card sales with associated fees. Also deduct 2% every month from the revenue as "bad debt," or uncollectable accounts. Bankers love to see this. It shows that you're savvy to the fact that you can't collect every debt, and they're right, there's a deadbeat in every crowd. On your spreadsheet, gradually build your income throughout the year as you steadily decrease the expenses and even out. By the last month, you should have a little money left in the bank – not a negative balance. If it is in the red, figure out what expenses you can cut first. Only then do you figure out how you can increase sales. In any budget, the amount of expenses always dictates the bottom line. You can control some of them, but most are like a big concrete monolith that isn't going anywhere. Revenue on the other hand, is very fluid, always elusive, and mystical. A client can decide overnight to stop coming to your studio. Someone can die or go bankrupt and not pay their bill. A sudden world-wide pandemic can come out of nowhere. Think those sound farfetched? They've all happened to me unannounced. This is why it's important to keep your expenses as low as you can so that you can weather the rough times.

After the first year, only build your spread sheet in quarters for years two and three, annually for years four and five. During my planning, I factored in a fairly good growth the second year (somewhere around 15-20%), but then gradually tapered off to around 5-8% the last year.[75] I felt that the customers would start rolling in after the first six months, then stabilize after 18 months. I would also reduce income during the quarters with "J" months, and go a little heavy in the last quarter. These decisions were based on my experience in running a studio for more than 15 years, so it may be difficult to visualize growth numbers if you've never managed a studio budget. I'd suggest scouring online for business

---

[74] Also be sure to completely understand the difference between a contract worker and employee. Not understanding it can get you into some deep and scalding water with the IRS.

[75] When I was running the studios at the corporation I worked for, our outside-the-company revenue typically increased 8% every year with modest marketing.

plans others have created. An industry that is very, very similar to ours is photography. Photo studios have corporate clients, advertising, and individuals, just like us. They're based on creativity, they need floor space, up-to-date gear, crazy schedules, etc. just as an audio recording facility would. In fact, when you talk to your insurance rep (you do need insurance, don't even think about not having it),[76] most will insure your business as a photographer, which is perfectly acceptable. Study their revenue predictions and how they grew different market segments.

One analogy that might be helpful to understanding budgets, is to think of your business as a factory that makes widgets. You need a factory, material, and workers. You also need customers. So, the factory employs salespeople to find customers that need widgets. As the demand grows, the factory ramps up and makes more widgets. What is your widget? Mine is time. There is only so much time in a day that I can give. When I reach the saturation point, I can't make any more widgets, or sell time, no matter the demand. How do I increase my sales if I've reached maximum productivity? You could make accessories to widgets. These would be service premiums such as license fees, talent markups, or publishing services. These are the problems you must work out for the kind of services you'll be selling. Always keep the widget analogy top of mind when running your business. It will help keep you levelheaded and focused on balancing your budget every month.

When you're in the planning stages of starting your own business, think seriously about your capital investments. These are pieces of equipment, furniture, computers, etc. You can drop a lot of cash right away on capital, so take a long hard look at what you really need to get started. Most, if not all, of my recording gear was purchased used. I bought items in bulk from a studio that had closed. I sold off what I absolutely didn't need – and that was painful, because there were some great vintage items in there – and kept what was going to make me money. I've done this several times over the years, buying equipment in bulk, and usually

---

[76] If you lease space, gear, or anything else, you're required to have business insurance.

breaking even by selling items individually that I won't ever use. Your gear has to have a reason to be in the rack when you're in business. If it's not making money or is taking up space, sell it. I have sold at least twice the amount of gear that I have now just by following this rule. I admit I've kept some items around that I just can't bear to give up, like that smooth-sounding Urei LA-4 tube compressor pair, or the warm Demeter VTMP-2b tube mic preamp, or the classic Lexicon MP-1 reverb. They still work and I occasionally take them out for a Sunday drive. I have almost cried when I've shipped off some other great gear, but having more money in the bank that I *can* use is better in the end.

When it comes to other capital items like furniture, buy used, clearance, on sale, or consider leasing. Scour Craigslist or Facebook Marketplace for local items, there's always someone getting rid of office furniture. Many estate sales feature home offices that are really nice. Unless you have a specific need, there's nothing wrong with consumer home office furniture for your first office. Even Ikea or Sam's Club/Costco furniture can be a wise purchase, we have many items around our offices that we bought from Ikea a decade ago.

Try to find a used laser photocopier, you'll need it for productions. Avoid inkjet printers if you can. The ink is like unicorn blood, even if it has ink tanks. We use laser printers for our main office needs, and only have one inkjet that we use for audio media printing. Our main workhorse is a multi-function printer. We have a second small B&W laser printer loaded with scrap paper for even more savings. You can't avoid buying office supplies, especially up front. I suggest joining a warehouse club like Costco or Sam's Club. They've been my savior since the beginning for everyday supplies.

And you'll only need one box of paper clips. I have a theory that your supply of paper clips can tell you how your business is doing. I feel like I've only bought one box of them, because many clients come in with scripts that have paper clips on them. I take them off and put them in a holder with mine. Eventually I outgrow that holder and have to get another empty one. Then another, and another. When I start throwing paper clips away, I figure that business must be going really, really good. I'll take a paper clip any day.

Wondering how I bought all that gear up front? Well, I arranged some financing on about half of it. I cherry picked the most important and expensive gear and got a lease on it. It's similar to getting a loan, but having a lease would free up credit for any loans I might need. And I did need one in addition to all my savings that I poured into the business. After I wrote my business plan, I shopped it around to various bankers. Many were impressed with my plan and intrigued by my business, but I didn't have enough capital to back up what I was asking for. Enter: An angel. *Cue the choir.*

An angel investor is someone of wealth that can either directly loan you money, or provide capital against a bank loan. I went the latter route so that I could establish business credit. The gentleman that so graciously helped me was the owner of a video production company that I had worked with. My timing couldn't have been better, as he was expanding the operations and needed a professional audio element to add to their services. From that first meeting was born a business relationship that still exists today. My first several years were spent embedded with the video company in the same building. Though separate businesses, we often worked on multiple projects together, feeding each other clients. To this day, we are still working together on television and web productions.

When you're working your numbers on your spreadsheet, be aware that bankers are looking for a crossover point where you start losing money and start making it. I worked and worked to make my crossover happen by year four. My theoretical point I settled on was 2 ½ years into it. I sweated that early of a crossover, but the new partnership with the video production company, which I always felt that partnering with a video house was vital to my success, gave me confidence. I'm proud to say I hit it to the month! Revenue wasn't as much as I had predicted, but I was able to control expenses during this time. By the start of year three, just six months after breaking even, I was debt free. I had paid off my lease and my loan. From this point on, I was able to take home a bigger paycheck, profits, and even save for a new studio.

I've talked a lot about the numbers part of running a business, but never forget that this is half of what business is. The other half

is relationships. I talked about how to build your name in the "Marketing Yourself" chapter (page 211). Much of what I advised is also true for marketing your business. But now you have to think about branding your company name. In the beginning, this couldn't be more important. You need to just hammer the market with your name and website. Identify your potential clients and where they will most likely be exposed to your name. To make your hard-earned money work best, I would avoid broadcast outlets like television and radio – unless your potential clients are also the audience. Having a commercial play in the middle of the afternoon during a talk show may fall on deaf ears. But one that plays during a business show, a music program, or maybe even the evening local news may get more bang for your buck. Social media/YouTube targeting may work better for your business as well as Google ads that place your name at the top of specific search results. Consider trading services for program and event ads. I occasionally do trades with local events that place my ads and logo in front of potential clients in return for audio services.

If your studio is focused on music, consider partnering with a radio station to offer a three-song recording session for the winner of a contest. It's a lot of press for you, especially for potential musician clients. You'll need to make sure everyone clearly understands the limits of the free session, but I would go out of my way to make the band very happy. Their word-of-mouth advertising is priceless.

Try to get some free press. If you've worked on a particularly interesting project, contact the local media and see if they'll cover it. If you're just trying to get them to give you free advertising disguised as news, they'll see right through your deception. So, be sure your potential story has an interesting twist to it.

Create foot traffic. I partner with various businesses and organizations that generate a lot of buzz and foot traffic for my studios. These partnerships, and the inflow of people through my studio doors, has led to even more business from people that weren't aware of our services. One partnership was with a local business news publication. We helped produce a regular television segment for a local television news station and podcast interviews with local movers and shakers. Another partnership with a local NPR affiliate for a radio show has not only created much foot traffic, but direct business from interview guests as well. We also get daily underwriting announcements on that station that my clients and potential customers hear. There are so many potential tradeoffs to partnerships like these, so find out where your potential customers are engaged in getting news, information, and entertainment. Many media outlets have audience breakdown reports that will help you determine if your future clients are listening, watching, or reading their content.

However you plan on marketing to your potential customers – by cash, trade, or a combination – make sure you're getting value out of it. You must match your customers with their audience. An example of a match that doesn't work for me is a school calendar ad. I'm often asked by local schools to place an ad on their sports calendar. I feel bad not contributing, but my small ad will be among barbershops, pet shops, restaurants, and roofing companies. I don't see how a recording studio that produces film soundtracks and corporate communications can woo someone that's waiting for the next big Friday night game. If my focus was on recording bands, then this ad might work. There are plenty of garage bands hoping to make it big, and a recording studio down the street would sure come in handy.

All these spinning plates one has to manage when running a business can cause major stress, and this is my last piece of advice. Separate your private life from your business life. It's easy to come home and pick work back up by checking emails, crunching numbers, etc. You and your family deserve a break from the company, no matter how good or rough things are going. Your company will still be there in the morning, so relax and decompress. If you must keep in touch with the business world, schedule time with yourself. For instance, only check email when you get home, and again at 9 PM. All other time belongs to you. Some other tips are:

- Change clothes when you get home. This creates a mental separation between work and play.
- Think about your day on the way home and mentally sort out what you'll do tomorrow. When you arrive home, stop thinking about work.

- If you work at home all day, quit at a reasonable hour every day, like 6 PM. Change your clothes.
- If you still can't decompress after working at home, go for a short drive and come back in the house like you're coming home from a long day at work. Throw your hat on the coat tree, kiss your children hello, and go change your clothes.
- If you feel overwhelmed with emails, office work, and other small tasks that build up, schedule times throughout the day to get them done. Don't do all of them after your workday ends, do them on schedule. I check emails and make calls for the first 15 minutes after I arrive. I also use the last 10 minutes of my day to do the same.

Your mental health is vital to your psyche, of course. But it's also vital to the health of your business. If you're constantly overworked, stressed, and tired, your business, and your customers, are at stake. You need to be at the top of your game in order to deliver your best to clients. And you will make better decisions that affect your business if you are not stressed or burnt out. Remember, it's just a business. Your life is irreplaceable.

If you find yourself stressing about your business failing, then first take stock in what you have in your favor. You have your health, your family, your friends, and many, many skills. Because you're a business owner, you might have even more skills than someone in a similar position. Therefore, you're more likely to get hired than that other person if you must close your business. Companies like former business owners because they see the big picture.

Second, build a few triggers into your business financial outlook. Decide what the drop-dead exit point is for you to throw in the towel. How much debt will you have to pay down *after* your businesses closes. Do you have enough assets to cover that debt? Work your way back from this ending point and put in a few red flags to watch out for. These may be revenue figures, expense figures, calendar days or months, or even world events. Plan steps to take if any of these red flags pop up but try not to increase the debt you're willing to absorb if the business closes. I've seen too often people mortgage their entire life away to save a business that was going to fail anyway. Sometimes only the first red flag pops up, you execute your plan, and things work out.

Third, be at peace with the possibility of closing the business. Look at it as the end of one chapter in your life and the beginning of another. This, even more than the financial crush, is probably the hardest to fathom. You might be thinking that you've put your heart and soul into starting, growing, and running your business, only to have it crumble at your feet. This is a natural thought and one that I dread having some day. But there are usually great opportunities on the other side. Plus, you will have killed the enormous stress that may have led up to your decision.

As a potential business owner, I've given you a lot to unpack. I would never try to sway you away from pursuing your dream. I just wanted to share my experiences, good and bad, so that you can go into this with eyes wide open. In my experience, I've had way more ups than downs. In fact, when I am faced with new challenges that I'm not sure I will survive, I tell myself, "Relax, you've got this. You've made it through tougher times. Remember those times you overstressed about the unknown and it turned out okay? You've recorded orchestras. You've engineered national broadcasts. You produced a documentary that played around the world. You started a friggin' business that is still going after twenty years for criminy sake!" So, I stretch my shoulders, pop my knuckles, and dive in. If you ultimately decide to take the plunge into owning a business, then every day you come to work, look up at <u>your</u> sign on the front of the building, pinch yourself, and tell the boss that today is going to be a better day than yesterday because you own a business!!! How many people can say that? You'll earn a lot of respect from just that one fact. Go ahead, pat yourself on the back. It's okay to gloat a little you've earned it.

18. CREATIVITY

"Art is the elimination of the unnecessary."

Pablo Picasso

Creativity is one of the most elusive and nebulous parts of my profession. It's not a skill per se, it doesn't come with a certificate and ID card. It's also not a switch you can flip on and off. It is, however, something you can nurture and exercise over time. If you have done any kind of creative endeavors in your life, like play or compose music, paint, sculpt, take photos, write poetry, or act, then you know that there are times when you have spurts of great creativity. And there are times when you sputter out. So, what exactly is creativity?

A simplified definition of creativity is that it transcends old ideas and conventions while making new ones. We live in a world of familiarity, from concepts and words to visuals and sounds. But sometimes there is a unique combination of the usual that becomes something unusual and grabs our attention. And when a creative piece hooks us, we're usually struck by how simple it really is. We sometimes think, "Oh I could do that," or "Why didn't I think of that?" But it's not that simple. The English language contains more than 170,000 words, but Langston Hughes only used 51 in his iconic poem "Harlem." I wonder how many words he threw out before he finished. Our eyes can detect millions of colors, but we praise Edvard Munch's two-color "Scream" painting. Do you think he started with three and agonized over which one to trash (maybe that poor soul screaming is him trying to decide)? Music occupies 20,000 frequencies on the sound spectrum, but Chopin created masterpieces on an 88-note piano. Did the low pounding beat in his "Funeral March" originally have more notes?

These geniuses probably started out with too much of their medium, but knew how to unceremoniously get rid of words and pigments and notes that weren't central to the core idea. They also probably started with a few simple rules. I'm not going to pretend to know their processes for creating their masterpieces, but I think I can help you unleash your creativity. And it starts with simplicity.

K.I.S.S. – **Keep It Sounding Simple**. In the world of communication –this can entail journalism, literature, art, music, and even entertainment – simplicity drives effectiveness. Writers, producers, performers, artists, and musicians are always striving to find the best path to get their message understood. When a producer brings a project to me, the script has already been whittled down by removing extraneous words and refining the message. It's my job to parlay that effort into an equally cogent soundtrack that will immediately inform the listener of its intent. Here's a concept that you probably hadn't given much thought to: *The simplest and most effective message is the hardest to achieve.* If you see the newspaper headline below, you might think, "I could write that!"

TITANIC SINKS

But it might have started out as:

WORLD'S LARGEST SHIP HITS ICEBERG, HUNDREDS FEARED DEAD

This headline tells us more but takes longer to read and sort out what the news is about. At the time, the Titanic had been in the news almost daily leading up to its maiden voyage. Readers probably knew that it had taken off four days prior. They probably also knew that it was "unsinkable" and carried many famous people aboard. The purpose of the headline is to quickly tell the reader what the following story is about, not tell the whole story. The short, to-the-point two-word headline informs the reader – even if they've never heard of the Titanic – what has happened. Something sank, probably a ship. It must have been big because of the name. It had people on board. Probably a lot because it's on the front page, therefore a lot of people probably died. This might have been the process a news editor went through to deliver an immediate knockout punch. Try defining the biggest event that happened to you yesterday in two words, it's hard!

The concept of a two-line headline should be your goal when constructing your soundtrack: immediately inform the listener where you're taking them. Using only the minimum to get the basic message across is perhaps the most challenging part on the path to creativity because the bare-bones essential elements of the piece must be defined. What raw emotion are you trying to elicit from the listener or viewer? What state of mind should they be in at the first moment they hear or see the work? Stripping down the elements of your work to build its foundation can be found in all mediums:

- Visual – a one color background
- Music – a simple rhythm on a hi-hat, solo bass, or a sustained single angelic note
- Soundscape – light ambience, or even complete silence

Only add color, instruments, or sound effects that <u>have a purpose</u>. I can't emphasize this enough. Don't add anything that doesn't have any value or meaning. If you're building a cemetery soundscape, begin with a simple exterior ambience, add in a light whistling wind gust here or there, and sprinkle in a raven or crow after several seconds to establish the creepiness. Any other sound must be central to the story. Any sound that is extraneous or unrelated will pull the listener's attention away from the magic of the moment. If your cemetery story involves zombies, then sneak in a distant and muffled scratching sound after the raven. Follow up with a creaky hinge opening from a grave. These are all audio markers that cue the listener to watch out, something terrifying is about to happen. At first the listener was inquisitive when they heard the ambience, then a little on edge when the wind began howling, maybe they became uneasy when the raven cried, and the beginnings of real fear started when the casket opened. This would all be moot if there was a leaf blower in the background.

The great director Alfred Hitchcock, well known for his chilling movies, capitalized on the audience's *anticipation* of a dreadful event rather than the event itself. Uneasiness, fear, then terror would slowly unfold before the stabbing, gunshot, or plunge off the cliff. It's a lot like simmering a stew in the crockpot all day, penetrating the olfactory senses of everyone in the house and building high anticipation for the evening's meal. Your job as a sound designer is to lead the listener down the path you want them to take. You can control their emotions with sound cues, and the simpler they are, especially at first, the quicker you'll tap into the rawest of emotions.

I'll leave you with one last thought on simplicity of sound. What are some of your most memorable experiences that included sound? The roar of the jet engine the first time you flew or the lapping waves the first time you saw the ocean? In the Preface, I told of my childhood memories on Lake Erie − the ferry boat engine, the waves against the hull, the transistor radio − there were other sounds that hit my ear canals that day, but these singular sounds were engraved in my memory. This is how your soundtracks should be constructed, as if it is the final, finely honed sonic imprint in a listener's memory.

Real life is boring. Let me zoom in on a point that you should never forget when designing sound: Making a scene sound "real" is counterintuitive to creativity. "Real" life sounds boring, "cinema" life is hyper real. Designing soundscapes involves borrowing from the brain's ability to laser-focus on small details while ignoring unrelated ones. This is called *psychoacoustics*. But when designing sound, you become the brain. You pick and choose what you want the listener to focus on. Understanding psychoacoustics is the fundamental bedrock of sound design, as well as studio design, microphone choice, live sound, etc.

Here's an experiment I often do with students. As they're intensely listening to me explain psychoacoustics, I remind them of the sounds in the room that they're *not* hearing: the clock, the HVAC, the car going by outside, the subtle clothing movements, the stomach gurgles, etc. Your brain filters out what isn't needed during critical listening. This all goes back to caveman days when humans needed to hear approaching threats. In fact, hearing is the only sense that stays active when we are in deep REM sleep, activated to warn of approaching threats like lions, tigers, and bears. In our modern world and comfy bedrooms at night, we're now alerted to alarms, storms, or our partner snoring.

When I use a microphone, I'm keenly aware that it is dumb. It has no brain. It hears everything around it and can't filter out unwanted sounds. That's why we use specialty microphones in quiet studios that reduce and filter out surrounding noises that can interfere with the source sound. They're not perfect, but selecting the right one for each environment and situation is critical to success. A great example would be using a "shotgun" microphone on an outside film scene when we need its hyper-directionality to hear more of the dialog and less of the surroundings. When you design sound, use the same principles as microphone choice: what do I *need* to hear and what do I *not* need to hear. Choose wisely and you'll successfully guide the listener's emotions and keep them immersed in the story.

Don't think outside the box, think *inside* the box. Being limited in options will often force creativity. Having dozens of choices versus a few choices will force you to think about the first rule: keeping it simple. Try this exercise: look at the movies currently playing in your local theaters. Go down the list sequentially by pairs and decide which one of the two you'd prefer to see, 1 or 2. Circle that one and move on to 3 or 4, and so on. Then pair up all the circled movies and again make the thumbs up/thumbs down choice until there is just one left. Hopefully this is a movie you should be excited to see and will feel good about your choice. You can do this same exercise when building your project foundation. Black or white. Snare or bass. Silence or ambience.

I used to produce the soundtrack for a weekly college football show on the Fox Sports Network. It ran for 3 or 4 years and could become monotonous at times, especially given the time crunch we were under to meet the broadcast deadline. The show itself was very good and had human interest and college tradition stories which required music underneath the narrative. We subscribed to four or five music library services (see **Tech Tip** below) and usually picked music from all of them when producing show segments. Near the end of one season, I was in a creative rut. I seemed to be picking the same music over and over again. So, one day I chose 20 albums from the smallest library we had. That's about 200 cuts of music from our nearly 15,000 cuts in all the libraries combined.

And I didn't cherry pick them, I selected them as one big group – numbers one to twenty. After struggling the first day, I eventually freed up my anxiety about the limitations and got on a roll. I had more fun on that one show than I had the entire run. And people noticed, too. I got a lot of compliments from the producers that week. I often go back to that tactic of boxing myself in when I'm in a creative rut so that I'm forced to focus on the most important elements.

Tech Tip

Music library services license background music for TV, movie, radio, etc. to a production company. These are generally meant to be used under dialog or narration to create a mood or support the story. These are not popular recordings heard on iTunes or the radio, but some may mimic a particular song or genre's sound. Fees and usage rights are structured around potential listeners and mediums.

Photo 5.

Do something unexpected. It's important to recognize that familiar and routine elements can be the foundation for your project. It's when and how you do the unexpected that gets attention. You can sprinkle in the surprise: Imagine a picture of dozens of white eggs placed neatly in even rows and columns on a white background. Now imagine that one of those eggs down near the right corner is yellow. It's not at all what you expected, and that splash of happy yellow has just lifted your spirits a little. In music, Bruce Springsteen and the E Street Band's sound had the familiar rock-and-roll foundation. But the subtle addition of the high-pitched glockenspiel in "Born to Run" was an unexpected bit of delicacy in a sea of sound. It's an instrument that we're familiar with in another context such as a cartoon or children's song, not in a rock ballad. These deviations from the norm work because they're tasteful and reserved, leaving the familiar intact.

You can also dramatically veer in another direction. What if those dozens of white eggs contained one charcoal black egg instead of a yellow one? That's a bold statement that will have the viewer on edge a little trying to figure out why this egg is dramatically different. Beethoven was known for his bold modulations[77] in his symphonies. He would lull you with gentle shifts to a related key, then modulate into a totally unexpected key[78]. The Ninth Symphony is a great example of bold modulations.

Now here's really something unexpected: Imagine all of those eggs are now black, except that lone yellow egg. It looked so sweet and innocent before, but now it has a macabre feeling. In the audio world, this might be represented by using seemingly inappropriate music for a scene in a movie. Some great examples of *soundtrack dissonance* are:

- In the 2000 film *American Psycho*, the 80s pop song "Hip to be Square" by Hughey Lewis and the News plays during an axe murder.

---

[77] A modulation is the movement from one musical key to another. For instance, a song may start off playing in C major, then shift, or modulate, to F major. Some modulations are direct with no "bridge" between. Others have a series of notes and/or chords that step into the key with more subtlety.

[78] The new key would usually have some relation, though distant, to the original key.

- In Quentin Tarantino's 1992 film *Reservoir Dogs*, a police officer is tortured while Steelers Wheel's bouncy "Stuck in the Middle with You" plays.
- In the 1999 film *Office Space*, the gangster rap song "Still" from Geto Boys blares over three white collar office workers angrily bashing a laser printer with clubs.
- And one of my favorites is *Monty Python's Life of Brian* from 1979. As the eponymous Brian is being crucified, Eric Idle, who's also hanging from a cross, gleefully sings "Always Look on the Bright Side of Life".

Using soundtrack dissonance may seem contradictory at first, but it may actually clarify and emphasize the storyline better than any standard approach might accomplish. But be careful, overuse of this device can come across cartoonish or insincere. It's usually reserved for the most important part of your soundtrack, like the apex, arc, or payoff.

Hide Easter eggs. Speaking of eggs, another way to drive creativity is to hide Easter eggs, understated sound cues that have a meaning, within your soundscape. They should have a subtle effect on the listener and only be identifiable upon close inspection. One Easter egg many film sound designers use began with Ben Burt. While designing the sound for Star Wars, Burt was digging through old sound effects libraries for screams. He ran across a series of short painful screams performed by an actor that were recorded in 1951 for the Warner Brother's film "Distant Drums". They were used in several other movies over the subsequent years as a matter of convenience. This set of scream sound effects was eventually labeled "Wilhelm Scream" after one of the characters it was dubbed in for. Burt used a particularly spirited one in the first three Star Wars movies, the Indian Jones movies, as well as many others. It's become a cliché and overused sound cue these days (I've even used it several times), but film enthusiasts will eagerly hunt for the *Wilhelm Scream* in newly released action movies. It even has its own IMDB page.

I've used my own Easter eggs as a thread to hold productions together. For instance, in a Civil War documentary, I used a bell every time a death count was mentioned. I pitched it to match the key of the underlying music and feather it in to the song. In another documentary I used a crow to signify death, such as an impending attack, a subject's death. or a graveyard. I've also used stirred up chickens and excited horses for approaching danger. By putting in little nuanced sounds into your project that have a meaning, it can ignite a creative fire and turn drudgery into a treasure hunt.

Borrow. Take cues from the story, character, or message to construct your soundscape around. If you're building a movie soundtrack for instance, something central to the plot can be morphed into a sound cue. If it's a submarine drama, take the pinging sound of sonar and manipulate it beyond recognition into a subtle cue under music – a PING-ping tuned like a bell wouldn't sound like an effect, only a musical element. A few noted examples in film and TV are:

- In the 2017 film *Dunkirk*, director Christopher Nolan supplied composer Hans Zimmer with a recording of his wristwatch. The movie, which follows the chaotic evacuation of British Soldiers from France as the Nazis are bearing down on them, revolves around the idea that time is running out quickly. Zimmer incorporated this watch sound into the music to build intensity.
- In the beloved British mystery series *Inspector Morse*, composer Barrington Pheloung based his theme song on the rhythmic pulse of the Morse code signal for M-O-R-S-E.

I wrote a musical piece for my former employer's demo reel by borrowing from Big Ben in London, England. Ed Commons (see page 47) had cleverly named his film company "House of Commons." His logo included London's House of Commons, which houses the world-famous clock Big Ben. Everyone is familiar with Big Ben's 16-note song followed by hour strikes. Instead of playing those notes as a melody, I put them in the bass. They played very slowly, each long note lasting four measures while strings played a melody over top. I sprinkled in a cup bell every four measures and concluded the song with the recognizable Big Ben tune on bells. This approach allowed me to use the tune, but in an unexpected and indirect way.

Lions and tigers and bears, oh my. I like to use organic sounds when layering sound effects. I feel like humans can connect to complex and new sounds if they contain a familiar element. In the truck chase scene in "Raiders of the Lost Ark," Ben Burt ingeniously layered a lion roar under the throaty engine of a Nazi truck to give it a menacing sound. To make a tough biker even tougher, I pitched and slowed down a bumblebee's buzz by several factors, then layered it under an idling motorcycle. My inspiration was the "Killer Bees" skit from the original *Saturday Night Live*. If you slow down a cat meow, you can get some creepy sounds to liven up a jungle soundscape. A pitched-down dog growl makes a great monster growl. So, go put on your pith helmet and explore other creatures from the animal world and how they can fit into your soundtrack.

Turn everything upside down and inside out. When I was in music school, we used to flip a sheet of music over and play it backwards and upside down. It made for some interesting sounds. When you're stuck for ideas, try reversing sounds, pitching them up or down several octaves, running them through reverb and keeping only the reverb, running a voice through a distorted guitar amp simulator, running a guitar through a telephone simulator, recording and playing back on inferior technology, sticking a microphone inside a wrapping paper tube, etc. I once created a unique sound by recording a sound effect onto a cheap desktop cassette recorder with a built-in speaker. I then rewired one of my big speakers to act as a microphone (a basic microphone is the opposite of a speaker, and vice-versa). The speaker's woofer became the microphone diaphragm. I then played the cheap cassette player into the woofer. That new sound effect was a nasty, dirty, off the hook piece of crap. Lovely, just what I was looking for.

Look to other artists for inspiration. Earlier, I used visuals as an example of simplicity. I find that by examining the works of other artists – be they painters, sculptors, photographers, landscapers, poets, or composers – I can get inspiration. I mentioned in the preface of this book that I may have synesthesia (see page 13), because I sometimes see colors when I hear sounds, especially music. Even though experts say we all have some degree of synesthesia, you don't need to have a pronounced measure of it to equate other senses with sound. Many of our audio editing apps have some form of coloring or shading based on frequencies and intensity of sound. In the art world, boldness will often stir up the critics, as did Mark Rothko's 1959 painting No. 301,[79] which used two shades of red to hit you in the face. This might translate to the

---

[79] https://www.artst.org/famous-red-paintings/

audio world as a big sharp brass note, a thunderous drum hit, a scream, or all those combined. Chicago's "Cloud Gate,"[80]a teardrop-shaped sculpture by Sir Anish Kapoor, oozes smoothness and liquidity. This might translate to a serene, washing, and endless soundscape, like a calm night on an ocean beach. The Walt Disney Concert Hall in Los Angeles[81] almost mimics two mediums: music, with its big horn-like columns, and animated Disney movies (maybe Mickey Mouse conducting an orchestra in tuxedo coattails in *Fantasia?*) with its whimsical angles.

Hit RESET. Sometimes you just need to clear your brain and let it drain. During the worldwide lockdown from the COVID-19 pandemic of 2020, many creative professionals either hit a wall, or exploded with new projects. Although I haven't seen any studies or media reports about this, I suspect that those with the creative explosions were suddenly experiencing a different and unexpected way of life. Maybe the "forced" solitude was all they needed to let their minds go wild. Those that suffered a creativity block may have been anxious (I know we all were), sick, perhaps cramped with their family in a small and overactive space, or unable to use their tools or connect with fellow creatives that would typically fuel their output.

But when I hit a creative wall, I try to turn my world around and upside down 180-degrees. Go take a walk, run, or bike ride. Listen to music you wouldn't normally have in your collection. Go to a museum or art gallery. Go watch a game, or even play a sport. Go on a photography hike and try to take pictures of just one subject, like merging lines or scenes with red. Meditate, practice yoga, or exercise. Go see a play or stand-up comedian. Play with the studio dog or cat if you're fortunate to have one.

The whole idea is to hit RESET and get completely away from your project and your working environment. Even if I'm in a time crunch and can't go away for an extended period of time, I find that just taking a 20-minute walk can do wonders. The key is to get out of your studio and do something completely different. Try to avoid any activity that mimics what you're stuck doing. I try to avoid television, computers, looking at my phone, dark rooms (my

---

80 https://en.wikipedia.org/wiki/Cloud_Gate
81 https://www.discoverlosangeles.com/things-to-do/walt-disney-concert-hall-at-the-music-center

studio has no outside windows), people (if the studio is crowded, or I may call a friend or talk with someone on my walk if I'm working alone), etc. Hopefully you haven't thought about your mental block and can just release all that built-up tension. When you do, sometimes a funny thing happens – you see your project in a whole different light. Suddenly a light switch comes on and the creative juices flow.

Let it flow. Surfers talk about riding an ocean wave as if it's a spiritual event. I can see what they mean. They're standing atop a massive wave of energy that only exists because of many forces of nature – the ocean, the atmosphere, the moon – have come together to give this gift of a rolling wave of water. Killer dude.

When you have finally sparked the creativity you've been seeking, let it flow bro. Don't stop it, don't doubt it, just jump on that surfboard and ride it for as long as you can. Once the ideas start coming, roll with them no matter how crazy they may seem, because you can go back later and tweak things. When writing this book, I've had writer's block more than a few times. But when my creative juices began flowing, I just typed and typed, following my stream of consciousness. I didn't worry about grammar, sentence structure, or spelling because I always go back later and finesse sentences and thoughts. My audio creative process works exactly the same way. If that creative valve opens, I let it flow like a fire hydrant because I can mop up the puddles later. So, just relax and let the creativity come to you instead of trying to force it. Gently nudge it in your direction by employing some of the tools I've given you in this chapter and it will start trickling out of the water tap. But if you try and push creativity too hard, it will burst like a water balloon and leave a mess all over your project. Good luck!

19. ENGINEERING AND RECORDING CONCEPTS

"The noblest pleasure is the joy of understanding."

Leonardo da Vinci

You won't get very far if you don't understand the bare basics of the recording arts. I'm guessing most of the people reading this understand that to record a sound with modern technology, a device must capture acoustic waves and transduce them into electrical signals. From there it may get a little foggy to some, so let's dive in further. These electrical signals will fluctuate in intensity and voltage. These fluctuations are then logged, either to magnetic tape as varying degrees of polarity of the magnetic material; to a computer application which converts the varying signals to data represented by ones and zeros approximating the variations; to a passing strip of light-sensitive film that captures light intensity variations created by differences in electrical voltage; or to a rotating disk or cylinder that records the variations as irregular waves in a continuous groove. That's a roundabout way of saying we can record sound to a reel-to-reel magnetic tape, a computer/digital recorder, a film recorder, or a record.

CHOCOLATE MILK

If you've never assembled a multi-track recording (something with more than one sound recording), then this section is for you. In the earliest days of recording, only one microphone (or bell/horn) was used for capturing the sound. The performer stood in front of it and sang or played their instrument. If a second performer was needed, they simply stood beside the first performer and moved toward or away from the microphone for a good balance. As technology advanced, electrical recording in the 1920s allowed two or more microphones to be used at the same time. An engineer would electrically blend the microphones' audio signals together into a single fluctuating electrical signal that would mechanically move a needle back and forth as it etched a continuous groove onto a disk. Once that disk was cut, there was no way to separate the sounds back out into separate recordings. They were combined forever, like stirring chocolate mix into a glass of milk. Can you get the chocolate back out of the milk? Maybe with scientific intervention, but it's basically there to stay.

This concept is still true today. After two or more audio signals are mixed together, you can fenagle some sound elements to have more or less presence, but essentially they're all stirred into the recording forever (until artificial intelligence makes it easy to separate them). *Multi-track recording* is the art of recording each element separately onto individual tracks. By using a recording console, or *mixer*, an engineer can blend these tracks together into a single recording. This is the *mix* or *master* recording, and it's what everyone else hears on the radio, TV, etc. If one wants to remove an element or track, then the engineer must go back to the original multi-track recording and *remix* the project, creating a new mix or master recording. Multi-track recording wasn't possible before magnetic tape was perfected in the 1950s (see my *Sound Education* article "When Recording Writes the Music" on page 469). Tape allowed multiple recordings to be made alongside each other, in parallel and in time with each other, even in separate recording sessions. They were very simple at first, just two tracks (a track is a single recording in studio-speak). But the technology eventually advanced to allow 32 separate tracks to be recorded onto one analog reel-to-reel tape. When digital recording matured, this track count jumped to 48 when using a tape-based digital recording system.

Photo 6.   A Tascam 85 16B analog tape 16-track recorder (1979-1984).

The advent of multi-track recording meant that you could record a bass on track #1, rewind back to the beginning, and while listening to the previous recording of the bass, play a guitar while recording to track #2, and so on. We take this for granted today, but it was a difficult-to-understand concept until multi-track recorders became commonplace in the 1970s. I didn't fully appreciate it (or understand it) until I actually participated in a recording session when I was a teenager (see page 32). It was magical then, and though it's a basic function I use today, it's still a small wonder.

Magnetic tape recording was a *linear* way of capturing sound – everything happened from start to finish on the tape. If you wanted to listen to the end of the recording, then you had to fast-forward from wherever you were on the tape to play the end. If you wanted to jump to the middle, then you had to shuttle the tape there. This was a tedious way to move around a recording, but it was all we had. There were other downsides, like the possibility of wearing the tape out, wrinkling the tape, or even breaking it. The only non-linear playback system before the 1980s was a record. Want to go to the end? Pick up the needle and drop it there.

When digital recording moved from reel-to-reel tape to computers in the late 1980s, *non-linear* audio production was finally available. Early DAWs were very limited because computer processors and hard disks were very slow for the amount of data flow that quality audio recordings demanded. The first DAW I worked with only had 8 tracks available at one time, and it was bleeding edge. Audio was stored on the hard drives as non-linear chunks of data to make writing and access to all that data easier. This allowed an engineer to jump around a recording with ease (non-linear access). Some hard disk-based recording systems wrote hard disk data linearly and contiguous, believing this allowed faster read times and more available tracks to record onto. Indeed, it did work well because hard disks were generally slow at that time. However, any bad sectors on the hard disk resulted in dropouts. Normal PC data storage procedures spread the data out between platters and sectors, skipping bad areas in the process. Today's DAWs can easily record and play back hundreds of tracks simultaneously, depending on processing and storage capability.

UNDERSTANDING HOW SOUND WORKS

Sound is a variation of molecules bumping into each other. The faster the molecules quiver and bump around, the higher the pitch. Without molecules, there is no sound. A classic experiment that demonstrates this law of physics is to place a bell inside a glass jar. You may have seen one of these attractions at a science museum. You press a button, and an old school telephone bell starts ringing inside an inverted glass mason jar. Meanwhile, a vacuum pump gradually pulls all the air out of the glass. Bit by bit the ringing sound goes away, but you can see the striker still pounding the little bell. It's fun to watch (and hear the transition from loud to near silence). It always gets lots of *Ooh!*s. Move that bell to outer space (which isn't a complete vacuum, but close enough) and nobody will hear it ring.

Sound will move through gas, liquid, and solids. In fact, it moves better through liquid than gas, and even better through solids. That's because the molecules are more tightly packed together. The effect of solids or liquids carrying sound is like being in an overly crowded subway car, elbow-to-elbow, when the brakes are suddenly slammed on. Everybody jostles into each other, creating a cascade of *Sorry!*s. For gases, the effect is as if there are only several people in the car – it's very difficult to have the occupants bump into each other without some serious braking. This comparison shows us that the medium that we usually think of as the optimum way to carry sound – air – is actually the worst way.

Controlling sound: Isolation

Acoustic engineers who design recording spaces are interested in several methods of sound transmission. One is how it travels through wood, concrete, and metal. They know that a hard thump anywhere in or near the building will quickly travel through the structure and into the recording space. That's why they spend so much time and money isolating structural elements and building heavy isolation into each sub-layer of construction.

Sound travels through air at about 770 miles per hour. It travels through wood and concrete at about 7,500 mph, and cast iron at a whopping 11,100 mph.[82] This means that these solid building elements are great at bringing unwanted noise into your studio. By isolating each structural element, engineers and carpenters can reduce sound transmission at every step. For instance, when building a studio floor, the entire floor is floated on rubber spacers just above the subfloor with no piece touching it or the surrounding walls. It's an island. The studs and drywall are also installed this way, each piece of wood and drywall acting as a lone island. When you encounter noise problems, such as someone slamming a door three floors away, you'll quickly understand that standard construction techniques that call for all the elements to be tied together are bad for building studios.

---

[82] Most microphones are designed to capture sounds transmitted through air (gases). However, there are also microphones that are specially designed to operate in water (a hydrophone) and on vibrating surfaces, a.k.a. solids (a contact microphone).

Studs that hold the drywall are isolated with rubber. The floor, which is also floating on rubber "pucks," doesn't touch the studs.

To better understand the transmission of unwanted sound through materials, and how to isolate elements, I like to use the analogy of train tracks. In the Old West days, one could tell if a train was coming by planting an ear directly on the iron rail. Because all of these were connected for miles and miles, a train's rumbling wheels could be detected several miles away. If the railroad company were to pull up a few ties, the connection would be broken. Another example is the childhood toy of two tin cans and a string. Without that string, there are no sound waves traveling between the Campbell's Soup cans. Snip the string and you won't hear Timmy yelling into the Alphabet Soup container. So, when studio designers are planning construction, they use every opportunity available to isolate each element.

Controlling sound: Blocking

We've talked about how to isolate construction elements, now let's talk about blocking sounds. Some elements do a pretty good job of blocking unwanted sounds from passing through them, like concrete and stone. I say pretty good, because the lowest of frequencies are very stubborn and can blindly pass through brick and stone walls. Drywall is basically a ground mineral (gypsum) combined with fibers and glues that bind it together between a sandwich of paper. It can serve as a barrier to sound but will still let very-low to medium-low sounds pass. Studios will often install two layers of the thickest drywall available (5/8"), isolated of course, to maximize blockage. Wood will block less than drywall and can even resonate like a drumhead if not properly attached. I've even created resonators made of sheets of varying thicknesses of plywood in order to counter-attack unwanted frequencies in studios. This technique vibrates the panel at the same frequency of unwanted "nodes," or accented frequencies, in a recording space. The resonator will vibrate out-of-phase with the node, thereby canceling it out. These large panels are great for solving mid- to low-frequency issues that might occur in small rooms, rooms with parallel walls, or rooms with concrete, stone, brick, or cinderblock walls.

And beware of those cheap wood and metal doors – they're often made with two thin sheets of lauan plywood or aluminum sandwiching cardboard or foam filler. Glass is better at blocking sound than you think, but it must be thick and specially made in order to do so. Regular window glass is wimpy but adding a second panel of glass reduces transmission of sound more. Be careful that the two pieces of glass aren't the same thickness and are not parallel to each other, otherwise they will resonate and sing like a canary.[83] Those double-paned exterior windows at the home improvement store are a great example of what NOT to install in studios. The best glass to use is tempered (like the kind used in automobiles). For double-pane studio windows, install one pane of glass vertically, the second one at a six-degree angle. Only one of them has to be tempered. Float each pane on a rubber gasket for isolation from the wall structure.

---

[83] Have you ever been in a glass office building downtown and noticed that the traffic outside creates "singing" glass? This is the glass resonating with the noises outside, much like a drum head or open piano strings.

Insulation behind our studio walls. The horizontal metal strips are for hanging drywall via screws.

There are several options to blocking sound by using filler. Once common and useful one is fiberglass or rockwool insulation[84]. It's the pink or yellow fluffy stuff that makes you itch. Its usefulness for absorbing sound waves comes from the fact that it is a) dense and b) loose. When sound penetrates insulation, it decays rapidly because there is no structure to its makeup like wood and steel. The denser and thicker it is, the better. But insulation alone won't block the lowest frequencies. That's where sand comes in. For the most difficult situations where you need to absorb the most low sound frequencies, even those so low they rattle your teeth, use sand. Sand offers extreme density, heavy mass, and very little structure because it's so loose. One common building technique is to fill the individual holes in cinder blocks with sand during construction. It can be very expensive, but sometimes it's the only sound absorbing technique that will work in very noisy environments. By the way, putting a studio in a basement can achieve the same thing on five of the six surfaces because the basement walls are surrounded by dirt. One last option is to hang lead curtains around the perimeter of your studio walls. These are long sheets with lead infused into

---

[84] Rockwool is safer to work with but is harder to find.

the rubber. They come in different thicknesses that can be ordered from any major studio accessory retailer.

So, we've isolated components from conducting sound, we've put up barriers to block sound, now let's kill sound. We do this using a free and plentiful construction element: air. Since sound travels through air with the least efficiency, building air gaps between walls is almost as effective as putting up another layer or two. When studio walls are built, there is often a three- to six-inch air gap left between structures. It won't kill all the sound, but it actually helps. Of course, you lose floor space, but you would lose more if you were to build another wall to reduce the same amount of noise that the air gap does. There is a very dangerous aspect of air in studios, however. Air leaking into the recording space. All gaps, doors, windows, wall plugs, etc. must be tightly sealed with caulk and weather stripping to prevent *any* air – i.e. *sound* – from entering. You can sink $100,000 into a studio and have a tiny two-inch air gap ruin a recording.

Controlling sound: absorbing and diffusing

In the previous sections we've blocked all the *outside* sound from coming into our space. Now we have to control the sound that's happening *inside* the recording studio. If you look at pictures of recording studios, you'll often see padding on the walls. You might also see some crazy looking geometric panels everywhere. These are there to control the sound *inside* the recording or mixing space. Just as loose and dense filler like insulation can block sound, it can absorb it.

Here's an example of why we want absorption in a recording studio. Sound from a musical instrument, voice, and other object you might be recording must be heard clearly by the microphone. Any other sound that bleeds into the microphone will take away from the purity of the recording. If a room is untreated, uncontrolled sound bouncing of the walls back into the microphone can result in unwanted echo and reverberation. Imagine you're in a square room with a tennis ball. Throw it as hard as you can at the wall right in front of you. That ball will bounce off the wall and come right back towards you. Now substitute a sound wave for the tennis ball. If a sound bounces off the wall, it bounces back into the microphone a fraction of a second later, just like the ball. When it does, it has slowed down slightly because it has lost energy. When it collides with the microphone that millisecond later, the delay creates an echo. And because it is traveling slower, its pitch is slightly lower than the original sound. This creates dissonance. These two factors combined are called reverberation. Reverb isn't bad, but you might have wanted a dry recording.

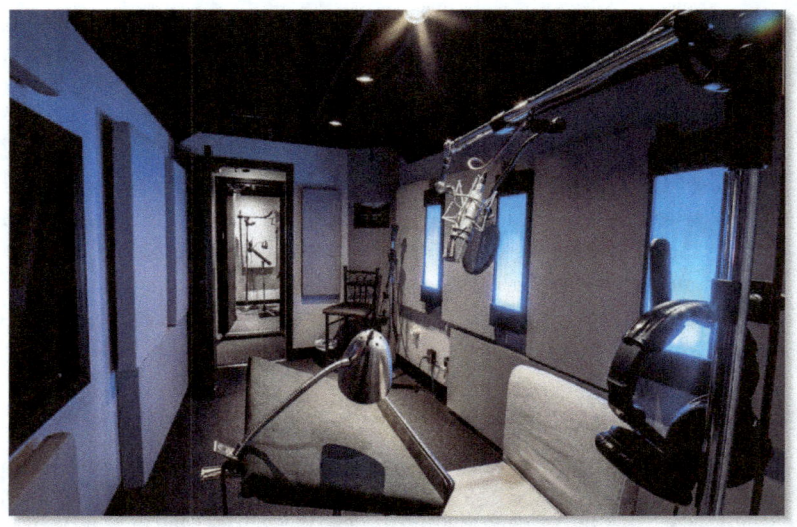

Sound absorbing panels are installed on the walls and ceiling in our studios.

If all the walls, floor, and ceiling are bare and untreated, this reverb phenomenon expands exponentially. You can experience this by walking into a public restroom and clapping your hands. The clap bounces off each slick and shiny surface and collides with other reflections. These reflections bounce off the walls and collide with other reflections, etc. You now have a feedback loop creating long reverberation going into the seconds. By hanging absorption panels on the walls, you can trap most of those sounds from reflecting and causing echo. We tend to put these panels on the walls, in corners, and on the ceiling. You don't have to cover all the surfaces completely in most situations, otherwise it will be *too* dry and uncomfortable to record in.

Tech Tip

Absorption panels can be made of fiberglass/rockwool, foam, or other material. It must be manufactured (or custom made) to sound absorbing specifications. Hanging mattress foam pads or egg cartons simply doesn't work, no matter how appealing the price is. Any material must also have fire retardant. If regular foam caught fire, it would ignite rapidly and release toxic fumes, quickly rendering anyone unconscious. Please take this bit very seriously if you are building a recording space.

Another useful technique in studios is to diffuse sound. A completely flat surface will allow sound to bounce back towards its source almost unimpeded. A diffusor will *redirect* that sound to another place, usually towards an absorber panel. A diffuser can also break up a sound wave into less distinct ones with lower energy and on random paths. Instead of bouncing directly back to the microphone, it meanders around the room and dies a quick death. Diffusing part of your surface area is not only cost saving but keeps your room from having that dreaded dead feeling by being over-damped. You can create a pleasing feel to your room with just a touch of almost imperceptible reverb created by diffusion.

Controlling sound: non-parallel rooms

The single best way to control sound is to eliminate parallel surfaces in your recording or mixing space. This isn't always easy, but if you're building a studio from scratch (or even retrofitting a space), you should skew your walls and ceiling six-degrees or more. This redirects any source sound to bounce away from the microphone. Not every wall has to be skewed, just two of them. Two adjoining walls that form an L can remain at 90-degrees. The opposing two walls can be constructed at a 6-degree skew. Do this to the ceiling by either skewing the whole thing, creating a cathedral-type angle, or hanging heavy-duty sound panels at 6-degree angles. You can even make a false ceiling or wall atop an existing one with a layer of drywall screwed into furring strips and 2x4 shims. If you have a studio window, angle the interior glass (you should use two panes of glass, remember?) down at 6-degrees so the sound bounces toward the floor.

Controlling sound: field recording

Now that you understand how to control sound in a studio, you can use some of these principles when recording in less-than-ideal spaces. Forgetting all the other problems of recording outside the studio, like HVAC noise, hum, traffic, etc., put on your studio designer hat when assessing a new space. I first pull out my imaginary tennis ball and look at what the sound will be bouncing off. I might position my subject and microphone at 10- or 15-degrees off-angle from the walls. I might place them in one-third of the room instead of dead center. I might throw up a sound blanket or pull the drapes to reduce sound from outside. Nothing will be as good as recording in a well-damped studio, but you can still get a quality recording if you take steps to find the optimum placement of your microphones and subject that produce the least reverb and slap back. Once you've done that, you can move on to the other problems.

USING MICROPHONES, ELECTRONIC INSTRUMENTS, PLAYERS, SPEAKERS, AMPS, AND RECORDERS

Modern audio production relies on using devices that either generate electrical signals, or can receive electric signals. Recording or amplifying sound relies on electrical signals, either generated by a microphone, instrument, or media player. For instance, a microphone transduces[85] air pressure differences into a varying electrical current. A speaker does the opposite, it turns electrical signals into air pressure variations. Your job as an audio engineer is to capture those electrical signals (recording) created by a microphone as faithfully as possible. You must then reproduce those and other electrical signals as true as possible over a speaker.

---

[85] A *transducer* is a device that converts variations in a physical quantity, such as pressure or brightness, into an electrical signal, or vice versa. *Oxford English Dictionary*

The microphone

A microphone by nature is an analog device. In the most basic form, a microphone has a circular diaphragm that looks a lot like a bowl or disc that is suspended around its edges. This diaphragm is pointed towards a sound source. As air differences (sound) hits the diaphragm, it causes it to move backwards and forward. After it is pushed back, it springs forward towards its resting position. At the back of this diaphragm is an electromagnetic coil and a permanent magnet. When the diaphragm moves back and forth, it also moves the coil in and out of the magnetic field of the magnet. This movement of the coil through the magnetic field sends small electrical pulses to two wires coming from the assembly. This is a very, very weak signal, so circuitry built into the microphone housing amplifies this very weak signal into a stronger one.

Most microphones use a 3-conductor wire with a 3-pin plug called an XLR. One wire is the hot, one the neutral, and the third is a shield which reduces noise. You will see this level in spec sheets noted about -60 dB or so.

The preamp

A microphone can then be plugged into a mixing console or other device that will further amplify its signal. This part of technology is called a *microphone preamplifier* (or just plain *preamp*). Of all the devices you will use in the studio, the microphone has the weakest electrical signal of all. Therefore, microphone, cable, and preamp quality must be very good to have a clean and noise-free sound. Manufacturers put a lot of emphasis on the quality of their preamps because a mediocre one can cause a lot of noise problems. Most mixing consoles and audio interfaces have built-in preamps, but separate preamp units are also made. A preamp amplifies the microphone and directly outputs a much louder electrical signal – *line level*.

Line level

A *line level* electrical signal is hundreds of times louder than the signal level of a microphone. It's the level at which most mixing consoles, recorders, and amplifiers operate. There are great benefits to operating equipment at this level rather than at microphone level. The topmost is the noise level. When audio signals (electrical pulses) are this loud, then inherent noise is very quiet. All electric circuits have noise, but line level masks it because it is hundreds of times louder. A comparison would be a drop of water on the ground would seem gigantic to an ant (microphone level), and nothing to an adult human (line level).

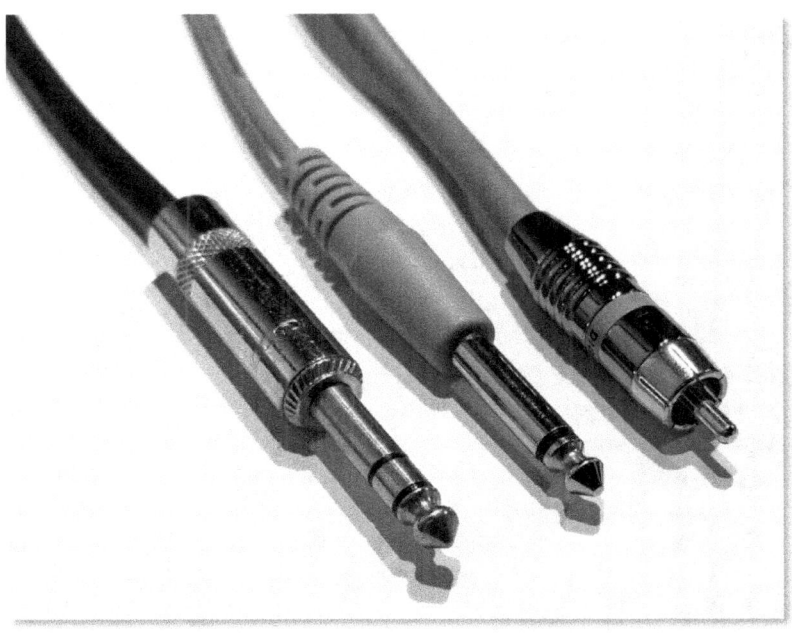

Left to right: Balanced ¼" phone plug, unbalanced ¼" phone plug, RCA-style plug.

Consumer line level cables generally have two conductors, either on an RCA-style connector (far right. Outer sleeve is ground, inner pin is hot), or a phone / guitar plug (middle. Tip hot, ring ground).

Professional line level cables will have three wires (like microphone cables) and either an XLR connector, or three-conductor stereo headphone-type plug known as TRS (tip, ring, sleeve) ¼" phone plug (far left. Tip is hot, middle ring neutral, bottom ring ground).

Consumer line level will be often noted in spec sheets as -10 dBV (0.316 volts), while professional level noted as +4 dBu (1.23 volts or higher).

There are two basic standards for line level that you need to be aware of: *consumer* and *professional*. Consumer line level is the economical version that has a lower electrical level, a tad more noise, and more cost-effective circuits. By comparison, it's a 10-year-old child looking down at that ant and water drop. It's what's found on the back of your stereo in the form of the two-conductor RCA connector. There's nothing wrong with it for casual listening, but it is limiting in a professional environment. For instance, there is no noise-reducing circuitry, so cables that are run more than 10 feet or so loose signal level and start to pick up radio frequency (RF) noise from electric cables and radio transmissions, and are susceptible to static and hiss. In comparison, professional-level cables can be run thousands of feet before signal level starts to wane and noise becomes a problem. You might ask why your home stereo doesn't use professional level? Cost, plain and simple. Your unit could easily cost 50% more for a feature you might not easily notice while rocking out in your living room.

Instruments

The signal level for electric guitars and other instruments with built-in pickups generally fall between line level and microphone level. Some mixing consoles and microphone preamp units have a special "Instrument" switch that will adjust the preamp to the right level for pickups. If your console doesn't have this option, the easiest thing to do will sound contradictory: lower the signal to microphone level and plug it into a mic preamp. We use a *direct box* to achieve this. These handy little boxes not only convert the signal to mic level, they filter out noise from the pickup circuit. Most guitar pickups have an unbalanced circuit, which means they only use two wires to carry the electrical signal, and lack the third wire that filters out noise. Many guitars made in the last 30 years or so now have an *active* pickup. These amplify the signal coming from the guitar up to consumer line level. They all require a battery to operate. I generally just plug this into my line level input on my mixing console and raise the gain. If you're sending it over a long distance, like from a stage to the back of the house, use a direct box. This also applies to most electric keyboards/synths. Note that some instruments, like stand-up bass, may actually have a small lavalier-type microphone instead of a pickup. Treat these as having microphone level. *Spec sheets will usually note pickups at -40 dB, active pickups at -10 dB, and keyboards at -10 dB.*

Digital levels

Many consoles, audio interfaces, recorders, and other gear have a variety of digital inputs and outputs. Some microphones even operate with digital-only outputs. What you need to keep in mind is that they all start as analog devices that convert varying levels of electrical pulses into a digital circuit. Following stringent noise-reducing standards and practices still applies to using these devices. To reduce noise, digital circuits are optimum, as long as the cables and analog-to-digital converters are doing their job nicely. The digital output of most of these devices is still an electrical signal, but instead of a varying voltage, it's a series of on/off pulses. One exception is fiber optic, which uses light in place of voltage. There are consumer and professional differences in digital circuits, just like analog. Consumer digital lines are also limited in length and can have digital dropouts if lines are too long or of inferior quality. Professional digital lines have many different varieties and are out of the scope of this discussion. But in essence, like their analog cousins, they can travel long distances with no errors. *The most common consumer digital connections are S/PDIF (either coax or RCA) and ADAT lightpipe (fiber optic). The most common professional digital connections are AES/EBU (XLR connector), USB, Firewire, Thunderbolt, and Dante (ethernet audio).*

Audio interfaces

Moving your audio from analog to digital requires a converter. A mixing console that has analog inputs and digital outputs is the granddaddy of them all. However, simpler options are available. One of the most basic devices is a two-channel interface with a USB, Firewire, or Thunderbolt connection. This device allows you to connect up to two microphones, line level devices, or instruments, or a combination of those. It will have a line level output (usually for a set of monitors) along with a headphone output. Most come with a simple piece of software that gives you limited control over the device, and some even include DAW recording software. The audio conversion is taking place inside the device before it ever is sent to the computer via USB/FW/TB. The quality of this conversion is usually reflected in the price, but recent improvements have drastically lowered the price of ones with very good quality. Quality conversion can also depend on your computer's software divers that control the digital timing and conversion of the audio to a digital signal. The one bane of these devices is keeping software and drivers updated. Some become obsolete after only a few years because drivers aren't updated by the manufacturer.

Larger and more expanded units are available. Most have a variety of inputs and outputs and controls. Some like to be controlled only by software, some have all the bells and whistles on the front. Regardless, a studio in the 21st century can have hundreds of inputs and outputs in a space no bigger than an apple box. When studio designers are planning how to interface all of their equipment, they're usually looking for interfaces that allow them to grow beyond their current needs. If you need 8 inputs right now, you might need 10 next month, so try to purchase an interface that has more than you currently need.

Amps and monitors

The final piece of the audio puzzle is listening. Headphones are great for listening to detail in a recording, but every studio needs a good set of monitors. Most studio monitors are *passive*. This means they only contain speaker cones and drivers and require a separate amplifier, just like your typical home stereo. Many other studio monitors are *active* and contain small amplifiers built into each cabinet. There are advantages to both. Passive monitors allow engineers to match an amplifier of choice to a speaker of choice. Passive monitors are usually less costly, but still require the purchase of an amplifier. Active monitors are easily installed and save rack space because the amplifier is built in. They are usually more expensive, heavier, deeper in size, and can generate heat. However, their amps are specifically matched to the speaker drivers and can operate more efficiently than passive monitor amps. I have both types in my studios.

The goal of listening to studio monitors is to hear the truth in your audio. You don't want an amplifier or speaker to color or alter the sound coming from your mixer. When a monitor delivers sound that is unaltered or uncolored, it is said to have a *flat response*. Many manufacturers that make consumer speakers color the sound for particular types of listeners. Beat-heavy listeners might prefer speakers with fat bass, while classical listeners might like a brighter response. These have no place in a studio, as they can give you a false report on your mix and cause you to overcompensate for either something that isn't being heard, or something that is overemphasized. If you construct your mix on flat response speakers, then each system it's heard on will, at the very least, reproduce the most important elements.

The same can be said for headphones. Mixing on headphones is usually avoided. The primary reason is that the stereo field is altered. When listening to speakers, the apparent center of the mix is forward, between the speakers (see the next chapter, page 374, discussing *phantom center*. When listening on headphones, that center part of the mix moves between your ears into your head space. Unless you know that your mix will *only* be heard on headphones, do your mixes on speakers. By the way, it's okay to use them while editing or tracking. Avoid consumer headphones, especially those with noise cancellation. Again, the primary reason is coloring or altered sonics. Noise cancellation headphones actually generate an audio signal that cancels out environmental sound. That "silence" you experience is actually sound hitting your eardrums. So, you're getting two signals hitting your ears: a negated noise signal, and the program signal. That is not the pure sound you need to critically listen. And because critical listening is energy consuming, ear fatigue might happen sooner while using noise cancellation headphones.

MIXING SOUND

We've discussed most of the equipment used, now let's talk about how to blend all your sounds into a final recording. Audio mixing consoles used to be big, gigantic pieces of gear with big knobs, switches, and large sweeping meters. They've steadily shrunk into space efficient consoles with touchscreens and virtual controls. They've even become software apps. The basic concept has been the same for several decades, however. An engineer uses a console to blend different audio signals together into one signal. A physical console is really just a big electrical control rig I remember seeing a stage lighting console in my early days of learning audio and struck by how it looked just like an audio console. Duh! It's also mixing electrical signals, but for lights. As you mix your different track signals together, you will hear what the final version will sound like. You can also temporarily hear each individual audio signal alone without disturbing the final version. You can alter the equalization of each signal, control the volume levels so there won't be distortion, place each sound in the stereo (or surround) field, mute certain parts, and blend in effects like reverberation. Mixers can range from smaller than your hand with just a few basic controls, to several feet long requiring multiple engineers to operate.

Inputs

Whether your audio signals are coming directly from microphones or from other sources, a mixing console blends them together. A mixer will usually have one volume control (*fader*) per signal or track *input*. This fader adjusts how much of the audio from each input is sent to the console's outputs. If you have 8 signals, then you would have 8 faders to control. The first control at your fingertips on a *channel strip* is the raw signal level: mic, instrument, or line level. A channel strip is a column of various controls for each input on a traditional mixing console. At the top are input controls, in the middle are EQ and AUX options, and near the bottom are output assignments. The very bottom will have a sliding indented finger pad (fader) used for raising or lowering the audio signal going to the outputs of the console.

Next, there is a *trim* control that adjusts the audio level before any other controls in the channel strip. With the trim, you adjust the input signal so that it isn't too low or high in volume. Each input may have other adjustments before the signal reaches the fader. These might include EQ, reverb, or compression. A mixer allows you to select to which *output*(s) you want each input signal to go. Some have multiple outputs beyond stereo. If so, each input will have *bus* assignment selectors (an output matrix). The last place in the signal path of audio through your mixer's input is the fader. This is usually an indented finger pad that slides about 100mm up and down a narrow slot (like a light dimmer). Sometimes just simple round knobs are used. If the fader is all the way down/left/off, then no signal goes to the outputs. Raising the fader sends a comparable amount of audio to the outputs. Faders of the sliding type are far easier to use for graceful mixing over rotary knobs, mainly because you can fit eight of them under your eight fingers, curling them to make adjustments.

Left: A typical input strip on a small mixer. The photo on the right from top to bottom: XLR input for microphone; ¼" input for line level; A low-cut rumble filter; the trim/gain control. On the far right are Stereo aux return jacks for signals from outboard gear like a reverb unit; Two ¼" inputs (L-R) for channels 5-6 and 7-8 stereo inputs.

Outputs

At the bottom of the input strip (below the blue knobs) is the output select section. The control labeled "Pan" allows the user to pan each signal left-center-right. Pushing in the white square buttons labeled "MUTE / ALT 3-4" will turn the selected channel off (mute). It also reroutes that channel's audio to a set of alternative outputs (ALT 3-4). This is useful for cueing up sources such as media players or even microphones, or providing an alternate mix for special purpose programs.

The "Pre-fader Solo" switches allow instantaneous audio of that channel to be played in the monitors without affecting the main stereo mix. It's great for listening to just one source without hearing the entire mix.

The bottom white knob is the "Gain." This controls the level of each channel going to the main stereo outputs.

The output of your mixer will go to something that would either record or reproduce your mix, like a recorder, or it would go to a live audience via an amplifier or broadcast/live stream path. As you mix, you raise or lower each input for balance. So you don't overload the output, mixers have *VU meters*[86], which give instant readout of your total overall signal level. The old school meters with

---

[86] VU = Volume Units of dB

a needle that swings back and forth like a speedometer are in fact measuring electrical signal.[87] Modern mixers have LED or on-screen digital meters that are more accurate than sweep needle meters.

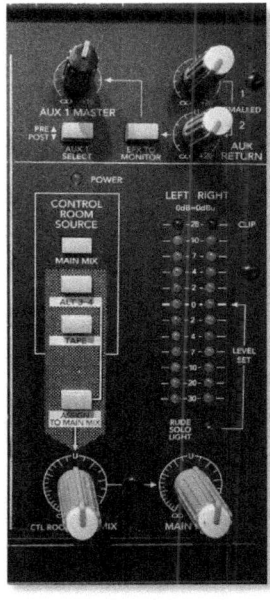

The output monitoring section. At the top left is the gain control for Auxiliary 1 master with an option to send the signal "Pre" regardless of if the channel fader is up or down, or "Post," only when the channel fader is active.

To the right of that is a similar control for the Auxiliary 2 return.

The "Control Room Source" section lets the user choose what to hear in the monitors. The "ALT" and "Tape" sources can also be assigned to the main outputs from here.

To the right is the LED meter section. This includes a red LED indicator for when any solo button is activated.

At the very bottom are volume controls for the speaker volume and the mix level directly going out of the main outputs

Mixing consoles usually have multiple outputs, the most common is stereo (2 channels), although some mixers have dozens and dozens. Each input fader will have a control (*pan pot*) for placement in the stereo listening field. This control allows you to precisely place that channel's signal anywhere from left to right. Most mixers also have additional auxiliary outputs called *AUX channels*. These are utility outputs that may send signals to headphones, stage monitors, or an effects unit. Each input channel will usually have at least one of these AUX controls. These are independent from the main outputs and will not be heard in your mix.

---

[87] That electric tester in your workshop with the similar looking meter can be used as a VU meter in theory, but I wouldn't rely on it.

EQ

Each input channel may also have equalization controls (*EQ*). This allows you to add or subtract bass, mid-range, and/or treble frequencies. Some recordings benefit from altering the equalization of some channels so that the recording can be more easily heard. For instance, enhancing the treble of a vocalist might make the voice brighter and heard better over a piano.

The equalizer (EQ) section. This small console offers basic but handy controls for shaping the sound of each channel. Each control (low-mid-hi) will either boost or cut the signal with a bell-like curve, peaking at its indicated frequency (such as 2.5 KHz on the mid control) Above the blue EQ controls are the sends for Aux 1 and Aux 2 as seen in the previous output section picture.

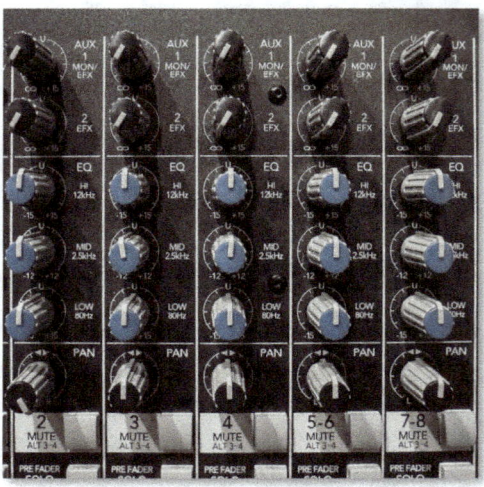

Effects

Lastly, many mixing consoles have built-in effects like *reverb*. Each channel will have AUX controls that send the signal to a built-in reverb unit (like in the previous picture of the EQ section). That reverb's output is mixed into the outputs along with all the other input fader signals. You can control the reverb's output so that it doesn't overwhelm the final mix. A console may also have built-in *compressors* or *limiters* that can tame the volume level of some audio signals. Controlling sudden audio surges or peaks can prevent distortion.

Here is a typical medium-sized analog mixer from Yamaha. This one has 16 inputs, 4 group outputs, 2 stereo outputs, and 4 aux outputs. The configuration would be labeled as 16 x 4 x 2.

Starting with the inputs, channels 1-8 have a dual input receptacle. Either a ¼" or XLR can be plugged in. There is a 26 dB pad, or attenuator, to reduce the signal from XLRs if line level is used. The "HPF 80Hz" switch enables a high pass filter to reduce low rumble. Further on down is the input "GAIN" control along with a built-in compressor control for each channel.

The yellow controls are for compression on each channel. These are very useful to control unexpected loud sources. The green controls are for EQ. The high and low controls are fixed frequencies, but the mid-range has a wide selectable frequency between 250 Hz and 5 KHz. Four AUX sends are possible, with AUX 1 being pre-fader only, AUX 2 with pre or post option, and AUX 3 and AUX 4 post fader. Each channel has pan control and an ON/OFF switch.

Each input channel has selectors for where to send the signal. In this case, Group 1-2, Group 3-4, and/or Stereo. The pan control above pans between each group pair or stereo. PFL (pre-fade listen) is the same as Solo.

Finally, the output section. Each of the four AUX send masters control the overall output signal from each channel's AUX sends. The monitor and Phones pots send audio to either speakers or headphones, with selectable source. The Group and Stereo faders control the overall output from the input faders as assigned.

Powered mixers

Most mixing consoles are designed to send your final mix to line level outputs. These can be used to send to a recorder, audio interface, or amplifier (such as the PA system at a live event). Some have speaker amplifiers built right into the console. These are called *powered mixers* and are designed to operate in small live venues. The mixing console has speaker cable outputs that the engineer would run to a matched pair of speakers. Mismatching speakers and amplifiers can result in damage to your equipment, so make sure you read the specs carefully when selecting speakers. Powered mixers also sometimes have one or more powered AUX outputs for on-stage monitor speakers (those wedge-shaped speakers you see at a performer's feet). For small bands or performers, these powered mixer combinations can greatly reduce set-up time and expense.

Digital mixers

Many newer mixers in the last 20 years or so have analog inputs and outputs, but also digital inputs and outputs. In addition, all controls, such as signal level, pan, AUX, etc. are processed digitally. They also have fully integrated compressors, limiters, noise gates, and other signal enhancers that formerly only existed in the physical world as separate devices. Digital mixers also have motorized faders that allow it synchronize to a DAW and be used to control a software mixer, as described in the next section.

Software mixers

Your recording software usually has a mixer built into it. It will usually look exactly like an actual physical mixer, with faders, pots, and meters. Each track on your software DAW program will have its own fader, as will each output. Control of each parameter is done by mouse or hot keys. However, there are physical fader controllers (*fader packs*) that look exactly like a mixing console, but control the levels and parameters of the software mixer. These can be quite helpful because you get a tactile feel of the faders, bringing more precise control. Some fader packs have built-in motors for each fader. As you raise or lower the track level in the software, it memorizes your movements. When you play that section back, the faders magically move along with your previous adjustments.

These fader packs can also control almost every function on your DAW mixer such as AUX levels, EQ controls, mutes, reverb levels, etc.

The mix window in Steinberg Nuendo. It's very versatile in what you can view, with custom windows, faders that can be hidden or moved, plug-in information, and much more. Notice that the first 12 channels from the left are tracks, the next four are group outputs, and the last on the far right is the main stereo out. The meter on the extreme right is also customizable in how you can view your mix.

EDITING

Data

Recording a sound opens up the possibility of altering it. Sound that is recorded is most commonly captured digitally. This can be to a variety of devices such as a stand-alone recorder, a computer, or video camera. It's captured as ones and zeros, and encoded within a data file with instructions on how to rearrange the data into something playable. Because it's just data, we rely on computers and processors to handle all the mundane tasks of storing and retrieving it. As computer technology improves in general, so does digital audio technology. But the bare bones of capturing that data have remained amazingly constant for decades.

Audio waves are digitally captured and stored as Pulse Code Modulation. PCM audio is just a stream of ones and zeros, but are sorted in logical groupings. These instructions for how to unlock the groupings and rearrange them for listening is stored in each file's container package. Each container package also has additional instructions, depending on what file format the data was recorded in. Let me simplify.

Let's say that a manufacturer makes soccer balls. They are all round, as soccer balls are, they are all white, and they all bounce exactly the same way as each other. The factory inflates all of them and puts eight of them at a time in generic boxes labeled "SOCCER BALLS". The balls inside are PCM audio, straight and forward data. The label on the side of each box is the container.

One of their customers wants to add a little pizzaz and have all the balls be painted with glow-in-the-dark paint so teams can play at night. They make the balls, paint and inflate them, and send them on. The boxes all are labeled "GLOW-IN-THE-DARK SOCCER BALLS". The balls do their job, but the description of what kind they are tell the players that these are special and can be used at night. Think of this as a basic WAV file, the content is the same but there is more finesse and usefulness to what's inside.

Another customer wants all bright yellow soccer balls so teams can see the ball better in the daytime. They also want to include some simple instructions inside for how to kick the ball, when to use the ball, and how to clean the ball after each game. These are inflated and labeled "BRIGHT YELLOW SOCCER BALLS-SEE INSIDE". This is an AIFF file, same basic soccer ball, but with some additional capabilities.

The soccer balls are popular, but transporting each box of eight balls is becoming cumbersome. The customers want more in each shipment, so the factory expands. Now they can make more balls, and more importantly, they make bigger boxes that hold sixteen balls at a time. This is akin to having a more powerful processor and more storage space, allowing for better quality audio. PCM audio went from low sample and bit rate to higher and higher rates. File sizes grew, but processor speeds advanced as well.

Everything's going fine, but it's getting expensive to ship soccer balls to their customers that are very far away, so the factory decides to ship deflated balls in smaller boxes, saving on shipping materials and transportation. The customers like the lower cost, but they must pump their own air into the balls when they get them. This is analogous to a compressed file such as an mp3. Once inflated (with some effort), the balls (and audio file) resemble the fully inflated balls (WAV files) but may have some creases or wrinkles from being shrunk.

Learning all the audio file formats can be challenging, but the standard WAV or AIFF formats are found across almost all recorders and DAW software. Keeping to this standard simplifies production work flows and ensures quality is retained through the editing and mixing process.

The Digital Audio Workstation (DAW)

The main work area in Steinberg Nuendo. The blocks (a.k.a. clips or regions) contain graphical representations of the audio. Quieter passages show less information. Notice the topmost track in green that has been sliced up and moved around. It started as one long recording and is now made up of several portions (clips or regions) of that recording.

The most efficient way to edit audio is on a DAW. The audio information, such as amplitude and frequency, is visualized as waves and colors. You can either record directly into a DAW onto an input channel, or import from an external recorder or file. Once in the DAW's timeline or work area, it can be cut up, moved around, muted, pitched up or down, stretched, squeezed, and a bevy of other manipulations. What's helpful to know when editing, is how the original recording's data is handled.

When you record or import audio into a DAW, the file remains untouched when any alterations are made. When you do something simple like create a fade out, the DAW actually writes a new, small audio file with the fade that replaces just that small section. The original audio file plays until it reaches the fade out segment, then plays that file. The editor doesn't see the seam where the two audio clips are butted up against each other, just a fade out line.[88] This is called *non-destructive editing*. This is what's happening each time you alter the audio clip – that section is replaced with a tiny audio clip with the change. You can usually find these little clips in your project's "Edits" folder. The original file will be located in the "Audio" folder. When you cut a clip into two pieces, cut out a part, move your cut clips around in a different order, or even delete it from the timeline, this is still non-destructive, because the DAW is simply jumping around the original file and playing the different sections.

Destructive editing is when you purposefully alter the original audio file. There are a few reasons to do this, but the most common for me is to process an intermediary file that is a duplicate. I might be applying noise-reduction or applying compression to it so my DAW doesn't do it real time. I also sometimes destructively edit final mixes because I'm under a time crunch to fix an error. It's rare that I need to, so I always do it with caution and make sure I have no other way to accomplish the same thing.

If you're ever in doubt about whether your DAW is inadvertently doing destructive editing, duplicate your entire project folder to another hard drive before you start. That way you'll have an unaltered original of everything.

Most portable recorders (like Zoom, Tascam, etc.) that have editing capabilities, do destructive editing. Any professional video editing app will use non-destructive editing, but phone apps are questionable so proceed with caution.

---

[88] In the earliest days of DAW editing, we did in fact see the butt edit. We could even grab the fade out clip and move it around. Some editors still show the edit point, but the two clips are "glued" together and move together seamlessly.

Editing in a Digital Audio Workstation

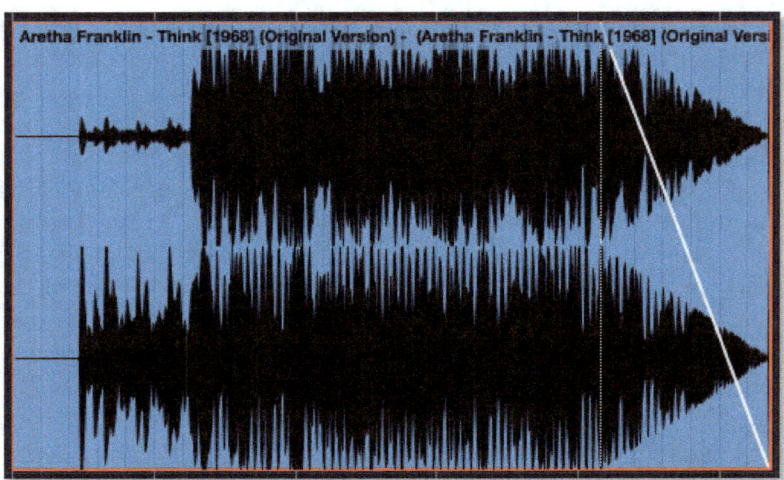

This is a stereo waveform of Aretha Franklin's "Think" from 1968. Notice the uneven part on the left. That is the piano intro in the right channel (bottom wave) and a distant microphone across the room (top wave). The song then goes full tilt in both channels when she starts singing. The diagonal line on the right represents an added fadeout. The waveform picture corresponds.

Each recording in a DAW project is typically called a *clip*. A clip looks like a children's play block, but has a *waveform*. A waveform is a visual representation of the amplitude and frequency range of the audio contained in that clip. A clip can be further cut up into more clips. Some DAW apps call these *regions*, others call them *segments* or *parts*. These are created when you slice a clip up into two or more parts. They can be moved around in time and between tracks. You can name each individual clip, adjust its volume, or apply processing or an effect to it. Clips can be mono, stereo, or surround.

The editing toolbar in Steinberg Nuendo. From left to right: Object selection; Range selection; Draw; Erase; Slice; Glue; Cut; Zoom; Move; Tempo; Parabola (for drawing volumes or notes); Audition clip; Colorize clip. Many of these have additional tools hidden underneath.

The basic editing tools in a DAW include:

- **Object Selection**. This tool is usually shaped like an arrow. Click on any clip to select it for editing, volume adjustment, processing, or moving.
- **Range Selection**. This tool usually looks like a sideways "H". It defines portions of tracks, clips, and time to edit.
- **Combo Tool**. This combines the first two tools into one, so the editor doesn't have to continually switch back and forth.
- **Split**. This usually looks like a pair of scissors or knife. It cuts a clip where it is clicked.
- **Erase**. This looks like a pencil eraser and deletes clips that are clicked.
- **Glue**. This looks like a bottle of glue and will "glue" two clips together so that they can be moved or processed together.
- **Draw**. Looking like a pencil, this tool can draw automation curves, volume curves, or silent clips used for spacing.
- **Scrub**. This tool looks like a speaker sometimes. By dragging it back and forth on an audio clip, it slowly plays the audio at the speed you drag it. This helps to find subtle audio events for editing. It sounds like an LP record being scratched slowly.

Other standard tools include:

- **Nudge**. Finely trims audio clip heads or tails.
- **Colorize**. Change track or clip color, making track organization easier. I usually color vocal tracks green, effects tracks yellow, music or instrument tracks blue, and reverb tracks purple.
- **Locators**. Drop bookmarks and pins in various places in the timeline. The *In* and *Out* locators define the section that will be mixed down.
- **Automation**. This tool set will help make fine adjustments to fader, pan, EQ, and other automated functions you've created.
- **Inserts**. Real-time effects like EQ, compression, and reverb for each channel.

These are just the basic tools available. Modern DAWs have layers upon layers of editing tools and functions. I suggest taking online tutorials for whatever system you will be using, or anticipate using. It also helps to watch videos of editors doing their job. Just seeing and hearing it happen will help you make sense of how DAWs work.

Timelines in Digital Audio Workstations

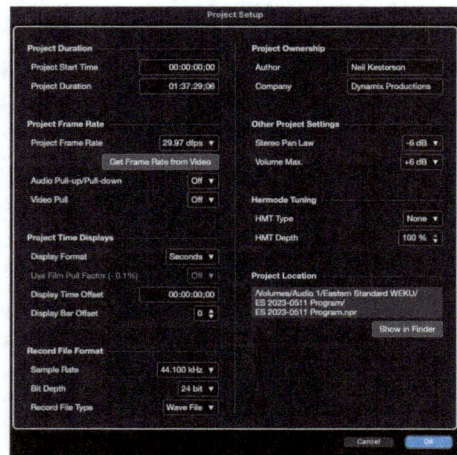

A typical project setup window. This one happens to be an hour and thirty-seven plus minutes. It's frame rate is 29.97 drop-frames-per-second. The display format is in seconds. It will record and import audio files at 44.1 KHz, 24 bit as WAV files. Other useful information is shown at the right.

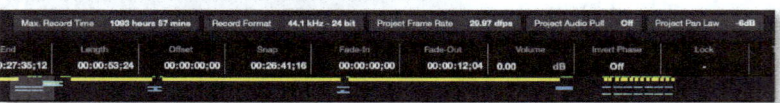

On the actual timeline, that setup information is always available (see top). The next line down is information about the clip I have selected. The very bottom colored lines are like a birds eye view of all the clips on the timeline.

When you start a project in a DAW, you'll be prompted to choose a sample rate, bit rate, and time base. The timeline displays your time base setting, which may be *seconds, timecode, bars and beats, frames,* or *samples.* Another choice you must make is the *project frame rate.* This is useful for video projects, but can otherwise be ignored. If you're creating audio-only programs for a podcast, radio, etc., choose *seconds.* Your time window will display *hours:minutes:seconds.* If it's for video or television, choose *timecode.* The *Bars and beats* timeline is good for music, especially if you will be using a *click track,* which is a built-in metronome that players will hear in their headphones as they're recording. At the top of the project window will be a long strip that displays the selected time base.

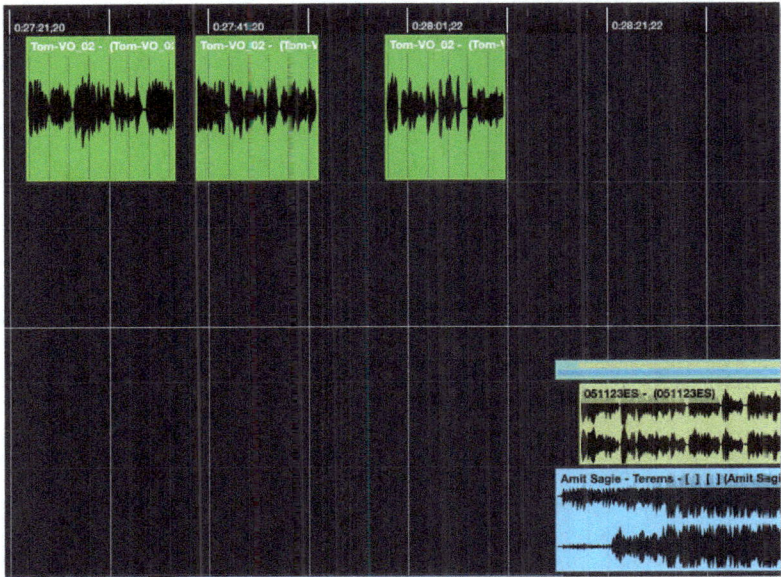

Notice the time counter at the very top. The vertical lines extending down are time divisions to help you place clips and quickly see their length.

There will also be a numeric counter window that will display the current position of the play bar/line. The background of the work window will have faint vertical lines denoting divisions of the time base, depending on how far you're zoomed in or out. For instance, each vertical line may indicate one second. This is handy for quickly aligning clips or visually timing sections. There is a *snap to time* option that will edit, cut, or align clips to those vertical lines if desired. Another useful function of the division lines is for adjusting time signatures when recording music. Many DAWs let you retard or ramp up time changes. These will also affect the click track, allowing the musician to hear the metronome change tempo with the timeline.

YOUR FINAL MIX

We've followed a sound from its origin in front of a microphone, through a mixer, into a computer, and back out to the world. Your mix can end up in an audio file, on a video, streaming over the web, on television or radio, or played through a PA system to a crowd.

Audio files

By far, the most common destination for an audio mix is to a computer file. When we record to a computer, we're creating individual audio files for each track, edit, or session. The usual procedure for mixing is to blend all the tracks together within the DAW's software mixer. Most DAW software programs allow you to adjust volume levels of each track with automation. Each parameter of each track can be adjusted and memorized. One common automation function is to record mouse movements of a volume fader as the program plays. After the automation is written, the software allows the engineer to go back and make minute corrections. This procedure is repeated for each track and parameter. These internal software mixers, coupled with automation, allow the engineer to finesse a balanced mix that would be nearly impossible to do in real time on a traditional analog mixing console.

When everything is balanced, the engineer will *mix down* (sometimes called *bouncing* or *bouncing tracks)* to a single audio file. This is the chocolate milk phase. Because everything is taking place inside the software, this usually happens faster than real time. That audio file is then distributed to wherever it will be heard. As an audio engineer, your goal is to maintain the highest quality possible throughout the entire process, from capture to mix. Even your mixed audio file needs to be high quality. This is your master mix and can be used to create different downstream formats, such as mp3 or AAC. But your final mix should be high-resolution, like WAV or AIFF. I usually keep this final file in the same format, sample rate, and bit rate as my entire project. This avoids any conversion errors or confusion.

Video

A documentary being produced in Steinberg Nuendo. The timeline contains the video track at the very top. On the left screen is a video window for reference (this would typically be shown on a third monitor). This project has more than 40 tracks, many of which are hidden within track folders, such as the green and yellow tracks.

If you've created an audio track for a video, the audio is assembled in a separate program from the video. The most common workflow is for a video editor to send a video file with separate audio elements. The video is then imported into your DAW software along with the audio elements. The audio is then aligned and synchronized with the video.[89] The software allows you to add and move new audio elements, like sound effects or music, around in time while remaining synchronized with the video. After adding all the elements and adjusting their levels, the final mix happens like any other software mix you've done. An audio file is created and sent to the video editor. The editor imports the new audio mix into their software, replacing the original audio. Some audio software programs allow you to directly replace the video's audio track, but in most professional applications, each element is handled by separate entities.

Other types of projects that your audio mix would be adjoined with video are live broadcast, live stream, or live-to-tape. Your mix would be live and happening in real time. The outputs of your mixing console would go directly to either a television transmitter, web streamer, or video recorder. You really have to be on your toes for a live mix.

---

[89] How this is done and what formats to use are out of the scope of this discussion.

Radio

Just like live television or streaming, your mix may go to a radio transmitter or audio streaming service. In live broadcast or streaming situations, mixing consoles are usually simplified in appearance to facilitate easy operation. All the bells and whistles found on recording consoles are usually hidden or eliminated, so the operator can focus on adjusting levels of speakers/performers, actuating commercials and announcements, switching to network audio feeds, and other high-attention tasks. Most radio engineering positions require the ability to also announce. This is true for music-heavy stations as well as talk/news/sports stations. Most independent radio stations have small on-air staffs because most of the programming is automated, so engineers may also have administrative duties. Larger stations, radio groups, and networks may have a dedicated audio engineer on staff that is tasked with only creating commercials, announcements, and/or operating live news and sports programming. The equipment used by production engineers is usually more complicated than most on-air staff will use.

Live Sound

The live mixing console at the University of Kentucky Kroger Field stadium. Each bank of eight faders (4 on extreme left, 2 on extreme right) contain inputs from various sources. They are grouped for quick access. Counterclockwise from top left: hardwired field mics; video production; TV/radio stations; talkback/intercoms; crowd/closed caption/remote feeds; wireless mics. The four faders left of center are stereo inputs for CD/turntable/media player.

The eight faders under the touchscreen mirror whatever eight-fader section is selected (in this case the bottom left bank), bringing control of that section under your fingertips. It is also customizable with select faders for optimum control.

Mixing for a live audience can be a huge thrill and a terrifying experience, all at the same time. Like live broadcast mixing, the fewer controls, the better. However, live sound requires many precise and minuscule adjustments beforehand. Many live sound consoles are similar to, or can double as recording consoles. They usually contain additional controls and functions that only live sound engineers use. The main goal for a live sound engineer is to prevent the main speakers from bleeding back into the stage microphones and causing squeal. Live sound engineers reduce this feedback by cutting (muting) very small slices of equalization out of each microphone input at the frequency where feedback occurs. Sometimes computer-assisted feedback reduction is employed that automatically finds and cuts the problem frequencies. During the live show though, more small adjustments are usually necessary.

The second main goal of a live sound engineer is to obtain as much *gain* out of the amplifier and speakers before feedback occurs. If the amplifiers and speakers are correctly matched to the size of the venue (square footage and audience size), then this is usually not an issue. Problems arise when the power output of the equipment is undersized for the audience. Pushing the equipment's output beyond its limits will usually create uncontrolled feedback, distortion, and a lot of dissatisfied patrons. Having an *over*-powered PA system can also create problems like feedback, hearing damage, and overheating of the amplifiers if they are operated far below the intended working range.

The third goal of a live sound engineer is to know the "script" and cues of the program. Concerts and stage events are usually rehearsed, notes are taken, and the engineer will practice fader movements. Digital consoles allow different *scenes* to be created. The *scene* function on a console memorizes default fader positions, mutes, EQs, etc. Each scene can be recalled for each program segment. Well-funded large arena concerts, Broadway shows, and other recurring events will use mixing consoles that can memorize fader, mute and EQ adjustments. These consoles use motorized faders (like software mixers and fader packs) for a semi-automated live mix. The programs are usually timed with a master clock that the performers, lighting, video, and other production personnel can also use to automate cues and effects.

Smaller gigs face more uncontrolled chaos than large productions. Each venue will have different characteristics, may not be optimized for live sound, and have budgetary challenges that prevent the addition of adequate personnel and/or special equipment. Good basic skills in live sound engineering and production can reduce problems before they arise. For example, positioning microphones and speakers to avoid feedback and never driving the amplifier above its rating will produce more successful results. Keeping a good attitude going into small gigs can reduce stress. For example, knowing that problems will arise because of the room or audience size, available equipment, lack of sound absorption, etc. will place these problems on your "Can't do anything about it" list and leave you to concentrate on what's important: the performance. Unanticipated problems during a production can be extremely stressful and affect job performance. So, if you anticipate which problems are the most likely to happen, then they aren't surprises.

20. AUDIO ENGINEERING TRICKS AND ADVICE

"Never tell the audience how good you are; they will soon find out for themselves."

Houdini

Now here comes the fun part. We get to peek behind the stage curtain and learn how the tricks are done. As with any magic trick, you'll need get the basics right before you can move on to the sleight-of-hand. And any magician will tell you to practice, practice, practice. So, within this chapter are tricks I have learned over the years, some by making mistakes, some by design, some from other pros, and some by dumb luck. I'll also offer some advice and technical details that I think you need to know. You won't find in-depth how-to segments for specific software or equipment unless it directly relates to the topic. There will be some specific technical basics however, but I'll try to teach them to you in layman's terms. Some of you will be more technologically advanced than others, so please don't roll your eyes when I'm getting down to basics, you just might learn something new.

STARTING A RECORDING SESSION

One of the first things you should master is how to quickly set up a recording session. Before you even plug in a microphone or hit RECORD, you need to plan your session carefully.

Do the paperwork first. The very first thing I do is set up an account for the client if they are new. Get all pertinent information from them such as name, business, address, etc. If your policy is to get a down payment, process that first before starting your session. If you have an assistant that can do that while you're getting mics set up, then that will speed things along, which your client will like. Also assign a job number to your new project if your company does that. Hint: You should do it even if you're a solo studio. That job number should be on everything associated with that particular job, such as the invoice, any purchase orders, filenames, hard drives, tapes, and any correspondence relating to it. It can be as simple as YYYYMMDD-01, or like we do, a 4-digit counter that started at 1000. We keep a master Google spreadsheet that everyone can access. It's really easy to get projects confused with each other as they pile up over time. You'll thank me later for this tip.

Count your chickens. The next thing I do is figure out how many mics I'll need, how many tracks I'll be recording, and how many musicians or actors or narrators I'll be working with. If it's a fairly involved job, like recording a concert or a large number of actors, I'll chart out every source I'll be working with and assign them to any channels, groups, or tracks *on paper* first. The assignments may change a few times once we get rolling, but I generally follow my original plan I laid out in the beginning. Be sure to remain flexible as the session gets going so that you can add / delete channels or tracks *when* things change. Don't get bent out of shape when they do, because no project ever ends the same way it started. Be sure to keep your paperwork with your project's notes for at least a few years because you never know when you're going to have to go back in and revise something. If space is a problem, digitally scan everything and keep the files with the project media <u>and</u> on a separate hard drive/cloud backup service. I will sometimes even save emails as PDFs and file away because there may be important instructions buried deep in the email chain. If you don't keep any notes, then later on you'll be scratching your head wondering why you recorded that guitar on two different tracks.

Know your delivery specs – Sample rate. The next thing I determine is: Who is listening to this, and where and what will they listen on. This will guide me on how to set up my DAW project and mixer. Are they listening on television, radio, streaming audio, a theme park, a movie theater, a toy doll? This will determine the sample rate (such as 44.1 KHz, 48 KHz, 96 KHz), the sound field (such as stereo, mono, surround), and file type (AIFF, WAV, mp3, AAC). I generally record, master, and deliver in the same or multiplied sample rate. For instance, audiobooks are almost always recorded and delivered at a 44.1 KHz sample rate (though filetype and bit rates will differ). Most video / film dialog and voice-overs are recorded and delivered at a 48 KHz sample rate. Music is a mixed bag, but most producers like to record at a high sample rate of 96 KHz (and beyond), then downmix to 48 KHz (a division of 96 KHz) for mp3s and iTunes files. Most television shows are delivered at a 48 KHz sample rate, but a lot of cinema-released and 4K movies are mixed at 96 KHz. That dialog that's recorded at 48 KHz is easily up-sampled to 96 KHz, its double. You might be wondering why not record dialog at 96 KHz then? A few reasons, the first of which is the difference isn't easily heard. The second is the economy of file sizes. Audio files are being transported all over the internet these days between studios, and if there isn't a glaring sonic difference, then why wait twice as long for an upload?

Tech Tip

Up-sampling refers to converting a lower-sampled recording into a higher-sampled one. It's strictly done for sample rate matching in most instances, because all elements embedded in a DAW project must be at the same sample rate. Here's an example: A 96 KHz film soundtrack has been built upon music and sound effects that were also recorded and mixed at 96 KHz. The dialog has been recorded and mixed at a lower resolution of 48 KHz. The dialog must be converted into a 96 KHz recording while retaining speed, pitch, and volume. The sonic quality of the dialog doesn't improve, but now it will play at the same speed as the film soundtrack instead of being sped up double-time like Alvin the Chipmunk. Because there is little discernable difference between dialog that is recorded at 48 KHz and 96 KHz, audio recordists can save file space while on location.

Know your delivery specs – Bit rate. When you're setting up your recorder, be sure to record in the highest bit rate you can, based on the source, disk space, and bang for the buck. I record exclusively in 24-bit unless the specs or source dictate something different. There is a big difference between 16-bit (audio CD and mp3 standard), and 24-bit. Higher bit rates can capture much more dynamic range. Music and field sound effects especially benefit from high bit rate because of the highly variable dynamic range. Voice-overs can be recorded at 16-bit if it's a measured delivery like an audiobook (most audiobook producers actually require that all files be delivered in 16-bit because there can be 10, 20, and even more than 30 hours of raw files to edit). Your final delivery specs may be at a lower bit rate, but by keeping a high bit rate through every step until the final output, you can make a big difference between something sounding flat, and something with some life in it.

Tech Tip

Besides recording at 24-bit, 32- and 64-bit are also options. Not all recorders or software actually record in 32- and 64-bit, even though they have it as an option. Make sure your hardware's bit rate has a 32- or 64-bit capability. Check throughput on the USB/Firewire/Thunderbolt bus and cabling to make sure it will pass it. And finally, check the specs of the hardware/software to make sure it captures in 32- or 64-bit, because some devices and apps only use the higher bit rate for processing effects and edits on files. Do you need to record in these high bit rates? Not really, but only the most experienced ears on the most expensive equipment will hear the difference. Most DAWs perform processing in 32- or 64-bit floating integer. The extra 8 bits of 32-bit are where post processing occurs while maintaining the original 24-bit material. 64-bit performs the same magic on native 32-bit recordings.

Know your delivery specs – Sound field. If you don't know what the sound field will be when you're beginning, play it safe and start in stereo. You can always retool to surround later (which is tedious but achievable) if your beginning sources don't need to be recorded in surround. For instance, you might start out recording voice-over or a solo singer in mono, which is the normal way to record the voice. Once the project gets going, you discover that the background material is in surround. No problem, start a new project in surround and import your mono tracks. If you're fairly deep into a stereo project before you find out it needs to be delivered in surround (this has happened more times that I can remember), then figure out if switching to surround or staying in stereo until the output is best. Stereo material can usually be "faked" into a surround mix by mixing some tracks into the rear channels with a slight delay and assigning the mono voice to the center speaker. If you do find out late in the mix that it needs to be in surround, then do all your mixes in stereo, start a new project in surround, and import the stereo mixes. Apply the surround simulators to the mixes and output in surround. Now you also have a brilliant stereo mix that you can send along with the other files

---

Tech Tip

Most surround projects require stereo mixes as well. Many DAW apps include downmix tools that allow you to mix all or some surround channels down to stereo. Surround decoders on the listener's playback equipment will also downmix the surround channels to stereo if they are listening in stereo or mono. Since you have no control over this, it's always good to check your surround mixes with a downmix tool to see if the surround channels are competing with the main front channels.

Mono a mono. Another thing to consider is how your project will sound in mono. You're probably thinking, "I'd never listen to anything in mono!" But a surprising amount of audio is indeed heard that way. Your smartphone may have two small speakers, but at arm's length it's heard mostly in mono because it's so far away. If you go to live events, most of them will be in mono. A stereo mix to a large, wide crowd would sound different to each listener, depending on where they are. If your music or commercial mix ends up on radio, chances are someone will hear it in mono. With all this in mind, it's prudent to check your mixes in mono to make sure everything still holds up. I've discovered serious phasing errors by summing to mono. Most DAW apps or consoles have a way to sum the stereo channels to mono. Be sure it's not just the left or just the right channel being played. It must be *both* left and right summed together.

Follow the law - the stereo pan law, that is. Most DAW apps have a monitor section that lets you switch between mono, stereo, and surround. Click that MONO button and listen back, making sure the important stuff translates properly. If the tracks that were panned to the center, like vocals or lead guitar, seem louder than the side channel material, then you may have a "pan law" issue. We don't have to call in Judge Judy to fix this. Go into your DAW's project setup menu and look for a setting called "Stereo Pan Law," "Pan Rule," "Pan Depth," or something similar. You will usually be given several options: 0 dB, -3 dB, -4.5 dB, -6 dB, and "equal power." The pan law options allow you to mix your project in stereo while adjusting for:

- Material that may be played in mono by summing left and right together (mono summing), as in radio, TV, live venue, etc.
- Listening in stereo on speakers with material that is panned from one speaker to center, or the other speaker.

Here's why we have all those choices. In stereo, we have two speakers, but *three* potential channels. Huh? We have left, right, and a "phantom" center. Any sound that is equally distributed in *both* the left and right speakers will appear to come from a third unseen speaker sitting right between your two real speakers. Common sounds that appear in this magical middle are narrators, singers, solo or lead instruments, or just about anything else that has importance. Some things just land there by accident, like the middle octave on a stereo-mic'd piano, bass, kick drum, etc. When we plan the stereo soundscape of a project, we must choose how strong that center channel is in relation to the left and right channels. Let's use an example of a recording with a stereo piano, stereo drum kit, and a mono vocal. In this example, you mixed a song with the pan law set to "off" (or set to 0 dB). Selecting different pan law settings, here's how the phantom center will sound for each in stereo and summed-mono. Keep in mind these observations are somewhat subjective and can vary depending on your monitoring system or your relative position to the monitors in the room:

- 0 dB setting, or "none". STEREO: Instruments even, vocals sit in the middle/phantom center. MONO-SUMMED: Piano and drums are even, the vocal sounds louder and more dominant than the stereo version.
- -3 dB setting. STEREO: Instruments sound even, vocals sit in the middle/phantom center but are just slightly lower. MONO-SUMMED: Piano and drums are unchanged, the vocal sounds even in relation to the instruments and similar to the stereo version.
- -4.5 dB setting. STEREO: Instruments sound even, vocals sit in the middle/phantom center but are lower. MONO-SUMMED: Piano and drums are unchanged, the vocal sounds somewhat even in relation to the instruments and somewhat similar to the stereo version. -4.5 is a compromise between --3 dB and -6 dB that works in situations that may be heard in both stereo and mono.
- -6 dB setting. STEREO: Instruments sound even, vocals sit in the middle/phantom center but are noticeably lower. MONO-SUMMED: Piano and drums are a little lower, the vocal sounds lower in relation to the instruments and the stereo version.

When you start a new session – and let me emphasize that this is when you make this setting, not after you've already mixed – choose the pan law setting that will best fit your final mixes. Test your DAW using sine waves in the different channels first, because not all DAWs handle panning the same way.

The -3 dB setting should be your default if most of your mixes will be heard in stereo. You can't go wrong with this setting in *most* situations.

The -4.5 dB setting is what I default to on stereo mixes that will probably also be heard mono-summed, like radio, theater, stadiums, etc. It's a great in-between that doesn't harm the mix when it's heard in mono.

If I'm mixing down mono material to a mono audio file, such as an audiobook or narration, I choose -6 dB pan law so that the volume of the mix matches in the left, center and right meters when mono-summed during the mixdown. Using any of the other settings (0, -3, -4.5, equal power) will make your mono-summed mono mixes louder and may clip or distort. Until I discovered the pan law, I was vexed when I would carefully set my mono material to -20 dB, mix down to a mono file, and have it be bumped up 3 to 6 dB louder.

Here's a little history about the pan law. The first stereo consoles had no "pan law" built in. In fact, many early stereo consoles had a 3-position switch for each channel with the choices of left-center-right. But when the *pan pot* came into existence, it allowed for exact placement of a sound in the stereo field. Pan pot is short for a panning potentiometer, or a knob that when turned all the way to the left will move the sound to the extreme left channel. Turning to the right sends it to the right. Parking it in the middle, or 12 o'clock position, will distribute it evenly between the two channels. This pan pot will be mouse-controlled in DAW software.

Sometimes a mixing engineer would intentionally "pan" a sound back and forth between the channels, for instance to simulate a car going by. When that car sound would pass through the center of the mix, it would sound slightly louder in the center than from the left and right speakers. People that are way smarter than a whole truckload of Neils theorized that having equal amounts of one sound in both speakers produced four times the volume (6.02 dBSPL[90]) in a room. In practice, it's been measured at about 3.00 dBSPL, or twice the volume. The average is about 4.5 dBSPL in well-made control rooms with top-of-the-line equipment.

So, engineers began building pan pots with a -3 dB or -4.5 dB gradual dip in the center of the arc. That is, when something is panned dead center at 12 o'clock, its volume has been reduced by 3 or 4.5 dB to compensate for the bump in volume that naturally occurs. When panned across the stereo field from left to right, it will sound even all the way from the left speaker, through the phantom center, and in the right speaker. In the old days when I

---

[90] dBSPL, or dB-SPL, is a measure of sound pressure level in decibels. It's basically a measurement of acoustical energy. Examples would be: 40-60 dBSPL-normal conversation, 100 dBSPL-jackhammer, 130 dBSPL-trumpet. We can also measure dBSPL coming from speaker systems. This shouldn't be confused with "dB" which is a generic term used to measure volume changes in software, consoles, and recording equipment.

had to mix everything on an analog console that didn't have a pan law, I had to manually reduce the fader by 3 dB when I passed through the center when panning something from left to right for effect. When I had to send mixes to radio stations, I usually sent a stereo mix to the FM, and a re-mixed mono mix to the AM. I had to lower all the faders that had mono material (like the voice-over channel) by 3 dB to make sure we still heard the music under the radio spot. It was a huge improvement when we got our first console with pan law. I'll discuss using the pan law a little later in this chapter.

MANAGING THE SPACE IN YOUR SOUNDSCAPE

Part of a listener's experience beyond content and quality is where sounds emanate from in the soundscape. The number of speakers, the environment, and playback equipment have bearing on that experience, but concentrating on where your sound elements come from can have subtle or dramatic effects on the listener. For instance, let's make a stereo television soundtrack. In our scene, we have a wide shot of a family eating dinner in a kitchen. There's a knock at the door, so little Sally runs over to the right of the screen to open the back door. The knock should come from the right speaker if we want the viewers to feel engaged in the story. It would be jarring of course if it were to come from the left. Leaving the knock in the center wouldn't be a disaster because that's also where the television screen is, and we're used to hearing sounds coming from screens and devices.

Let's finesse this scene a little bit further. In a wide shot, the family is at the center of the screen with the rest of the kitchen to each side. The sounds of them eating and talking should also come from the center of the soundscape. We *could* enhance it more by spacing out the fork and knife sounds slightly to the left and right, but I'm not sure it would add anything to the scene if it didn't mean something to the story. If, however the camera view was positioned as a guest at the table, then I would definitely spread out the utensil sounds across the stereo (and perhaps surround) field.

If we wanted to hear our visitor arrive in a car (or horse, or jetpack) I might pan that distant muffled vehicle from slightly left to hard right upon arrival. This would cue the viewer that someone was coming to visit from the right of the screen. I'm not a big fan of exaggerating panning effects unless it's central to the story or will create an interesting musical signature, so go easy on these types of audio cues.

Watch your SFX spread. Pay attention to the stereo spread of sound effects when building soundscapes and spotting sounds to video. If your scene shows someone walking at a distance, let's say 20 feet, be mindful of the spatiality of any footstep sound effects (usually called "footfalls") you might dub in. Far too often I hear a closely miked stereo sound effect dubbed onto distant action. Most distant sounds are pinpoint located in the soundscape instead of surrounding our ears. I convert these sounds to mono, then place them in the field left to right (or front to back if in surround) according to what I'm seeing. If I need a little realism, such as a door closing in a big room, I send that sound effect to a stereo reverb channel where it will then have some more depth and match the visual environment. This applies in reverse to sounds that are recorded in mono but need to have a stereo spread. These might be ambience, close-ups of objects being moved or operated, or close-up body sounds. For ambience, I try to fake the stereo by using any plugin or app that "stereo-izes" a mono sound by altering phase, equalization, and/or pitch. Try not to overdo it because it may start to sound "fake" and draw attention away from the story. For objects, I usually just leave it alone or send part of the signal to a stereo reverb channel for more depth. Again, don't go overboard.

Tech Tip

A *plugin* is a separate daughter app that runs inside a DAW app. These add additional functions to a track or clip, like reverb, compression, equalization, delay, analyzer tool, etc. Most DAWs have built-in plugins, but there are many third-party software companies that offer more nuanced plugins. Some DAWs use a common framework for developers like VST (Virtual Studio

Technology) or AU (Audio Units), while others use a proprietary framework (Avid ProTools uses AAX).

Keep dialog, voice-over, and lead singers in the middle. This seems like a no-brainer, but I've heard soundtracks where someone just discovered the pan pot and thought they were cute by panning two people's voices hard left and right. I'm not against it in the right situation, but if you want the listener/viewer to focus on the message or story, keep things simple. When we watch a movie in surround sound, 99% of the time the dialog is coming from the center channel. This lines up well with the screen and is, quite frankly, easier to mix. If you're creating a radio spot with two people talking, try not to pan them left and right. Instead, create a stereo ambient environment around them. As a media ingesting society, we're conditioned to hear the main voice from the center.

You could pan them slightly away from each other, but to stay close to convention only do a small percentage. I listen to a podcast that features two people in discussion who are panned slightly left and right. It disturbed me at first, but after a few episodes I got used it. Interestingly, their guests are panned straight up 12 o'clock, as if they're sitting between the two.

If your voice sources are antagonists, bystanders, or some other non-central part, go ahead and play with stereo location if it will help the story. If they are back-up vocals in a song, spread them out if will help thicken your mix (hint: if they can't sing very well, panning them will reveal their less-than-accurate crooning). I like to start at about 30% left and right for two singers. If there are more voices, try spreading all of them out at different widths. Sometimes just leaving the chorus in mono is better, especially if your instrumentation is already spread pretty thick across the stereo field. Sometimes a wide stereo chorus will fight with instruments already in that space.

Keep tab of stereo perspective with music groups. With music anything goes. But if you and the band want to create something that mirrors the group playing live, then pay attention to where each instrument sits in the stereo field. When legendary engineer and producer Tom Dowd started recording The Allman

Brothers Band, he set the band up in the studio exactly like they played on stage. This also translated to the stereo field in the mix and truly mirrored the experience of listening to the band live. When engineer and producer Bruce Swedien recorded most of Michael Jackson's hit albums, he preferred to record most instruments in stereo, exactly where he was going to place them in the stereo field. He knew he could save precious tracks by recording an instrument in mono and panning it hard left in the mix, but he felt that it had more depth if he had the player stand on the left side of the room in front of a stereo microphone. He ought to know, he won five Grammys.

Plan out your locations of instruments as best you can before hitting RECORD for the first time. In large ensembles where you place spot microphones,[91] be sure to pan them exactly to where they would be heard in the front stereo microphones. Also don't forget to time-align these spot mics with the front mics so you don't hear them a hair earlier than the front mics.

I've had some interesting challenges while recording ensembles. During the COVID-19 pandemic in 2020, a local college was forced to cancel an annual concert by the choir. The event moved online, and I was tasked with recording their songs in the gymnasium. Because of COVID protocols, they had to be a minimum distance from each other. We had recorded a smaller ensemble earlier that spread out in the bleachers with no problem. But the sheer number of singers in this choir prevented that. So, we put them in a circle around the basketball court. If this was going to be in surround, it would sound like magic. But alas, it was to be in stereo. So, I had to make some serious choices.

---

[91] Spot microphones are additional mics placed within an ensemble to fortify the main microphones in the front of the ensemble. An engineer might place spot mics in front of a piano, the percussion section, a soloist, harp, or other instrument or voice that needs a bit more clarity in the mix.

A 360 panorama of the choir recording.

First, I determined how many microphones I would need by spacing them out and pulling them back from the singers. I placed six microphones on the floor: two stereo pairs and two mono mics. The two stereo pairs went on either end of the floor near the backboards. The two mono mics covered the long ends. By moving the mics around and having groups form a lazy arc around each mic stand, I was able to get everyone covered. Now the fun part: what is my stereo field?

I had to choose one direction, and then match the other mics to that. I chose one end of the court because it was evenly split between the sopranos and tenors. I then reverse-panned the other stereo pair so that left and right would match. I then fit the other two mono mics into the mix to approximate the choir's standard set-up while on stage. I had to be careful of bleed between sections, so I made sure that one group that I had panned left wasn't bleeding into another mic's right channel. It was very confusing at first, but once I mixed it, it sounded almost heavenly along with the gym's excess reverberation.

I ran into a similar situation when recording the Alltech Celebration of Song concerts, as I detailed on page 179. Picking stereo forward was easier on this job, but it still has its challenges. Bleed from one stereo pair to the other was a constant battle. One thing that helps if you are in this same situation, is to play with the angle of the microphone's backs to one another. If you're using directional mics, they have a null point in the back. You can fiddle around with their orientation to one another to achieve the least amount of bleed.

Using the pan law. As promised, let's revisit the pan law. Most engineers cringe when they hear this term. It's a lot like the infield fly rule in baseball[92] – it's often misunderstood. Apart from

---

[92] For those that want to know, Major League Baseball defines the infield fly rule as "If the ball is near the baselines, the umpire shall declare "Infield Fly, if Fair." The ball is alive and runners may advance at the risk of the ball being caught, or retouch and advance after the ball is touched, the same as on any fly ball. If the hit becomes a foul ball, it is treated the same as any foul." In other words, when a runner or runners are on base and an infield fly is hit, the same rules as an outfield fly apply. The ump must call it for it to be in effect.

three scenarios, you shouldn't have to worry too much about the pan law. But you should always consider examining your pan law settings when these possibilities come up:

1. You will be panning a mono source from one channel to another for effects.

2. Your material will be mixed in stereo, but may be heard in mono when the two tracks are summed by another engineer, other software, or other listening device.

3. Your material will be mixed by you into a one-channel mono audio file or onto a device with a single mono input channel.

I find it easier to just employ a conservative pan law (-3 dB) on most of my stereo projects and adjust for special situations. You'll need to explore each setting on your console and DAW to see what settings work best. I recommend doing controlled mixdown experiments with a calibrated tone (-20 dB 1 KHz sine wave) so that you can find out how your DAW or console handles mono summing and panning. If you don't, you may get some surprises in audio levels of your mono files after mixdown. But let's break down how panning and summing work in some very simplistic examples.

Here's what would happen if I were creating a stereo mix with the pan law off (set to 0 dB). I put a guitar in the left channel, a piano in the right channel.

LEFT   CENTER   RIGHT

Guitar- 100% Left	Piano - 100% Right

Listening to this in stereo with two speakers would sound like two distinct sources in two discrete channels. If I sum them together using the pan pot for each channel and create a mono mix, then it would put equal amounts of each instrument in each speaker. However, the two instruments would sound as if they're coming from a center position between the two speakers. Their apparent volume would not change and they would sound blended together in mono.

LEFT   CENTER   RIGHT

50% Left - Guitar- 50% Right
50% Left - Piano - 50%Right

As I discussed earlier in the pan law section (page 374), and it's worth going over again in more detail, the center is really a "phantom" channel. This means that if you listen with two speakers at a 60° angle (which is the preferred professional stereo set-up), then the vocals would appear to come from a non-existent speaker exactly between your two real ones. If you listen on headphones, which is never a good idea when you're crafting a stereo mix[93], the center channel would seem to come from the middle of your head. This is because the stereo field is exaggerated by having the headphone speakers at a 180° angle instead of the traditional 60° angle of room speakers. Unless a stereo audio program is intended to be listened to with headphones (like a binaural recording), then you are experiencing hyper-stereo that over-emphasizes side-channel material and is most likely not the way the producers intended for it to be heard.

Next, let's use a simple lead vocal and nothing else. The track is in mono, so we'll pan it 12 o'clock right up the center into both left and right channels. This will appear in that phantom center. But if we measure the amount of the lead vocal, it's actually sending 50% to the left channel and 50% to the right channel.

LEFT   CENTER   RIGHT

50% left - Vocals - 50% Right

Now let's put that lead vocal into the mix with the guitar and piano. We're going to leave the vocal panned at 12 o'clock. This

---

[93] Unless you use special software or an external headphone that compensates for the discrepancy by emulating a monitoring environment with speakers.

will again appear in that phantom center. The vocal is still sending 50% to the left channel and 50% to the right channel, and the guitar is still 100% in the left channel, and the piano is still 100% in the right.

LEFT   CENTER   RIGHT

50% left - Vocals - 50% Right	
Guitar- 100% Left	Piano - 100%Right

Listening to this in stereo with two speakers would seem somewhat balanced because there are three distinct sources in three somewhat distinct channels. The guitar in the left, the vocal in the phantom center, and the piano in the right. Using the example above, if I solo[94] the guitar track, then I only hear it in the left channel. If I solo the piano track, I only hear it in the right channel. If I solo the vocal track, I hear it in both channels equally, but it again sounds as if it's coming from that phantom center channel.

If I turn off the right speaker, from the left I would hear the guitar *and* the vocal together. If I listen to only the right speaker, I will hear the piano *and* vocal together.

Another way to understand this is to imagine we're making a fruit salad. We'll start with a pear and an apple. Remember, we're listening with the pan law setting "off" or to 0 dB.

---

[94] On recording consoles and in DAWs each channel usually has the ability to be listened to while all others are muted. This usually doesn't affect the live mix and can be a way to isolate problems or to check a sound cue. This is sometimes called PFL, or "Pre-Fader Listen."

Next, let's add an orange in the middle. These represent the guitar (the pear), the piano (the apple), and the vocals (the orange). Our intention is to have an equal balance between all three fruits (at right).

But it tastes like this (below):

With both channels playing, that phantom center channel is now creating a third channel. The vocals (oranges) can now be

heard in all three channels – a little bit in the left, a little bit in the right, but loudly in the middle. With the pan law "off" or set to 0 dB, the phantom center channel dominates the middle. What's really happening is the orange (vocal) is being distributed into the left and right channels equally, essentially doubled. Play them together, and the phantom center channel is the sum of two oranges from each channel, thus each channel contains an orange (at left).:

If we mix it all together into one bowl (or combine the left and right channels into one mono channel) the equal number of vocals (oranges) in each channel will now double the vocals (or double the oranges) when mono-summed. <u>One</u> pear and <u>one</u> orange, plus <u>one</u> apple and <u>one</u> orange, equals <u>one</u> pear, <u>one</u> apple, and <u>two</u> oranges (at right).

This is the paradox we're put in without the pan law activated in our DAW. It sounds fine in stereo, but once we start summing channels, the fruit salad blows up. Luckily we can compensate by choosing the right pan law setting for our final mix. The fruit salad will then taste like we imagined it (below):

Now we're going to see the pan law in action. Let's turn the pan law setting off (set to 0 dB). First, let's mute the guitar and piano tracks. Now we grab the pan pot for the vocal channel and pan all the way to the left (You can try this on your own using a steady tone like A 440 Hz.), sending 100% of it to the left channel. It will sound as if it drops off in volume because it's only coming out of one speaker, but the signal is the same in the left channel meter as when it was centered. The right channel meter shows no signal. Pan the voice over to the right channel and the same happens. Now center the pan control, and the sound is coming from the phantom center channel. The left and right meters are equal to each other. What's happening is that when we *listen* through speakers, the phantom center is the *sum* power of the left and right speakers. With the pan law off, the sound is doubled into that phantom center but remains constant in both channels of the mixer.

Now, with the vocal (or A 440 tone) still panned in the middle, listen in mono by either panning the DAW's left-right faders to mono, or engaging the "mono" switch on your playback monitor system. If we gradually pan the vocal from left to right and watch the meters, they will stay the same, but the vocal will gradually get louder as it approaches center, and gradually fade as it recedes from center. Not by much, but it will become apparent when you hear it. Here's a graph of what it will sound like through the speakers:

Pan Law = 0 dB

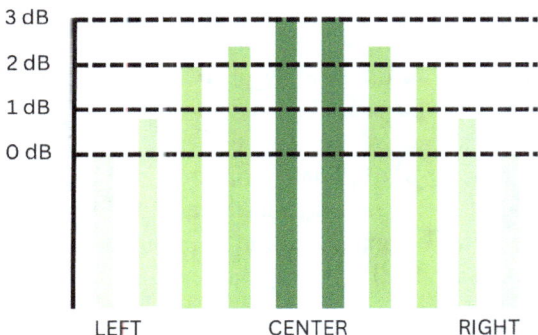

Signal rises and dips as it is panned from LEFT to RIGHT

Pan Pot

Non-compensated pan across left-right.

This is happening with the sound in the room only, as the DAW or console only has two channels on the meter (left and right) and the listening space has three (left, phantom center, and right).

On the meter, the level will read equally in both channels during the entire panning process.

Now let's set the pan law to -3 dB. You will immediately notice the master output meter behaving differently. It will be -3 dB lower in both channels, and it will sound slightly softer. Using the same exercise of panning from left to right in both stereo and mono monitoring modes, you will perceive the vocal (or A 440) sounding more even across the listening area from the left speaker – in the phantom center – and from the right speaker.

Now here's when using the -3 dB pan law for most of your mixing duties will come in real handy. If we were to mix down your project to a single mono file (one channel only) where you have guitar, vocal, and piano all panned up to 12 o'clock, then your file's output level will match your stereo output bus's meter exactly. You can experiment with this yourself by generating a known sine wave (I like the standard -20 dB 1 KHz sine wave) on a track, mix it down to a mono file using the -3 dB pan law, and check the statistics.[95]

If I were to mix it down without the pan law enabled (set to 0 dB), the new mono file would be 6 dB louder and possibly clipped and distorted. I know this may be confusing, but doubling a signal raises the output by 3 dB. That signal that is in both channels (the vocal or A 440 tone) is raised 3 dB in each channel: 3 dB in left + 3 dB in right = 6 dB of gain. Doubling the signal to the speaker has the potential to be 6 dB louder, but in most environments, it is *perceived* as only about 3 dB. Doubling the left and right channels of an identical source into a single mono channel will raise it by 6 dB unless an adjustment is made, like employing the -3 dB pan law or lowering the master output by 6 dB. The -3 dB pan law applies its magic of -3 dB into *each* channel, thus totaling 6 dB of reduction when mono-summed. Still with me?

I find that leaving the pan law at -3 dB gives me a more even mix and no surprises when I build my stereo mixes. You can also use a setting called "Equal Power" that delivers about the same results as -3 dB. The other two common settings, -4.5 dB and -6 dB can be used for special circumstances, if you are having mono sum issues, or if it sounds more pleasing to your ears to mix with. When

---

[95] Most DAWs have an audio analysis function. The free program Audacity has a dB scale built into the left side of each track.

you are exploring these settings, just be sure to listen back to your mixes in a media player and analyze their final levels to make sure nothing is out of whack.

Another advantage of using the -3 dB pan law when mixing is if you have to split your stereo mixes into two files, such as left and right. I do this all the time when delivering final mixes to television networks. For instance, they may want all the tracks mixed down to separate audio files. In addition to a full mix, there are "stems" (sometimes called "splits"), which are various portions of the project that can be blended back together later if there are last-minute edits or changes to be made. It also serves as an archive for future engineers:

1. Program mix stereo – left

2. Program mix stereo – right

3. Mix-minus[96] - left

4. Mix-minus – right

5. Sound effects – left

6. Sound effects – right

7. Music – left

8. Music – right

9. NAT sounds[97] – left

10. NAT sounds – right

11. SOT[98] – left

---

[96] Mix-minus refers to a sub-mix that contains everything but the voice-over. This is usually done for international versions that will replace the original voice-over with one in the local language. The mix sounds exactly like the final stereo mix with dialog, sound effects, natural sounds, and music, but lacks any voice-over.

[97] "Nat" is short for "natural." These are sounds coming from what we're seeing on camera and aren't altered.

[98] "SOT" is short for "sound on tape," a classic term for when you see pre-recorded footage, such as a clip from another video, and has sound already accompanying it.

12. SOT – right

13. Dialog – left

14. Dialog – right

15. Voice-over – left

16. Voice-over – right

Each one of these 16 tracks will be 3 dB lower in volume if the -3 dB pan law was employed. When they're married back up to video later, they will sum at the correct levels needed. If I were to leave the pan law off, the program (and each stem) would be too loud when played. The television technical engineers and the FCC doesn't like that to happen.

Surround yourself. We've talked extensively about stereo because it's the most common format we hear (and we hear in stereo with two ears). Surround sound, which is constantly evolving, is the next thing to conquer. Planning a surround mix is, by default, more complex than planning a stereo mix. But there are essentially just two major zones to worry about: what's in front of the listener and everything else (behind / beside /over / below). When planning your mix, you should focus on these baseline decisions first, only later assigning individual sound components within a zone. For instance, you can easily decide that all vocals/dialog will go in the front zone, and most ambient sounds or reverb will be in the surround zone. The exact location or level in a zone doesn't need to be determined yet. In a TV sound mix, I might dictate that all music, sound effects, dialog, and narration go in the front, and some sound effects like ambience, sweeping sounds, music reverb, and a few character or filler walla voices will go in the back[99]. In a music mix, I might decide to have the live band in the front, and the crowd in the back. Or I might get wild and put the listener in the middle of the band, with the vocals and lead guitar in the front, and all the other instruments in the surround.

Next in my planning stage I will designate where each sound will live in the front zone. Dialog and narration will go in the center channel only. Music cues and most sound effects will go to the stereo speakers. For the surround zone, most ambience and music

---

[99] See the footnote for "walla" on page 153

reverb effects will be routed to those speakers along with other sound cues that are central to the story. In my DAW, I will stack and group tracks from top to bottom on my worksheet mirroring where they are in the sound mix. For example, all dialog, which is front and center, will occupy the top tracks as one group. Under this Voice Group is the Music Group,[100] which will be heard primarily in the front stereo speakers but may also fall into the surround zone. And finally, the SFX Group contains all sound effects, which are generally up front, but may also make a wide swath into the surround zone. Within each group I will stack sounds top to bottom similarly according to how they fall into the surround mix and their relative importance. For sound effects, I consider general ambience such as birds, traffic, air conditioning hum, etc. as a foundation sound because a scene may sound dead and lifeless without it. Therefore, it goes on the bottom. Because those ambient sounds will be in both the surround and front zones, and they are foundational, those tracks will be at the bottom of my track grouping. Other sound effects (or character dialog) that may move around between zones or speakers will get special placement with a color-coded track or waveform. Organization is always important, but it's vital with complex projects like surround.

You're probably wondering how you place each sound in a zone. Most DAWs that have surround capability have special surround panners for each track. The tracks must be created as surround tracks (as opposed to mono or stereo options). Your master output must also be configured as surround. The surround panner can usually be configured with many options, from simple click and drag to a physical joystick on your desk. Each track can also bypass the panner and be directly routed to a single output bus. This is how we assign dialog and low frequency effects (LFE, or the ".1" in 5.1, 7.1, etc.).

If all your elements are only recorded in stereo or mono, you can either pan them through the front and surround zones to immerse the listener or apply a surround simulator plugin on their channels. These simulators use equalization, phasing, and even delay and reverberation to spread the stereo sound throughout all

---

[100] Except "diegetic" music, which is music that is within a character's environment. For instance a radio might be on in the background that the character hears. I try to make this part of the scene by reducing fidelity and adding in room reverb. I would group this track with all sound effects.

zones. These are especially helpful for spreading music tracks from the front zone into the surround. Like stereo panning, do this with a light hand so that the listener isn't pulled away from the story on screen.

Regarding the LFE channel, I rarely use it in the type of projects I do. This is not a channel to feed a subwoofer in your typical home surround system. Home amplifiers use "bass management" to distribute all low frequencies to a single subwoofer. In theaters and theme parks however, there is a separate subwoofer system just for that ".1" channel. Since a subwoofer doesn't produce midrange and treble frequencies, only low frequency effects like booms, thuds, and bottom-heavy music cues will benefit from being assigned to this channel. If my mix will be played on a true 5.1 surround system, then I will sometimes use the LFE channel as a 40 Hz big bottom enhancement to other effects. Home theater amplifiers will put that LFE channel in the subwoofer along with all the other low sounds from the other channels. Therefore, this LFE effect may get muddied or masked by all the other low frequency sounds that it is competing with.

Surround technology is advancing every year with completely new software and playback devices hitting the market. Virtual reality seems to be driving the current trend of research and development. A few decades ago, it was theme parks that were driving the tech. Where it will be in ten years is only a guess. But I would suggest that you learn the fundamentals of the basic 5.1 surround system first. It's the most common surround system for broadcast, disc, streaming, and music. Once you can create a realistic or immersive experience in this most basic format, you will understand how to work in 7.1 and beyond.

BUILDING A BETTER MIX

I've already spoken about how project organization is important. Organizing your DAW or console mixing setup is just as vital. By employing simple structural methods throughout your process, you'll develop good habits, work more quickly, and be free to focus on creativity.

It's all about that bass. When I build a song, I organize my tracks from the bass up. That is, I put the bass on the bottom and the vocals on top. Everything in between builds upon the foundation of the bass in a logical order (at least to me). Bass, drums, keys, rhythm guitar, lead guitar, brass/woodwinds, backing vocals, lead vocal. I may deviate from that on occasion, but that's the way I think about the "order" of things. It also happens to be the way we built songs on multi-track reel-to-reel tape decades ago. Because of technological quirks of recording on analog tape, we started by recording the bass onto track #1. We would then leave track #2 unrecorded at first because the massive signal from the bass would "bleed" onto track 2. If there was something already recorded on track 2, then the bass bleed would forever be part of that track. We usually went back after the bass track was cut and erased track 2. Any new sound we recorded on track 2 would usually be an instrument that *didn't* have any bass (such as a tambourine) so we could filter out any residual bass bleed. The other reason for recording bass on track 1 was that the edge tracks on reel-to-reel tape were usually less responsive in the treble. Anything on an edge track (1 or 24 on a 24-track recorder) had a little bit extra hiss and sounded dull. We would just filter it out on the bass and nobody heard the difference.

Next would come the percussion. Depending on how many tracks you had available, we would build the drum kit from the kick drum up. This pecking order went all the way up to lead vocals on the highest track. On the console and tape machine meters, it went track 1 to 8 / 16 / 24, whatever your tape machine could record. I kept this habit as newer technologies came along, like digital multi-track tape (Alesis ADAT, Tascam DA-88), digital hard disk recorders (Alesis HD24 ADAT), and eventually direct to computer. The way to think about it is that the bass isn't the least important, it's the foundation of the song, much like our lesson in surround sound track-stacking.

When I'm building soundtracks for broadcast advertising, corporate videos, or other productions with narration and other elements like music and sound effects, I employ a similar "foundation" approach. I'll group the music at the bottom of my DAW worksheet, SFX next, any on-camera/secondary voices next, and finally the narration on top. Since what's being said is always the most important, it sits atop the mountain. When I mix these types of projects, I tend to get the best mix I can with just the voice and music. I'll then go back and blend in the SFX to fit. I do this because the music is the foundation on which the message (the voice) sits. If a sound effect is a key part of the message, then I make sure that its level matches the voice and can be heard over the music.

In live productions, some mixing consoles are set up in a similar hierarchical way with voices and solo mics starting at position #1 and going up (actually to the right) in tracks. Another way to organize a live console is to put mics/sources into faders that match the visual set-up on stage. For instance, the keyboard player might be on the extreme left, so that instrument is in track #1 and his/her mic is in track #2. Next is the bass player in track #3, and so on.

For me, arranging tracks in order of importance, soundscape position, or stage position allows me to find sounds easily or to quickly grab the right faders. If you're constantly hunting for sound cues or faders, you're wasting your time. Stop and re-organize your tracks into something that makes sense to you.

It's *not* all about that bass. The area at the very bottom of the frequency spectrum, the bass, can be a crowded place. Those heavy amplifiers, those big woofers, those huge cabinets – they take the most amount of energy to get working. You want a clean, tight, and fat bottom on your mix, right? So why does your bass sound muddy and undefined? It's probably all the unintentional bass frequencies in your mix that are making those big honking woofers work overtime. Your problem is an accumulation of low-end rumble that bleeds into microphones. If you're recording a vocal, regardless of whether it's a male or female, there is usually unwanted rumble down below about 70 Hz. Filter that out by using a high-pass filter. An HPF lets frequencies pass through that are *above* a frequency threshold that you specify. It's usually a gradual slope (it looks like /‾) downward from that frequency. So, if you set the HPF at 70 Hz, everything *above* 70 Hz will be heard, and anything *below* 70 Hz will be gradually attenuated. As your tracks build up, along with unfiltered rumble, the bottom end of your project will sound muddy. If you have sounds with natural bass, then those will fight with all that unneeded rumble. Make it a routine to roll off the bottom frequencies of all your tracks that have rumble.

Maybe it is all about that bass. Once you've cleaned up the excess rumble, fatten up your bass. There are hundreds of tricks and plugins that give you bigger bass, but keep in mind that bass that is too strong will easily "eat up real estate." That is, it will take over your levels and meter if you don't tame it. Here are some basic things to remember and employ.

Compression is your friend. I always stick basic compression on a bass track (or low-end sound effect). You have to play with attack and release some, but generally electric bass compression can be set to a quick attack with super long release times. This evens out any musicianship issues and lets the bass just roll at the bottom of the mix. I like vintage compressors or plugin simulators when compressing bass. The vacuum tubes (or simulation algorithms) give a nice warm and gentle compression, especially to electric bass.

You can also have even more control and success with multi-band compression. This is a compressor plugin that selectively compresses certain frequencies, while leaving others alone. Multi-band compression can also boost the apparent level of some frequencies. Using the bass as an example, select the very bottom range of frequencies the bass is playing in. Select a compression ratio (start at 4:1) and *raise* that frequency band instead of decreasing it. This will fatten up that bottom while controlling peaks that would have normally peaked your meters.

Another trick is to duplicate the bass track, over-compress one version and blend it into the untouched version. This allows more expression to come through that might get squashed using heavy compression.

Similar to the mic rumble fix in the previous session, employ a low-pass filter on bass tracks. This works the opposite of a HPF and reduces the treble of a track. If there are no overtones (as a string bass would produce), then get rid of those highs with a low pass filter, which looks like ‾\ . These build up just like bass frequencies and add an overall hiss in your tracks. If you're recording an upright string bass or acoustic bass guitar, you might think about keeping the treble frequencies because of the unique overtones that come from these instruments.

Chain gang. Since we're talking about compression, let's touch on using multiple compressors in a chain. You can stick just one compressor on your master output and be done with it, but I guarantee your mix will have issues. I like to put compressors and limiters[101] throughout the audio chain so that specific problems are addressed at each stage.

Let's start at the master output. I insert a limiter as the very last thing audio passes through before it gets mixed. I'll set this at whatever my mastering specs indicate. For music, I just set it at -0.5 dB or -1.0 dB as a safety net. For broadcast, it's a lot lower because of transmitter and streaming specs. I will use limiters in my audio channels *before* they feed the master output, because every track that you add to your mix will increase the master output level, potentially overloading it. Look at each limiter as you build your mix. If you see (and hear) the limiter working all the time, then your tracks are too loud. You'll need to lower the level of all your tracks before going any further.

I will also use compression on the master output[102], but it is usually built into a mastering suite such as Izotope's Ozone plugin that offers other tools to maximize the final output. It's wise to put compression on all of your individual tracks that you have recorded. Pre-mastered audio, such as a commercial music bed, usually doesn't need any more compression than what another engineer has applied to it. Sound effects with transient spikes will probably need both compression and limiting. Voices can greatly benefit from compression because of the peaks and valleys of speech and singing. I like to use vintage compressors or plugins that give vocals a smooth and warm sound.

I will also sometimes use compressors on group channels. A group channel is a submaster that is fed from individual tracks. One example is a vocal group submaster. In our example we have a lead singer and two backup singers. I would assign these three channels

---

[101] A limiter is a special type of compressor. It controls the dynamics of only the loudest peaks in a program. Think of it as a lid for a cup of coffee. Any sound below the level setting is undisturbed, while any peak that hits it is squashed. If maximum loudness is 0 dB, then a limiter setting of -3 dB would stop any sound on that channel from going over -3 dB.

[102] A master output is the very last output on a mixing console, or within a DAW's mixing chain. It usually is what's also feeding monitor speakers. This will be the main channel you'll monitor when making mixing decisions.

to a separate submaster group fader called "Voice Group" instead of the master output fader. I would then assign the Voice Group submaster to the output fader. This allows me to control the overall mix of all the vocals. When I pull that Voice Group fader down, *all* the voices come down in volume at the same time. It looks like the following figure.

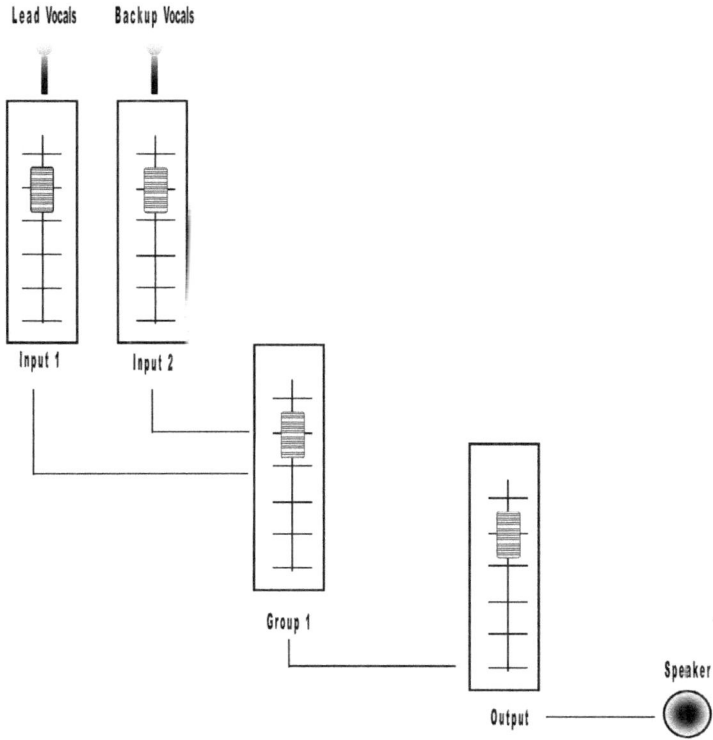

Using group channels.

I can continue to add additional vocals to this submaster. I can also create different submasters for other groups of sounds such as a submaster for all the percussion, another for the guitars, etc. Once I get my individual tracks balanced, I can then make fine adjustments to groups of sounds using just a few faders. Using groups in large projects is very helpful.[103]

---

[103] When creating groups in a DAW, you use the usual "add track" command, but choose "group" instead of "channel," "effect track," "instrument," etc. There

Now let's talk about the compressors and limiters in my vocal chain. Each channel would look something like this, with the audio flowing from the vocal channel and through a compressor and limiter on its way to the output (below):

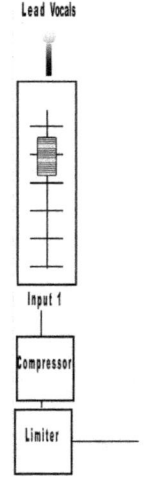

is usually no limit to how many group tracks you can create. Mixing consoles however, have a finite number of group tracks.

With the full chain, it would look something like this (below):

The full chain of inputs, compression, limiting, groups, and output.

That sounds like a lot of compression doesn't it? Well, the secret is to go easy and apply only what you need. On the originating channel, use light compression and limiting to gently control the peaks and bring up the weakest parts. Keep increasing each parameter until you hear the compressor working. This is just over the edge of how much you want. Now back the parameter off by 10%. If you still hear it working, back off a little more. The key is to set the parameter just shy of the point where you hear it working. That sounds contradictory but believe me the compressor wasn't designed to be heard, it was designed to control sound levels from going out of bounds. As you adjust each parameter using this method, your track should now start to fall into the meter range you want. Do this to all your individual tracks in your group before adjusting the group submaster's compressor. I usually make even subtler adjustments on this compressor, only trying to tame the loudest of sounds. Remember, this compressor is now hearing sounds from three channels, so the dynamics of all your vocals together will change from how they sound individually. I work back and forth between all three places in the chain when setting compressor levels. Making a small change on one can affect another one in the chain, so work in groups to avoid getting confused. It's helpful to solo your group or channel in large projects so that you actually hear the changes you make in the parameters.

Don't overload your master. When building a large mix, I often overload my master output at some point. Many of us would immediately reach over and turn down the master fader. But that's a big no-no. The master needs to stay on 0 dB, or whatever the DAW or console has designated as "unity." Your individual tracks or submasters need to come down. If you've followed my advice and used group submasters to organize your mix, you can look at each subgroup's meter to find out where your volume problems are coming from.

If the input to a submaster is overloaded, then backtrack to each individual channel. You might not see any one channel peaking, but it may be the sum of all of them at their current fader levels that are overwhelming the submaster. If you're happy with the balance of each track on that group, then you can lower their levels a few different ways.

1. Highlight all the channels on your mixer and link their volume together. Now you can grab one fader to bring them all down at the same time. Lower the fader well below where the meters peaked.

2. Highlight all the automation for the tracks involved and lower all the nodes together.

3. Highlight all the clips/events on the affected tracks and lower the volume. Go one dB at a time until the group submaster's meter no longer peaks, then go one dB more for safety.

4. Reduce the input gain on individual source channels if this parameter is available. Any track that is peaking should have its gain lowered. Lower one dB at a time until the meter stops peaking, then go one more dB for safety.

5. Reduce the input gain on the group submaster if it has this parameter. Like a source channel, lower one dB at a time until the meter stops peaking, then go one dB more for safety.

CREATING LAYERS IN YOUR MIX

This may seem obvious, but it can get overlooked when you're building a mix with increasingly complex sounds. All programs and music recordings, no matter how simple or complex, should have distinct groups of sounds that influence what the listener hears. I divide these up into what I call "layering." It's not a button to push or software plug-in – it's a concept. Let's use a simple example: a musical piece by a band with singer. The rhythm section contains drums, bass, and guitar. When the vocalist sings the lyrics, she can be considered the top layer, or in the forefront. The rhythm section supports the vocals and is on the bottom layer, or background. Simple enough. We can take it further and divide the rhythm section into sub-layers: the drums on one layer, and the bass and guitar on another since they complement one another.

Now let's move layers around. When the song lyrics take a pause for a guitar solo, the guitar moves to the top layer and the bass and drums stay on the bottom layer. This is all pretty straightforward, but if you let the bottom layer overwhelm the top layer, you'll confuse the listener. An example of this would be mixing the guitar at the same level as the vocalist during lyrics. When the guitar is relegated to the bottom layer, it should blend in with the bass and drums and stay out of the way of the vocals. Adjusting its volume level is one way to do this, another is to dip the guitar's equalization (EQ) in the same frequency range where the vocalist's voice is. Most vocalists, whether male or female, have pronounced range from 3K – 5KHz. This is the area where you should dip the guitar's EQ when it's on the bottom layer. The guitar will maintain its presence, but will pleasantly "wrap around" the vocals. When it's time to play the guitar solo, restore its EQ to flat[104] so that it sounds natural and not dull or clamped down. You should also pay attention to the drums that are in the same frequency range as the vocals and apply multiband compression[105] during the lyrics.

As instrumentalists and vocalists are added to a song, assign them to layers and sub-layers. You should maintain this hierarchy to keep clarity in your mixes. Sure, you can break the rules, but know what rules you're breaking so that your mischievous ways will be more effective.

Apply this same layering technique to all your mixes and you'll have more control of your sound. In videos, I put the narrator and "talking heads" (people on camera) on the top layer and build everything under. Again, you can employ sub-layers for even more control. For instance, my mentor Ed Commons always advised me to put the talking heads on the very top layer, and the narrator just slightly below. He felt that what people were saying is vitally important, and the narrator is there to fill in the gaps and move the story along. I've found this technique works very well. I've never once had anyone compliment me, complain, or mention that they heard this subtle technique. That tells me I've done my job and guided the listener to what I want them to hear and feel.

When you're building your mix using the layering technique, mute every other element but the top layer (by soloing the channel that the top layer is on). Adjust its level so that it sits right where you want it to on your meter.[106] Next, apply any compression you desire, but keep in mind that you may need to change some of these parameters once other elements are added. The same goes for any

---

[104] "Flat" equalization means no equalization at all. No frequencies are either boosted or cut.

[105] Multiband compression is dynamic control of levels in a specific frequency range. These tools let you dial in compression in this EQ range while leaving the other parts of the signal alone. All normal compression parameters are employed. An example would be reducing the dynamics of a guitar from 3KHz to 5KHz with a 4:1 compression ratio while a vocalist is singing.

[106] You'll need to decide where that is based on what kind of material you're producing and where it will be heard. Using the K-scale as reference, K-12 has an RMS average of -12 and has 12 dB of headroom. K-14 had 14 dB headroom, and K-20 has 20 dB of headroom. K-12 is a popular pop song and radio commercial value, while K-20 is similar to film and television dialog levels. The next section "Know the Numbers" discusses dB values in more detail.

EQ you apply at this stage. My preference is to make this layer full and rich with a little brightness.

Next, unmute the bottom layer and see how it fits with the top layer. It should not be too close and tight to the top layer, nor should it be barely heard. I find that the bottom layer needs the least compression and EQ fiddling of all, but you should still tame peaks, transients, and bass levels that might dominate the mix.

And lastly, unmute the middle layer. This layer will need the most attention because it usually contains material that's somewhat important and may be sonically similar to the top later. Your goal is to not let it interfere with the other layers, but still be heard. More compression, EQ, and other trickery will need to be used to make this layer fit up against the top layer. One simple trick that will help is to solo this layer and adjust the metering so that it averages 3 dB less than the top layer. Use this as a starting point to adjusting levels between all the layers. Getting all three layers to blend and complement each other is hard, that's why you're a pro. But don't despair, there are a few more magic tricks you can use with your mix.

When I have a complex mix with three distinct layers that are starting to fight with each other, I try to analyze where the problems are happening. Look at the entire mix on a spectrum analyzer and try to determine the part of the frequency spectrum that the sonic clashes are happening. Now solo the top layer and watch the spectrum analyzer in this same area to see if that part's EQ can be reduced, boosted, or have multiband compression applied. Next solo the middle layer to see if this is the source of the colliding frequencies. If so, dig down into each track to find the source of the EQ peak and carve that out. I'm sometimes surprised on which track I find the issue. It's usually an overtone or unneeded lower frequency that can be reduced without affecting the quality of that sound. When trying to crowd a lot of sounds together, especially with vocals that need to be heard clearly, you must go back and forth, and back and forth again between layers and individual tracks and make minute adjustments to fix sonic clashes.

When vocals or dialog/narration is involved, I find that reducing the lower frequencies and boosting the upper ones of the voice around 4Khz to 5 KHz help it stand above those bottom layers that are thick and bass heavy. If you solo the voice after making these adjustments, it may sound a little thin and very bright by itself, but don't worry because when it's blended with the other layers it will stand out enough to be heard clearly.

One phenomenon that I feel compelled to mention is the phantom sound. As audio tracks start to stack up into the dozens, there are sometimes weird and odd sounds that seem to be self-generated from the stack of sounds. You can solo individual tracks and never hear it, but it may only be heard in a certain pairing or grouping of tracks. If you locate which combination of tracks are producing these sound spirits, try making a quick fader dip under one track, or even muting that short clip for a fraction of a second. Sometimes DAWs will have write errors to audio clips that were processed. I've had problems clear up when I've deleted the clip and replaced it with a duplicate. I've also had success by moving a very small segment of an audio clip forward or backwards just one sample (that's about 1/48,000th of a second).

There are so many other techniques and tools available to help you blend complex layers, but knowing these basics of EQ and compression can help you grab the right tools to fix problems. Artificial Intelligence is starting to make its way into audio tools that help you with mixing, but I want control over my mix. I think it makes you a better engineer if you don't rely on AI or automatic settings for most of your work. I would only consider using AI if I were under a horrific time crunch and the material was for a small audience. Stick with manual control, because if you apply AI to your mix, can you *really* take credit for it?

SILENCE IS GOLDEN

What is the most recognizable sound on the planet? Silence. Just as a bass drum hit, a cymbal splash, a thud, cricket sounds, or other sound can punctuate and enhance a song or program, silence can be just as effective. In my chapter on creativity, I suggested using silence as an option for constructing a foundation for your soundtrack (see page 319). If used effectively and judiciously, it can sometimes have a stronger effect than any other sound can. Much as "negative space" is used in art and photography to balance a composition, silence can be inserted into a soundtrack for balance. It's usually preceded by some kind of introduction or build-up so that the audience understands that it's part of the listening experience instead of an audio glitch.

Music is full of moments of silence, more than you think. Mozart said, "The music is not in the notes, but the silence in between." And that silence does not have to be seconds long, it can be fractions of a second. Playing a staccato note is one example. In the classic rock song "You Shook Me All Night Long" by AC/DC, the 15-second flowing solo guitar intro lulls the listener into a false sense of relaxation before the last note decays into near silence. The silence is then suddenly interrupted by an authoritative drum hit as the rhythm guitar and drums play an aggressive and gritty riff. Technically, it's not complete silence at the 15-second mark. The silence is underneath the solo guitar – no other instruments are playing.

Maybe a better example is Elvis Presley's 1957 performance of "All Shook Up." The song pretty quickly establishes that it will use silence within the first 20 seconds: "I'm in love…(full stop by the band and a snare hit)…I'm all shook up." The boogie-woogie piano, which has a rolling tempo like a big truck barreling down the road, comes to a sudden stop. When the truck slams on its brakes, it gets everyone's attention. And so does Elvis.

Perhaps the ultimate music example of silence is 4'33" by composer John Cage. It's a three-act composition from 1952 that can be performed by any instrument or combination of instruments. If you are in the audience during a performance of 4'33", you would witness the performer(s) sitting silent for four minutes and thirty-three seconds. Nobody plays anything on their instrument or utters a word. But there really isn't silence. You hear the environment, breathing and other body sounds, and maybe a few giggles or whispers. Each performance is unique and has a different effect on the audience and performers. The idea came to Cage from studying Zen Buddhism. The original title was "Silent Prayer." His concept was for a piece that would mimic the length of a typical *Muzak* song (3 ½ to 4 ½ minutes). *Muzak* was a supplier of "canned" or "elevator" music that was ubiquitous in office spaces and retail stores across America for decades. Perhaps 4'33" was a rebuke of the ever-present sappy music that was supposed to calm nerves and urge more purchases from consumers.

Pure silence in a soundtrack is rare, it's usually an underlying element with light ambience or even hiss from the microphone or media. An example of using dead silence is when films or television programs portray people with hearing loss. This is usually an effective method when the camera is shot from their point of view. I've also heard it used this way in radio PSAs[107] for hearing loss.

A long period of complete silence must have a reason to be there. It must challenge the viewer/listener to be a participant. When designing a soundtrack, we often introduce sounds as a way to guide the listener to a particular mind space we want them in. Chicken and cow sounds put them on a farm. Sounds of water rushing by puts them on the banks of a river. Explosions and gunshots put them on a battlefield. With silence, the listener can actually be more engaged with the story. You, as the sound designer, are not guiding them with a specific sound. You're allowing the listener to guide themselves through that space with their own thoughts, because there are no sounds to distract them from the story. If we go back to the white space idea from the creativity chapter, placing a character (and the viewer) in a completely blank white space with complete silence allows the viewer to conjure up multiple scenarios in the mind. What's going on? Where are they? What's going to happen next? Why is there no sound? It can be a very powerful moment, and one you can capitalize on. What's the next thing they hear? It's up to you. You have a clean slate to work with at this moment, so the next sound they hear will be more captivating than the silence. Why? Because you've introduced a thirst or craving for sound, any sound, by starving them with silence. The silence is the "…" between the "I'm in love" and the "I'm all shook up." We know something's coming, and we're relieved when it arrives. In music, the next sound that breaks the silence is often the "chill bump" moment. The next time one hears this musical moment, they know what's coming. And

---

[107] Public Service Announcement. It's a radio or television spot for an organization or cause. It's usually inserted into programming when no advertisers have been sold that opening in the schedule, however broadcasters are required to run a certain number of PSAs within a given period. All PSAs are broadcast at no charge, unless the organization has paid/traded for a certain time slot for maximum exposure.

when it does, it satisfies the brain's craving. *Chill bumps.* And it's this moment that usually defines our memory of the song. We don't remember "I'm in love," we remember "I'm all shook up." We don't remember every note of AC/DC's guitar solo, we remember the drum hit. *Chill bumps.* When you can manipulate the listener into that same bit of euphoria when the silence is broken, you've got them in the palm of your hand.

As I pointed out, we rarely use completely dead silence. There's often some environmental ambience underlying a scene. There are only a few places on earth where there's complete silence, and most of those are anechoic chambers.[108] So, when I'm putting together television programs that have long periods without music, such as in a DIY show, I'll put a steady low volume HVAC sound under all the interior scenes. We aren't always using sound from the hosts' microphones, so that sudden gap in audio between cuts creates a big silent void. The HVAC hum fills that in with a controlled silence until the next host speaks or swings a hammer. In this case, silence is more of a filler between action or conversation. We don't always need to hear music in these types of productions, as that would wear out the listener over a full hour.

You can also use silence to differentiate characters in film and audio productions. Let's take one example that has a brash and bold character, and a quiet and methodical character. The scene will flip flop back and forth between the two going about their day. First, the quiet character is painting toy soldiers in a study. Quick cut to the brash character running a loud juicer. Cut to quiet one reading a book and a clock ticking. Cut to brash character mowing the lawn. And so forth. The silence, or quietness in reality, has a profound effect on how the viewer interprets both characters. The dichotomy between the two is enhanced with sound and silence.

By including silence in your toolkit, you have a powerful way to enhance your soundtracks. In the previous section about layering sounds, I probably should have defined silence as the very bottom

---

[108] A specially built room that completely eliminates exterior sounds from entering, and sounds from within from reverberating. It's a completely dead-sounding room that is dangerous to enter without noise-generating headphones. They are built to accurately measure sound levels generated by equipment. Even in a well-built recording studio, some sound bounces around the room and back into the microphone, spoiling a pure recording of a sound source.

layer. I often preach that every sound should have a purpose. If it doesn't, then get rid of it. What you're left with is silence. It's your blank canvas to start your next masterpiece.

SPACE, THE FINAL FRONTIER

If silence is a tool, then space is cool. If you were to read that aloud, you'd first hear that I made a rhyme. But if we break it down further, you'd hear a space between "tool" and "then." The comma is a separator of thoughts in writing, and a pause or breath in narration. Try reading the sentence aloud without the comma and the timing will seem off and sound rushed. Paying attention to little details like this when you're constructing soundtracks or producing music can make all the difference in the world. I often hear narrations that have no space between sentences. The editor chose to delete the entire space between the end of one sentence and the beginning of another, mashing them up together as if the narrator never takes a breath or pause. Maybe they were trying to save time, or maybe they didn't understand the software. But the rapid-fire voice is jarring to the listener and immediately takes away from the message. This constant machine-gun pace reminds me of books from a thousand years ago that had little to no punctuation. Looking through those books is eye watering because there are no periods or commas, just a page of words.

When editing narration, I try to put natural pauses throughout. If I must remove a breath or long pause, I listen from the end of the previous sentence and stop playback at the exact point where I think the next sentence should start. I place the following audio clip at that point and listen back. If it isn't exactly right, I nudge it the direction it needs to go and listen back again. The average timing of a pause between sentences is anywhere from 1.25 to 2.5 seconds in most situations. In addition, I'll edit 2 to 3 seconds between paragraphs, and 4 to 5 seconds between sections. If a narrator takes an unnatural breath in the middle of a sentence, I usually cut the breath and slide the following clip back halfway into the gap, dividing the silence in half. I listen through the edit to make sure it doesn't sound weird. Butting two words up together in narration or dialog is pretty much a no-no unless you're trying to fix an error. You will sometimes have to do this when someone stutters or pauses unnaturally. Listen through a few times to make sure it doesn't sound manufactured. Timing the human voice is a "feel" thing. You can't use a boilerplate to time your edits, otherwise it will sound robotic. Listen to long passages, know the intent of the reader and author, and put yourself in the seat of the listener to get an idea of the overall tempo. I sometimes close my eyes and imagine I'm sitting in a comfortable chair listening to the narrator. Does it sound too fast? Too slow? Too jumpy? Too plodding? Every project is different, so make sure you're not timing this afternoon's soundtrack like the car commercial you edited this morning.

Other places to pay attention to spaces is when assembling documentaries, programs, interviews, or other productions that have multiple elements. If sound bites[109] are being edited into a narration, make sure you don't butt them up against the narration (unless it's intended). Give them a little breathing room. I try to edit in the same natural sentence pauses that I would in a straight narration. Like before, play back the audio about a sentence before the edit and listen through to see if the sound bite beginning is placed about where the narrator would naturally say the next sentence. It's really a timing and tempo thing. I produce a lot of programs for public radio and television, and the pacing on most of these productions is very deliberate and slow. We try to let the information sink in, instead of force-feeding it like a celebrity gossip show would do.

And when/if you have to produce a celebrity gossip-type show, spacing is a factor here as well. It's just super-fast. I try to look at the grid on my timeline to guide me on spacing in both slow and fast-paced situations. Most DAW timelines can display an overlapping grid that divides vertical lines into seconds, half-seconds, etc., depending on how far you are zoomed in or out. This gives you a visual guide to placing audio clips so that you can be consistent. If a half-second sounds good between sentences in the narration, then edit with this in mind, using the grid as a guide. Be sure to listen back to see if it's too tight for the listener.

---

[109] A short audio/video clip of someone talking, doing something, an event, or other sound that is descriptive to the story or feature.

These spacing rules also apply to spotting sound effects or musical cues. I often produce videos and TV programs that have a lot of whooshes and sizzles that are synced with visual graphic effects (VFX) . These are usually quick and punchy, so I routinely cut off and fade the end pretty quickly. This is part of my rule on sound effects: Establish it, then get it out of the way. These don't need to hang around very long, because another whoosh is coming in fast. The only times to let an effect go on is to fill in gaps or follow on-screen motion.

Timing of spaces is also critical when placing cues for comedy or drama. There are no rules, but for call/response or cause/effect scenes where the sound effect or vocal cue is a character (meaning it's become critical to the story), experiment with its placement. I try nudging it sooner or later while listening through the cut. If I think it's right, I go back a minute or two and listen to the program without watching my timeline as it plays. If the timing sounds organic and doesn't jump out, then I've got it right. If there's the slightest question, I change the timing. In my experience, sound cues have the most impact with more space between them than less. Let the sound breathe.

As you can see, spacing and timing are very important in helping your soundtrack. Even if the audience doesn't specifically pick up on your deliberate timings, such as music beat-driven spacing, maintaining a rhythm of event timing and spacing helps the listener digest your soundtrack. If every edit and space were random and without thought, you risk creating a chaotic and unordered soundtrack. It may agitate the listener and pull their attention away from the story or music. A more ordered and timed soundtrack eases the listener's tension in a way, and brings a familiar and satisfying "beat." By knowing these loose rules of timing and spacing, you can pull the listener along more easily.

You can also break the rules when you need the element of surprise. One example is if you are working on a horror scene that is building up tension. Try to place beats or sound effects in a loose rhythm. When you need to spring the big surprise, skip a beat or two to create even more tension. The audience is subconsciously wondering why the beat stopped. Then on an upbeat or beat that's completely out of sync, hit them with the music stab or scream. I guarantee the surprise will have more impact if you first follow the rules and then break them.

One more control of spacing is with sound effect timing in commercials, theatrical and radio plays, and other audio-only presentations. When you need to make things quickly happen in a limited amount of time, don't let your sound effects happen in real time. Edit them closely together, even overlapping them, to simply establish the cues. It's like the no-no of filmmaking, don't show a car pull up, the person get out, lock the door, go around the car, walk up the sidewalk, knock on the door, and wait for an answer. Just cut to the last few knocks for crying out loud. The same sensibilities can be applied to a sequence of sound effects that establish or help along a scene.

THE BREATH OF THE SUBJECT

The majority of my job is to record and edit people talking. It's mostly narrations, but there are many interviews, instructions, podcasts, and other productions. One of the decisions I must make when beginning an edit is whether or not to edit out breaths. Taking out a breath will alter timing, so that's the first consideration: Do I need to leave the timing as is, or do I need to reduce the voice recording to fit into a shorter time frame? Editing out breaths and closing the gap is the best way to make up time.

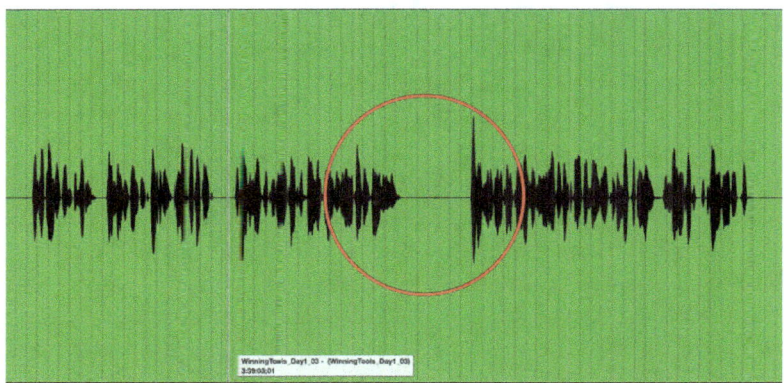

The gap in the circle contains a breath, however it's difficult to see.

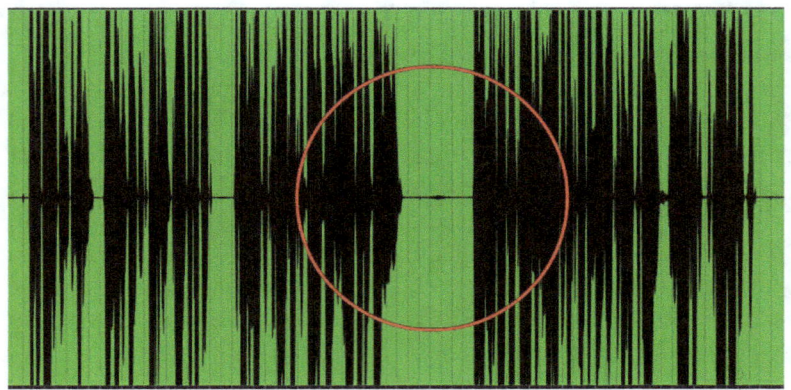

By increasing the vertical view of the waveform (not raising its audio level), breaths are easier to see. In short time, you'll be able to spot breaths without listening.

Another casualty of taking out breaths is making the narrator sound like a robot, especially if all the breaths are edited out and there is no supporting music underneath. I must consider how the track will be heard before doing a full breath edit. If it will sit atop music in a commercial, then I usually go ahead and edit all breaths out. Commercials are usually tightly edited anyway, so I can always use the extra few seconds I gain by removing breaths and reducing the gaps. I WILL NOT edit breaths that are part of the performance, like sighs or gulps.

If the voice track will be naked (with no other sound underneath), such as an audiobook, then I leave most breaths in. I may remove odd breaths or ones between paragraphs. Some inexperienced readers tend to breath in the wrong places and sound out of breath, so I remove the oddball breaths and leave the natural ones. If an unnatural breath is taken, such as in the middle of a phrase, reduce the gap you left by about 50% after removing it. That way there isn't a weird pause in the middle of nowhere. As always, play through your edit to make sure it sounds natural. Replace all of these gaps with room tone. For every session, record a minute or so of the room the narrator will be in, but empty with the door closed. Edit out any clicks, surges, or other noises, then place this on your timeline under your voice track. Mute the track so that it doesn't get mixed into the master. I duplicate the room tone multiple times so that I can quickly copy and paste it into the gap I left after removing the breath. I created a macro shortcut in my DAW (Steinberg Nuendo) so that I could highlight the gap, press one key, and copy and paste the room tone from the track underneath onto the edit track (see picture below).

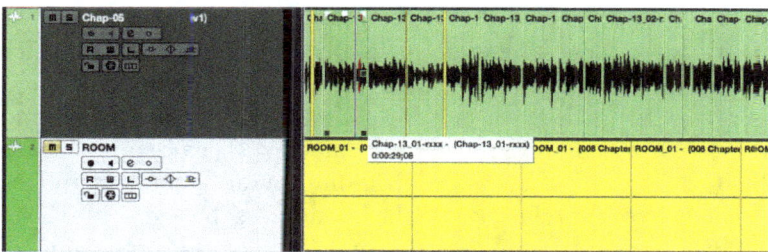

Room tone is in yellow, narration in green. Note the track 'ROOM" is muted (the yellow "m" button on the left is highlighted) so it doesn't add extra noise to the recording.

You can also massage the breaths you want to leave in for performance or context. Some may be too loud, clicky, gurgley, or too long. Separate or highlight that breath and reduce its volume. I will sometimes go to the length of exporting it to a noise-reduction app and remove the clicks, whistles, or whatever else is ruining its purity. If I'm trying to reduce timing on a narration that will remain naked, I select each extra-long breath and time-squeeze it. Sometimes this is enough to fit the read into the time limit without altering the speed of the entire file. Setting aside "good" breaths is another tactic. Like the room tone method, copy and paste several good-sounding breaths to a work track that you can cut into your vocal track to replace ugly ones.

Editing breaths in music performances is nearly the same for me. I try to leave them in if they don't distract me, but I am ready and willing to remove them if they detract from the music. Highly produced hit singles will usually have breaths edited out because there has been so much tweaking done on the voice. Plugins such as pitch correction, harmonizer, chorus, and others may magnify the breath so much that it's too noticeable. I nearly always remove breaths from backup singers, mostly because the breaths are too random or uneven and not part of the performance.

SQUEEZE ME, S'IL VOUS PLAÎT

What happens when you have to squeeze 10-pounds of voice into a 5-pound sack? When you're faced with narration that is too long, a great problem solver is the modern time-squeeze tool found in most DAW edit programs. I say "modern" because as recent as 2010 or 2012, these time compression programs would introduce artifacts into audio clips. But in the last decade, the algorithms have become increasingly sophisticated and seamless. The time-squeeze tool can successfully reduce most spoken word recordings up to 6-7% without distortion, artifacts, or noticeable processing. You can push to 8-10% if the style and read are more relaxed. Upwards of 10-20% can be successfully achieved for legal disclaimers, contact info, and taglines. More time savings can be achieved with editing out breaths and reducing gaps. My rule of thumb is that I can easily reduce a narration track down by 10% with editing and time compression. To have the most success, there are some general guidelines you should follow.

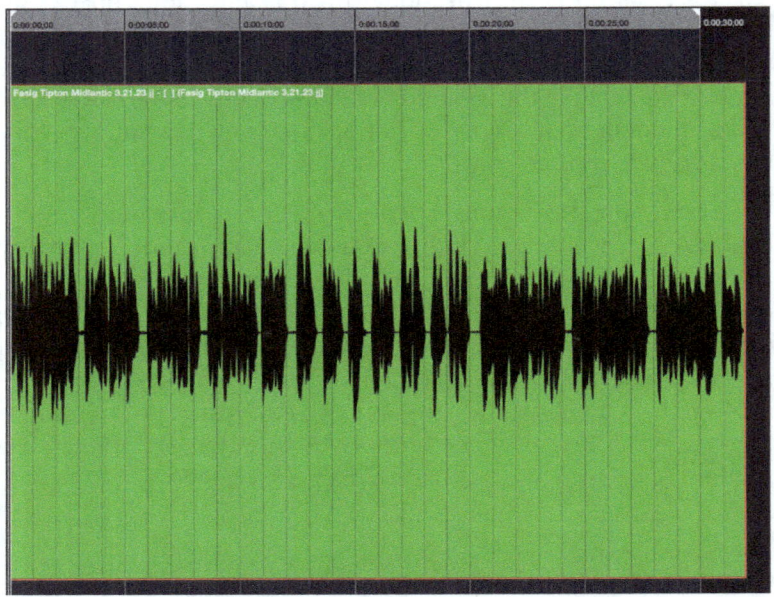

Here's a voice-over unedited. It's 32 seconds long, but needs to time out under 30 seconds. Notice it hangs over the shaded area by two grid lines, which represent seconds.

Before using the time squeeze tool, edit your narration so that its timings are pleasing and natural. Then, close all the longer gaps, usually between sentences, by half. Measure the overhang time to see if it's in that 6-7% time-squeeze range. An example would be a 35-second voice-over that needs to fit in a 30-second slot. After editing, it is now 32-seconds. 32 x 93% = 29.76 seconds. It can successfully be time-squeezed by up to 7% with little to no artifacts. This is a rule of thumb only, so you must actually try the compression and critically listen to the results.

When I'm using the time-squeeze tool, I use it several different ways, depending on what I'm trying to accomplish. The simplest method is to edit the audio to the shortest time that's comfortable. Copy and paste that edit to an inactive track in case you need it later. Highlight all the edited clips on your original track and bounce/replace them with one long single file. Apply the time-squeeze tool to this bounced audio clip.

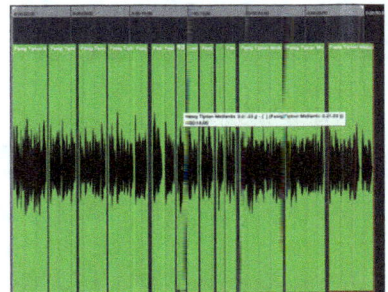

On the left example, the breaths are removed, and the clips are tightened up. It's still too long, so we'll consolidate the clips into one clip (right example) before using the time-squeeze tool.

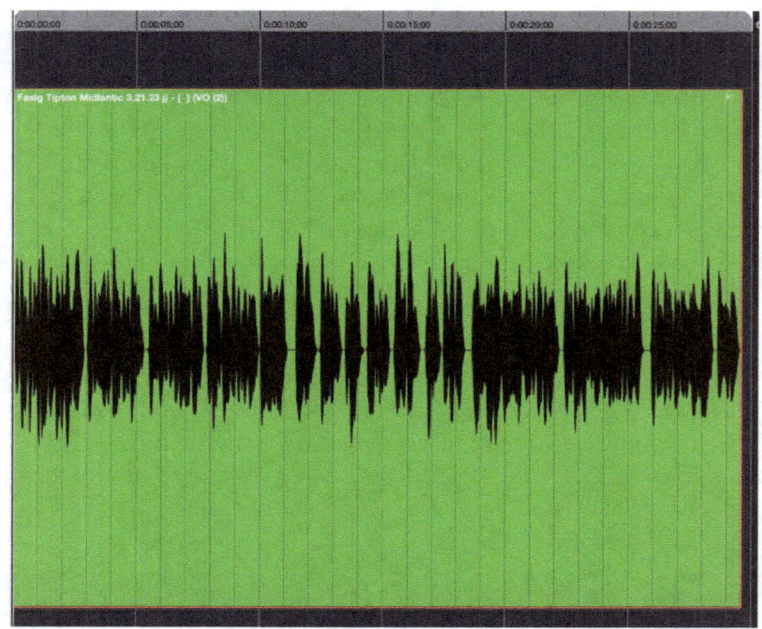

The consolidated clip is time-squeezed to fit under 30 seconds, in this case 96% to 29.6 seconds.

Another way I use it is to apply the time-squeeze to one small clip at a time. I will use this method when I want to nip and tuck a track into a fixed time slot one phrase at a time. I often do this to minimize words sounding too fast (more on that later). If I have certain phrases spotted to exact places on the timeline, then I might want to only squeeze select portions *around* those anchored clips so that I don't mess up all the timing with a global time-squeeze. I might also apply a more aggressive time compression on parts of the narration that are less important to the story or script, such as location and contact info, small print details, or tags.

I also time-squeeze parts of words. If someone drags out a vowel too long for instance, I will grab that vowel and squeeze it down until it sounds more natural. It's pretty amazing how useful this tool is and how well it fixes small speech errors or timings (and just as useful on sound effects and musical notes).

When you know you must time-squeeze speech before you actually record it, such as an over-wordy legal tag, instruct your narrator to read the tag slowly and deliberately while overenunciating the consonants. Short sounds like Ks and Ts will get extra short and disappear when they're time compressed, so you must save them *before* you time-squeeze.

Another use for time squeezing is on music vocals. Does the singer hang on a note too long? Squeeze down the ending so it cuts off in time. A duet will often have one singer holding onto a note longer than the other singer. Time squeeze that note down to match. If a note is too short, extend, or time *stretch* (see below) that last note out to match the cutoff of the other singer.

The parameters for a time-squeeze tool vary, but the best algorithms for speech are "solo" and "musical." These two settings seem to maintain clarity and quality the best. Settings for time-squeezing sound effects vary, depending on the software and complexity of the sound, so choose the parameters that best describe the effect you're working on. Experiment liberally to make sure it doesn't sound surreal. Or go crazy and experiment more if you want to change the sound to something otherworldly by pushing the parameter settings to their limits.

Music is perhaps the most complex and fidgety to time-squeeze. There are so many settings that, depending on how complex the material is, you really need to sift through and try several different algorithms. The most efficient workflow is to use the "preview" or "audition" mode of your time-squeeze tool to quickly figure out the time-compression needed. Then, sample a short 5 or 10 second clip that you can try different algorithms on. Once you find the setting you like, apply it to the whole file.

You can also expand time in files using the time-squeeze tool. I find that there's about a 105% maximum time expansion for the human voice before someone starts to sound drunk. For a real funny party trick, crank up the time expansion to 115% or more of your friend's voice for a real sloshy performance. Unfortunately, I've seen this technique used by nefarious on-line persons to make a politician or other important person sound drunk. Please don't be a jerk and post that party trick online, you could cost someone (maybe even you) their job.

USING REVERB REVERB REVERB REVERB REVERB

Using reverb can be one of the most polarizing applications in the studio. The volume, roominess, decay, timbre, and feedback can be scrutinized to death – usually by me! I never know what's "right" or how much to apply. I'll mix a song with what I think is beautifully mellow reverb under the vocals, only to have it shot down by the artist. It doesn't hurt my feelings, it only makes me think harder about how to get inside the head of the performer.

There are many types of reverb units, software, and DAW plugins. In fact, these seem to be one of the most popular types of plugins available on the market. Reverb is the shiny object that gets people excited. Nobody gets excited about the latest compressor plugin or dithering tool. Reverb can create exciting new soundscapes and even out performances. It is the most noticeable tool you can use, as compression and equalization are problem fixers rather than fairy dust. But like those problem fixers, it can be easily overused.

Here are a few rules-of-thumb to help you decide what type of reverb, how much to use, and on what kind of material. Remember, these are only guidelines, as your creativity and outside-the-box thinking should drive your choices.

Pick your room

The choice of the space your source will be in is the most important reverb decision you make. Where is your source? Inside a large hall, medium church, small bathroom, or inside a coal bucket? Each of these can have a big impact on the sound. I like to put my program in loop mode and try out different reverb settings, keeping the reverb level low (about 15%) so that I hear it blended with the dry signal. When I stumble on an interesting setting, I raise the level to 100% wet (all reverb and no dry signal). I want to hear the characteristics of the reverb itself. I'm usually listening to hear if it's too bassy, thin, ringy, and other made-up-words that might interfere with the overall sound. I'm looking for a room that doesn't overwhelm the dry signal, but blends with it as if it's an extension of the original sound.

Large rooms with long reverb trails tend to work best under short sounds that leave room for the reverb to trail off. Large rooms will also even out singers that have trouble staying on pitch or finishing notes. But more importantly, the reverb program you choose can influence the listener. Do you want to create a moody sax solo? Try a medium to long reverb in a medium to large room. Do you need to fatten up a drum kit? Try a drum room preset or a backwards reverb setting. Are you trying to match an ADR (see page 91) line to existing dialog recorded in a house? Try an unfurnished room preset or small room setting with a very short decay. There's a setting for almost any scenario or mood.

Real or surreal?

Reverb falls into two basic categories: <u>Real</u>, which either simulates a given space through conventional reverb control settings, or is calculated from recordings in an actual space; and <u>surreal</u>, which employs exaggerated settings to create otherworldly sounds. Your material will usually dictate which route you want to go. For music, I tend to start with basic presets like "large hall," or "small room" and then scroll through the presets. If I'm trying to match a new cut of dialog with an existing one in a film (ADR), I search for a preset that comes the closest to the original recording space. For fantasy and horror, I will usually try the more weirdly named presets that someone had a lot of fun creating, like "Unreal," "Afterburner," "Hall PREdator," or "Trauma."[110] These put the listener in a space that probably doesn't exist anywhere on Earth.

How much to apply?

Depending on how you're patching in reverb into your DAW, editor, or mixing console, your main control is "wet" or "dry." By blending the original signal with the reverb, you are controlling the wet/dry mix. 100% dry means that no reverb is heard. 100% wet means no original signal is heard, only reverb. Of course, you can adjust in-between, such as 70% dry / 30% wet.

---

[110] Real reverb preset names from Steinberg Nuendo's "Roomworks" plugin.

Most reverb software or hardware units have standard parameter settings in the app or on the face that you can adjust, such as room size, decay, feedback, equalization in/out, reflections, modulation, tail, and delay. By starting modestly and with most settings off or near zero, you can slowly adjust the parameters of each setting until you hear a change in the dry signal. Subtle reverb effects often go a long way when you're just trying to match an environment or add just a hint of effect. A heavy reverb mix may overwhelm the original sound, so be careful.

Surround, stereo, or mono?

Your dry signal may dictate your field width of your reverb. If it's a stereo recording, then a stereo reverb signal usually sounds more natural. If it's in surround, check to see if your reverb plug-in is surround capable. If not, you'll have to route extra stereo outputs of your reverb to the surround channels for a more natural space. If your signal is in mono, then match your reverb output width to your main width for a more natural sound. Some reverbs will split up a source signal based on frequency and send those to either left or right, creating a nice pseudo stereo effect. Sometimes you might want to match a mono reverb return with a mono signal, such as when…

Using reverb on vocals

Most pop songs of the 1950s and 60s used mono reverb on the vocals. Some of the larger studios had an actual reverb chamber that might have been the hallmark of their sound. Others used plate reverbs, spring reverbs, or tape delay (See Tech Tips below). Digital reverbs started to find their way into studios in the late 1970s. They exploded in the 1980s, giving that decade the nickname, "The Big 80s." Everything had reverb, and it was in glorious stereo. Today, we're a little bit more judicious with reverb.

I like to use it on vocals most of the time. When a performer is in the studio, I'll often sneak a little reverb into their headphones only just to make them relax. I will most often use stereo reverb on vocals because it spreads out the sound into a wide space, giving it more power.

Tech Tips

Reverb Chamber. In its simplest form, a signal from the mixing console would be sent to a loudspeaker in a separate room (usually a large reflective room in a basement). A microphone on the other side of the room would capture the reverberant sound and send that signal back up to the return bus on the console. Better-sounding rooms had maze-like chambers that bounced the amplified sound around many corners to lengthen the decay.

Plate Reverb. Actual large metal plates mounted vertically in an isolated room (or in a case) were fed an audio signal from the mixing console. The transducer, mounted in the middle of the thin metal plate, vibrated the plate. Pickups on the ends sent a signal back to the console. The result was a lush reverb, often with a long decay.

Spring Reverb. Very similar to a plate reverb, a spring mounted in a cabinet was fed an audio signal. Spring reverbs can often sound "boingy" if driven too hard. Many budget live consoles in the 1960s through the 1980s used small built-in spring reverbs.

Tape Delay. A channel's signal is sent to a separate reel-to-reel recorder. The output from that reel-to-reel tape's playback head is sent back into the inputs, therefore causing a feedback loop. Because the playback head is a delayed signal, there is a delayed echo sound. John Lennon was particularly fond of tape delay reverb for his vocals.

Using reverb on narration

I don't use reverb under most narration. But sometimes a soundtrack needs something to warm up the voice. It should be used sparingly and subtly, but it has a calming effect for spots and narrations that are heartfelt or reminiscent. This age-old trick can also give a voice more authority in advertising, marketing, or documentaries. It usually only works when music is underneath so that the reverb is masked and not obvious. Here's how I do it:

- Create a separate effects track in MONO. If it's in stereo, then sibilant sounds may bleed into the outer spatial areas and be revealed.
- Add a reverb plug-in to that effects track.
- Pick a preset that has a rich tone, large space, and medium to long decay.
- Adjust the wet/dry ration to about 30% wet.
- On your effects channel, insert a low pass filter and adjust until you don't hear anything above 5KHz-6KHz. The idea is to make it dark sounding with no treble.
- On the voice channel, send a signal to the effects bus through the AUX or SEND outputs, adjusting the level while the music is playing underneath. As soon as you hear the reverb, back off the send level until you don't hear it anymore.
- During any quiet passages or near the end of the program/ad, automate the effects track fader and reduce the reverb output so you don't hear it under the voice. The idea is for it to be subliminal. I usually fade out the effects track at the end so that the decay isn't heard and doesn't get cut off by the out marker.

Using reverb on instruments

One approach to using reverb on instruments is to send them all to one reverb channel, creating a room in which they're playing. Another approach is to apply a separate reverb channel for each instrument or group. Neither is right or wrong, but simply a preference. If I can get away with one, I will. But sometimes one instrument will overwhelm and dominate the reverb signal, forcing me to have separate reverb channels for a cleaner sound. Something I almost always do is have lead vocal, backup vocals, and instruments on separate reverbs. All three may be on the same preset, but I find the reverb is less muddy when they're separated. Don't be afraid to try different presets for each instrument/group, because music is art, and there shouldn't be any boundaries. I try to stick with similar settings so there is some cohesiveness to the sound of the reverb, but sometimes a wildly different preset can shake things up a bit and add some interest to a mix.

Using reverb on ensembles

If I record an orchestra, chamber orchestra, choir, or other group in a room that is on the dry side, I'll add reverb to soften the sound. I try to match the preset to a room that the ensemble would normally be heard in. Try to be subtle with the reverb level here, because ensembles are usually not closely miked, so the overall sound is wide and spread across the sound field, as opposed to a small, individually miked studio band.

Using reverb on sound effects

In film and television, many visual transition effects also have an accompanying sound effect. These whooshes, zings, and zaps can sometimes need a little help with reverb. I won't put it on every effect, instead creating a channel or two for certain effects that can benefit from the decay. A lot of these transition effects are computer-generated and very dry sounding. Adding a little reverb softens them so they're not piercing the viewer's ears.

I will also put reverb on some ambient tracks, such as a city at night, or a basement drone. Reverb smooths out any attention-getting spikes and crackles in the sound clip, as well as helping to create a subtle backing track that doesn't need a lot of attention.

KNOW THE NUMBERS

I love baseball, it's my favorite sport. The atmosphere of a ballpark brings back so many sweet memories of my beloved Cincinnati Reds[111] and the Big Red Machine. But the part of baseball I love the most is the statistics. Baseball is all about the

---

[111] I'm a glutton for punishment because the Reds have mostly had losing or mediocre teams since the breakup of the Big Red Machine in 1979. They did win the World Series in 1990, but have not even come close since then.

numbers: .366, .689, 4256, 762, 511, 5714.[112] What's the team's record? Which inning is it? How many outs are there? What's the count? What's the score? What's the batter's average? What's the pitcher's ERA? Growing up, I would check the league standings in the newspaper each morning and comb through the stats of the top 100 hitters in each league in Sunday's edition. I still enjoy keeping up with my favorite players and analyzing their numbers just for fun. But for a baseball player or manager, stats are critical. Pitch velocity, launch angle, spray percentage, pitch count, etc. are necessary tools the pros use to try to control the outcome of a game. Without the numbers, it's all guess work. And players don't like guessing. Neither should you.

Like baseball players, audio engineers are all about the numbers. But our numbers are 0, -10, +4. dB, RMS average, wattage, impedance, signal-to-noise ratio, track count, Q-factor, and many more. Don't worry if you don't know what any of these are just yet, but they will become as familiar to you as your favorite team's AP Poll ranking or number of championships. Just like how a pitcher uses batting statistics when facing every hitter, audio engineers use a set of values that can be applied to each situation. By knowing basic principles of how your equipment works, you can easily apply standard settings to just about any kind of live or recording scenario when setting up.

For instance, I know that the Shure SM58 handheld dynamic microphone is built to take a beating, both physically and with loud volumes. I can put this mic on stage for a vocal performer and know that a typical pre-amp gain will be about 90% if a vocalist is talking normally, and may need to be turned down to 50% if they are screaming like a lunatic. But it should still sound clean for both situations if the microphone is held about six inches from the mouth. But similar to how a pitcher adjusts to different batters in a line-up, I must test this mic on each mixing board or microphone pre-amp I use because there will be slight variances of level and quality. If I use another microphone of a different design, such as a Neumann U-87 condenser, I know from experience that it will have more output and cause distortion if someone yells into it. I

---

[112] Highest career batting average (Ty Cobb), highest career slugging percentage (Babe Ruth), most career hits (Pete Rose), most career home runs (Barry Bonds), most career wins (Cy Young), most career strikeouts (Nolan Ryan).

would therefore use different settings on my pre-amp and possibly insert a -10 dB pad in line to lower the microphone's level.

Knowing what your equipment was designed for and how it performs under different circumstances is crucial to getting consistent results. I'll let you in on a little secret. I didn't know a 0dB from -20 RMS for the first few years I was in the business. I learned all the basics on the job by not only watching other engineers work, but by experimenting with any equipment I could get my hands on. Much like revving a car engine to the red line before peeling out, I needed to discover what the boundaries were for each piece of gear. By asking a lot of questions, reading reference books and articles, and by experimenting, I was able to grasp the basics of how to set up and operate most audio equipment. Over the ensuing years, and when I was prepping to teach a college audio production class, I finally buckled down and learned what most of the numbers meant.

I'm no expert, and I will forget details if I don't use them in my work regularly, but learning the fundamentals of how your gear and software works is liberating. One of the big questions I always ask is, "Why? Why is it called that and why are those numbers or specs quoted that way?" If I understand the origins of gear and software or a spec or setting, then I'm more apt to remember its values and how to set the parameters. I can remember almost to the day when I finally understood what the settings on a compressor did. It was like a big dark cloud had been lifted. After that, I wasn't afraid to touch that box and turn those knobs anymore.

Knowing the fundamentals of how gear and software work will also eliminate much trial and error. I'll often sketch out my gear layout at my office before I ever go out to a complex remote recording job. I don't want to get there and try a zillion different setups. I need a well laid out road map that has had the kinks worked out before I pack my bags. On large recording jobs such as the Alltech Celebration of Song concert I detailed on page 169, I plot out every microphone's position on the floor, on the mixer, on the recorder, and how I will mix it. I plan which mic will need phantom power, which direct line feed I will need to convert from $1/4$" phone plug out to XLR input, and which mic stand will hold what microphone. This detail comes from going through all the equipment beforehand and charting any technical characteristics.

When I arrive on location, it's a fairly quick set up because I've already worked out 90% of the details ahead of time. This leaves plenty of time for last-minute changes or experimentation.

Audio engineers that design amplification systems for arenas, auditoriums, conference centers, and other places where large groups of people come for presentations use numbers to plan. Room dimensions, crowd size, type of entertainment, and other variables all go in to determining what amplifiers, microphones, speakers, and acoustic material to install before construction begins. They build in enough flexibility into their design so that adjustments can be made once the equipment is up and running. By using basic guidelines of how audio behaves in large spaces coupled with the technical capabilities of equipment, they are able to design effective audio systems on paper before installation.

You can employ some of these same planning principles to your projects by diving into some of the specifications of your gear *before* you set up. One example is a live gig for your band. If you're going to take a small amplifier rig to a nightclub, first go check out the space before your gig. Measure the room and check the seating capacity. A good rule of thumb for how powerful your amplifiers need to be is by multiplying the number of persons by watts. One person needs one watt of amplifier power, so a room with a 300-person limit will need about 300 watts. That's where I would start, but I'd probably take 500 watts just in case. So, if the place is packed with 300 quiet people, then your amplifiers would probably run at about 60% (300 watts-people / 500 watts = 60%). If they're a rowdy crowd, then you might have to bump up the volume to 80%. That means you still have more headroom before your system starts distorting.

I know this scenario is a *very* loose calculation, but it is a starting point for your planning session. Planning for overages, unanticipated failures, etc. is crucial. In the bar example, having extra wattage on hand is a good plan. Just be sure to not go overboard. Amplifiers that are built for live sound are designed to run at 80-100% power. You get a much cleaner sound by using amps and speakers designed for a particular output level. Plus, running live amps lower than 50% may dramatically shorten their life. Having an amp that's underpowered can be a problem as well. Driving an amp and speaker too hard results in harsh audio and distortion, which can quickly damage the components. So, you see, it's a fine balance when you're setting up something as simple as a bar gig. Dive into the numbers so you don't do a number on your equipment.

For other parts of your job, knowing the numbers can save you a lot of headaches down the road. You should learn what the different dB scales are, their range, and their uses. I won't go into much detail here, but you should know that a dB scale can be applied to any measurement of audio levels, whether it's power, sound pressure, or loudness. You will see generic use of dB as well as specific uses (like dB-SPL), so it can be a bit confusing at first when you see the different nomenclature. Here are six things to learn about dB that will help you:

1.   The decibel, or dB, is 0.1 Bel. Bel is named after Alexander Graham Bell. 1 dB is the smallest perceived volume change between two sounds that human ears can detect. In practice, we never really use the term "Bel." People might think you're a ding-dong if you do.[113]

2.   When we measure decibels, we are mostly measuring the difference of level between two sounds. Like the difference between complete quiet and a chainsaw running (110 dB). Or a 10 dB difference between signal A and signal B. Or raising the level of a signal by 3 dB.

3.   Decibel variations are calculated on a logarithmic scale. The numbers we use will not make sense at first, but after time the scales will become second nature. Here's a quick breakdown of what those numbers mean on a logarithmic scale when you increase or decrease sound levels:

Increase in dB	Change in Sound Intensity
+3 dB	Doubles
+6 dB	Quadruples
+10 dB	Increase by a factor of 10

---

[113] Pun intended.

Increase in dB	Change in Sound Intensity
+20 dB	Increase by a factor of 100
+30 dB	Increase by a factor of 1,000
Decrease in dB	**Change in Sound Intensity**
-3 dB	Halves
-6 dB	Decrease by a factor of 4
-10 dB	Decrease by a factor of 10
-20 dB	Decrease by a factor of 100
-30 dB	Decrease by a factor of 1,000

6. **Decibel scales look different on various applications and devices.** Think of it as Celsius and Fahrenheit on a thermometer. 0° Celsius = 32° Fahrenheit. 0 dB on an analog console meter = -20 dB on a digital console meter.[114] There are also different applications that will add a suffix to the decibel, like dBm for milliwatts, dBu for Root Mean Square voltage, dB SPL for sound pressure level, dBv for voltage, etc.

7. **Digital metering scales start at 0 dB at the top, or loudest, and go down in numbers into negative measurements as levels decrease.** When 0 is the loudest and not the other way around, it's contrary to the way we normally think of a scale, but there's a backstory. When digital recorders first started to appear in studios, there was no easy way to match its metering with analog equipment. What was understood is that if a signal hit maximum on the meter, then

---

[114] -18 dB on the EBU scale in Europe, but that's splitting hairs for a purely educational example.

severe digital distortion could occur. In the analog world, a maximum distortion level was almost theoretical, depending on the equipment and signal flow. One of my consoles started distorting at around +24 dB above average program, another would start clipping much lower. My reel-to-reel machines kind of liked distortion sometimes, it would fatten up the bass. But the digital and analog had to live together. So, manufacturers determined that most of what was being mixed at that time had about 20 dB of headroom above the average program. That would also work well with the new digital recorders. So, they put a 0 on top as an absolute maximum peak and put the reference level 20 dB below that at -20 dB. Therefore, the average program material would sound good at -20 dB on a digital scale, with another 20 dB above that for swells and peaks. If you listen to early audio CD releases, from the 1980s especially, mixes sounded generally soft and quiet. That's because everyone was used to mixing in analog, or about -20dB down from full-scale-digital. As more studios started working in the complete digital domain (recording, mixing, and mastering all in digital, or "DDD" found on early CDs), mixes became louder with less headroom. On an analog mixing console, the reference level was 0 dB on its analog meter (confused yet?), which read -20 dB on the digital meter of the recorder when properly calibrated. I have an easy way to remember this when you have to match an analog output with a digital input (or vise-versa). I call it the "Zero-Two-Zero" method. Generate a 1KHz sine wave tone on the analog mixer and set its output to 0 dB. Adjust the input of the digital recorder to -20 dB. Now you've matched 0 to 0, or 0 -20, or Zero to Zero. You can go in reverse as well when feeding out of a digital device into an analog mixer or recorder. This scale below might clear things up for you.

Analog Scale	Digital Scale
+20	0
+15	-5
+10	-10
0	-20
-10	-30

Analog Scale	Digital Scale
-20	-40
-30	-50
-40	-60

In the real world, a 1 KHz reference tone at 0 VU on an analog scale (see the bottom analog meter in the following illustration on the next page) is the same volume as minus -20 dB on a digital meter (right digital meter). A digital meter, as the one on the left, can be reset to display dB readings similar to an old-style analog meter. Keep in mind that analog equipment can't be driven too far past +5 or +6 dB (the red portion of the analog meter) without distortion. If you are recording audio <u>onto</u> an analog device <u>from</u> a digital device, synchronize your meters so that -20 dB on the digital output meter lines up with 0 VU on the analog input meter. Then adjust output so that no peaks on the digital meter go over -15 dB (-20 dB minus 5 dB). Digital's advantage of more headroom can be seen when comparing analog and digital range on these meters.

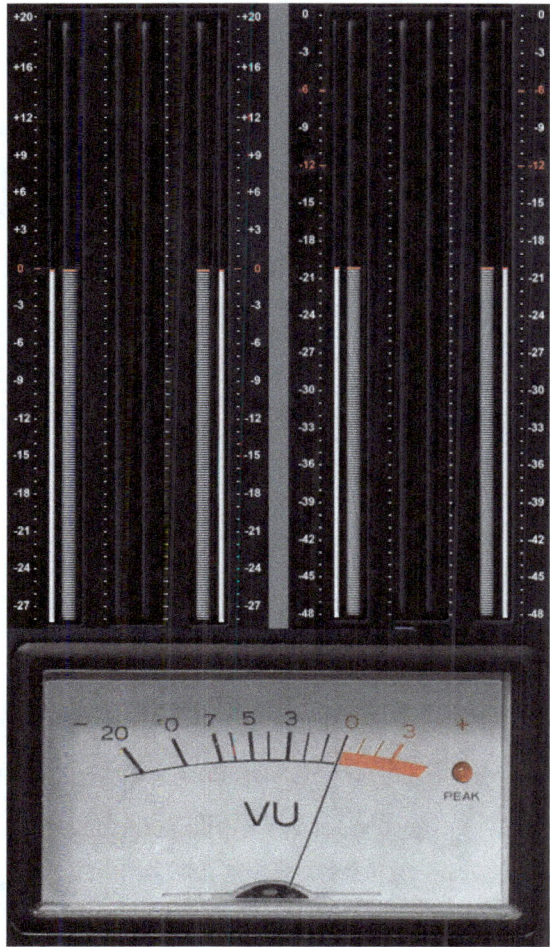

8. Decibels can be used to read average program levels.
For instance, an average level for voice-over on a radio commercial is -12 dB. The average level for dialog in a movie is -20 dB. The average level of a K-Pop song is -3 dB. I'm mostly making up that last one, but contemporary pop music is very, very loud with very little headroom. Watching a program or song play on the right kind of meter will show a slow-moving section that hovers around a certain range on the meter. This is usually the average RMS level. Above it you will see faster moving pulses up and down. These are the transients and peaks that occupy the headroom. The larger this area is, the higher

amount of headroom you have. This material will sound more open and airy. The example below has an **RMS** average of -14 dB with 14 dB headroom for peaks.

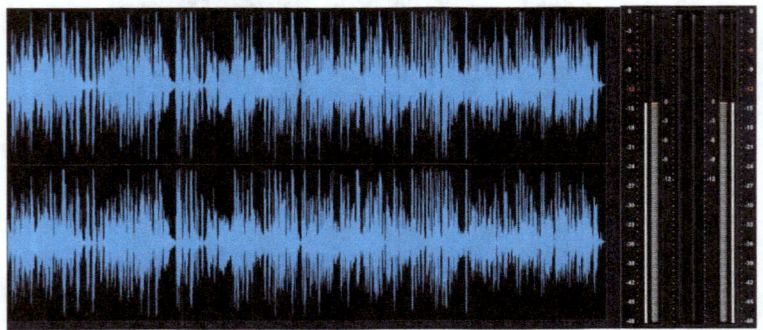

Waveform with RMS average of -14 dB. Notice how much space is above the energy plot on the meter at right.

If that headroom area above the average **RMS** is very shallow and small, then these programs will have little headroom and sound crunchy and forceful. The example below has only about 6 dB of headroom.

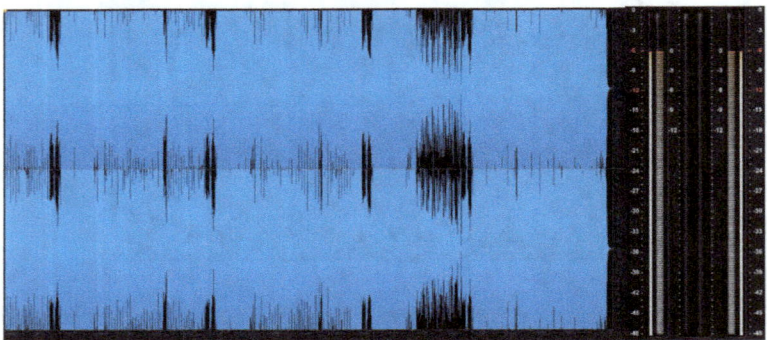

Waveform with RMS average of -6 dB. Notice how little space is above the energy plot on the meter at right.

KNOW YOUR ROOM

With any new recording situation, I first scout the room. I'll assess the location's potential sound problems first. Because it's an uncontrolled site like a studio, I assume that there will be more noise problems than not. If I'm recording on location for a video, I go all around the room and building to spot potential noisemakers like air handlers, people, alarms, etc. I locate all the light switches and HVAC controls. I test the flooring to see if there are any loose boards or tiles that may creak. I clap and listen to the slap back and reverb to see what kind of problems my recording might have. After I've located all the bad things about the space, I go looking for the good things. Like what position in the room is the quietest, or where there is minimal noise from outside, or where I won't get slap back from the walls. In any team sport, defense is usually stressed more than offense. The same can be said for recording remotely. In a recording studio, the builder has eliminated most of the problems through acoustic materials and careful construction. On location, there will be more problems than good things happening. By getting to know the space, I'm making sure the cards aren't stacked too high against me by reducing the problems before they have a chance to surprise me.

Here are some tips on reducing problems on remote recordings.

- Scout the site as far ahead as possible. Take pictures and/or draw sketches of the space. By going early, some problems can be eliminated or reduced by the on-site staff well ahead of your recording dates.
- Assume that there will be continuous mechanical noise. Most spaces will have HVAC. Find the controls and learn how to turn the system on and off. Some spaces will not have this option (such as a large complex that has centralized control), so learn where the quietest place is to record. Most continuous noise can be reduced or eliminated with software, but only if it's a much lower volume than the source you're recording.
- Assume there will be exterior noise. Traffic and weather are the biggest culprits that ruin recordings. These are very difficult to eliminate with software, so finding ways to reduce it before recording goes a long way towards a clean product.

- Assume there will be people noise. Getting the space reserved during off hours is helpful. Putting up signs in hallways helps a little, but people don't understand how loud they really are. I've had people read the QUIET sign and start laughing loudly as they joke about being quiet. Cut! Another take ruined.

- Assume there will be radio interference. If you're using radio mics, then you need to scan the spectrum[115] when you first get there. Also assume things will change once recording begins. Check with other crew members to see if they're using wireless equipment so each of you can avoid cross talk. Most venues have a "frequency czar" coordinator that registers and assigns all wireless transmissions.

- Assume there will be video equipment noise. Some lights and cameras have cooling fans, so talk with production people about either turning them off or placing barrier flags between your mic and the equipment. If there are dolly moves, the tracks will likely squeak. Make sure the grips have powder to sprinkle on the tracks.

- Assume the actors will make noise. Aside from clothing making noise in your lav mic, inspect the actor's shoes if they will be walking on the set while talking. Have them walk around to check for shoe noise. To solve, either have a carpet put down or apply Hush Heels to the bottom of the shoes. In a pinch put several layers of gaffer tape on the soles. Check all props with the script – actors might be handling or setting down objects that may ruin the recording. I'd rather keep the props silent on set and spot in sound effects later.

- Assume *you* will make noise. I try to locate my gear ten or twenty feet away from the on-set action. This way I'm not too far away if I have to run in and adjust a mic, but I'm far enough away that if I flip a monitor switch on my mixer it doesn't bleed into the recording. I'm also reducing my body noises (like shifting in my seat, stomach growls, accidental sniffs, etc.)

- Assume every recording will have noise. Recording remotely is very unnerving if you're used to recording in a super quiet recording studio. You will go from having a very quiet studio

---

[115] Most wireless mic systems have a band scanner that scans through the spectrum to find interference or other transmissions, allowing you to custom tune your transmitter to clear frequencies.

with a noise floor[116] below -30 dB to a room with -50 dB cr louder of background noise. It's even worse outside. Your goal is to record the source as high above the noise floor as possible without distortion or clipping. We use lavalier and boom mics that can be placed as close to an actor as possible so that the noise floor is lowered. The farther away a microphone is from the source, the louder the background (noise floor) will be. The same principles can be applied when recording music remotely. Get the mics as close to the performers as possible if the room is noisy.

Another room you should get to know is a new control room. This can be in a recording studio, remote truck, arena, stadium, concert hall, church, etc. There will be times when you're called on to step into an unfamiliar environment and operate unfamiliar equipment. It may be a new job or a one-time gig, but it's important to understand how the room is put together. When I first started my job mixing for the University of Kentucky football games (see page 149), I was thrust into a very unfamiliar situation. As I discussed in that section, they were still assembling the equipment on game day, so I had little time to learn how things worked. I understood the basics of course, but if something went wrong, I didn't know how everything was linked up. During the off-season, I got permission to go into the facility and trace all the wiring down so that I could see how it was all put together. One challenge I was facing was the existing systems and wiring that was integrated with the new PA system. It had been added to, repaired, re-wired, and finagled for decades. The new system was clean and pure. The two didn't interface well at all.

I started with the production booth because it had the newest gear and wiring, and it was where I would be working during the games. So, I traced every connection, cable, and piece of gear in that room. I learned where each setting was by experimenting with levels and controls (the main PA amplifiers were NOT on during this time, I would have a whole bunch of neighbors mad at me if

---

116 The "noise floor" is the quietest possible residual noise level you can achieve with given equipment and the space your microphone is in. Most well-built studios have a noise floor below -30 dB.

they were). After learning that room, I traced all the wiring that went to and from the booth. It fed a back wiring center, which in turn fed the scoreboard amps, the CCTVs, the concourse speakers, the radio and TV booths, and the production farm[117] outside the stadium. The main production booth also had connections from the field level. On-field microphones and other audio sources and intercoms used these connections.

I spent more time figuring out that big mess of a wiring room in the back than any other part of the stadium. I traced each wire or bundle from that room to its marked destination in the stadium. I was climbing up ladders and down on my knees finding them all, but I did. I even went up into the massive endzone scoreboard that housed the big TV screen and speakers. There were several racks of amplifiers, each one feeding a single speaker. That room was cooled and heated year-round to protect the equipment. The speakers were like little modular housing units stacked on trusses. I swear a small family could probably live behind one of those giant subwoofers.

Once I had learned where each and every connection went to in that stadium, I was very confident about solving problems on the fly. In the season before if someone would breathlessly run up to me and say that such-and-such isn't getting audio, I would have no clue how to solve that problem. But after spending a whole day tracing wires and connections, I could usually solve those out-of-the-blue issues pretty quickly.

When you step into a new control room, don't feel you have to go to the extremes I did in the stadium, but do peek behind the equipment racks if possible. It's organization (or lack thereof) will clue you in to what experiences you might have while working the console. Here are some tips on what to do when you work in a new production room:

- Look for user manuals and glance through them for reference. Bookmark chapters that you might need to quickly reference.
- Pull any master faders or control room pots all the way down before powering up anything. No matter if it's a studio or

---

[117] A production farm is an area set aside outside arenas and stadiums where all the remote TV production trucks park. There are multiple connection boxes for power, video, audio, and intercoms. Some have porta-potties and craft services.

arena, if you don't know what's going where, you may blow a speaker or an ear drum when you power up.

- Bring some familiar music with you to play over the speaker system. Something that you've heard in a hundred different ways will either sound better or worse in the new room. Adjust your brain to what's different to improve your mixing IQ.
- Bring your own set of headphones if you'll be doing critical mixing or monitoring on them. They should be professional, non-noise canceling headphones.
- Talk with other engineers that have used that room to see if there are quirks or unusual characteristics.
- Check out as much cabling as possible to learn how everything is interconnected. Go from rack to rack, even room to room, and trace cabling and jack points. Knowing the basic flow of signals between devices and rooms will speed up any troubleshooting you might have to do.
- Put yourself in the place of the talent. If you are recording talent in a recording studio or on-stage, go stand where they will be and experience how it will sound to them. This way you can adjust headphone levels or other foldback audio devices to acceptable levels *before* they come. There's nothing worse than the talent having their eardrums blown out when they first put on their headphones.
- If you will be working multiple days on the equipment, create and save your own settings in the console software so that you can instantly recall everything each day. Some venues have multiple events, so last night's rodeo may have ruined your jazz band settings you worked so hard on yesterday. It's also a good idea to take a photo snapshot of your console faders before you pack up each night. This way you can reset them easily if there is no software recall or some other issue.
- Take copious notes on settings and signal paths. You may not need these later, but I always found that if I write it down, it gets more easily cemented into my memory.
- Mark your faders and settings. I like to put white camera/gaffer's tape or removable masking tape just below the faders and mark each input or group output. Even if the

console has an electronic scribble strip[118], I like to mark important faders with tape so that I can quickly find them. I will also put a patch of tape on the face of any outboard gear so that I can either write setting parameters or mark the location of a knob value.

- After your gig, clean up your mess. Return everything back to how you found it. Remove all tape, notes, papers, etc. from the room. Reset any software back to default. Pull the master faders down. Remove your coffee cups and McMuffin wrappers. Push the chairs back in to the counters or console. Turn off the lights and say, "Good night, Gracie."

When you start a new permanent job at a new studio/arena/facility, you should perform the same look-around I described above. As your days and weeks go by, you'll have more opportunities to explore the finer details of your new home. Don't pull any connectors loose or change any software parameters yet until you're trained properly. But I do encourage lots of experimentation and exploration of every component and software app. Your new job will be to get the most out of the equipment and software, so knowing how everything works – and how to work everything – will propel you to the next level.

KNOW HOW TO LISTEN

The most important tool you can have as an audio engineer is a pair of ears. You must listen, without haste, to every element of your production. You must evaluate each sound to make sure there is no noise, distortion, or other problem that will ruin an otherwise good recording or live mix. You must also listen to content: Are the notes right? Is it in tune? Are the words right? But we can often be distracted or pressured for time. Don't make the mistake of doing

---

[118] A scribble strip actually derives from using white tape on a console. On modern consoles, it's a little LCD or LED window on each fader strip that gives track info.

cursory checks of inputs or mixdowns, because it will come back and bite you later.

Something that's happened more than once in my career is to "fix" a recording that wasn't listened to. One I remember without fondness was a videotaped press conference. The camera operator plugged the line feed from the press distribution box[119] into his audio inputs on his camera, checked that the meter was moving, and hit RECORD. The problem? The line feed was a +4 dB line output, and his camera was set to receive a -60 dB microphone input. There was distortion beyond belief because the two levels weren't matched. This is more common than you think. It's hard to fathom how a camera operator can look into a viewfinder to make sure that video is being recorded, but NOT put on a pair of headphones to make sure that the audio is too. When you're on a location that requires feeding your audio mixer to a camera, make sure the camera operator is wearing headphones at all times.

Another similar thing happened, but this time the camera was set to LINE input with a microphone plugged into it. The level was WAAAAAAAAAAAYYYYY low. The team not only failed to listen, but didn't even check the meter. Wow.

On one location job, I was mixing eight wireless lav mics down to a stereo/split feed to one camera that was all the way on the other end of the set we were shooting on. I was relying on the camera operator to monitor the feed because I didn't have the ability to listen directly out of his camera to make sure it was being recorded. About a half-hour in to one of the takes (it was a pseudo drama for an E-learning lesson), I looked over to see he had taken off his headphones. I silently motioned to him to put them on. He did, and his eyes got really big. "Cut!" he barked, "no audio!" My feed to him via two cables were laying on the ground next to him. Unbeknownst to me, he had removed them to move camera positions and forgot to plug them back in. Had he also put his headphones back on, he would have immediately known there was

---

[119] This is a one-input, multiple output device that different news organizations can tap into for audio. Usually, there's one microphone at a podium or desk that is fed into the box. This one audio feed is then sent to 12, 24, or more duplicate outputs. These are usually all line-level, all microphone-level, or a combination. Camera operators and reporters then run an XLR, ¼" or 1/8" cable from the box to their camera or recorder input to have a clean sounding direct feed from the podium.

a problem. Now who's fault was this? I took the blame because I should have checked and double-checked at the start of every take. I don't remember every detail of that production, but I remember being caught short on cables and couldn't rig a Y-split from his headphones to monitor. But still, it falls on the audio engineer. I will say that he never worked for that director again.

When you're mixing a song, program, commercial, audiobook, or other project, listen all the way through in real-time before mixing down to an audio file. If you've fully tested that workflow on that computer and software numerous times, you can spot check the final file afterwards. But if it's relatively short, like 5 minutes or under, listen to the whole audio file back in real time to make sure there are no glitches or mistakes. Several times in my career I've rushed out long format mixes that ended up having errors in the audio file that I delivered to my client. Some of these were digital glitches, some had audio clips that shifted on the timeline somehow, some had editing errors, and some contained wrong content that had been revised but didn't make it into this version. Mistakes happen, we're human. But had I listened back in real time before mixing down, I could have saved the time (both mine and my client's) it took to fix my stupid mistake. You will have this happen to you more than once, but by making listening back a habit, it will reduce how many times you have to slap your forehead and say "Doh!"

(Previous page). My Control Room A with speakers near ceiling and on stands near computer monitors. The surround center speaker is hidden behind the monitors. When I need it, I raise the articulated arm it's mounted on.

Another important way to listen is to check your mixes on various speakers and formats. I have five speaker systems in my control room. The main pair I use are self-powered medium-sized two-way (woofer and tweeter) speakers on short table stands that are near-field. That means that they are very close to my normal sitting position and are about 6 feet away. I chain a sub-woofer to these for some bottom end clarity (because physics dictates that the lowest bass frequencies aren't fully heard/felt at least 15 feet from the source). My second set is a pair of big 3-way (woofer, mid-range, and tweeter) speakers mounted way above the near-field speakers near the top of the ceiling. They're passive and powered by a separate amplifier. These are professional grade, but to my ears sound more like really nice home stereo speakers. They also fill the entire room, so they're great for playing stuff back to clients in the back of the room. My third set is a pair of small 5" square-boxed monitors that have only one speaker. These lack bass and treble, but are professional grade and flat in response. My room rounds out with additional rear and center speakers for surround mixes, and a little wedge-shaped speaker on the wall to one side for cueing up phone and internet calls.

Each one has a purpose, so here's how I use them. Set #1, the near-fields, are my everyday workhorses. They reproduce everything I need to hear with a flat frequency response and clear detail. If something doesn't sound good on these, it won't sound good on any speaker.

Next, my #2 set, are big and bold speakers that I like to use to do final checks of mixes that might be heard in stadiums, arenas, and even homes with big stereo systems. They have a sharp mid-range that I think mimics some sound systems that are being driven a little hard. This helps me find problems with harsh vocals and sound effects, because they really jump out on these. I don't use these for my nitty-gritty recording, editing, and mixing. I only use them as a final check before mixing down.

Next up are my #3 speakers, the little boxes. I use *Avantone* MixCubes, which are designed to mimic the discontinued classic

Auratone 5c Sound Cubes. These only have a frequency range of about 90 Hz – 17 KHz (I think the Auratones were probably even narrower in bandwidth). I mixed on the classic Auratones for years, and appreciated the straight-up, no fooling around sound they gave. By eliminating the bass and treble, they allow you to concentrate on the part of the frequency spectrum that is the most important. If all your main content (vocals, solos, etc.) can be heard on these clearly above the other layers, then your mix should sound great on any other speaker system. They are the definitive final check for any important mix.

Next are my surround speakers, which fill out my surround mixing system. I keep my near-fields and add these. I have my system calibrated so that I get equal signal out of all speakers at my mix position. You can do this by feeding pink noise[120] to each speaker one at a time and calibrating with an SPL meter. In a pinch, you can use a smartphone app that registers dB-SPLs.

And lastly, I have a small wedge-shaped mono cone speaker on the wall at my side. This is actually a vintage speaker like you would see in a classroom that blared school announcements. It's great to hear sources on my console in a cue mode. I feed my telephone and other call-in sources to this speaker so that I can monitor the input without bringing it up in the mix. This is vital if you do any kind of live broadcast. It's also a great crappy speaker for checking your mixes on. If you can hear the vital parts on this, it will play great on other crappy speakers.

Hearing your mixes on different speaker systems is a great way to make sure your mix will translate to other sound systems. When you're learning a new room, console, or monitor speakers, take your mix home with you. Listen to it in your car, play it on your home stereo, listen on your smartphone with earbuds, and listen over an Alexa. I have a little FM transmitter that I can plug into my headphone output of my console. I can then tune my old 1970s table radio to hear the mix "dumbed down" through the inefficiencies of radio transmission. I can even go out to my car in the parking lot and hear it over that system. Beware that radio stations will usually crunch your mix, so don't compare your studio mix directly to what's playing on air. Any different way you can

---

[120] See my article "The Color of Sound" on page 249 for a definition and usage of pink noise.

hear your mix will help you to fine tune how all the layers fit together.

Another trick is to turn down your monitors to just a click above OFF. Have them so low that you can only hear the vocals (or lead instrument). If you can understand every word or lead note without it being sucked down into the lower layers, then you're on your way to a good mix. Another technique to try is to start your mix playing over the speakers, leave the control room, shut the door tightly, and listen outside the door. If you can hear the important parts, then your mix should translate to other speaker systems.

If you're learning how to mix radio commercials or music with vocals, put a track of traffic sound effects in your project's timeline. Turn it up pretty high and mix your spot so that the voice comes out just above the car noise. Now mute that traffic track and listen. What you were just doing was simulating, to the extreme for sure, how your mix would be heard inside a car. You can also use this technique for arena and stadium mixes (cheering and crowd underneath), truck pulls (loud mufflers and hot rods), bars (rowdy crowd), etc.

Tech Tip

Commercial radio stations almost always apply aggressive compression and equalization to their audio signal before transmission. They're trying to fit a lot of information (dynamic range) into a small space (the radio wave). Most public radio stations use conservative compression, that's why they "sound" lower in volume. They are all actually transmitting within the same volume parameters. Here's a fun experiment: tune your FM radio from the lowest channel (88.1 MHz) to the highest (108 MHz), stopping at each radio station. Most public radio stations will be on the lower frequencies. As you progress through the stations, you'll notice they'll get louder and more in-your-face. None of them are louder in peak volume than the other, however. The rock, modern country, and beat stations are just squashing their dynamic range to sound "louder" than the other stations, sacrificing the difference between soft and loud passages. If you lower your volume to just above zero, these over-aggressive stations can be heard clearly, while the conservative ones will sound very soft.

TAKE NOTE

Keeping good records and taking detailed notes is a must in my profession. My approach to record keeping is to notate and organize everything as if some other person has to dig into the project years later and quickly figure out what the hell is going on. Imagine you're a police detective that might have to testify in a court case 5 years later. You would appreciate a binder of detailed notes to jog your memory.

When I started in the industry, analog ruled. Reel-to-reel tape, analog mixing consoles, rack gear with knobs and buttons, printed scripts – you get it, the age of dinosaurs. Well, we had developed good habits that enabled us to restart or revise older projects. It all started with taking good notes. If it was a scripted project, we took copious notes during the production. When recording voice-over, I would reset the tape counter on the reel-to-reel machine to zero before recording. Before hitting RECORD, I would enable a 1KHz reference tone on the machine. Next, I would record 30 seconds of tone so that the next engineer could match levels on their console to what I recorded. During recording, I would mark events on the script such as retakes, new sections, etc. with the current tape counter time. When playing back this tape, the engineer would reset the tape counter to zero when the tone started so that they could fast-forward to events on the tape. That was the best way to navigate through a half mile of tape (about 2,500-feet). The other, less elegant way was to slip thumbnail-sized pieces of paper into the tape path on the take-up reel for a visual indicator of where events were.

My scripts then and now have many markings, all of which are descriptive. I tend to mark scripts in red or blue, which is in contrast to the black ink on white paper. If I'm sending the marked-up script to another facility, I put a note code at the top of the page as a guide. For instance:

// = take 2. Take 1 is the original read[121]

O = pause. Editor needs to close gap

[text] = this phrase or sentence has been re-read

PU = Picked up reading here

FS = quick false start or stutter

* = noise (click, thump, etc.)

BR = noisy or odd breath

ST = stomach noise[122]

I will also mark file numbers in places, such as "VO_01" or "02." I will write other notes in the margins for clarity, such as "Multiple retakes here, use next to last one," or "Car sound outside, check recording." I will also mark running recording time at the top of each page of a long project such as an audiobook. These times aid editors searching for words or phrases to fix errors. Any kind of note, however miniscule it might seem, can be helpful.

Keep notes on any microphone, console, outboard gear, or software settings. If you can, write down general settings and backup software to the cloud or thumb drive so you have a copy. As discussed in the section about working in a new environment on page 437, take a photo of all the gear and settings so you can reference them later. In the ancient analog days, we used pre-printed line drawings of our console to mark settings for each

---

[121] I include this because some engineers mark a single / for the first retake. I developed my // habit decades ago from working in film, as the first take is always "take 1." It's been a difficult habit to break, especially when I have to follow a certain note-taking convention for some clients. I will also draw a line out from the retake point to the margin to aid in locating edits. Hash marks are easy to overlook if they are within the body of text and too small. If you decide to mark within the text body, make sure your marks are big and fat.

[122] Yep, bodies are noisy. The longer you work in the studio, the more unfazed you become to hearing gurgles, burps, farts, and other bodily noises that can be embarrassing to the performer. Reading, singing, and performing is a physical act that requires muscles and tendons within the torso to flex and move repeatedly. This in turn jostles all the liquids and gases around within the intestinal system. So, a burp or groan is inevitable – even with celebrities, priests, politicians, and grandmas. Your best way to spare their embarrassment is to just politely ask for a retake without mentioning why.

complex project. This method could still be viable if you work on an analog console.[123]

If your project's notes will go to an old-fashioned file cabinet, print out all emails and other notes from the project and include in the file. Think about creating a project numbering system like I discussed in the section about paperwork on page 370. Hunting down old project elements without an easy reference code can be maddening. If you keep elements in different places, like paperwork in the backroom, digital files on a hard drive in the studio, and references on spreadsheets in the cloud, having one code number that ties everything together can make your life easier.

THE ABCS OF A-B-ING

One of the staples of production is the ability to do multiple takes. Thanks to miles of magnetic tape, then buckets of data space, doing second, third, and thirty-fourth takes of a performance has been one of the chief benefits of recording. In the earliest days of recording, a wax cylinder or blank record signaled the performers that this was it, one mistake and we have to toss the disk. Many performers in those days probably only thought linearly anyway, the concept of a second take was novel to artists that only played to live audiences. This glorious new technology however, enlightened performers and gifted them a mulligan.

As magnificent as it was, recording to disk made it challenging to precisely blend parts of two or more performances together. Engineers could use two record players and one record cutter to re-record a new master. They did this by playing back one record with take 1 while blending in a second record with take 2 at a specific point in the song or program. Clumsy by today's – or even 1950s – technology, it was all they had.

---

[123] Many recording facilities, stadiums, churches, etc. still use analog mixers. In fact, it's a fail-safe way of ensuring rock-solid performance for critical applications. It's also common in boutique studios as well as mega-facilities to have a reconditioned analog classic console to track and mix through.

When optical recording (recording sound waves onto movie film via a pulsating light source) came along in the 1930s, it made it a little easier to make tight edits. This was commonly used in the film industry, as the music industry was mostly still recording to disk and radio was primarily broadcast live. It wasn't until after World War II that editing and multi-tracking made life in the studio so much easier.

The post-war discovery that the Nazis had developed advanced reel-to-reel tape technology revolutionized the recording, film, and broadcasting industries. By the early 1950s, studios were recording direct to tape, radio stations were "tape delaying" programs, and television was recording video to open reel magnetic tape. Engineers took the splicing methods they learned in film and applied them to tape. Multiple takes, no problem. As in film, an engineer would cut out each take and hang them beside each other (in film, the cut segments, or "clips," would hang from an overhead rod down into a cloth bin, hence the terminology "bin" for a collection of "clips" that's often used in video and audio editing programs today). The audio editor would then linearly tack the clips together and play them back so they were heard one after the other. This is a good way to detect subtle differences that might not be heard if the takes were played back with a longer time in between, say several minutes or hours. You can use this method of picking takes today with editing software by lining up the clips on a single track.

When you have many takes to choose from, divide your picks into pairs and make binary choices. From pair 1, select A or B and set aside. Move onto pair 2 and select A or B, and so on. After all pairs have been whittled down to a winner apiece, pair these heroes up and perform the same routine. It's best to play all these selections (or "selects / heroes" in industry parlance) in context with the main recording. For instance, if it's a guitar solo, insert or activate each hero take in the surrounding material and start playing several bars before the solo, through the solo, and into several bars afterwards. If it's voice-over or dialog, simulate this method. Playing each take only by itself will not give you the whole picture as to how it will affect the rest of the song/film/program.

Each time you listen to a take, focus in on a different element. For instance, first listen to the notes (or words). Next, listen to the tone, then speed, then energy, and so on. This will help eliminate takes that may have seemed good when they were cut, but now have flaws that are revealed under scrutiny. Take detailed notes when listening, and don't be afraid to merge one or more takes into a single one. After all, you have miles and miles of tape...err, data space.

There are other ways A-B-ing can be useful in the studio. If you're trying to match a previous mix, but with some new or improved material, flipping back and forth between the old mix and new can help you make level, compression, or equalization choices. Many modern DAWs have an easy A-B function built in, so that your reference track (aka old mix) will not go through any processing that your new mix is using. You can even match stereo spread, overall level, and other facets of the original using analysis tools. These days, many classic albums are being pulled apart, cleaned up, and remixed to match the original, but with much more clarity. A-B-ing is an essential tool for success.

Researchers also use A-B-ing to compare audio samples with test subjects. It's traditionally binary choices, but A-B-ing can also include several choices (A,B,C, or D) if necessary. One example might be in comparing differences between audio compression algorithms, such as mp3 vs. AAC. Having comparative studies greatly aids researchers, as single sources have nothing to be compared to. We all know what happens when only "one voice" is heard.

A-B-ing is an essential part of my everyday workflow. I use it for spacing edits, adjusting levels, picking narration takes, choosing music or sound effects, directing talent, etc. I'm never satisfied with the first choice out of the gate, although sometimes that's the version I end up using. I always want an alternative to choose from.

Tech Tip

Many DAWs have a time-saving feature called "lanes" or "versions" built into each audio track. These are essentially multiple layers/versions within each track. The project's worksheet is usually two-dimensional, with tracks laid out from top to bottom. These "lanes" become three-dimensional, falling below and underneath each audio track and are revealed with a toggle button. As new takes are recorded on that track, the most recent is brought

> to the top or front, superseding previous takes. However, you can solo an older take or edit two or more takes together. This is very hard to explain, but it's like a vending machine. You normally see just single candy bar selections behind the glass. As you buy one of them, a replacement will pop up to the top. Open the vending machine and you'll see a whole stack of those Mars Bars in the chute. Those chutes are your "lanes" and the candy bars are your "takes."

DIVIDE AND CONQUER: TIME AND PROJECT MANAGEMENT

Organizing your project and schedule can greatly increase your chance of success. At first, you may have no idea where to start. But if you compartmentalize and divide your recording project up into sections or chunks of work, you can stay on track Do step 1, decompress and then shift your focus to step 2, and so on. Trying to multi-task by jumping around between basic tasks and finishing tasks will jumble your mind, and the project. Think of it as painting a room: First mask edges, then lay drop cloth, then cut in, then roll walls, then paint the trim. Do one thing at a time. Not all projects will follow this flow I've outlined below, but most will:

1. **Pre-production – Get your ducks in a row.** Before the record button is pressed, you must plan and collect information. First, talk with your client about specifics like audience, format, number of musicians, actors, or narrators needed, if any backing tracks are expected, etc. Schedule the session(s), collect any upfront fees, prepare any documents, scripts, music beforehand, etc.

2. **Production – Capturing the moment.** Record all the elements and ingest any other audio elements needed. This is the part where the artist, actor, or narrator is behind the microphone and performing. Any editing or other sound manipulation is usually only performed in order to aid the recording, such as editing good takes together into one take to

determine if more recording is needed or to give the producer a good idea of what the final product will sound like.

3. **Post-production – Organize.** Once recording is done, the first phase of finishing begins. This is where you edit, move clips around, organize takes and build your tracks. If it's audio-for-video, you would de-noise and clean up voice-over and dialog takes, edit the dialog track into a smooth single take, add ambience tracks to balance dialog track edits, create group tracks, apply general compression and limiting, and do other chores that prepare the tracks for a final mix. If it's music, you would use this time to *comp*[124] voice and instrument tracks, equalize individual tracks for clarity and fullness, create group tracks, apply general compression and limiting, and do other tasks in prep for mixing.

4. **Post-production – Mixing.** Now you're ready for the final mix. Satisfied that all your tracks and elements are sounding their best by themselves, it's time to gather them all together for the party. This is where you would adjust volume levels, equalization, compression, and limiting; add reverberation or other effects; and blend all the tracks into your final output. This may be the shortest production phase, but it's no less important. You are following guidelines and specifications lined out in the pre-production phase.

5. **Post-production – Final checks.** It's now time to make sure you've done everything correctly. Listen to your final mix. Check to make sure that your mix translates properly to all formats and monitors. Check the final mix files for errors, out-of-range specifications, and correct format.

6. **Post-production – Delivery and wrap.** Make any alternate format copies, upload or copy your mix to appropriate destinations, and follow up with your client to see if there are any errors or problems. Fill out and sign any paperwork like invoicing, data logging, or contracts. Back-up your project.

If you're producing a live show, your time is divided up a little differently:

---

[124] Make a *composite*, or single track out of several takes.

1. **Pre-production**. This is the same as before.

2. **Load-in and set-up**. Trucks arrive, equipment is loaded out, and gear is set-up. This can take hours or days, depending on the size of the show and venue.

3. **Testing and balancing**. Test all components, align monitors, eliminate feedback, check all mics, instruments, and other sound sources and destinations.

4. **Sound check**. The band/performers come onto the stage so that the crew can fully test sound, lights, and effects.

5. **Production – Live show**. Everything should be tested and working at this point. All sound crew members are anticipating any problems and are ready to leap into action to fix.

6. Tear down and load-out.

Livestream and broadcast are very similar to live shows:

1. Pre-production.

2. **Load-in and set-up.** This is moot if you're working in your studio. But some remote broadcasts can be extremely complicated and involve a lot of equipment.

3. **Testing.** Test all components, mics, return feeds, and other sound sources and destinations.

4. **Broadcast check.** Perform a short simulated live broadcast/stream and check levels. If it's a remote, the aggregator or transmitter should be also listening and testing audio coming from and returning to the remote site.

5. **Production – Live broadcast/stream.** Everything should be tested and working at this point. All broadcast crew members are anticipating any problems and are ready to leap into action to fix.

6. **Post-broadcast.** Many broadcast outlets require logs to be kept during the broadcast that track commercial playback. These are usually hand-written as they happen, as well as electronically recorded by software used by a board operator to play back audio elements used in the broadcast. The final documents are called *affidavits* and help the sales department

determine if obligations are met for their clients (advertisers). Other tasks after the broadcast has aired may include archiving recordings of the broadcast, editing and distributing recorded highlights from the broadcast, disconnecting and packing up transmission and production equipment, and producing audio elements and paperwork for an upcoming broadcast.

I try to divide up all of my projects into chunks so that I can manage my time. I'm usually familiar with how each part will go, so I will estimate the time needed for each phase. I'll sometimes set alarms for when each part should wrap up. If I need to steal time from one chunk to get another one done, at least I'll know that I will have to work quicker to make my deadline. Before I start, especially the production phase, I will back-time from the last phase. If, for instance, I must deliver by 5 PM, I calculate how long that last phase will take. Then I step back another phase and estimate how long it will take, and so on. My mental countdown looks something like this for a 15-minute video that I'll be finessing and mixing down in one day:

5:00 PM. DEADLINE

4:00 PM. Final outputs and mixing must start now. Mixdown will take 20 minutes, listening back will take 20 minutes, upload 5 minutes. 15 minutes to spare as long as everything works perfectly.

2:00 PM. Start final mix. Balancing main dialog tracks will take 45 minutes. Balancing music to dialog will take 30 minutes. Balancing sound effects will take 30 minutes. Getting final levels to specs will take 30 minutes. 15 minutes to spare.

1:00 PM Continue editing.

12:00 PM. Lunch and 20 minute walk.[125]

10:00 AM. Begin editing, balancing narration, dialog, sound effects, and music clips.

9:00 AM. Ingest all audio elements, align sound to picture, create and organize basic workflow, submasters, groups, and final output channels.

---

[125] Notice that I set aside a mental buffer block of time? It's mandatory to keeping your wits. Try 5-10 minute breaks throughout the day if you finish a section earlier than expected.

This imaginary timeline wouldn't include searching for background music, which can add a day or more. It might include a few sound effects to support on-screen action. If it had one or more streams that might be intense, like sound effects for graphic moves or really bad location audio, I would budget more time. It takes real discipline to stop one section and move on to the next. The secret is to tackle the hardest and most laborious tasks first. Then if you have time, move on to the less involved, and so on. Starting each phase on time can help you finish the project on time. We have a saying in the production world: *You never really finish a project, you just run out of time.*

FUTURE-PROOFING YOUR WORK

There is no true way to fight father time, but if you take careful steps to preserving your projects from the ravages of time, you can share those great mixes you did today with your grandchildren in the coming decades.

Don't trust the cloud

The cloud we all rely on is useful for day-to-day data management. But to expect it to be here five or ten years from now is foolish. How many great online services or apps have you seen disappear over the last five years? Two years? Only use the cloud for immediate data safety needs. I've even experienced reputable cloud storage systems fail and lose data. I lost years of data when I transferred files from a certain well-known cloud service to my new computer. All I was left with were 0K files and a touch of heartburn. I'll discuss more permanent solutions later.

Don't trust your computer

Always have a back-up for your back-up. Even when I'm recording into my DAW, I also record on a separate fool-proof backup recorder. My computer will sometimes say that it's recording, show me the waveforms as it's chunking along, and then unceremoniously dump all the data it just received, leaving me with a blank recording. It's often a sync issue, but sometimes the drive hiccups, or the power fluctuates, or the planets momentarily went out of alignment. It's not something you can predict, so always run a separate recording device as a safety measure. If possible, have that backup on a different system as your DAW (I sometimes run a separate hard-disk recorder that is fed by an analog signal off my console). I find myself going to my backup audio at least three times a year. That's three jobs that were saved!

But you should also look at what you're recording to. I like to record to a dual RAID hard drive system. This can be either real platter-based hard drives or solid-state drives (SSD). The key is to have the second drive mirror the first drive. You sacrifice a little speed and throughput using this method, but in audio recording, it's usually not an issue. What you gain is an exact duplicate of your recordings in case a drive crashes. The drive enclosures that hold these RAID drives are more likely to fail than the drives. In fact, this happened as I was finishing this book. I was able to retrieve all of my projects safely from both mirrored drives.

If speed is your game or you only have one fast drive to record to, dedicate a second drive as a backup. You can use software that will mirror the first drive to the second drive simultaneously or at time intervals. Another option, and one I deploy regularly, is a dedicated project back-up drive. Since I'm using a dual RAID system while recording, at the end of a day I will transfer my major can't-lose-projects to this back-up drive. Each day I work on a critical project, I'll drag and drop it to this drive as a safety net. Just because your big fat RAID drive worked when you left yesterday, does not mean it will work this morning. Yet another option is to use a cloud service specifically designed to back up media files to the cloud. These work by only uploading when the app detects a pause in computer activity. Play it safe and back up your money gigs, to more than one place if possible.

Looking on down the road, how are you going to get your data off your main drives and back it up? Finding a permanent data storage solution is impossible because technology changes every week. Being flexible and staying just behind the cutting edge may solve that problem until the next big data storage solution comes along. The problem you must solve is to get the most data storage, the most robust medium, and the longest surviving medium you can get for the lowest price per gigabit. You can pay high dollars for the latest and greatest data storage medium, but will it even interface with a computer in five years? The crux of the matter is that you're going to put data on a shelf for years before you may, if at all, retrieve it. How much are you willing to pay to have it just sit there unused? How much will you pay to ensure that one as-of-yet-unknown vital project can be pulled off the shelf in five years and make money again?

My solution for years has been data disc. At first it was CD-ROMs, then DVD-ROMs, then dual layer DVD-ROMs, then Blue Ray-ROMs. I still store a large amount of my projects on Blue Ray and dual layer DVD-ROMs. Most of these are smaller projects that I'm pretty certain I may never need again, but I can still quickly retrieve them at a moment's notice. By keeping them in an air-conditioned storage room, I've only lost one or two discs to data corruption in two decades. From what I've read, the DVD-ROMs have the best long-term stability, with the dual layer DVD's next best. I'm not sure about Blue Ray's stability, but I've had no problems after five years. The data disc has been the cheapest per gigabyte solution I've found, but disks are quickly going away. If you decide to use them, make sure they are of good quality, a name brand, and are rated for data. The consumer versions may be attractive for the price, but you'll quickly regret it. Go for ones designed for business and buy in bulk. I also use a data cataloging program (currently NeoFinder)[126] to scan and catalog the contents. I label each disc and keep them organized in binders with special sleeves, sorted by client. A quick search in NeoFinder for a project tells me which binder and disc to find it in. I can usually search and retrieve a project in just minutes using this method. The "key" is to use keywords, dates, and job numbers in your project names and contents. This way the data catalog will easily find any element and direct you to the accompanying disc or hard drive. My rule of thumb is that you can never include too much information when naming and organizing a project.

My larger projects go to a removable hard drive. I currently use new internal drives that fit in a USB3 drive caddy. I can simply

---

[126] https://cdfinder.de/

drop the drive into the slot, and it pops up on my computer. I have less faith in hard drives, however. I've had numerous failures with them, mainly from NOT using them. If you don't spin them up periodically, the platters will freeze in place rendering them useless. I haven't stored long term to SSD, so I can't speak to its longevity. I also scan the contents of these drives into NeoFinder for quick retrieval. NeoFinder's catalog is backed up as well on Dropbox (a cloud data service), where it is always backed up and ready.

From articles I've read in the last few years, old-fashioned magnetic tape still seems to be the best long-term solution for large amounts of data storage. LTO, or linear-tape open, has been around decades. In the 1990s and 2000s, we used a predecessor of LTO called DDS, or digital data system. Both of these tape-based systems store data on a tape sequentially, writing a table of contents at the tape head. Most systems offer data compression (usually 2:1), thereby doubling capacity. I'm afraid media files can't be easily compressed without destroying quality, but LTO still offers huge capacities over hard drives, like terabytes vs. gigabytes. The downsides are cost and speed. It's very expensive to set up a system, but the data cartridges are quite reasonable in cost per gigabyte. They seem to have reliability measured in years and years, and capacity per square inch doubles every two or three years. Experts currently see magnetic tape storage a viable option until at least 2030, but they keep pushing that date out with new developments.

Whichever data storage system you use, you should expect to periodically move to newer technology every several years. For the most important projects, you should transfer from the older format to the newest right away. Keep your old archive around just in case! But being human, you'll probably forget to transfer all your old data and run into a technology panic when your old format won't interface with your new system. I have piles of old data archives that I'm hoping one day some genius will come up with a way to read them on new computers. I keep older technology around for as long as I can exactly for this reason. When I retire a computer, I try to repurpose it somewhere else, like on an office desk or as a server. I have an old Dell computer that I bought when I started my business in 2003 that still works 20 years later! For years after I put it out to pasture, I used it to cruise websites when I lunched in. When it got sluggish, I installed a Linux operating system to breathe new life into it. I've also done this with older Macs and

Macbooks to extend their lives. I took my old Mac Pro tower home and still use it to edit projects on. Plus, it has DVD-ROM drives that I can use to access old projects if I get in a pinch. In summary, old tech may save the day. So, try to hold on to working computers and peripherals you once used on a daily basis. You never know when it will come in handy again.

Make stems and different versions of your project

On large projects I typically make "stems," which are sometimes called "splits." These are really just separate sub-mixes of the elements. This way you (or another engineer) can go in and re-balance the mix at a later date. They can also be used for dubs, remixes, alternate versions, etc. Mastering engineers love stems so they can have separation of the elements while they rebalance and equalize the parts. I discussed one way I do this for television programs in the pan law section on page 389. For music, I will make stems for all major elements, like drums, bass, keys, rhythm guitars, lead guitars, backup vocals, lead vocals, etc. I'll also export stems of broader sub-mixes like rhythm, leads, vocals, etc.

I sometimes get stems of original scores for films or documentaries from the composer. This allows me to get a better blend of the music under any dialog or narration. For instance, if the horns are competing with the narration, I can dip that stem while maintaining the levels of the other instruments. I can also take an isolated stem, like percussion, and pluck out measures to be used in other parts of the program for emphasis.

Not creating stems for an important project is like hoping that technology doesn't advance beyond today. Hoping that a DAW project will work several years from now is foolish. I sometimes have problems opening projects from only six months ago because my software has changed. Trust me, you're going to get burned if you don't get into the habit of making stems of your most treasured (or important) projects.

One type of a stem is "undipped." All automation, equalization, plugins, etc. on the stem channels are turned off and the master output is bypassed. This is the ultimate version for future remixing and balancing projects. In film and TV, it's essential for remixing foreign versions.

The other type of stem is a "mix" or "dipped" stem. You would go about your merry way when mixing, but separate group stems would be created along with your stereo and/or surround mix. These stems would have all your fader movements, equalization, reverb, etc. that you intended for the final mix. These are more for mastering engineers and subtle rebalancing mixes. When in doubt, create both "dipped" and "undipped" stems along with master stereo and/or surround mixes. You might also want to consider a mono version if your project might be heard on toys, smartphones, AM radio, or some other device with limited-quality playback.

You should also put your most prized final mixes on separate mediums and store them in different locations. Put your mixes on an audio CD, thumb drive, hard drive, in the cloud, etc. Give one version to a family member or put it in a safety deposit box or fire safe. The key is to spread the different copies out to avoid a disaster.

PART IV

FOR THE CURIOUS MINDED

21. A SOUND EDUCATION

"An investment in knowledge pays the best interest."

Benjamin Franklin

Throughout my career I've written short essays for newsletters, teaching, and marketing efforts. My goal with all of these has always been to share interesting audio-related trends and facts in an easy-to-understand style. Here is a collection of these musings that I hope you'll find interesting, educational, and when intended, humorous.

THE BIRTH OF RECORDING

Dreamers in the 19th century seemed to be driven by the need to capture things. Animals were captured and put into the first American zoos in Philadelphia, Chicago, Cincinnati, and New York. Light was captured by Joseph Niépce and Louis Daguerre in France. And sound was captured in France by Édouard-Léon Scott de Martinville. Scott? De Martin--who? I always thought Thomas Edison had been the first. He was the first to record *and play back* sound, an important distinction. Scott's phonautograph recorded sounds as early as 1854, 24 years before Edison. But there was one problem, Scott didn't think about playing them back. They were simple lines drawn on a sheet of paper, not a physical etching into tin foil like Edison's invention. Explore the first sounds on the First Sounds website.[127]

---

[127] http://www.firstsounds.org/sounds/scott.php

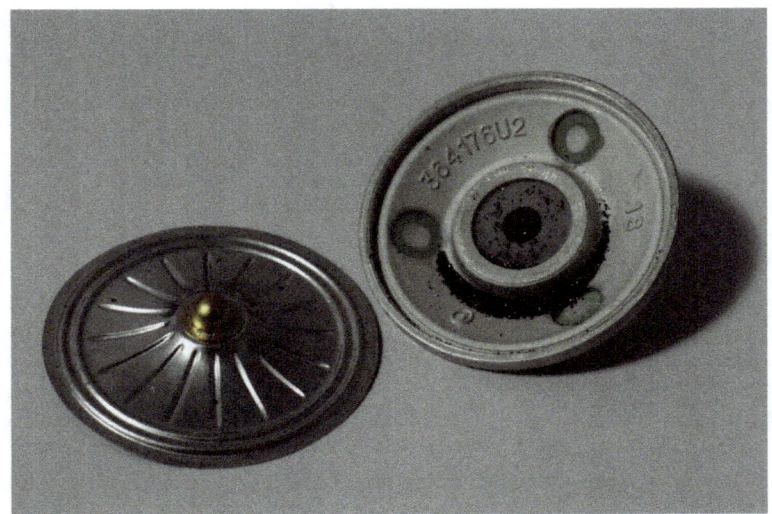

Photo 7.   Carbon Microphone

Other inventions started to pour out of laboratories, like the telephone, the electric generator, and the light bulb. While these men were rightly made famous, it's usually the people who improve the invention that push it into everyday use. Take Emile Berliner, a German-born Jewish immigrant that came to the U.S. in 1870 at the tender age of 19. By the time he was in his late 20's, he was filing patents for telephone-related improvements. His carbon microphone got the attention of Alexander Bell and soon after was working for him. Although the carbon microphone was also independently invented by Bell and David Hughes, Berliner's vastly improved upon Bell's with much higher output. The carbon microphone became a staple of telephony and was used well into the 1980's. Early radio broadcasters used them as well. You can even still buy one new, the Shure 104c, to interface with legacy equipment.

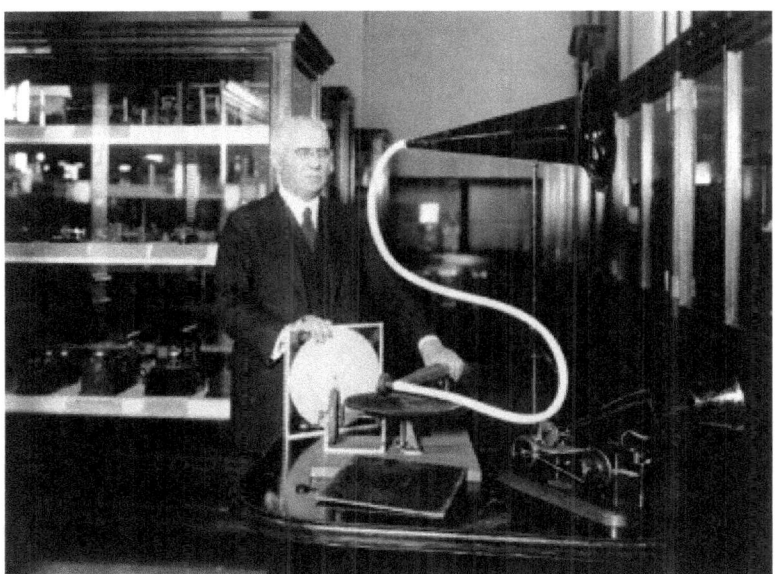

Photo 8.   Emile Berliner with his Gramophone

But Berliner is probably best known as the inventor of the Gramophone. Edison's recordings were done on a cylinder. Berliner put his on a disc. The disc would become one of the most common devices in the twentieth century to store data, such as the record, the CD the DVD, and the hard drive. But Berliner wasn't done with audio inventions yet. He also created the acoustic tile that recording studios, radio and TV stations, and performance halls rely on today.

Emile Berliner would also invent a new type of loom, floor covering, and an early helicopter utilizing a lightweight rotary engine. Whew!

Like other inventors of his magnitude, he was wrapped up in legal battles for many years. The Berliner Gramophone Company was forced to operate out of Canada while his former collaborator started the Victor Talking Machine Company using everything he learned from Berliner. His carbon microphone patent was trumped by Bell in court on a technicality. He was a philanthropist and advocate of public health and sanitation issues, especially when it came to children. He was also deeply involved with Zionism, writing several articles for newspapers and journals.

Berliner made many contributions to recording, especially the microphone. His improvement leapfrogged any existing technology and allowed telephone service to be quickly extended long distances because of the greatly increased output. This high-output microphone would also allow early radio experimenters to transmit the voice further. Thank you Mr. Berliner.

Did You Know?

There are many similarities between Thomas Edison's first recordings and Édouard-Léon Scott de Martinsville's early recordings. Both used a bell to capture sound waves that vibrated a stylus. This stylus rested on a rotating cylinder. Scott's etched waves into soot-stained paper. Edison's etched waves into tin foil. Edison's could be considered "mechanical," while Scott's "optical."

Early filmmakers desperately tried to include sound with film, but the awkward technology of record discs made it difficult to synchronize the two. The first commercially successful "talkies" used optical sound. Optical sound exposed film to a light that pulsed with the sound vibrations. As the film passed in front of the light, wavy lines are exposed on the edges just inside the sprockets. Much like recording sound separately from film/video today, on-set recordists relied on audible and visual slates to begin each scene. Mechanically stable motors to run the optical film recorders were vital so that sound and picture would later synchronize without lag.

Since the 1990's, many films have been distributed with optical digital tracks, such as Dolby Digital and SDDS. Later some also included optical synchronization pulses that would allow digital discs containing digital surround tracks to synchronize with the film for even clearer sound.

Tech Notes

When trying to play back Édouard-Léon Scott de Martinsville's early recordings, researchers used a technology originally made for particle generators. As they had previously done with antique cylinder and discs, they generated digital maps of the surface without actually touching it. They would use image analysis to reconstruct the audio with the added benefit of reducing noise. They first approached Scott's recordings like any other mechanical recording, by decoding the wavy lines as though they were mechanical record grooves. This didn't work, as the lines seemed malformed. But by approaching the recordings as if they were optically recorded, they were successful.

Early experiments by Scott had no reference to what speed the cylinder was rotating. These recordings are thus far unrecoverable. But Scott's later recordings included a 250 Hz tuning fork trace that can be used as a calibration aid.

This method of using a set frequency for calibration would enable the first "talkies" to be produced. Film cameras and optical, and later magnetic, sound recorders both used a set frequency for playback motors to operate at. We use it today with digital recording technology with sample rates and word clocks.

THE SOUNDTRACK OF THE PROHIBITION

It's been just more than 100 years since the beginning of the "noble experiment" – Prohibition.[128] The 18th Amendment banned the "manufacture, sale, or transportation of intoxicating liquors." Heralded in as a way to curb crime, especially domestic violence, it actually created a whole new cottage industry for organized crime and others to sell alcohol, sometimes with the help of law enforcement itself. When bars closed down, illegal nightclubs called "speakeasies" began to pop up. A club was often hidden from plain sight or disguised as another business, and a whispered password or secret knock got you in. When in public, patrons were asked to "speak easy" about its location.

The "Roaring Twenties" got its nickname from these speakeasies, the newly liberated women who were patrons, and the

---

[128] 1920-1933

raucous jazz music that played in these illicit "gin joints." In most cities there were many more speakeasies during Prohibition than there were bars before the ban. To entertain these lively new crowds, owners often hired local African American musicians to play a new up-tempo style of music. The crowds, a radically new mingling of men, women, blacks and whites, shared not only drink together, but a love for this new sound called "jass" – as it was daring and exciting. Jazz wasn't really new, but few had heard it prior to the 1920s. Jazz had been played live in local clubs and traveling shows for the first few decades of the century. The first recordings of jazz weren't made until 1917. As those records spread to other cities and towns, musicians were listening and copying this radical new sound.

Simultaneous to the rise of speakeasies was the beginning of commercial radio, which also fueled the popularity of jazz. During the decade, those local jazz musicians began recording their music. These records were played on the nascent radio stations, and soon jazz was being heard by large numbers all across the country. Jazz was the first multi-racial music genre in America, and it was played by, listened to, and liked by both blacks and whites. Jazz music became the soundtrack of the Prohibition.

The earliest days of commercial radio were like the Wild West. Amateur and experimental stations, most of which transmitted with irregular schedules and changed radio frequencies throughout the day, grew in numbers after the World War. There were no assigned frequencies, and a license had to be issued to anyone that requested one. As technology improved, more got into the game. Department stores and manufacturers such as Powel Crosley, Jr. in Cincinnati bought transmitters and used the airwaves to sell their wares. Entertainment and news programs grew as the cost of owning a radio fell. Record sales fell as well because the public was now hearing "free" music on the radio. The Radio Act of 1912, set up to license maritime and amateur stations, never foresaw the rapid growth of commercial radio. As more technologies like television and FM radio emerged during the decade, the government struggled with licensing and regulations.

The honor of the first station to be commercially licensed and broadcast in the U.S. is "up in the air." Most scholars recognize KDKA in Pittsburg as the most probable one to claim the prize. An amateur station started in 1916, it transmitted sporadically for several years under the call letters 8XK and 8YK. Their inaugural commercial broadcast as KDKA came on November 2, 1920, reporting the Harding-Cox presidential election results. Of all the earliest commercial stations, KDKA is the only one to retain its call letters and remain in its city of origin.

Speakeasies that either couldn't afford to hire a band or were limited in space used coin-operated phonograph players, known as jukeboxes today. The first models were acoustic players with big bells that channeled the vibrations from the needle. In a noisy nightclub, these were very hard to hear. When electric amplification came around in 1925, suddenly a record player could fill the room with jazz. In 1927, AMI released the first coin-operated electric machine that could play both sides of a record. These machines typically had a 20-song selection at 5-cents per play. Because record sales were hit hard by radio, so were coin-operated machine sales.

Another medium that propelled jazz into the consciousness of Americans was film. Talkies, or motion pictures with sound, started showing in cinemas in the late 1920s. Many of these early films during Prohibition featured famous jazz and swing groups that played in speakeasies, such as Duke Ellington, Louis Armstrong, Ethel Waters, and Paul Whiteman. By the time Prohibition ended in 1933, jazz and swing had become mainstream. And thanks to a do-good movement by tee-totalers, we have a true American art form.

WHEN RECORDING WRITES THE MUSIC

When commercial radio really took off in the 1920's and 30's, it was fueled by advances in recording. You could even say that each drove the other. Early music recordings were mostly documenting what was already being played to live audiences - classical, early jazz, folk, etc. As bands got bigger and louder, the music got more exciting. Dixieland was new, records were all the rage, and radio was just beginning to transport the new sounds across the country, just like the transcontinental railway brought the ideas of the gilded age to America a half-century earlier.

As those songs got louder, instruments such as the guitar got squeezed out. Enter the banjo, an instrument previously associated with steamboats and old west saloons. The banjo's inclusion in Dixieland bands was mostly because it could be heard despite the blaring horns, piano, and drums. When recording one of these bands, each musician would sit around one or more "microphones," which were actually large bells configured to collect the sounds as they cut the record. This was an all-mechanical process, so if the trumpet was too loud, that player would stand further back. And they played LOUD. They had to, the recording technology at the time couldn't record anything subtle.

Photo 9.   Recording the Victor Salon Orchestra, 1925.

But the lonely guitar was about to be asked back to the dance. A new kind of music was starting to swing in and take over. The amplified guitar was a backbone of the rhythm section of swing music. There was much experimentation and development during the 1930's and 40's with the electric guitar. Early examples suffered from problems such as feedback, distortion, and uneven sound between strings. But by the early 1950's, the electric guitar as we know it today was taking shape. By the 1960's guitar wizards like Jimmy Hendrix were using distortion and feedback to create new sounds. That's lemonade from a lemon.

Many erroneously credit Les Paul for inventing the electric guitar, but he only perfected what already existed. He did, however, use recording technology to forever change the way music is created. It all started with the Nazis. Inside Germany near the end of World War II, Allied troops discovered a previously forgotten technology - reel-to-reel recorders. Initially invented in the early 1900's, it was abandoned because the recording material (magnetized metal ribbon) was too cumbersome to manufacture. The Germans secretly developed and improved it, exploiting its quality and portability to distribute Hitler's speeches to radio stations for synchronized "simulcasting." The Allied countries seized and transferred many of Germany's technologies, including these recorders, and distributed them among themselves. In America, the Ampex Corporation was the sole manufacturer of reel-to-reel recorders and tape for a time. Les Paul was the recipient of the second model made from friend and Ampex part-owner Bing Crosby. With it, he invented sound-on-sound, the simultaneous playback of a previous recording on one track while mixing it onto a second track while playing a new part. It's similar to what we now know as overdubbing. But in the 1940's, it was an unusual thing to hear the same musician accompanying himself eight times. He also experimented with half-speed recordings, which when played back at normal speed, doubled the pitch and speed, giving a virtuoso effect if done properly.

Photo 10. Les Paul and Mary Ford

Paul also owned the first true 8-track recorder capable of selectively choosing different tracks to record onto while playing back previously recorded adjacent ones. However, using multi-track recorders to layer multiple instruments and vocals wouldn't come to prominence until Frank Zappa, the Beatles, and the Beach Boys started pushing its limits in the 1960's. The Beatles' Sergeant Pepper album is probably the best-known example of the early experimentation with a reel-to-reel machine to create music: backwards effects, vari-speed recording, tape delay, automatic double tracking, flanging, and other staples of recording today.

Photo 11. Doc Herrold is shown at the microphone of KQW, early 1920s.

The microphone, one of the earliest components of recording (remember, bells were used to vibrate the cutting needle at first), has also influenced music. Early models were offshoots of telephony, but as the technology got better, some artists were using the close miking technique to change the way they sang or played. Bing Crosby, Les Paul, and Mary Ford were early pioneers of the "proximity effect" to make their voices sound richer and fuller. When a sound source, such as a voice, gets very close to a microphone, the bass frequencies are greatly exaggerated. This allows the performer to use less effort, but also gives a more intimate sound. It's hard to imagine a modern recording using any other technique.

There are a multitude of other recording technologies that influence music, but at the root of it all is how musicians adapt, take advantage of, and push technology to create what is in their soul.

Did You Know?

The game of golf may have helped usher in magnetic tape to broadcasting. After the war, Bing Crosby was by now a superstar and wanted nothing more than to travel and play golf, rather than perform live on radio several times a week. The newly formed ABC Radio was interested in building a competitive network, and that meant signing big stars. Their promise to Bing and other performers was to record several performances for later playback. Some even pulled double paychecks by playing bigger-paying gigs on the weekends at the same time the pre-recorded broadcasts were airing.

Tech Notes

Sound-on-sound, invented by Les Paul, is the method of recording on one track, then playing that back while recording new material onto another track. An example using a two-track recorder is:

Using a mixer, record a drum track onto track 1 only. You now have track 1 with drums, and track 2 silent.

1. Rewind the tape and put track 2 into record.

2. Bring the output of track 1 into the mixer and raise the level.

3. The second instrument, such as bass, is also brought into the mixer.

4. Both the output of track 1 and the bass will be recorded onto track 2 at the same time.

5. Press record and play the bass along with the pre-recorded drum track from track 1. You now have track 1 with the drums only, and track 2 with drums and bass.

6. Rewind the tape and put track 1 into record.

7. Bring the output of track 2 (drums and bass) into the mixer and raise the level. Mute the output of track 1.

8. The third instrument, such as guitar, is also brought into the mixer.

9. Put track 1 into record and unarm track 2. Both the output of track 2 (drums and bass) and the guitar will be recorded onto track 1 at the same time.

10. Press record and play the guitar along with the pre-recorded drum and bass track from track 2. You now have track 1 with drums, bass and guitar, and track 2 with drums and bass.

11. Repeat as necessary, bouncing tracks back-and-forth.

Pros about this process is that it was a cheap way to have multiple instruments and voices. Cons were many, beginning with the fact that once you recorded over a track, you couldn't get it back. You had to get the balance between the recorded track and the new instrument exactly right early on. You couldn't adjust it later. Also, noise build-up and loss of clarity, known as "generation loss," could become overwhelming if noise-reduction wasn't used. Even then, it was tricky avoiding it. When the Beatles recorded Revolver and Sergeant Pepper, they used a modified version of sound-on-sound by bouncing a stereo submix from a 4-track to tracks 1 and 2 of another 4-track. They would then record 2 new tracks on tracks 3 and 4. Then they would bounce a stereo mix of those 4-tracks back to tracks 1 and 2 of another 4-track. Engineer Geoff Emerick and the other EMI engineers were amazingly able to keep noise low. Because they mostly used fresh tape for each bounce, most of the original tracks remained in archives. George and son Giles Martin were able to mine the original tracks for new mixes and realizations for Cirque du Soleil's Love show.

THE FATHER OF HI-FI

Arthur Haddy may not a household name, but his achievements are. Haddy is considered by many to be the "father of hi-fi." He may single-handedly be responsible for some of the greatest consumer audio advancements of the late 20th century: High-fidelity recordings, Stereo LPs, and Cassette Dolby noise reduction.

You could say that Arthur Haddy's leap into high fidelity began on a dare. Arthur was born in Newberry, England in 1906, educated in electronics, and eventually became a radio engineer at Western Electric. While attending a 1929 recording session of his future father-in-law, the singer Harry Fay, he found the recording equipment appallingly primitive. He jokingly remarked that he could build something better on his kitchen table. Six months later, the director of that studio at the Crystalate Company (the Rex and Panachord labels) challenged him to do just that. After he delivered on his promise, Haddy was hired at twice his Western Electric salary.

During his early years at Crystalate, he worked to improve the fidelity of cutting heads and dynamic cartridges. Wax disk frequency ranges at the time were limited to about 8,000 Hz (AM radio quality), but his developments greatly increased recording clarity. In 1937, the Decca Record Company bought Crystalate. Haddy continued his long career with Decca and made his greatest accomplishments while there. In 1939, he was just beginning work on a new extended range disk cutter when World War II broke out. It was by sheer luck that the British armed forces needed an extended range recorder for identifying differences between friendly and enemy submarines and airplanes.

Now working for the war effort, Haddy and his team at Decca were able to extend the high-frequency fidelity of wax discs from 8,000 Hz to 12,000 Hz (somewhere between AM and FM radio quality). One particular operation this helped with was for intelligence and training teams examining the subtle characteristics of water movement of German and Allied submarine propellers.

After the war, Haddy and his crack engineers at Decca were able to parlay their military advancements even further, now thankfully for entertainment and not war. The wax disk's frequency range was extended to 16,000 Hz, better than FM radio. Decca marketed this new "full-frequency range recording" as ffrr. Not very catchy, but it took the world by storm and others had to play catch up.

Arthur Haddy then turned his attention to reducing the noise floor in records. His application of pre-emphasis (boosting weak frequencies during recording, de-emphasizing them during playback) was an early form of noise reduction that is employed on all records today (RIAA standard). By 1950, Haddy and his engineers were considered the best in the industry.

He developed many other improvements to the sound quality of disks, disk cutters, phono cartridges, and other components of the turntable that are taken for granted today. His developments allowed Decca to be the U.K.'s first company to release long play (LP) records. As stereo recordings gained popularity, he guided the audio industry to use the now standard 45° by 45° record groove (instead of the sidewall and floor of the groove for left and right channels).

When Dolby A noise reduction was introduced for recording on reel-to-reel multi-tracks, Haddy championed its use during the mastering and dubbing stages as well, furthering his quest for noise-free recordings. Among other improvements to audio cassette technology, he also pioneered the use of Dolby B noise reduction in cassette players and recorders.

Arthur Haddy was a huge proponent of digital recording, and was even a pioneer of the first video disc in the late 1960s. Haddy devoted his life's work to making high quality, low noise recordings for entertainment.

Haddy received many accolades from the industry, including the AES Emile Berliner Award, was an AES fellow, and was awarded the CBE from Her Majesty the Queen. He retired from Decca in 1980 and passed away in 1989. Let's all spin an LP on the old hi-fi for our "father." Maybe "Arthur's Theme"?

THINGS THAT GO BUMP IN THE NIGHT

I can tell when Halloween is just around the corner. It's when the decorations start showing up on people's houses in August, or is it July? Those pumpkins and ghoulish displays remind us that October is a great month to watch a horror movie after a day of raking the leaves, putting away the deck furniture, and burying bodies behind the garage...

Just kidding.

Maybe.

Filmmakers have been trying to scare the wits out of us since the dawn of cinema. The earliest known horror film was 1896's "The House of the Devil." There were many more great horror films of the silent film era, like "Frankenstein" (1910), "Dr. Jekyll and Mr. Hyde" (1908 & 1920), "The Hunchback of Notre Dame" (1923), "The Monster" (1925), and "The Phantom of the Opera" (1925). The special effects and makeup on some of these films were groundbreaking, but there was one missing element that could scare the bejeezus out of audiences - sound.

The period from about 1926 to 1931 was a huge transition for cinema as silent films gave way to "talkies." There wasn't a sudden shift for movie houses from organ and piano players to amplified sound because installing sound equipment was a major investment. So, many continued to play silent films until dwindling audiences forced them to upgrade. Amplification in movie theaters was a new technical field, and many early sound systems lacked fidelity and loudness that are commonplace today. Further slowing down the transition was the difficulty and lack of a universal method of synchronizing sound to picture.

It seems completely natural to us today, but audiences in the late 1920s did not instantly acclimate to hearing actors speak on screen. Many felt the actors to be "bloodless," unrealistic, and contrived. Much of this was due to sound synchronization problems that became very evident during closeups. The voices of the actors also sounded disembodied, partially from low-tech sound systems, and partially from adjusting to the nascent idea of marrying sound with picture. Today we take foundational basics of cinema for granted, such as jump cuts, cutaways, and cut-in edits. But movie-going audiences usually need time to adapt when a new technique or technology is introduced.

Horror movie producers during this silent-to-sound transition period took advantage of the uneasiness that audiences were experiencing in adjusting to voices coming from the screen. In 1931's "Dracula," Bela Lugosi's appearance, diction, and voice seemed otherworldly to the former silent film watchers. The film also uses to great effect the one thing that movie studios were shunning – silence. At the time, using silence had tremendous impact when it was juxtaposed against other sounds in the film, especially non-linear sounds that were intended to jar the audience. Examples of non-linear sounds include the howling wolves in "Dracula" or the violin stabs in the shower scene in "Psycho." Humans react negatively to sounds of distress, and when a soundtrack is built up (or left silent) to present a non-linear sound, the effect can hit hard. Though "Dracula" may be considered a campy horror film today, its impact on the industry was profound. It can be viewed as a working experiment in cinema sound that informed future horror film directors about what works, and what needs more work.

"Frankenstein," also from 1931, has had a considerably longer shelf life than "Dracula." The famous scene where Dr. Frankenstein's monster first comes alive has compelling lightning and electrical sound effects. It's a very dynamic scene that lacks music but still works today, even with modern cinematic production sensibilities. As Dr. Jeckyll drinks his concoction and hallucinates in 1931's "Dr. Jeckyll and Mr. Hyde," dissonant music and eerie voices magnify the tension as he transforms. This technique has been copied again and again throughout cinema history.

During the silent-to-sound transition period audiences were very enthusiastic about the new technology, so they had a heightened sense of awareness to soundtracks. This played right into the hands of horror film producers who understood the newfound significance of sound in their films. When we watch some of their horror movies today, the impact they had on contemporaneous audiences is sometimes lost on us because production techniques that were cutting-edge at the time have become either standard or cliché. And that's a shame. My parents were growing up during the 1930s and 40s, and they considered some of these movies as gold standards of the genre.

The horror movie genre has gone through many phases in the last century – lows and highs – and yet keeps pushing boundaries as new technologies emerge. It's our generation's turn to experience a new bleeding edge of cinema – virtual reality – in both visual and sound. As we tremble and scream at even more realistic monsters in the VR world, we owe it to Dracula, Frankenstein, and Dr. Jeckyll (let's not forget Mr. Hyde) to acknowledge how much impact they had on a genre of cinema that continues to reinvent itself.

FANTASOUND

In 1940, before the world would be plunged into a half decade of devastating conflict, a larger-than-life cartoon creator teamed up with a wild-haired orchestra conductor and unleashed a fantastical film that would forever change the way we experience movies. The morning after the gala event at the Broadway Theater in New York City, The New York Times critic Bosley Crowther said,

> *"The music comes not simply from the*
> *screen, but from everywhere; it is as if a*
> *hearer were in the midst of the music."*

Even with all the wondrous characters, vivid animation, and whimsical storytelling of this new film, it was the sound that stole the show.

Fantasia from Walt Disney Productions has delighted audiences for years, been resurrected from imminent decay several times, and overcome its initial box-office failure. The animated feature's soundtrack featured the Philadelphia Orchestra playing eight orchestral pieces (one with a vocalist) from composers such as Stravinsky, Bach, Beethoven, and Tchaikovsky, and conducted by the world-famous Leopold Stokowski. There were many rules that Walt Disney broke when he dreamed up the film: it's length (125 minutes, the longest ever animated Disney feature), it was a full-length animated musical (called a "long-haired musical" by RKO Radio Pictures), the cost of producing the soundtrack ($400K, or 17% of the film's budget), and the expensive sound playback equipment ($85K per theater, $1.7MM today).

Fantasia was the first commercially released stereo / multichannel audio film. But the most groundbreaking part of the film was how the soundtrack was played back in theaters. *Fantasia*'s soundtrack was at its heart stereo, but it wasn't just played back through two speakers behind the screen. It had a third recorded channel that helped to immerse the audience "into the orchestra." Dubbed "Fantasound" by Disney, engineers had installed 96 speakers throughout the theater that surrounded the audience. This wasn't lost on Crowther:

> *"As the music sweeps to a climax, it froths*
> *over the proscenium arch, boils into the*
> *rear of the theatre, all but prances up and*
> *down the aisles."*

This was literally the earliest beginnings of surround sound, and it was waaaaay ahead of its time. It would be years before films were routinely released in stereo, and decades before surround sound became the norm. For *Fantasia*'s Fantasound, separate rear speakers independently played back a third recorded channel. It was manually turned on and off during screenings for effect. What was in this third channel? Soloists and a distantly placed microphone of the orchestral recordings that gave more realism to the sound. Today we call it a "room mic" which adds natural depth to drum and ensemble recordings.

Only 12 theaters ever played the film with Fantasound (and all 15,000 pounds of its equipment), so those that experienced these early Fantasia screenings as it was intended were very fortunate. At first, Walt Disney was so enthralled with the film that he wanted to put new music segments in every year and rerelease it over and over again as a "new" film. But World War II killed the movie, the profits, and his dreams.

Photo 12. Leopold Stokowski

Leopold Stokowski was the person most responsible for the film's technological breakthroughs in sound. By 1939, the conductor had already reached "rock star" status. When Disney first met Stokowski in Los Angeles, someone described the history-making encounter as "maestro meets mouse-tro." Disney was interested in pushing the technology envelope in his films, and Stokowski was already doing that with sound recording. In 1931 and 1932 he had recorded the Philadelphia Orchestra (of which he was the conductor) in the first orchestral stereo recordings. Working with both Bell Labs and RCA (Disney's partner) throughout the 1930s, they did numerous recording experiments, mostly in Philadelphia's Academy of Music opera hall. This is also where the soundtrack for Fantasia was recorded.

In 1933, the seeds of Fantasound were planted when the Philadelphia Orchestra's performance at the Academy of Music was transmitted via telephone lines to Washington, D.C. There, Stokowski manned the audio controls and mixed three channels of sound over separate speakers to a live audience. In 1937 he recorded the soundtrack for the film *One Hundred Men and a Girl* in stereo, though the picture was released in mono (he also played himself in the film). By the time he met with Disney, he was fully vested in multichannel sound and film.

Photo 13. Fantasia recording.

Recording the soundtrack was almost as groundbreaking as playing it back. Over 7 weeks and 42 recording sessions, 33 microphones were spread around the opera house, most of which were specifically placed within the orchestra for more detail from each section. But instead of engineers mixing these multiple microphones down to one recorder "live" and in real time, 8 groups of microphones were recorded onto 8 separate optical film recorders – all synchronized together (see picture). Recording onto optical film was one of the highest-quality ways to capture sound at the time, and Fantasia used more than 90 miles of it. Using optical film was crucial to not only maintain synchronization between tracks, but to the final film itself. Something else they did that is commonplace today was to overdub soloists in another studio in Los Angeles. Overdubbing is a mainstay in recording today, but in 1939 it was a new concept. So was the click track, a separate channel that contained a recording of a metronome

To mix the soundtrack, audio engineers blended the eight separate channels down to three and, using devices fashioned with gears and bicycle chain sprockets, playfully panned some of the instruments back-and-forth around the audience. Techniques and devices considered Audio 101 today were either created or invented just for this soundtrack.

Fantasia has lived on in many forms over the last 80 years. When RKO Radio Pictures released it to the general public in 1942, its length was cut to 80 minutes and the soundtrack was in mono. In the 1956 re-release, the stereo version was restored. The first soundtrack of *Fantasia* was released as a stereo LP set in 1957. Disney digitally re-recorded the soundtrack for the film's rerelease in 1985, which was the first film to be publicly shown with full digital sound. However, the original optical soundtrack in Fantasound was restored and recreated in digital surround for the 50th Anniversary release in 1990. The VHS and laserdisc versions had a similar, but less dramatic, surround version. In 1991 (and a 2001 rerelease) the soundtrack was released on CD and sold 100,000 copies in the first year alone. You can now find the original soundtrack on services such as iTunes and Spotify.

Before *Fantasia,* no film audience had ever experienced this kind of "surround" sound. It was a moment in cinema history not to be forgotten. And Bosley Crowther, in a 1940's kind of way, couldn't have said it better:

> *"Mr. Disney and his troop of little men, together with Leopold Stokowski and the Philadelphia Orchestra and a corps of sound engineers, have fashioned with music and colors and animated figures on a screen a creation so thoroughly delightful and exciting in its novelty that one's senses are captivated by it, one's imagination is deliciously inspired."*

A wonderful and detailed article from WHYY in Philadelphia about the recording process, complete with pictures of artifacts from the actual recording can be found at https://whyy.org/articles/modern-movie-sound-was-born-in-a-philadelphia-basement/

And a contemporary article published in the August 1941 *Journal of the Society of Motion Picture Engineers* is at http://www.widescreenmuseum.com/sound/fantasound1.htm.

THE LASTING LEGACY OF BELL LABS

To really appreciate that smartphone in your pocket, that music you're listening to on your stereo, and the newest episode of your favorite TV show, the important work of Bell Labs deserves our full attention. It was born more than a hundred years ago out of the need to improve the nascent telephone. It grew into a pure research facility that made an astounding number of scientific discoveries, improved or invented new technologies, and even influenced art and music.

In 1907, Western Electric, the manufacturing subsidiary of a young AT&T, started a research department to improve, develop, and patent telephone technology. By 1925, the department had grown to 3,600 employees. AT&T split the department into two groups, one of which was for pure industrial research–Bell Telephone Laboratories, Inc., aka Bell Labs. Because their efforts required much experimentation, some interesting new technologies were developed in the early days of Bell Labs, such as:

- Electrical sound recording
- Television transmission
- The fax machine
- The quartz electric clock
- A wearable electronic hearing aid
- An artificial larynx
- Transatlantic telephone system
- And the sampling theorem – or more precisely, digital audio and communications.

All of these were conceived by the brain pool of Bell Labs *before* 1930. The next decade would bring even more unbelievable new discoveries and technology:

- The moving-coil microphone (basically the modern microphone)
- Radio astronomy
- Stereo sound recording, transmission, and phonograph

- Raster scan television (standard TV until Hi-Def came along)
- Vocoder speech synthesis
- Boolean Logic Relay Computer

When, as one author put it, "The Second Great Inconvenience" broke out in 1941, many Bell Labs inventions were, ahem, "convenient" for war:

- Vocoder Speech Secrecy System
- Acoustic Homing Torpedo
- Horn-Reflector Antenna
- Echo-Ranging Sonar
- Synthetic Rubber
- Computer Controlled M5 Gun Director
- Nike Anti-Aircraft Missile

From after the war until the early 1980s, Bell Labs invented, developed, or improved:

- Coax cable
- The silicon and photovoltaic solar cells
- The words "software" and "bit"
- Wireless cellular communications
- The transistor
- Computer music
- Digital computer art
- The "laser"
- Satellites
- Electret microphone
- Big Bang radiation detection
- Van Allen belt detection
- UNIX operating system (Apple, Linux, etc.)
- C, C++ programming language (leading to Java, Python, Perl, and other internet programming languages)
- CCD (video and digital photography sensor)
- The hologram

- Fiber Optics

This list is by no means exhaustive. They produced thousands of theorems, discoveries and innovations that surround each of us every day. There were hundreds of scientists who worked at Bell Labs, many of whom won the Nobel Prize, that are now legends in their respective fields:

- **Joseph Maxfield** - recording and acoustical engineering work on the phonograph and movie sound recording
- **Harvey Fletcher** - acoustic engineering work on the electric hearing aid, stereo recording, and stereo transmission
- **Harry Nyquist** - communications engineering on thermal noise, television transmission, and the sampling theorem that led to digital audio and communications
- **Arthur Keller** - audio engineering on stereo recordings, and sonar systems for the US Navy
- **John Bardeen** - electrical engineering on the transistor and semiconductors
- **Chapin Cutler** - communications engineering on Telstar and Project Echo satellites
- **John Pierce** - electron theory and devices for NASA's first communication satellite Echo 1, the Telstar 1 satellite with the first intercontinental TV broadcast, and the electron gun used in CRT televisions and computer monitors

Bell Labs continued to be the world's largest and most significant industrial lab after the war through the 1970s. In 1984 when the Ma Bell monopoly was broken up by the courts, Bell Labs was broken up into smaller units as well. With unlimited funding virtually gone, it was no longer dominant. Today, the much, much smaller Bell Labs is part of the Alcatel-Lucent Corporation under Nokia. It still creates, enhances, and produces innovative technologies for voice and data communications. With all those big brains over there, I wonder if I can get them to fix my iPhone dropping calls whenever I walk into my kitchen?

3D AUDIO ON THE RIGHT TRACK

It's said that when an early motion picture was first shown to the public, women fainted, and men ducked from an approaching train. The director made a bold new decision that would alter the course of filmmaking for the next century. Instead of just placing the camera in front of all the action like an audience watching a stage, the director moved the camera to a new position - within the action - to create perspective. There were more changes on the way. About a hundred years ago, the first color and 3D films were being created. In an Avant Garde era when artists were distorting reality, most filmmakers were trying to recreate reality and immerse the viewers into it.

Realistic sound is no exception. In fact, stereo sound was first demonstrated in 1881, and multiple speaker playback in the early 1930's. These early attempts at locating sounds for the listener were impractical though and required expensive and ungainly equipment. By the late 1950's, consumers could finally experience stereo with LPs and tapes. But until home theater systems became popular, most had to go to a place like a theater or theme park to experience anything beyond stereo sound.

Since digital audio and video have pretty much taken over the world, we've seen a rapid growth of new technologies. Virtual reality is one of those, like the Oculus Rift, a VR headset for the masses (first introduced in 2012). This is a visual VR device. But what's lacking is auditory VR.

Enter the researchers at Microsoft. They've created a way to fool a listener into thinking sounds are coming from a specific location using ordinary headphones. To make it work, the listener's head and shoulders are scanned into 3D software, which then builds a custom filter. Add motion sensors and a camera to track the listener's position, and the fun begins. Sounds can seem to be coming from objects or areas in a room. Imagine making that stuffed Teddy bear in the corner of your child's room actually talk. That model hot rod on the shelf could rev its engine. The uses seem endless.

It's obvious that this new device will be used as a companion to a visual VR headset. But there could be many more uses. Theme

Park attractions could be revolutionized by creating more realistic environments while eliminating costly sound systems. The movie industry could enhance the viewer's experience. Music artists could create the ultimate mix, with that lead guitarist standing next to the coffee table.

I think the largest user of this technology will be the advertising industry. Imagine walking down the street with your headphones listening to some music when a voice from your left whispers, "Pssst! Hey buddy, wanna buy a watch?" You turn and see the sparkling Bulova timepiece in the window of the jewelry store.

Did You Know?

- In Paris in 1881, Clément Ader demonstrated the first two-channel sound utilizing telephone transmitters. As part of an exhibition, the Paris Opera performances were heard at a remote location by listeners wearing headphones. *Scientific American* immediately picked up on the aural spaciousness compared to a single receiver.
- Adre's process was later marketed in France for over 40 years as the Théâtrophone. These coin-operated devices were popular in hotels, cafés, and clubs. There were also many homes that had the Théâtrophone by subscription.
- Similar services were the Electrophone in England and the Telefcn Hirmondó in Budapest. In the U.S., there were only one-time experiments.
- The Théâtrophone service also included short news readings, making it a prototype to the *telephone newspaper* as well as the first example of electronic broadcasting.
- The popularity of radio and the phonograph killed the Théâtrophone by 1932.

Tech Notes

One of the fundamentals of recording and mixing is deciding what kind of spatial experience the listener will have. Creating a realistic one is difficult. If accuracy is not adhered to strictly, the result is a false space. An example of a near realistic auditory recording and playback is to place two microphones closely together in front of a performance. During playback, the listener is positioned in front of two loudspeakers at about the same angle and distance as the microphone were placed. This is a fairly pleasing experience but isn't 100% accurate because everyone's playback systems and environments are different.

A false spatial method is called "pan-pot" stereo. Mono or stereo tracks are "panned" in the mix away from center. An example might be a cowbell panned slightly to one side ('More cowbell!"). Most contemporary pop and rock songs are constructed this way because the tracks were built one performer at a time.

Recording engineer and producer Bruce Swedien (who recorded and mixed the biggest-selling album of all time, Michael Jackson's *Thriller* pre-planned his stereo mixes. If Swedien wanted that cowbell on the left side of the mix, he would record it in stereo with the performer standing to the left. In the analog tape days this required careful planning because engineers were limited to a finite number of tracks. Most multi-track recorders had 16 or 24 tracks. If all instruments are recorded separately in stereo, then that limited the sources to 8 or 12.

Most stereo recordings are intended to be heard on speakers. Once the listener uses headphones, the aural space changes dramatically. Instead of left and right sounds coming from forward of the listener (from the speakers), they are now coming from extreme left or right. Anything that was intended for the front middle (like the vocalist or lead guitar), is now coming from inside the head, right in the middle. It's a hyper-real experience, and immediately going back to front speakers elicits a lifeless experience.

There is one recording technique that requires listening only on headphones. This ultimate 2-channel spatial experience is called binaural recording. Two microphones are placed either in a mannequin head with false ears, or over the recordist's ears. Whatever the recordist hears is correctly translated to the listener. A common use for binaural recordings is an audio tour. How about a stroll through Chinatown on a busy Monday morning? Or a walk through a submarine as she makes her dive to 300 feet. The listener is instantly transported to the locale.

I did this on a project that required me to be in a crowd at a sporting event. I wore headphones that had small microphones (lavalieres) clipped on the outside. To the unsuspecting person, I was just someone listening to some beats. To the listener, I was their portal to the game.

LISTENING TO LIGHT

For generations, humans have been trying to link sound and light together. In 1704, Sir Isaac Newton, one of humankind's most celebrated thinkers, put forth an idea that the seven colors of light that a prism splits white light into (red, orange, yellow, green, blue, indigo, and violet) are related to the seven musical tones of the diatonic scale. To the non-musician, these are all the white keys on a piano. Besides being next to each other (most a whole step away, two of them a half-step), the notes have a harmonic relationship to each other. Starting on the F key, they are all a perfect fifth away from each other (F-C-G-D-A-E-B) and are part of music's Circle of Fifths.

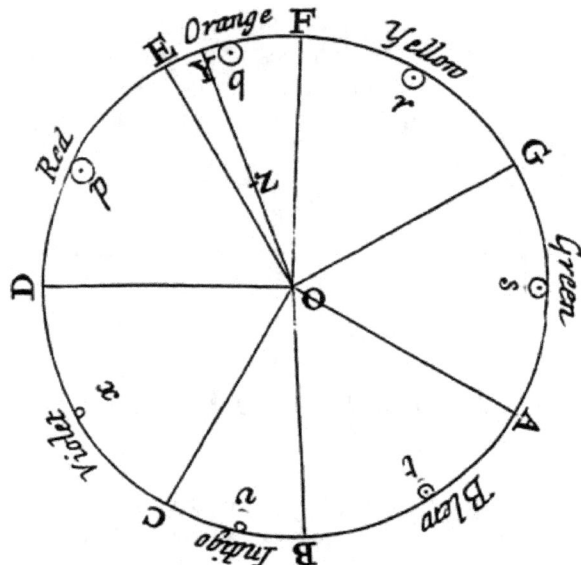

Diagram from Opticks, 1704, Sir Isaac Newton

Newton assigned these notes to opposite colors on a circle of colors in a convincing way, thereby beginning a fundamental 18th century theory of universal harmony for scientists and musicians. This theory was so well regarded, that French mathematician Louis Bertrand Castel invented a modified harpsichord, popularly called the "ocular harpsichord" or "color organ," that employed seven different colored lamps that were exposed for corresponding notes and harmonies. A "harpsichord for the eyes." While the theory was pooh-poohed by some, Baroque composer Georg Philipp Telemann wrote several pieces for it. The theory was eventually discredited, but not before musicians, artists, and writers embraced this new "visual music."

In 1880, Alexander Graham Bell and Charles Tainter sent the human voice over a beam of light using their invention called a photophone. This technology would lead to fiber-optics a century later. A few decades later, German physicist Ernst Ruhmer realized he could expose the fluctuations from the photophone's arc-light onto a moving roll of film. By reversing the procedure and shining a light through the moving roll of developed film onto a selenium cell, that original sound would be produced. This method would be the anchor technology of motion picture sound for nearly a hundred years.

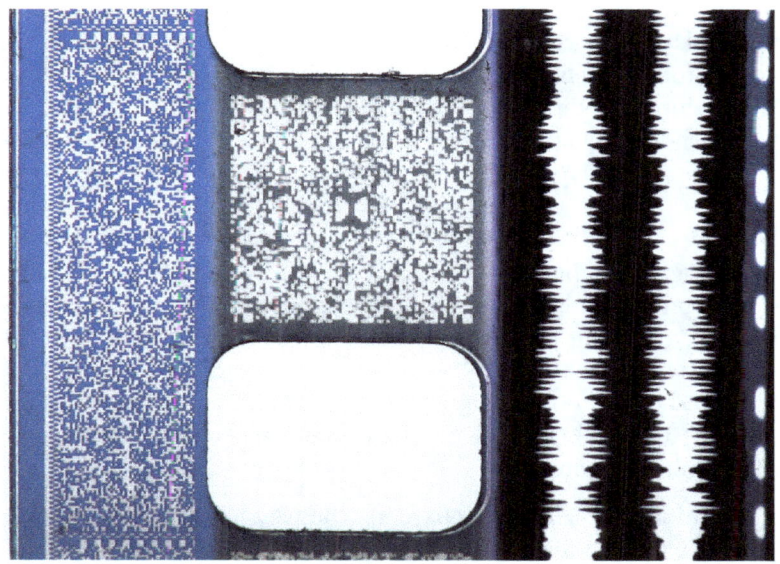

Photo 14. Macro of 35mm film audio tracks. Left to right: Sony SDDS, Dolby Digital, analog Optical. DTS time code.

Early attempts at synchronizing sound and visuals on film were clumsy and inexact. These mostly involved cutting a disc or cylinder while filming. Synchronized playback of a disc with motion pictures was next to impossible. The obstacle was finally overcome by using light to record sound onto a separate, but synchronized sound film recorder. For the theater release, the final film had the edge around the sprockets of a motion picture exposed with an optical soundtrack. Because the sound and picture resided on the same medium, the sync problems of two separate technologies were history. Today, presentation and archival 35mm motion picture prints still include an optical soundtrack, both analog and digital.

The next frontier for the harmony of light and sound is in data. We are now able to store light as sound. Current computer technology is "electronic" and based on the electron, which moves much slower than a photon, a particle of light. The next generation of computers will be based on light. We can already move data at light speed (fiber-optics), but we just can't store or process photons using tortoise-speed electron technology. That's why we slow the photonic data in fiber-optic channels way down to a pokey electron speed. New light-based computers will process data at near light-speed. Here's how it works: Photonic information, basically a pulse of photons traveling like a freight train, passes into a photonic microchip one direction through a maze-like path designed to lengthen its travel time. Those photons collide in the middle with a separate "write" pulse of photons sent into the maze from the opposite direction. This train wreck at the center of the chip produces a small acoustic wave in the microchip. As the chip is still vibrating like a bell (less than 10 nanoseconds later), a separate "read" photon pulse is sent into the chip. This pulse passes through the still vibrating chip, is converted back to photonic data, and directed out of the chip to be processed. Though the photonic data is slowed down to below light speed, computers utilizing photonic circuitry will be 20 times faster than what can be achieved now with electronic computers.

And finally, lasers are changing the way hearing aids operate. Amplification of a sound wave can be inefficient and problematic with traditional hearing aids. Scientists know that certain types of light can hit a surface, have their photon energy absorbed and converted to mechanical waves, which then generate sound waves. Researchers found that they could stimulate the inner ear with a laser, which then produced electrical impulses that were sent to the brain and interpreted as sound. By taking advantage of the fact that sound waves move much slower than light, a sound wave is captured by this new device and converted to laser pulses as the original sound hits the ear canal. This eliminates the feedback, distortion, and other problems with acoustic-amplified hearing aids. While still in development, these new "laser" hearing aids could change the world for aging rock-and-rollers.

VIDEO ON VINYL AND OTHER TURNTABLE TRANSGRESSIONS

Vinyl is the format that won't die. It'll probably still be around after humans are extinct and our sun has gone supernova. Perhaps in eons, Voyager spacecraft with the golden records aboard will meet distant stars and future vinyl lovers. But in this eon, people will not stop pushing vinyl to its limits. Mad scientists and crazy artists like putting something other than music on it - or in it. More on that later.

(Drop needle onto record, scratchy gramophone sound effect)

Let's start in 1927 with Scottish inventor John Logie Baird, the first person to demonstrate television. Logie, as he probably didn't like being called, was looking for a way to record and play back video. He turned to gramophone records, the kind that Duke Ellington and Rudy Valentino were on. We think of the 1950s as being the birth of video recordings, which were on magnetic tape. But the 1920s were right in the middle of the mechanical recording age, and it only seemed natural for Baird to attempt to capture this infant technology to a mature format. Ultimately, he failed to *play back* video, but he was successful in capturing it to disc, a process he called Phonovision. Half a century later, Donald McLean rescued the images, as well as other video-to-disc recordings from that era.

(Heralding trumpet sound)

In the mid 60s through the 70s, RCA tried to put video on discs. Making a Capacitance Electronic Disc (CED) was a very difficult process that involved cutting grooves 10 times denser than conventional LPs and coating the disc with a thin layer of metal and silicone lubricant. Each side of this fragile CED held 1 hour of video, had limited playback life, and had inferior quality to VHS. By the time of its release in 1981, VHS was winning over consumers.

(Sad trombone wah-wah-wah)

And speaking of Voyager, NASA and Dr. Carl Sagan *("Billions and billions" sound clip)* crammed 115 images plus 90 minutes of voices and music onto gold-plated lacquer discs. They included a cartridge, needle, and instructions on how to play it back. One spacecraft is headed to a star called AC +79 3888, the other to Sirius. Let's hope whoever finds it has ears.

(Drum kit "bucket-of-fish")

But experimenters weren't done trying to squeeze more than grooves into grooves. Austrian artist Gebhard Sengmüller created the VinylVideo format in the 1990s, and it has been revived today by the German company Supersense. For about $140 in 2022 US dollars, you can buy [129]a decoder that converts VinylVideo on a special release LP into a video signal. There are four discs available ($13), one from Motorhead, and one from the Courettes, which feature a really creepy dancing skeleton with a top hat.[130] The video quality is...ahem...artsy at best. One reviewer recommended watching only "if you hate your eyes."

("Psycho" violin stabs)

In the 1980s, a few artists and bands such as Chris Sievy, Pete Shelley, The Thompson Twins, and Shaky Stevens put software on vinyl. These were usually simple programs that contained lyrics, games, pictures, or crude video that supported the music. The idea of digital data as audio was not a new idea, as home computers used cassette decks to store and retrieve data, and phone lines carried data back and forth via modems.

("Pac-Man" sound effect)

Other interesting vinyl mods over the years include pictures and holograms on the surface, hidden tracks, backwards-playing hidden messages, double-grooved sides with two programs, and clear or colored vinyl. Consumers love things that are different, and some artists have pushed the envelope to satisfy their fan base.

("Ta-da" music cue)

We've talked about trying new things on the record, but what about "in" the record? Several artists have attempted, with some success, to put liquids inside the vinyl, essentially manufacturing a clear LP with a cavity under the grooves that contain injected liquid. Jack White put blue liquid in his "Sixteen Salteens" album;

---

[129] http://vinylvideo.supersense.com/
[130] https://i.kinja-img.com/gawker-media/image/upload/s--H9m2JY9R--/c_scale,fl_progressive,q_80,w_800/fkfwa5agvh5lyxaarexw.mp4

Worthless put red and green inside their "Greener Grass" LP; the "Friday the 13th" soundtrack album had blood-colored liquid inside; and not to be cutdone, the Flaming Lips put real blood inside the "Heady Fwends" album. All of these were limited release. Thank God only ten blood-filled albums were ever pressed.

(Evil laugh sound effect with echo)

With vinyl records selling very well to new audiences, what will some enterprising artist try next? Putting their live Instagram feed on the label? Projecting 3D holograms from the grooves? Communicating with vinyl lovers on a planet orbiting Sirius?

(Morse code sound effect, fade out)

IS THE MIX TAPE BACK IN THE MIX?

What, another old audio format is making a comeback? Yessiree! If you want to be hip, then dust off your old Sony Walkman. But like me, you've probably dumped all your old cassettes along with your floppy disks and Trivial Pursuit. These days, my pocket can carry the same amount of music that drawers and drawers of cassettes can.

But there are people who want to drag this once noble king of convenience from its analog obsolescence. These "people" are the new generation (and some older generation holdouts). They not only cherish the dejected and ejected cassette, they find it useful and economical. Sure, hipsters have latched onto the little magnetic wonder as a cool throwback, but resourceful indie musicians are leveraging the 50-year-old format as a distribution method.

Rewind

Before we find out if Maxell has cast a spell on these analog lovers or if there really is some merit to keeping these relics around, let's rewind back to the beginning. In 1962, the same year the Beatles released "Love Me Do," Philips released the "compact cassette." With some sound quality improvements over the next decade, the cassette replaced 8-track and reel-to-reel tapes as the consumer preferred recording format. Further improvements in the 1980s and 90s made the cassette a staple of radio reporters, home music studios, police departments, courtrooms, and schools. As a radio producer, I routinely recorded field interviews, sound effects, and programs on cassette. By the late 1990s, a top-end cassette deck mated with the latest high-biased tape could yield an incredibly satisfying recording worthy of the most critical audiophile snobs (including me). But it was too late, digital audio tape (DAT) had already become the new portable standard.

Six Percent

Compared to recording studio master tapes used in the day, the cassette used just six percent of the surface area and ran at just six percent of the speed. The audio fidelity is limited (worse than FM radio), the audio is over compressed (to fit into the tiny recording space), and there is considerable hiss. But during its heyday, it was the most convenient way to shuttle sound around, akin to the mp3 today.

Cassettes weren't limited to recording audio, they were also used for data storage. Computers in the 1960s and 70s utilized the small and affordable format. Interestingly, data storage onto cassette is still viable. In 2014, Sony squeezed 185TB of data onto a modified cassette. That's 185 terabytes, as in 370 BlueRay discs - or 3,936 DVDs - or 28,460 CDs - or 7 months of music.

The Home Studio Revolution

In 1979, Tascam introduced the long revered *Portastudio 144*, the world's first 4-track cassette recorder. It enabled tracking and overdubbing, just like the big boy reel-to-reels in recording studios, but on a budget. To reduce the obvious noise and low fidelity issues that cassettes have, high-bias metal tapes running at double-speed were used. Later on, eight tracks were squeezed onto an audio cassette, only made possible by employing noise reduction. The quality was acceptable enough that a few major artists actually released albums produced on these 4- and 8-track recorders.

Have They Gone Mad?

Why on earth would a musician sell their music on an analog cassette when we have CDs, mp3s and Soundcloud? I remember tape hiss, wrinkled tape, and the warble of tape dragging on the heads. Why would someone risk these drawbacks? Because releasing tunes on the more desirable analog format, the vinyl record, can be cost prohibitive. To cut just one-hundred vinyl records will set you back a minimum of $10 per disc. Having a hundred music-quality cassettes duplicated will cost about $3.50 each, and a lot less if you dub them yourself. In addition to cost, a cassette can be unique. Handing someone a cassette can pique their interest. They're more apt to play your little plastic fantastic than wade through lists of mp3 files.

Why don't you have your next production sound "classic." Come on into our studios, I've just resurrected a 40-year-old Tascam professional cassette deck. We'll give your radio spot that unmistakable cassette warble...flutter...hiss. And I'll throw in the wrinkled tape for free.

ANALOG RULES!

There's a growing trend in the music business - recording to reel-to-reel tape. Wait, I thought we got rid of that when we went digital. The truth is it never went away. Much like the recent boom in sales of records and film, reel-to-reels are gaining new fans and bringing back old ones.

Vintage analog outboard gear, like mic preamps, compressors, and reverbs are still coveted by both young and seasoned professionals. But analog tape took a serious backseat to digital by the time we partied like it was 1999. Most studios abandoned tape for the new highly efficient Digital Audio Workstations (DAW) like ProTools. Those still using tape did so out of economic necessity or defiance. Digital enthusiasts touted the DAW's noiseless recordings, fast workflow, unlimited track count, and endless plugins. Analog purists decried digital as harsh and soulless, with some vowing that tape would be pried "from my cold, dead hands."

It turns out that those old school purists are having their day. Those of us that made the transition from tape to digital know firsthand that it doesn't have the same sonic resolution. But because there were so many compelling features, we overlooked its shortcomings. Later on, we pined for some of those old analog sounds, so the market brought us software plugins that emulated vintage gear like vacuum tube compressors, classic EQ strips, vinyl record noise, and reel-to-reel tape recorders. DAWs now make it easy to integrate vintage hardware into our sessions. There is even a device that flows audio through a recorder, onto reel-to-reel tape, and into a ProTools DAW.

The things we don't miss about analog tape are the slow workflow and machine maintenance. The tape hiss can be managed with noise-reduction, but there is significant sonic detail lost when bouncing from one tape to another (called generation loss). Tape wear from shuttling back and forth while building a song is a real problem as well.

Things we miss about analog tape are the warmth from the magnetic reproduction of sine waves. The frequency bandwidth is far greater than standard digital recordings, which can capture valuable harmonics and deep bass. Analog stereo recordings have a proven time-spatial advantage that more accurately translates the recorded space - in other words, listeners feel like they're in the same room as the musicians.

We have all been overexposed to compressed sound, such as the mp3 and streaming media. Even the trusty audio CD is sonically limited. This may be one reason why we're looking to the past to put some juice back into our recordings. John Mellancamp's recent album "No Better Than This" was recorded with a vintage RCA 77DX microphone on a 1950's mono Ampex 601 tape deck. Taylor Swift, Jack White, and Lenny Kravitz are analog aficionados.

Analog tape's restrictions are actually helping some musicians. Taylor Swift's producer Nathan Chapman says Taylor's young, and she has the energy to go the extra mile it takes to record in analog's more limited number of tracks. Five-time Grammy-nominated producer Cookie Morenco of Blue Coast Records says that the high cost of recording tape forces producers and artists to make quicker performance decisions. This makes for a faster session with less fatigue.

Analog tape's archival qualities are another reason to believe. Recordings from 30, 40, and even 50 years ago can usually be played back. Digital formats and files can disappear without careful archiving and re-archiving. All but gone are DASHs, ADATs, DA-88s, DATs, and minidiscs. However reel-to-reel players and replacement parts are becoming scarce.

With the price of recording tape at an all-time high because of low demand and costly raw materials, it will remain a niche recording process. But in the never-ending pursuit of a unique sound, some will embrace it until the next thing comes back. Just to be unique, I'm going old-school here in my office and installing candlestick telephones. If you want me, just call EDison 5-1101.

GET IN THE GROOVE!

It's 1992. You make that trip to the basement carrying something that once was the centerpiece of your living room. Not the coffee table, not the couch, but your record player. Your turntable is kind of like Buzz Lightyear in Toy Story 3 who gets stuffed into the attic with the other toys. You've grown up to the CD now. No more static, no more skips, no more flipping the side over.

Well, there's a new generation that has discovered that old dusty record player. They're wondering why you ever stopped playing records. What is wrong with these kids?

What's wrong is they crave something they can hold in their hands and see. You can't hold an mp3. CDs aren't hip. LPs are real. And what's real is that LP sales are the highest they've been in more than 25 years. It's the same movement that's going on in film photography. It's also going on in the book world. People are rejecting digital for analog.

Why records? To quote my daughter Mara, "I enjoy being more involved in the listening process." Records are collectable. How many CDs have you purchased that you thought might increase in value? Records have a different sound. They've been described by new listeners as "full," "warm," and "rich" sounding. What was your first description of a CD when you heard it? Mine was "I don't hear any scratches." They didn't sound warmer, fuller, or richer. In fact, I remember early CDs sounding harsh and gritty.

The sound of audio CDs have improved since then. But curiously, CDs have the same sonic specifications from 1980, while recording technology has leapfrogged those specs several times. It's like watching *Avatar* on a TV from 1980. But LPs have retained, and even improved on, the sonic quality that apexed in the 80's.

To fully capture the full frequency spectrum of a well-mastered and pressed LP, one must at least quadruple the sampling rate (or number of snapshots per second) of standard audio CDs and increase the dynamic range resolution (or bit rate) from 65,000 possible levels to nearly 17 million. Even then, digital is not a true representation of a waveform, records still come closer.

The young are not the only ones playing LPs. Many of us old folk are rediscovering vinyl. And the record companies are rewarding us with LP-only bonus tracks, re-releases, and specially mastered discs. Jack White's LP Lazaretto has brought together many "tricks" from the old LP days, like double grooves, inside-out play, locked grooves on each side, and a first-ever hologram. He also had a new trick up his sleeve - playable labels. That's right, the round labels in the center on each side also contain songs, one at 45 rpm and one at 78 rpm. Watch a video with White and Ben Blackwell of Third Man Records as they explain all the details at http://www.npr.org/blogs/allsongs/2014/05/06/310156717/ul tra-lp-version-cf-jack-whites-new-album-has-some-crazy-surprises.

You know what else is crazy? Cassettes are making a comeback. Now this has to just be a fad, because cassettes cannot top the sonic quality of records. But there are musicians that will only release their material on cassette.

I think I know what the next craze will be. The children of today's young parents will dig through the boxes in the basement and pull out these small round objects in wonderment. They will marvel at their shiny surface and "Ooh" and "Aah" at the motorized drawer that snatches them from their hands. They will sit mesmerized by the glow of numbers just counting up, up, up, while brittle music slams into their ears. They will be the new CD generation.

Did You Know?

Here's an old trick we used to do: Hand someone a record. Have them examine the surface and then ask them to count how many grooves they see on one side. You may get answers like, "350," "1,000," or "there's too many to count." The correct answer is "one." It's actually one long spiral from end-to-end. Most of the time the spiral runs from outside-inwards. But some records, especially short-run records from the 1940's and 50's, went inside-out.

Some records actually had two or more grooves on one side. Depending on where you set the needle down, you would get a different program. One classic example is Monty Python's

"Matching Tie and Handkerchief," a "three-sided" record. Jack White's Lazaretto album has one song that starts with two grooves (one groove has acoustic guitar, the other electric guitar) that eventually blend into one groove.

In modern stereo LPs, one side of the wall of the groove contains the left channel, while the opposing wall contains the right channel. Early stereo records used both walls for the one channel, and the valley or floor between the walls for the other channel. Although the sound quality was superior to double-wall stereo, the "floor" channel would wear out rapidly from friction.

Tech Notes

Mastering for records is much different from for other media, like CDs or mp3s. When heavy rock came along in the late 60's, producers pushed mastering engineers for more bass on the records. But the engineer faced a dilemma. Because bass waves are large, the needle would just bounce right off the record if the bass was too heavy and loud. Both parties compromised by lowering the overall level of the music and adding more compression than previous records.

Without taming the dynamic range through compression, the needle will fluctuate and vibrate too much, resulting in poor audio. Keeping this from happening while maintaining a pleasing dynamic range is difficult. When Alan Parsons was engineering Pink Floyd's Dark Side of the Moon, producer Chris Thomas insisted on compressing everything. Parsons argued against it. As a compromise for the final mix, Parsons compressed vocals and instruments, leaving the drums alone.

AUDIO LETTERS TO HOME

"It was easier just to say it out on a tape
than trying to write it because it will take a
lot of writing paper in order to get it
straight."

Private First-Class Frank A. Kowalczyk

Long Binh Post, Vietnam, 1969

Back when it was expensive, or impossible, to call someone long distance, friends and family members would send messages on records and tapes to each other through the mail. Not only was it more affordable, but it was also a more personal way to stay in touch with each other and have some fun doing it. When I digitize some of these audio letters for customers, I feel like I'm transported back in time in a way that a paper letter can't take me.

Let's look back at a time when audio letters were very popular – 1966. Humans had yet to go the moon, but they could go to the Astrodome. Batman and Star Trek premiered on television in color. You could fill up your car for less than six bucks on your way to a movie that cost $1.35 to see. There were lots of choices for consumers in fashion, food, and entertainment, but not in telephone service. Ma Bell absolutely ruled the telephone industry. They controlled not only the price, but the choice of phones you could have. The average monthly telephone bill was $5, or about $40 today. That's roughly what a basic cellphone plan costs. But the first three minutes of an average long-distance call was $12, or $100 in today's dollars. Yikes! Most families reserved long distance calls for emergencies and bad news. If you wanted to communicate with family or friends afar, you stuck a 5-cent stamp on a letter. Or...you recorded an audio letter on tape.

Before magnetic tape became affordable for consumers, people could make their own records in a small booth or kiosk at a record store or arcade. One such device was a Voice-O-Graph, which was essentially a telephone booth with a microphone, a record cutter, and of course a coin deposit box. For about 35-cents, you got a three-minute record. The record was a "one off," and usually included the sounds of the turntable motor and cutting mechanism for free. By the mid-60s these self-serve studios were all but gone. These days, they're being restored and can fetch a high price. The Voice-O-Graph is even making somewhat of a comeback in the recording world. Neil Young recorded an entire album in one at Jack White's Third Man Records in Nashville. You can too if you make the trip to Nashville.

Sony-Matic TC900

By 1966, reel-to-reel tape machines were affordable. A low-cost small reel-to-reel recorder like the Sony-Matic TC900 (which is on my office shelf if you want to see it) was $67.50, or about $550 today, the price of an economical smartphone. The 1960s television show *Mission: Impossible* featured a number of tiny reel-to-reel players in the opening scene. I'm hoping real ones didn't self-destruct and go up in smoke like the TV props did.

Back of a box for a 5" reel-to-reel tape.

Little mono recorders like the Sony-Matic could accommodate a small 3" reel with about an hour of recording time on each side at low speed. Tell your story, pop the reel in its box, scratch an address on the outside, and drop it in the mail. Your recipient would listen to Mom tell the latest neighborhood gossip, Dad would provide updates on his latest new gadget, Johnny would talk about his baseball team, and

Front of a box for a 5" reel-to-reel tape.

Susie would brag about how well school is going. There might even be a short piano solo as a bonus. On the other end, Aunt Sally and Uncle Joe would record all their news on the flip side of the reel and send it back. It was a great way to stay in touch, and hearing someone tell a story in their own voice was much more emotionally satisfying than a letter.

For soldiers overseas, it was a boon if they could get their hands on a reel-to-reel machine. The Smithsonian National Postal Museum features a detailed and heartwarming story[131] about PFC Frank Kowalczyk form Calumet City, Illinois. Frank and his family regularly sent audio tapes back and forth during his nearly year-long stay in Vietnam in 1969. He took advantage of the military's free postal privileges for those in Vietnam and other designated zones. Each little package made an expedited flight on a commercial airline back home to Illinois. He had bought a reel-to-reel recorder from another soldier while stationed at Long Binh Post, Vietnam. Other soldiers not so lucky could go to recording stations at USO and American Red Cross centers and take advantage of the "Voices from Home" program. The 3M Corporation supplied "Living Letters" brand tape and shipping boxes for the soldiers.

---

[131] https://postalmuseum.si.edu/collections/object-spotlight/audio-correspondence.html

My most memorable transfer of an audio letter was from a man who had lost his mother when he was a baby. His family was living in Hawaii in the early 60s when his parents recorded an audio letter for my customer's grandmother. In the background, you could hear a baby cooing and giggling – that was my customer as an infant. When he came to pick up the CD, he wanted to hear it right then. He and his young daughter stood there and listened, enraptured. Then with a tear in his eye, he turned to me and said, "That's the first time I've heard my mother's voice."

WHEN OLD IS OLD AGAIN

Buford T. Justice: Breaker, breaker for the Bandit.

Bandit: Come on back, breaker.

Buford T. Justice: Bandit, I got a smokey report for you. Come on!

Bandit: Well, talk to me good buddy.

Buford T. Justice: You got trouble comin...

Bandit: Well, what's your handle son, and what's your twenty?

Buford T. Justice: My handle's Smokey Bear and I'm tail-grabbin yo ass right now!

Smokey and the Bandit (1977)

Just when you thought CB radio was dead, the Federal Communication Commission passed a rule that might have every "Smokey and the Bandit" fan yearning for another sequel. The FCC is allowing FM transmission on CB radio!

Though not in the forefront of the American conscience anymore, Citizens Band radio has been around since 1945. Twenty-three channels (later 40) were carved out of the 11-meter shortwave band between broadcast AM radio and old-school VHF television. From the beginning, CB radios transmitted by amplitude modulation (AM), which was more economical and common than frequency-modulation (FM) in the 1940s.

At the height of its popularity in the 1970s and 80s, the CB craze was everywhere: TV, movies, music, and magazines. Millions of radios were sold, and everyone seemed to have one in their home or car (including our family). Even new cars like the Pontiac Trans Am (the one the Bandit drove) could be ordered with an AM-FM-CB radio. Back then, this instant communication with people in your community was almost parallel to today's social networks, except way more civil. But after a while most folks burned out on it and left the airwaves to the truckers. Go to ten yard sales on any given Saturday and you'll find at least one dusty old CB radio for sale.

What killed CB radio? Crowded airways, boredom, static and noisy transmissions, and eventually mobile phones and the internet. Truckers, farmers, hikers, trail riders, and some businesses continued to use CBs because of the economical way to have short-range communications. Sure, they have a squelch feature to block out background static, but they've always been limited in range from power restrictions and susceptible to noise from auto engines, power lines, and atmospheric interference.

In the mid 1990s the FCC opened up the UHF spectrum to create the license-free Family Radio Service Band (FRS). Initially proposed by Radio Shack, FM-transmitted FRS has a lot less noise than AM-based CB radio. But like it's sister, FRS is limited in range. Now called HT (handy-talkie), it has been widely adopted by businesses and outdoor enthusiasts.

Who still uses CB radio in the U.S.? Mostly truckers for real-time alerts about road conditions from other truckers. Large family-owned farms and ranches may still use them, as well as some businesses with simple communications needs. Some newer transceivers include superior noise reduction plus an optional SSB (single side band) mode that makes everyone sound like aliens. Like the dark web, SSB even has its own community and terminology. But curiosity seekers will probably quickly grow disillusioned while trying to find anything interesting to listen to. Some may graduate to ham radio, never admitting that they took a step up from the "Chicken Band."

So why would the FCC suddenly allow CB radios to operate in FM mode if it's unpopular? FM does have increased fidelity and reception over AM, but that's not the driving factor. Is it because the FCC is trying to lure people away from the increasingly crowded FRS band? That's probably not a factor. Is it because the public has been loudly crying for FM on the CB Band? No, most pleas have been for more power and a wider frequency band. It's most likely because one manufacturer just simply asked them to.

Cobra, a long-lived but dying manufacturer of CB radios, filed a petition with the FCC in 2017 to add FM to CB's 40-channels. President, another manufacturer of CBs, went on record in support of it. You see, Cobra and President already manufacture CB radios that transmit on the CB band with FM. Those have been sold in the United Kingdom since 1981 when the Brits created their own Citizen's Band spectrum. Its channels reside very near ours, but CB operators in the UK have had much clearer transmissions because they operate in the FM mode. Cobra, President, and other manufacturers who already supply the UK and European market will only need to slightly modify its FM circuitry to sell these as new models in the U.S.

This is where the controversy in the amateur radio community begins. The FCC apparently is allowing AM and FM users to use the *same* channels simultaneously. That means that AM users will only hear garbage when an FM user transmits, and vice-versa. This risks clogging the channels with unintelligible radio waves and effectively squelching millions of existing CB radios. In order to "breaker-breaker" on the channels they've been freely using since Truman was president, CB users will have to – you guessed it – buy a new radio. Radio buffs are really PO'd that the FCC ignored the power and frequency upgrades that the larger community has wanted for decades, only to have one company's petition come to fruition in just a handful of years.

What does the future hold for CB radio? I see a big race to the line between AM and FM, like a thrilling movie chase scene with a big rig built for speed and a sports car built for agility. There's only one cop that can police this situation and it's not the FCC. It's Sheriff Buford T. Justice.

WAGNER, VADER, AND THE VIKING

Richard Wagner, the 19th century German composer, would have loved *Star Wars*. He may not have understood what a light saber or X-Wing fighter was, but he would get it. He would know that Darth Vader was bad, Luke was troubled and lonely, and that the Rebels were the heroes - even with his eyes shut. That's because the *Star Wars* films are rich with composer John Williams' scores that employ a musical tool that Wagner himself was a master of — the *leitmotif*.

Leitmotif literally means "leading motif," or a recurring short musical phrase that identifies a character, place, or idea. Wagner's operas, particularly the *Ring of the Nibelung* (which Williams is a big fan of), used hundreds of motifs to tie everything together. Later masters of the leitmotif in opera were Claud Debussy and Arnold Schoenberg. I've always said that operas were the cinema of their day. The music, dialog, characters, and set all worked together to give audiences a total visual and sound experience.

When silent films hit the screens, composers borrowed from Wagner and wrote "bad guy" and "pretty girl" sheet music for the local pianist to play during the film. Think of the poor girl tied to the railroad tracks looking at the train barreling down on her — what music do you hear? Then the hero cowboy in the white hat shows up just in time to cut her free. They kiss — now what music do you hear?

When the Roaring Twenties came to a close and "talkies" pictures took off, film composers took the leitmotif to new heights.

Fritz Lang's *M* is an early masterpiece and uses film soundtrack elements that are taken for granted today: a narrator, sounds off camera, and silence as suspense. Using the leitmotif, Peter Lorre's character whistles a tune, which later cues the audience that the antagonist is nearby.

Modern films with leitmotifs that you will instantly recognize are:

- *Psycho* - the stabbing orchestra during the...errr...stabbing
- *Jaws* - the slowly pulsing orchestral thumps precede the shark
- *James Bond* - the twangy guitar implies our favorite spy is on the move and about to kick some butt
- *Harry Potter* - the chiming theme represents "good magic"
- *Lord of the Rings* - nearly a hundred, but The Hobbit theme invokes the calm and serenity of the shire
- *Toy Story* - a western theme for Woody, and blaring horns for Buzz Lightyear

In film, leitmotifs aren't restricted to music. Much like the visual element that uses colors, lighting effects, camera angles, or other subtle cues, sound can do the same. Some excellent examples are:

- Darth Vader's mechanical breathing in *Star Wars*
- The drill sound inside the head of Max in *Pi*
- The helicopter sounds, first woven into the Doors' music track and a ceiling fan, and later before an attack in *Apocalypse Now*. And bonus: Wagner's "Ride of the Valkyries" from the *Ring* opera
- Pitch shifting down not only music, but surrounding sounds as the characters progress into deeper dream states in *Inception*.
- The heavy breathing of Michael Meyers in *Halloween*.

I've used them in some of my productions as well. For instance, in the documentary *Retreat from Gettysburg*, I blended a bell, which represented a funeral bell, with the music score during narratives about soldiers dying. In the documentary *Daniel Boone and the Opening of the American West*, I used frightened horses during attacks to symbolize the fragility of the pioneers.

Whether you're aware of it or not, films and television programs manipulate the hell out of you. Like a magician, they've already performed the trick before you realize it. When that music shrieks or the bomb explodes, they've either built up the tension or lulled you into a false calm. They make you love or hate a character through music. They put you inside the scene with carefully constructed sounds. When the leitmotif starts, you know something important is about to happen. Just like in Wagner's *Ring* opera when Brunnhilde stalks out on stage in the Viking garb and horns, you know it's time for the fat lady to sing.

THE REBIRTH OF AM RADIO?

Maybe you haven't noticed, but AM radio has pretty much sucked the last twenty years or so. Maybe you didn't notice because you weren't listening. A lot of people aren't, and the FCC is out to change that. The FCC? You bet – this isn't your father's FCC. We're so used to hearing "FCC" and "restrictions" in the same breath, that broadcasters were pleasantly surprised in 2015 when the FCC announced an "AM Revitalization" initiative.

The FCC is trying to undo some of its doings from the last ten decades and relax some regulations for AM broadcasters. They hope their actions will entice station owners to become more involved with and provide more interesting programming to their communities. The unravelling of AM radio really started back around 1990 when the FCC wanted to cram more stations between 550 KHz and 1600 KHz. They were also wanting to reduce interference between neighboring stations that bled into each other. One way to do it was to reduce the frequency range of audio from a respectable 10 KHz down to 7.5 KHz. Good enough for talk radio, but bad for music. Their thinking was that FM radio had taken over that genre, and AM radio could survive as talk/news.

Now they're backpedaling and admitting that AM radio, the century-old bastion of broadcasting, may be dying a slow death. And because the listening audience has very few youngsters, there won't be a future generation to support AM radio. Their plan, parts of which are still open to discussion, was rolled out with some immediate solutions to kick start the revitalization. The most noticeable is the use of FM translators. In lay terms, the AM program is simulcast on a low power FM channel.

Other efforts by the FCC involve relaxing standards for scheduling, coverage area, radio power, and other mind-numbing regulations that only a slide rule carrying broadcast engineer would understand. But the wheels are turning, as they say. Though medium- and long-term plans are still under discussion, some radio broadcasters and analysts are crying for more changes, even more regulations.

Thankfully most of those arguments are for the listeners' benefit, not the broadcasters. The big elephant in the room is the noisy nature of AM radio. Without going in to why, AM has always been susceptible to noise. Manufactures of radios have the ability to filter out much of that noise but choose to build the cheapest AM tuner that they can. The FCC does not regulate AM receivers as it does FM and television, but they could, says broadcaster Larry Langford in Radio World. Langford says the FCC could improve distortion and set bandwidth standards "that would start the slow improvement of receivers as new ones hit the market, especially in cars. And isn't this all about sound anyway?" Paul Litwinovich of WSHU public radio in Fairfield, CT notes that many vintage radios still outperform most modern radios in AM fidelity and noise suppression, particularly his pre-1930 Atwater Kent Model 55.

And speaking of noise, many offenders are nearby electronic equipment such as computers, appliances, and power tools. They're supposed to be regulated for noise suppression, but the FCC has little resources to police the manufacturers. Power and communications companies are also a big violator of radio noise. That buzz and scratchiness you hear on your AM radio as you drive the streets is coming from power lines, transformers, and other equipment that don't meet FCC criteria.

How else can the FCC help the sound? They could revert back to the broader 10 KHz bandwidth, or even wider, as AM stations drop out of clogged markets. Others propose eliminating the high-power "clear channel" stations to open the AM band up to more local stations.

But the last, and I think most important change, should be the programming. Give the next generation something they want to listen to today. Today's young generation seems to be into everything retro – records, film, long beards, plaid shirts. They gotta sell AM radio as cool and hip. Spin some Rat Pack and martini lounge music mixed with Arcade Fire and LCD Soundsystem. Play a little beatnik poetry mixed with beats. Run old Pabst Blue Ribbon commercials along with West Sixth Brewery spots. You know, I think I would probably listen to that station. I feel young again!

HEADS, TAILS, GROOVES, AND NEEDLES

Most of you reading this know us at Dynamix Productions for creating new sounds with new technology. But did you know we also like to resurrect old sounds? In the 1990s, magnetic tapes and records were standard formats we worked with every day. Now, they're just "antiques" and items taking up space in a closet. But many people are discovering (or re-discovering) analog, and they want it in digital form. For many years, we have been helping people resurrect old recordings by transferring their tapes and records to CD. Many of these analog recordings are of family, but others are important historical archives.

Our main challenge when restoring an old recording is improving the condition of the archive enough to capture an audio signal. Scratches on an old record are obvious, but many are warped, dusty, oily, and even muddy. Reel-to-reel tapes often exhibit "shedding," where the magnetic coating flakes off the acetate base as you play it, destroying it forever. They can also be "sticky" when the adhesive gets gooey and seeps through the magnetic material. This can also pull magnetic coating off the acetate while gumming up the tape machine heads and other parts. Although not all recordings are recoverable, we've had great success with most. Tapes can be "baked," or slow-heated and slow-cooled to temporarily restore the adhesive that holds the magnetic coating on. Records can be cleaned, and if warped, flattened.

We have a multitude of analog equipment for transferring old recordings, including:

- 1/4" reel-to-reel decks with multiple speeds and track configurations
- A turntable capable of playing 78-, 45-, and 33 1/3-rpm records
- Standard-, micro-, and 8-track cassette playback decks
- Digital decks for DAT tapes, ADAT tapes, and minidiscs

Some of my more memorable restoration projects include:

- A 78-rpm recording from 1947 of Man-o-War's funeral that was broadcast on the radio. The record came in warped like a salad bowl.
- An "audio postcard" from a young mother that passed away shortly after its recording. Her son and granddaughter finally heard her voice for the first time.
- Pilot chatter from a practical joke where five seasoned pilots secretly replaced trainees. The instructor had many Barney Fiffe moments as they performed aerial stunts, disregarded orders, and buzzed the tower.

Many old recordings are disappearing quickly. Reel-to-reels are especially fragile because the magnetic material is not only flaking off, but also slowly losing its magnetic field. Another enemy of tapes is temperature fluctuation and mold/mildew from improper storage, such as in attics and basements. Records are at risk from temperature fluctuations as well, especially heat. So be a hero! Take a look around for a treasured recording to rescue.

Did You Know?

A tape that is stored "tails out" means it has to be rewound all the way to the head so it plays forward. Storing a tape "heads out" allows you to play without rewinding - but at a cost. The magnetic coating burns through the layer above it causing a pre-echo effect called "print-through." It's a lot like water leaching through a cloth or print from one page of a book sticking to a facing page. This causes the song to faintly be heard before it actually starts, like in Led Zeppelin's "Babe I'm Gonna Leave You." What about when the tape is stored tails out, is there still print-through? You betcha, but it's post-echo and not usually heard because it's being overpowered by the program.

Tech Notes

To use noise reduction or not in old recordings? It depends on the intent of the transfer. If it's a historical archive, the answer is usually no. We sometimes provide an alternate version with noise and scratches reduced, but the official version would be "flat." For anything else, it's all about taste and budget. If it's a music transfer, such as an LP, I often like to make it as pristine as budget will allow. These days, it's easier to do a fast but good sounding cleanup because of mature digital software. For critical transfers, like mastering projects for instance, we spend a lot of time squeezing out as much noise as we can without losing the signal. We may spend a day or two on just one music track.

WALLA, RIPPLE, PLOP!

When I was recently explaining to our intern about how we used to synchronize sound and film together, I realized how many industry terms are borrowed from other tasks or re-hashed from another era. Most make sense, like "copy," "paste," and "edit." But with others you have to make an association. For instance, when you edit film, and I'm talking honest-to-goodness cellulose, you might cut out a bit of a scene to use later. You would hang each piece of film, or "clip," with an actual clip over a rolling cloth bin (like a laundry or mail bin). Many video editing programs use a "bin" to hold all the "clips" of video. Our audio program calls it a "pool," which is similar to a pool of office workers. Though I still think I hear a splash when I open it.

"Spotting" in photography means to retouch the negative with dye using a small brush or dropper. In weightlifting, it's being ready to help someone while they attempt a heavy lift. Both involve using the eyes. In film/video, it's placing sound effects, music or dialog on the exact frame that matches the picture.

Here are some of the words we use every day. If you didn't know these were industry jargon, you might think we were just plain kooky.

You'll see us jog, scrub, nudge, ripple, and jam. It's good that we have headroom, bias, and handles. We'll sometimes send a donut, a streamer, and a plop to a bus, and sometimes to a child bus with a daughter card. Would you rather see us heads out, tails out, on-the-fly, or rough cut? You might think we're hard-nosed because we use a guard band, full coat, master, punch-in, or hard-knee. Or maybe we're softies because of soft-knee, pink noise, layback, and flutter. Sometimes we boom with a shotgun, a blimp, a sock, or a dead cat, but never with a figure-of-eight. Sometimes we bounce with pull-up or pull-down, patch a slate, send a stem, loop walla, and solo a mike. Most days, we have to make a choice between a feather, overlap, cross, or a butt. But we rarely encounter wow, combing, crosstalk, or clipping.

Maybe we are kooky after all.

Tech Notes

Old fashioned film sound sync is coming back. When I started out in the mid 1980's I worked for a production company that produced most of its content on film. Unlike most video formats, film doesn't have a way to record sound when shooting, so a separate recording is made at the time and synchronized later. This is called "double system" recording. There must be a way to synchronize the sound and picture later in edit, so the most common method is to "slate" each recording. With the popularity of DSLRs and mirrorless cameras to make video now, the old problem is back. DSLRs and mirrorless cameras record sound with the video, but it is poor at best. Low-quality built-in microphones and audio inputs make it a choice for amateurs or for reference only.

"Roll camera. Roll sound. Slate it. And...ACTION!" That's the most common verbal sequence on the set. The camera starts rolling while zoomed into a handheld slate (or marker). The sound begins rolling. Then a production assistant snaps the top clapper so that the camera sees the exact moment that the hinged top clapper meets the slate board and makes the "crack!" sound. The audio is of course recording this "crack." Each time a take ends and a new recording starts, it must be slated.

Later in the editing room, the editor finds the exact film/video frame that has the clapper meeting the slate board. The audio for that take will have the "crack" sound near the beginning. Visually there's a thin vertical line in the audio waveform (a graphical representation of the sound file). That vertical line is lined up with the exact clapper frame. Now the entire take will be in sync.

We used to do all that on film. The good takes and scenes were transferred from reel-to-reel field recordings to sprocketed magnetic film. Because you don't see a waveform with analog recordings, you had to... (drum roll) ...listen. When you heard the clap, you stopped the playback, hit rewind, stopped when you heard the clap (backwards), and then jogged the sound film back and forth until you heard the exact point of the clap. You could then lock the picture and sound together to maintain sync. This entire process of locating, transferring, and locking all footage to picture could take several hours or days. That's not counting the time to develop and log the film.

There's now a new and rapid way of synchronizing DSLR footage with separate audio files. During the shoot, audio is recorded separately as in a traditional film production. The DSLR will also record audio, either from the built-in microphone, or a separate feed from the audio mixer. In edit, the video editing software, or a separate program named PluralEyes, will quickly lock up the sound from the audio file with the sound/video from the DSLR file. It looks for matching waveforms of each audio file. This can be done in seconds.

There can be a few problems using this method. If your camera audio has more noise than signal, the software may have a hard time matching. If your subject is more that 15-20 feet away from the camera and you're using the built-in mic, the audio will be off by one frame or more.* If this is the case, just drop a split from the audio mixer and feed into the camera.

*Because sound travels at approximately 1 ms every foot, and 1 frame of video is 33 ms, at 17 feet, the sound is hitting the camera's mic on the borderline of a half frame of video. Which exact frame to match would then become ambiguous.

2-BITS, 4-BITS, 6-BITS...

We love convenience. Drive-throughs, same-day delivery, automatic transmissions, instant coffee. Uh, maybe not that last one. Convenience often drives technology. And when it does, something has to go. What are you willing to give up for convenience? Taste, comfort, money, quality?

Convenience also influences new audio technology, and the result is portability, because we are a society on the go. So, what did we give up to take Elvis along for the ride? In the early days of records, players got smaller and smaller so they could be moved from room-to-room, house-to-house, and even house-to-car. As the players got smaller, so did the sound. In the 1950's, engineers threw away the large vacuum tubes (and the warm sound) in radios for the tiny transistor. Now you could hold Elvis in your hand. In the 60's, a wonderful little pocket-sized storage unit called the cassette tape came along that allowed you to take 2 or 3 records' worth of Elvis with you - but not the big sound.

And then came the iPod. Apple wasn't the first portable digital file player, but they made it a household name. Small device, small earbuds, small audio files - what's not to love? I admit that as a fan of convenience, I'm a huge fan of the iPod. The mp3 had been around for a while when the iPod came to town. This unique way of compressing large audio files down to smaller ones was created to speed up file transfers (remember, we were still using pokey dial-up modems at the time). So, we sacrificed audio quality for speed.

At least Apple tried to address the loss-of-quality issue by authoring their own codec (code-decode algorithm). The AAC (Advanced Audio Coding) codec offers excellent audio quality with even smaller file size, plus it does so much more than the ancient mp3. If it's superior to an mp3, why isn't it more popular? Because Apple wants to sell Apple products. They usually keep a tight control on their technology but have relaxed a little on licensing AAC. You'll now find it on YouTube, Nintendos, PlayStations, Wiis, and most smartphones and car stereos. But it still isn't as popular as the venerable mp3. Sorta sounds like the old VHS - Betamax war doesn't it?

The reason for all the audio codec wars is to save time and space. Not something Arthur C. Clark would lay out in a textbook, but something of convenience - faster downloads and more tunes in your pocket. At ground zero in this war is the bit.

You generally win and get higher fidelity with more bits in a digital media signal. But convenience wins when you have fewer bits. Fewer bits, less time and space. The digital audio CD spits out 1.4 million bits per second of data (1,411 kbit/s). The highest quality mp3 produces 320 kbit/s - or 23% of what a CD does. Is the sound quality 23% less? It all depends upon your perception.

Mp3, AAC, Dolby AC3, and all the rest use perceptual coding technologies. In a basic explanation, what's really important gets less compression, and what isn't gets heavily compressed or thrown out altogether. Think of it as a stage play with real props on stage and a painted scenery backdrop. We trick the mind into thinking something faked is real. In audio codecs such as an mp3, the parts of the sound that take up the most file space (like the bass), are highly compressed. When playing them back, those parts are faked, just like that backdrop. A long time ago, someone in a computer lab decided how much bass you won't really hear.

When you stick that audio CD into your computer to make an mp3, you must make a few decisions that will affect the quality of your future entertainment. Do you want small size, or big sound? Choosing a small bit rate (like 64k, 96k, or even 128k) will reduce the file size considerably but throw out a lot of those important stage props. Detail is lost. When it's played back, it may sound watery, jingly, or muffled - not quite the real thing. It's kind of like a sloppy paint-by-numbers scenery backdrop. But if you use a higher bit rate like 320 kbit/s, more detail is preserved. Better yet, use a modern codec like Apple's AAC to preserve even more.

Of course, bit rate isn't the only deciding factor in audio quality, but it's the greatest. Consider this. A full-fledged cinematic motion picture is recorded and mixed at 96KHz, 24-bit, 7.1 surround - 18.4 <u>million</u> bits per second. An mp3 on your iPod is probably recorded at 128 <u>thousand</u> bits per second. That's less than seven-tenths of a percent of that movie sound. That's like Weird Al Yankovich vs. The Avengers. Bits will be flyin'!

Did You Know?

The mp3 format is, unfortunately, a standard file format to send audio over the internet. Even with blazingly fast internet connections, many radio broadcast facilities still prefer commercials and programs to be sent in the mp3 format. Once these files are downloaded, they are often ingested into the station's audio file server, recompressing them into a new compressed format. This original audio file has been compressed (and compromised) twice at this point.

If the radio station's transmitter is at a remote location, the main audio signal is often digitally compressed over a transmission line from the studios to the transmitter site. The original audio has now been compressed three times.

If the radio station is transmitting a digital signal such as HD Radio or satellite, the original audio has now been compressed four times. If the original audio program or commercial contained any material that was in mp3 format, such as the voice-over or music, it has now been compressed five times.

This is a lot like playing "telephone" in grade school - but in different languages for each person. Each interpretation and retelling is dependent on who is hearing and retelling the story. A lot can be misinterpreted.

Tech Notes

The mp3 codec is formally called MPEG-2, Layer III (1995). It was first introduced in 1993 as MPEG-1, Layer III. MPEG is an acronym for Moving Picture Experts Group, a technical standards organization.

The mp3 format was developed by the Fraunhofer Institute in Hanover, Germany. It is actually a trademarked brand and for many years required licensing for implementation in software or devices. It's now free to use and embed in software and hardware devices.

The mp3, WMA, AAC, and AC3 use "lossy" compression, meaning audio information is "lost" when encoded.

There are "lossless" codecs that successfully reduce file size but retain 100% of the audio information. Some of these codecs are Apple Lossless (ALAC), FLAC, ATRAC, HD-AAC, and WMA Lossless.

Compression codecs take advantage of "perceptual" coding, first discovered in 1894 by American physicist Alfred M. Mayer. He discovered that a tone could be rendered inaudible by another tone of lower frequency.

Small file size is the "pro" of an mp3. Decoding is the "con." It takes a lot more processing power to decode and play an mp3 than playing the original uncompressed audio format. Modern computers and devices don't struggle with this, but they did in the early 1990s when the standard was developed.

Suzanne Vega's "Tom's Diner" was chosen as a benchmark during the development of the mp3. It is considered the "Mother of the mp3."

THE COLOR OF SOUND

How would you describe a sound to someone without using descriptors that are unique to sound, like: loud, bassey, shrill, whining, atonal, or noisy?

Not a problem, because we most often describe a sonic experience with words related to our other senses: sharp, warm, angular, raspy, piercing, even, warbling, soft, smooth, or flat.

What about blue? I think of that as more of a style of music or mood instead of a type of sound. Why don't we use more colors to describe what we hear? Probably because a "yellow" sound could be cowardly. A "green" sound may be eco-friendly. A "purple" sound is probably regal. A "brown" sound - well, we'll leave that one alone.

What if we could see sound? Aside from graphical representations of sound like waveforms and meters, we can't just look at an orchestra and see sounds flying out of the trombones. I wish we could watch the beautiful tones flow from Itzhak Perlman's Stradivarius.

But we can - sort of. As reported by NPR,[132] we can see certain sounds using a technique invented in the mid-19th century. Click on the link above to read about and watch a short video describing this process to get a clearer picture. To simplify, scientists watch the disturbance of heat waves by sound. Ever look down a highway on a hot summer day and see the heat creating wavy images? Scientists have used this phenomenon to "see" sneezes and aircraft wing turbulence. But Michael Hargather at New Mexico Tech uses it to study explosives.

So, what's next? I would love to be able to put on some goggles and see sounds and where they're coming from. Loud sounds would be bright. Bass would be blue, treble would be white, and green, red, and yellow would fill in the gaps. Imagine seeing green waves and ripples emanating from the violas, bubbles of blue from the tuba, and distinct columns of yellow and white from the violins. It would be like Peter Max was the conductor. With technology

[132] "What Does Sound Look Like?" April 9, 2014.
https://www.npr.org/2014/04/09/300563606/what-does-sound-look-like

advancing at such a rapid rate, this may not be so far-fetched in our lifetimes. Color me crazy.

Did You Know?

"White noise" in sound engineering describes randomly generating all the sounds in the frequency spectrum. Since the sounds aren't generated at the same time, they are measured over a period of time. Each sound is at a consistent level.

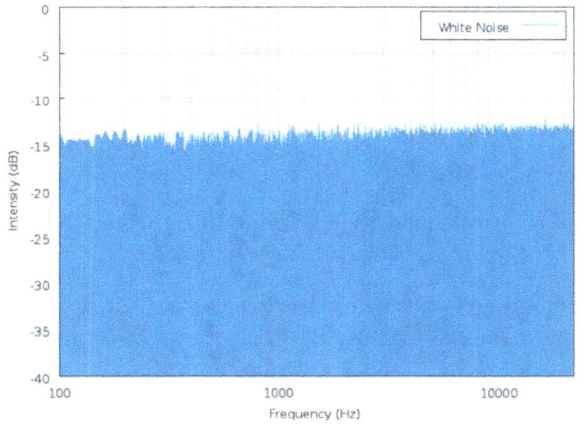

Photo 15. White noise spectrum

White noise sounds similar to a radio that is tuned to no station.

White noise is often used in large offices to mask sounds from workers, computers, and other office machinery. People also use white noise generators to aid in sleeping.

"Pink noise" is similar to white noise but decreases in intensity each ascending octave.

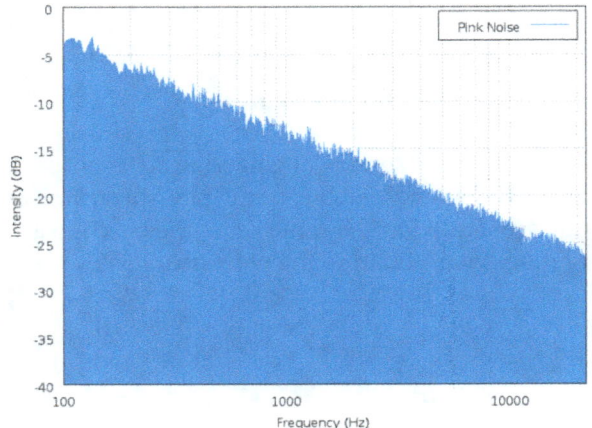

Photo 16. Pink noise

Pink noise is primarily used to measure the output of an audio device.

Sound engineers play pink noise over monitor systems to check frequency response and level of speakers. If measurements show that a speaker produces some frequencies differently than the pink noise (more bass for example), then it is considered to have a "colored" response. Pro audio speaker manufacturers strive for a "flat" response from their products. This way an engineer isn't fooled into compensating for the difference while mixing.

Live sound engineers use pink noise to reduce feedback and get maximum performance from speakers.

Other types of noise used in analysis are violet, brown(ian), gray, blue. Other informal names for sound used in measurement are red, green, black, noisy black, and noisy white.

Tech Notes

Reducing feedback in a live sound situation is very tricky, especially if good sound performance is desired. The "squeal" you hear when a microphone is turned on is from a buildup of a certain frequency. It's usually the point at which the microphone and speaker are the most efficient. If one points a microphone at the same speaker that is amplifying it, then serious feedback occurs. Most speakers are placed in front of or beside performers so there is no direct bleed back into the microphone. If speakers are placed behind the performers (think The Who), then eliminating feedback is a bigger chore.

How do you eliminate feedback? Let's use the simplest set-up as an example: one microphone and one speaker. A graphic equalizer (GEQ), a device that increases or reduces frequency by octaves, is inserted after the microphone channel and just before the amplifier. The engineer slowly raises the amplifier level until the first inkling of feedback. Using the GEQ, the engineer locates the offending octave, ex: 630 Hz, by actually increasing that frequency creating more feedback. That octave is then reduced until feedback goes away.

Next, the amplifier is turned up a little more until the next inkling of feedback occurs, usually at another frequency, which is then reduced. These steps are repeated over and over until the amplifier is at a suitable level without feedback. Of course, computer technology has simplified this process greatly with devices that rapidly reduce feedback "on-the-fly." And with software, engineers for permanent PA systems in large venues can even predict where feedback will occur before installation. They can then program in filtering or make changes to the architecture, equipment, or speaker placement.

LEFTOVER BEETHOVEN

In 2014 the Library of Congress inducted 25 entries into the Library of Congress National Recording Registry, I was excited to see U2, Linda Ronstadt, and Isaac Hayes get their due. Perusing the list, I saw a very influential (at least personally) album - *Copland Conducts Copland: Appalachian Spring (1974)*.

I was a music major in college and always found Aaron Copland to be the quintessential American composer. He seemed to capture what Americans idolize about America: hope, boldness, charm, intrepidness, looking forward but not forgetting the past. Copland had a sense that the audience didn't want to hear a European's take on America. His music was organically Americana by taking styles and songs from our heritage. He then boldly threw them into a fire and forged a new sound.

What's really interesting about Copland is to see him rehearse an orchestra for one of his compositions. There's a recording of him rehearsing Appalachian Spring [133] in which he gives direction that we producers, directors, talent, and copywriters can heed. Here are some excerpts:

"It's too sentimental...it sounds on the Tchaikovsky side. Make it more American in spirit, in that the sentiment isn't all shown on the face."

"The music by itself is warm, you don't have to help it."

"Round and noble, rather than violent."

"Light, bouncy, happy and American-ish."

He gives some technical direction during this rehearsal, but his emotive directions get more response. This is true during a successful recording or film session. The actor / narrator needs to be believable, and the best way to get there is for them to believe they are in a place. That place being "noble," or "happy," or "warm."

How does one get there? Each person is different in their approach, but imagery is the most common. Imagining one is in a field of flowers, on a beach, flying like a bird - whatever works. The tone of the voice or the flow of the body will follow naturally. I'm oversimplifying it of course, but you get the gist. Sometimes it can take a while to get to "that place." I remember one film of a Copland rehearsal where he quickly stopped the orchestra and said (and I'm paraphrasing here) "No, no, no! You're still playing the Beethoven you played last night. Softer, lighter." With our daily workload of ever-shifting projects and clients, we are all challenged

---

[133] https://www.youtube.com/watch?v=WfWMoHKZzfY. If unavailable, search the internet for "Aaron Copeland rehearses Appalachian Spring."

for new ideas. Maybe we should take Mr. Copland's advice to keep it fresh for our client today, by not having last night's leftover Beethoven.

Did You Know?

Copland enjoyed Cubism, an avant-garde visual art technique created by the artists Georges Braque and Pablo Picasso. Objects are basically depicted from different viewpoints instead of just one. Copland described his music as a "musical cubism," existing on different planes. He also incorporated jazz elements into his compositions to create energy and excitement.

Copland also enjoyed other forms of art. Drawing on his appreciation for folk art, Copland weaved "Simple Gifts," a Shaker melody, into "Appalachian Spring."

"Appalachian Spring" was originally written as a ballet, commissioned by dancer and choreographer Martha Graham

Tech Notes

Preservation of audio recordings, from cylinders, records, wires, and tapes; to digital-borne tapes, optical discs and hard drives; is a race against time. According to the head of the recorded sound section of the Library of Congress, Gene DeAnna, 50-100,000 recordings are acquired each year. But as DeAnna points out in an interview with NPR in 2014,[134] only 15,000 can be digitized in a year.

Recordings are put in a temperature-controlled environment to slow down the decay, but thousands will inevitably be lost before they can be transferred.

Although the LOC digitizes old recordings, they also use good old-fashioned analog tape to ensure a recording's survival. Digital

---

[134] "Preserving Audio For The Future Is A Race Against Time" March 23, 2014. https://www.npr.org/2014/03/22/291420005/preserving-audio-for-the-future-is-a-race-against-time

formats come and go, but analog tape recordings from the early 1950's can still be played today. Viva la analog!

BONG, BONG, BONG

"If it weren't for Philo T. Farnsworth, inventor of television, we'd still be eating frozen radio dinners."

Johnny Carson

Nine decades ago, three musical tones, "G-E-C," were played on a fledgling network of radio stations. What started as a technical cue for local stations, has become an instantly recognized trio of notes woven into the American identity. NBC Radio's musical logo is no longer used as a cue, but can be heard almost every day on NBC Television.

There's some question as to what radio entity first used chimes to cue local stations for program changes, but NBC definitely perfected it. They experimented with several combinations, one of which was seven chimes long. Radio hosts were expected to dutifully play the chimes in correct order without error. That was never going to happen, so they shortened it to four. Evidently that was still too complicated, and so history was rung in on November 29, 1929, with "Bong, bong, bong."[135]

During this time and even today, announcers were using strict phrases to cue local stations, such as "This is the NBC Radio Network." But busy station personnel would not always hear the vocal cues. NBC tried sending cues on teletype, but that didn't

---

135

http://web.archive.org/web/20070307110031/http:/www.uspto.gov/go/kids/soundex/72349496.mp3

work. Eventually, engineers found that radio hosts could recognize simple tones as their cue. The NBC executives also liked it because a musical identity would be a great branding tool.

Humans played the small xylophone-like chimes, albeit erratically, until 1932 when an automated machine was put into service. That music box-like unit was the brainchild of Richard Ranger, the father of the "modern" fax machine. The cue tones were eventually replaced with silent automation cues in the 1970's. Some radio and television affiliates continued to use the tones within newscasts for years. One holdout, WNBC-TV, still uses it today.

There has been one noteworthy alteration of the tones over the years – the fourth tone. In the early 1930's NBC executives needed a way to alert key network personnel that they were needed, such as in an emergency. They shifted to another key, G-major, and repeated the third tone. The sequence was played every 15 minutes until the necessary key people would check in. It was an early paging system.

The four tones eventually morphed into a special alert for radio stations and listeners that urgent programming was to follow. The Hindenburg disaster and the Pearl Harbor attack were notable examples. The four-tone alert was officially retired with the end of World War Two. It was played one last time in 1985 when NBC merged with General Electric.

The musical sequence of G3-E4-C4 is as familiar to Americans as Yankee Doodle. In music training, it's used to familiarize students with a major 6th interval (G3-E4) and a C-major chord in second inversion. It's been used in songs by Ray Charles and Isaac Hayes. It's been used in NBC slogans ("Chime in"). It's even been worked into sound effects on NBC -TV shows such as The Office (phones ringing) and Deal or No Deal (cash registers).

There are many songs that are part of the American psyche – "God Bless America," "This Land is Your Land," "Take Me Home Country Roads," "Take the A Train," "America the Beautiful," and "The Star-Spangled Banner." They say less is more, and this simple three-tone song is a heavyweight among all American songs.

Here are some great links to the history of the NBC chimes.

The NBC Chimes Museum at http://www.nbcchimes.info

History of the NBC Chimes at
http://www.radioremembered.org/chimes.htm

Listen to NBC Chimes past and present at
http://www.radioremembered.org/nbc_chimes.htm

NBC chimes machine at
http://www.oldradio.com/archives/stations/sf/chimes.htm

An electrical design for generating the NBC Chimes at
https://www.theremin.us/Circuit_Library/nbc_chimes.htm

I MIGHT NOT CAN SAY THAT WORD

Sitting in front of my studio speakers can sometimes bring loads of laughter. Nobody said this had to be a serious business, so I try to find humor whenever possible. But a lot of times, it happens all by itself. It's not easy for an announcer to sit in a vocal booth with a microphone stuck in their face, all ears and eyes on them, and have every word scrutinized. Talk about pressure, that's usually when the lid blows. I don't mean a tantrum or blow-up, although I've witnessed a few of those. I'm talking about bloopers, uncontrollable laughter, and just plain fun.

Most people that work in the sound and video business probably have a dozen embarrassing stories about themselves that they're willing to share, and a few they won't. As an engineer I've witnessed plenty, and I'd like to share a few. I'll leave out the names to protect the innocent, and I'll even share a few of my own gaffs as well.

I've decided that the tongue is the most important part of speech. Sometimes it won't perform as planned and has a mind all its own. We all have words we can't say very well, but when you're an announcer it stops the show. One well-known radio personality I worked with couldn't pronounce "abdominal." A dozen takes later, he just gave up and said, "Oh, belly muscles!" (He also couldn't pronounce "formidable," which resulted in more than forty takes.) If a particular word was giving him fits, he used to say amusingly, "I might not can say that word." The tongue can also play cruel jokes on people by not allowing them to say words they need to use all the time. What if you couldn't say the name of the city you live in? Unfortunately, it's been the one word that an announcer I know still can't say without effort. Announcers usually poke fun at themselves when these goofs happen because we always try to keep things lighthearted during a recording session.

Occasionally we get cracked up over the least little thing. You know, the uncontrollable laughter that just won't stop. One announcer I knew would get uncontrollable giggles if a certain common horse term was in the script – *weanling* – and it's used all the time here in Kentucky. The first time it happened, it took some twenty minutes to get back to the script. Sometimes the script is either poorly written or just asking for a Weird Al Yankovic makeover. When this happens, just making it through the script with a straight face is hard. Of course, there are sexual innuendoes flying everywhere with the right crowd, especially with a male/female combo in the booth that are revealingly very familiar with each other. Sometimes it's enough to make even Hugh Hefner blush.

Most recording sessions combine work and fun, or at the least work and pleasantries. But occasionally there are those who want to dispense with any pleasantries and go right to work. Sometimes this is necessary in a time crunch, but one session I did with a rather well-known national voice was all business. We dialed in to the studio in Los Angeles using our ISDN (a form of real-time digital audio connection between studios), and began. The announcer curtly gave the required hellos and then was silent awaiting instructions. The producer would describe the read she wanted, and the announcer wouldn't respond. We thought we had a dead connection, so let's give the announcer the benefit of the doubt and assume he must have been writing the instructions down. Well, he read the script and just went silent afterwards - no comments, no questions, nothing. We tried lightening things up a little with some jokes and such, but there was no response - zero. Without a window or video monitor to see him, you can only wonder what he was doing - filing his nails, looking at the ceiling, rolling his eyes. That was a session that seemed a lot longer than it really was.

Okay, it's time for me to tell a few on myself. It's always rewarding to hear your work on the air, but not when it includes your mistakes. As I'm driving home from work one day listening to the radio, a commercial comes on that I had just produced that afternoon. To my horror, the announcer stops in the middle of the spot, coughs, and says "Let's take that again." I about wrecked the car turning it around to head back to work.

Let's rewind to another gaff of mine, back to the good old days of reel-to-reel tape. I had been working on a project that required me to pitch the playback speed way down. Well, me being me, I forgot to reset the speed before dubbing off a radio spot. You guessed it, the announcer sounded like a chipmunk on the air. I got home late that day as well.

Did you ever have that sinking feeling that you've forgotten something big? Like forgetting to press "record" after spending hours in a recording a session? We're talking Titanic sinking here. The talent had come in from out of town, the producer was meticulous, and the stakes were high. After the talent left, I went to start laying off the good takes. KA-THUD!! That's when I felt like I was in the middle of a bad dream. At that moment, I just shot up out of my chair and screamed "I'll be back!" to the bewildered producer. I ran out to the parking lot hoping to catch the talent, but his car was gone. I ran around the building to the street just as his car was pulling out in rush hour traffic. Fortunately, he saw me waving frantically and pulled back in. Now I had some 'splainin' to do. I tell my students to just tell the truth when you mess up, no matter how much of an idiot it makes you look like. This was one time if there ever was one. I will never forget the look on the producer's face as he said, "None of it? We didn't get anything?" But this story has a happy ending. Because we spent so much time tweaking each read, the talent came back in and knocked it out in ten minutes. Plus, the producer thought this round was even better. What I brought out of that session was to always run a backup, always check and double-check as you're recording, and to swallow your pride when you act like an idiot.

Another story of idiocy by yours truly involved a location shoot for a high-profile client. I had packed everything well in advance...well almost everything. The location was many miles away, so I planned to leave early just in case. The producer called a few times and requested additional equipment, so I spent my "early" time packing up extra stuff (which he never used, by the way). He then called and moved up the call time. There goes any hope of getting there early, I would just make it. Out I ran, and started making good time, thanks to my new radar detector I had just bought that week on a lark. About of a third of the way there, out of nowhere, I thought "Did I pack the microphone?" Oh @#$%*&^%!!!! Cue the Titanic again. That drive back to Lexington seemed to take forever. I felt like I was that idiot on the beach during a hurricane trying walk against the wind. Well, my radar detector worked that day - I got there on time.

The next time you hear a commercial or program, just imagine what that recording session might have really been like: the straight-faced announcer stopping in mid-sentence after a goof, trying unsuccessfully several more times, and then finally declaring with a chuckle "I might not can say that word!"

THE GOLDEN YEARS OF PODCASTING

In the humble beginnings of radio, there were no rules, only groundbreakers. Independent broadcasters would fire up the transmitter at will, talk about whatever they wanted, and play whatever music they wanted, all without any outside restrictions. Of course, they had self-imposed restrictions like decency, but it was mostly a free-flowing medium for amateurs and hobbyists. Then came along the government. Seeing a need to regulate the ever-growing broadcasters and crowded airwaves, they began licensing stations. When KDKA-AM of Pittsburgh became the first commercially licensed radio station in 1920, the demise of the individual free-thinking broadcaster began.

Oh, I don't blame the government for regulating the airwaves. It was a promising new medium that would be total chaos if some ground rules weren't laid down. And that decency thing, they would regulate that, too. But commercial radio wasn't necessarily bad for America. After all, we wouldn't have Jack Benny, George and Gracie, and Edward R. Murrow. Nor would millions have had heard the New York Philharmonic, Louis Armstrong, or Hank Williams. It's just that the individual's ability to access many listeners would be extremely difficult for the next three-quarters of a century.

Free speech, a much-debated foundation of our Constitution, has always been at the heart of broadcasting. In the early days, most of those independent pioneers probably didn't realize that they were fully exercising their free speech rights. When the Federal Communications Commission started to regulate what was being said on the airwaves, you better believe those broadcasters knew exactly when they were exercising their free speech.

Throughout broadcasting history, there have always been rule breakers. But the most daring were the pirates. Pirate radio stations, or those without licenses, are often operated clandestinely, and their transmissions usually have an agenda, including propaganda, political, religious, or just plain wacky. But many existed solely for the reason that there was too much government regulation. These operators wanted to broadcast without restriction – and they did – at least until they were caught.

In the 1990's, along with the internet revolution, came a new way to broadcast. Internet radio stations began popping up all over the planet, literally. How cool was it to listen to a station from Antarctica? Those first internet broadcasters immediately took their cues from the earliest radio pioneers and started broadcasting whatever they wanted. The government and the Recording Institute Association of America (RIAA) eventually clamped down on them for playing music without paying the artists. Though still in flux, this segment of the broadcasting community keeps growing – under watchful eyes.

Then in recent years, the next revolution started. Though not "broadcasting" by traditional description, podcasting is a way to deliver one message to many. Technically, podcasting is just a fancy term for delivering an audio file to a willing listener. "Willing" is the key word. The listener must choose to click on the file to play the program, or click to "subscribe" to a series of programs until the listener chooses to stop receiving them. It's a lot like getting a magazine. You can either go to the news stand to buy a copy whenever you feel like it, or get it regularly delivered to your doorstep with only one action – to subscribe. If you don't like the magazine (podcast), you simply throw it away or unsubscribe.

If we look at the magazine world for inspiration, there used to be a magazine for everything. Want to cultivate marijuana? Want to know more about paving roads with blacktop? Do you collect Cupie dolls? The two most important things that magazines and podcasts have in common are free speech and target audience. Where newspapers and broadcasters seem to have too many regulations, magazines and podcasters can be bold, arrogant, and nasty if they like. Where newspapers and broadcasters are forced to water down their content to suit a broad audience, magazines and podcasters can hone down their message to a pinpoint and shoot it like an arrow, often striking the target dead center.

So, what is the future of podcasting? I won't be so bold to predict, but I would like to wish it would stay free and unrestricted. Right now, free speech isn't the only unique quality of podcasting. There is also a lack of formatting, formality, finesse, and quality – those must-haves of radio. This is not a bad thing, it's fresh, exciting, and more importantly – real. When I listen to some of these under-produced podcasts, I feel like I'm connecting with the podcaster who probably produced their program in their living room. The broadcast industry and business world have already discovered the power of podcasting. The broadcast stations now let you download copies of what they aired, or even offer alternative versions for the internet. Businesses have discovered that they can advertise on popular podcasts, or even produce their own. More and more podcasts are slickly produced (disclosure: I'm one of those producers), but there remains a large number of individuals throwing all caution to the wind and producing podcasts that are defying the rules of broadcast. This is what I wish for the future of podcasting – that those individuals don't give up because they can't polish the sound; that they don't stop saying what's on their mind; that they come out in droves to bring us into their living rooms and lives; and that the regulators don't step in. But sadly, something with so much promise for the little guy is usually sucked up into the mass ocean of regulations and sameness. If this is the future, then I guess we are truly living in the golden years of podcasting.

WHY YOUR LISTENERS MIGHT BE SLEEPING THROUGH YOUR EVERY WORD

Do you remember your high school English class where everyone took turns reading a literary classic aloud? Was there anything more boring? If you didn't have the book in front of you, it was hard to follow along – that is if you stayed awake. Okay, I'm not out to bash classic literature. I'm just raising an argument that the author probably didn't intend his or her work to be read aloud (especially by sleepy teenagers). But take Shakespeare – now that dude knew how to write for spoken word. He intended for hundreds of listeners to hear his words being spoken aloud.

The methods by which we communicate with words can be broken down into two simple categories: by eyes, and by ears. They're sometimes used together, but the most primitive form of communication was probably by sight. Caveman Gok would motion with his hands to caveman Krog to build a fire. The next form of communication was most likely a grunt when Krog told Gok to build it himself, followed up with a rude hand gesture.

Today we communicate with words, art, music, dance, and even laughter. The communicator's hope is that the full meaning of the message is perceived, but sometimes the way it's delivered is out of sync with the way it's being received. Like a review of a painting in the newspaper, one can't fully grasp the artist's intent until seeing it in person.

Perhaps the hardest way to communicate is using one form of communication to deliver another form, like that English class. Successfully writing for spoken word is not natural, it's complicated. The confusion starts with how the writer constructs the message – by writing. In school, most of our communication education was the written word. Very few of us had a speech or drama class. So, when a novice sits down to write narration, it's natural to write in a style that we have been using our whole life for essays, letters, emails, notes, etc. When that text is actually spoken, it's sometimes like we're back in English class.

What's happening? Why is the listener having trouble receiving the message? I believe that most of all, it's sentence structure. If you've ever read any of Elmore Leonard's novels ("Get Shorty," "Jackie Brown"), you probably recognized his unique ability to write believable dialog. Leonard just brushes it off as writing what people say, but on closer analysis I believe his sentence structure is the key.

"People talk in short sentences."

"Yeah. Often incomplete ones. Usually grammatically incorrect."

"Disconnected sometimes."

Why? Attention span, the slowness of oral communication versus written, body gestures, and many other things contribute to the compactness of speech. When reading a written piece, your eyes can pause or scan back to solidify what you just read. With speech, you can't reverse time and listen again. When reading, you see phrases and groups of words at one time. With speech each word is delivered one agonizing word at a time. You must wait for the next word to be said, even if you know what it will be. When writing, the author can use punctuation to group thoughts, sections, and phrasing. With speech, you must use tone and inflection to separate thoughts. Like this written sentence, the author can introduce a subject – such as how to make a box, expound on it for several lines to describe its shape, material, and workmanship, then veer off in another direction to talk about all the great boxes of the world and what they contain, and then return back to pound the final nail in the lid. In speech, the listener would be thinking about what to cook for supper before you finished the sentence.

So now you see the pitfalls. How then, do you write narration for the listener? Here are a few tips from a professional that is paid to listen:

- Remember to keep sentences short. Give the listener time to process each nugget of information before you move onto the next one.
- If the information is complex, reinforce it with short examples or analogies.
- Don't be afraid to break sentence structure rules from time to time.
- Read your copy aloud. Better yet, have someone read it to you. Be sure to read with a loud volume and take deliberate breaths. This will reveal problems with phrase lengths and timings.
- If the narration accompanies visuals, remember that a picture is worth a thousand words – don't dwell on describing the obvious. Don't have the narrator read the same works that are on screen (or better yet, don't put words on the screen when using narration).
- Don't give a lot of useless information that isn't vital and won't be remembered, such as phone numbers, addresses, dates, etc. If your narration is to only get your name out, the listener will look you up in the phone book.
- Don't wear out the listener. Trying to cram in too much information will actually have the opposite effect on the listener – they'll tune out.
- Don't just cut and paste your print copy to the radio script. Take the very basics of the idea you're trying to convey and turn it into a conversation or "theater of the mind."

Of course, there are many other aspects of writing, but I hope these few tips will help you avoid wasted studio time editing copy – or worse, lose the listener. Remember, it's an art and it takes lots of practice, so keep writing and reading your copy aloud. You'll know you're getting better at it when people quit falling asleep.

THE NEW YEAR '22

The year '22 ushered in an exciting new technology. Here's what has been said about it:

"The newspaper that comes through your walls."

"Anyone with common sense can readily grasp the elementary principles and begin receiving at once."

"It will become as necessary as transportation. It will be communication personalized. There will be no limit to its use."

What is it? You might want to ask what year is it? It was the year 1922, and it's when radio for the masses exploded into homes across America. It had been building steam for a few years since the end of World War One. That's when transmitting restrictions were lifted. In 1919, Westinghouse engineer Frank Conrad began spinning Victrola records of concerts from his home-based amateur station 8XK to a couple of hundred other radio enthusiasts. Then his listeners grew to several hundred, some even writing in requests. In 1920, he broadcasted one of the earliest live concerts: his son playing piano. Westinghouse relicensed the station as KDKA soon after, becoming the first station to broadcast live presidential election results. KDKA was an important early pioneer of live radio performances.

Radio popularity grew because the vacuum tube had recently been perfected and could reliably amplify a radio signal. As a result, transmitter equipment became smaller and more affordable for the average person to set up a "radio shack" in their house. Many amateur radio operators began transceiving with each other or putting on music shows like Frank did. Receivers were also coming down in price for some families ($200, or about $2,800 today), but a DIY crystal set with headphones could be built at home for less than $10 ($140 today) John R. McMahon talked about his own adventures of making a crystal radio. His story starts with his neighbor's attempts:

```
    He had bought about three dollars' worth
of raw material, which looked suitable either
for an embroidery party or a horse-doctor's
kit.  These  things  had  queer  names,  like
```

galena, cat's whisker and tickler. I surmised that the cat's whisker tickled the galena, and this made the radio laugh. An important part of the apparatus was a wire-wrapped cylinder of pasteboard, this having been an oatmeal box which the maker had abstracted from the kitchen when his wife wasn't looking, and in so doing had left a trail of oatmeal all the way into the living room.

The Country Gentleman, 1922

So popular was making your own radio equipment that retailers sold out of supplies. So, people resorted to outright theft:

Chicago, Ill.--From all parts of the United States telephone companies are complaining about the forays amateur radio operators are making on public telephones in order to secure equipment they think will be suitable for their outfits. The seclusion of a telephone booth affords a good opportunity for the radio nut to acquire a receiver. The thrifty and unprincipled parties are greatly disappointed with results of sets equipped with ordinary telephone receivers--they won't work on the wireless sets. Telephone men are hoping the daily newspapers will tip off their readers to this fact and cut down the losses of telephone equipment.

Telephone Engineer, 1922

Amateur wireless operators are blamed by the authorities for the disappearance of telephone receivers from public pay station booths in Paris and other French cities of late. So extensive have the raids on the telephones become that the government has sent out a "general alarm" circular warning station operators and merchants to be on the alert.

Disappearance of the receivers, which can be used in radiophony, began shortly after the Eiffel Tower wireless station started broadcasting concerts and news.

Telephony, 1922

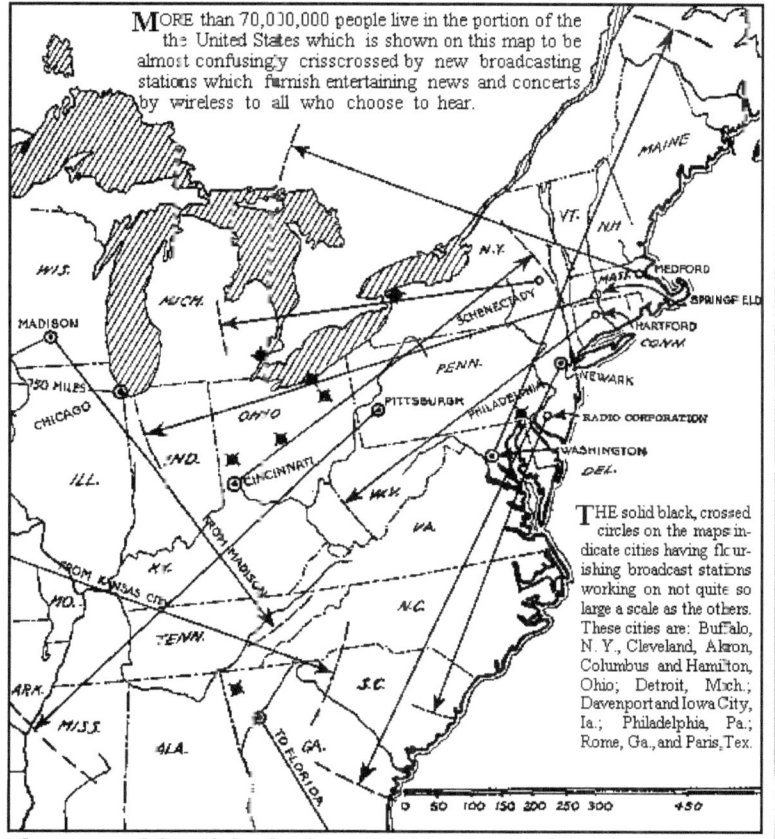

MORE than 70,000,000 people live in the portion of the the United States which is shown on this map to be almost confusingly crisscrossed by new broadcasting stations which furnish entertaining news and concerts by wireless to all who choose to hear.

THE solid black, crossed circles on the maps indicate cities having flourishing broadcast stations working on not quite so large a scale as the others. These cities are: Buffalo, N. Y., Cleveland, Akron, Columbus and Hamilton, Ohio; Detroit, Mich.; Davenport and Iowa City, Ia.; Philadelphia, Pa.; Rome, Ga., and Paris, Tex.

One or more of the radio broadcasting stations indicated by the circles on the map can be heard regularly, with adequate equipment and favorable local conditions, in 48 states of the Union. Find on this map the cities within whose radius you are; then refer to the article for details as to the programs of these stations. Completing the dotted lines will give you the reported "normal range" of these stations, but sometimes they cannot be heard for reasons reviewed in the article

The rapid expansion across the U.S. of both stations and radio sets was phenomenal. Then Secretary of Commerce Herbert C. Hoover said, "We have witnessed in the last four or five months one of the most astounding things that has come under my observation of American life. This Department estimates that today more than 600,000 (one estimate being 1,000,000) persons possess wireless telephone receiving sets, whereas there were less than fifty thousand such sets a year ago."

This growth of licensed commercial broadcasting stations in 1922 was enthusiastically chronicled by *Radio News Magazine*:

June 1922. Ninety-eight radio stations were broadcasting music, concerts, lectures, and market and weather reports, according to the Department of Commerce on March 23. Among the sending stations are 10 newspapers, a church, a Y. M. C. A., several large department stores, and two municipalities. Many manufacturers, radio sales and equipment shops, and five universities are also sending out amusement features in several forms so that today "all who listen may hear," just as all who "ran" have been able to "read" for many years. Even Hollywood, Calif., has a broadcast.

June 1922. Today there are broadcasting radio telephone stations in 26 states of the Union.

August 1922. The growth of this class of radio stations has been remarkable; it jumped from 67 stations a little over two months ago to 274 today. Applications are filed on an average of about three or four a day.

September 1922. The states of Kentucky and Mississippi went on the Department of Commerce's Broadcasting Map last week when stations in Louisville [WHAS] and Corinth [WHAU] were licensed.

September 1922. On June 30th the Department of Commerce licensed the 382d broadcasting station, issuing 21 during the past week...The future of radio telephonic broadcasting seems assured, as the remarkable growth still goes on at the rate of about three new stations each day.

October 1922. When KDKA, the first broadcasting call, was assigned nine months ago to the Westinghouse Electric & Manufacturing Co., East Pittsburgh, Pa., even the Chief Radio Inspector did not suspect that today there would be 451 stations broadcasting, one or more in every state except Wyoming.

December 1922. Broadcasting still continues in all but one state in spite of the pessimistic reports from some quarters that this service, which is likened to a fad, is falling off and likely to collapse.

December 1922. Broadcasting with the issuance of a license in Laramie, Wyoming, [KFBU] every state in the Union has one or more broadcasting stations.

Ma Bell (AT&T) was determined not to be left out of the sudden popularity of radio. It had already been developing radio techniques for extending telephone call service for several years, so AT&T easily stepped into the commercial radio business. Its first station, WEAF (now WFAN) in New York, went on the air in February 1922. AT&T's goal from the start was to build a radio network. Less than a year later, WEAF and WNAC (now WRKO) in Boston were linked together for radio's first network broadcast. Two more stations joined the network in the following months. What's important to know is that this was done over telephone lines, which they controlled.

As new listeners tuned in to news, sports scores, impromptu musical performances, records, and even bedtime stories, business owners took notice. This was a prime opportunity to advertise to a very captive audience.

When radio with the start it already has, receives the further thought and scientific development of the next few months it will be completely adapted for many kinds of commercial enterprises that do not employ it as yet. It will become as necessary as transportation. It will be communication personalized. There will be no limit to its use.

How to Retail Radio, 1922

The radio boom had created a whole new market for industries, some selling directly to the radio enthusiast:

It is in the sale of batteries for radio work and in the recharging of them that the battery man can 'cash-in' on the radio phone 'craze.'

The Automobile Storage Battery, 1922

Selling radios and the batteries to make them work was one thing. Selling on the radio became a whole new industry. The first radio broadcast advertisement was on WEAF on August 22, 1922 at 5 PM. AT&T had built its telephone business on charging by the minute, so it was only natural to parlay that business model over to radio. Hawthorne Court Apartments in Jackson Heights, New York bought 10 minutes of airtime for $50. By October, WEAF had sold $550 in advertising. Executives called their simple formula of trading airtime for dollars "toll radio." It was here to stay.

For advertising to be successful, the programming had to be enticing to listeners. Everybody was learning this new craft and stumbling through each broadcast, but a few started to develop regular programming in 1922. The previous year, Frank Conrad advertised schedules of music entertainment to be played on his little amateur station in Pittsburg. His listeners ballooned from 200 to 400 almost overnight. Horne's Department Store advertised that his radio station could be heard on radio sets sold by Horne's:

AIR CONCERT "PICKED UP" BY RADIO HERE

Victrola music, played into the air over a wireless telephone, was "picked up" by listeners on the wireless receiving station which was recently installed here for patrons interested in wireless experiments. The concert was heard Thursday night about 10 o'clock, and continued 20 minutes. Two orchestra numbers, a soprano solo- which rang particularly high and clear through the air- and a juvenile "talking piece" constituted the program.

The music was from a Victrola pulled up close to the transmitter of a wireless telephone in the home of Frank Conrad, Penn and Peebles avenues, Wilkinsburg. Mr. Conrad is a wireless enthusiast and "puts on" the wireless concerts periodically for the entertainment of the many people in this district who have wireless sets.

Amateur Wireless Sets, made by the maker of the Set which is in operation in our store are on sale here $10.00 up.

Gwen Wagner, another radio pioneer who did just about every job at the upstart WPO in Memphis, Tennessee, shared that station's program from its inaugural broadcast in 1922:

7 p. m.--Baseball results.
7:05 p. m.--News brevities.
7:20 p. m.--Cortese Bros. on harp and violin.
7:50 p. m.--Bedtime story.
8:10 p m.--Selections on the reproducing piano.
8:30 p. m.--New records on the phonograph.

Radio Age, September 1925

Music was often heard on this newfangled device – sometimes out of true desire by the operator to enrich the lives of listeners, and sometimes just to fill time. One thing was certain, live music sounded better than music from records. That's because radios used electrical microphones, and records were still being recorded and played back mechanically (you know, with the big bell protruding from the tone arm). Electrical microphones weren't being used yet to produce records (though telephones had been using them for decades), and they were still being played back with a steel needle that was amplified by a large bell. As a consequence, radio exploded, and record sales fell off. It wouldn't be until 1925 that records began to start selling in large numbers again. That's when RCA Victor started recording with the better electrical microphones. They also built an electrical reproducing turntable that didn't need to be wound up.

Since radio was so new, many were having trouble figuring out what the audience wanted to hear. George H. Fischer, Jr. of Pierce Electric Company in Tampa, Fla. complained that "too many stations have persisted in filling the air with 'jazz' and nothing else." He recommended more variety because he had heard too many Sunday School sessions, lectures, pick-up bands, and "long-winded orators with no time limit and uninteresting subjects."

The big corporations and government felt incumbent to control what the public heard on radio. Most felt that classical concerts would enhance the lives of listeners. Scholarly lectures, school lessons, and church services would round out acceptable programming. Said one writer in The Radio Dealer in 1922, "In the territory where broadcasting stations are found in great numbers the 'canned music' may have little appeal but in the territories at a distance beyond the daylight range of the big stations it is almost a necessity." However, the small independent radio stations were mixing up their programming, if you can call it that, with anything that came to mind, including jazz. These were heady days for both the radio operators and the listeners alike. They were experiencing the wild west of radio. But not for long.

The U.S. government wanted to be rid of playing music records on the radio all together "out of public good." The record industry and musicians' unions had called on U.S. Commerce Secretary Herbert Hoover to stop the practice. Part of the reasoning was that those industries depended on record sales, and the public was effectively listening for free. Soon after Hoover issued his moratorium, ASCAP and commercial stations entered into contracts to allow them to play music on the air. This started the growth of corporate-owned stations and networks, and the decline of small stations that couldn't afford the hefty fees.

Where one tuned on the radio dial to listen to their favorite station was also up for debate in 1922. The government, in its usual "wisdom," allocated two places in the radio spectrum for stations in December 1921:

Licenses of this class are required for all transmitting radio stations used for broadcasting news, concerts, lectures, and such matter. A wavelength of 360 meters is authorized for such service, and a wavelength of 485 meters is authorized for broadcasting crop reports and weather services, provided the use of such wave lengths does not interfere with ship to shore or ship to ship service.

On paper, having a separate place for farm reports and weather made sense. Farmers in remote areas would hopefully have a clear signal at 485 meters (about 618 KHz on the AM dial). Having everything else on 360 meters (833 KHz) had listeners quickly tuning back and forth throughout the day. As stations became plentiful, most occupying 360 meters, overlap became a problem. Stations had to vary their power throughout the day and night to avoid this, often without success.

The equipment that radio stations used was nascent technology in the early 1920s. When WLW went on the air in 1922, a broadcast engineer later noted that just staying on one frequency was impossible with early broadcast transmitters. The signal would drift up to 10 meters in either direction of 360 meters (810-850 KHz). The government eventually acquiesced and spread stations out across the now familiar AM radio dial. The only survivor from these early days in radio is the NOAA Weather Radio network, which maintains more than 750 transmitters and covers nearly 90% of the 50 states.

Radio had great potential, anybody could see that – including the newspapers. They saw doom and gloom ahead because their newspapers were being read on the air – without financial reward – though the real decline of newspapers happened later in the decade. Some publishers saw dollar signs instead and invested in radio to sell more copies. By the end of 1922, about 10% of the 570 stations in the U.S. were owned or controlled by publishing companies.

Today, media cross-ownership is as prevalent as ever, especially with television, the internet, and streaming mediums. Radio isn't as relevant as it was in the 20th century, but it's still alive and kicking. Edison Research says that 87% of all in-car ad-supported listening is traditional radio. 45% of all radio listening occurs in cars, 32% at home and 23% at work. The most listened to time period is mid-day (M-F 10 AM - 3 PM) which is about 27% of all radio listening. I hope there is still a big audience for that most important broadcast of the day: Bedtime story for the kiddies.

SOUND FARMING

Today's farm is not at all like your grandfather's farm. It's a high-stakes business for farmers who expect high-yields. And what's driving up those yields? Technology. Since the Newcomen steam engine of the late 1700s, the agriculture industry has been progressively adopting new technology and science to feed the world. And now high-tech farming is getting even more high-tech. Farmers are using exciting new sound technologies and practices to coax more out of their crops, keep their livestock happy, and keep themselves safe.

The smartphone is a ubiquitous device that's as easily at home at the stock exchange on Wall Street as a stock yard in Wyoming. With one swipe, farmers can monitor livestock health in real time, get immediate data on soil nutrients and moisture, and even be notified when a cow is about to give birth. These advanced technologies rely on cameras and sensors. Adding microphones to data collection opens up a whole new level of connected innovation for farmers.

An exciting new technology that Dutch and Canadian scientists are very close to implementing listens to pigs to determine how they feel. You read that right, they're trying to read a pig's emotions by listening to their squeals. "I am convinced we will see the mental state of animals being monitored on a commercial basis in the next few years," says Daniel Berkmanns, a bioengineering professor at KU Leuven in Belgium. He goes on to explain, "Pigs are intelligent animals, and we should use their intelligence. If you put animals in a pen they will behave like stupid animals, but if we recognize that they are individuals with different needs and responses, we can react accordingly. It will enable us to make things more interesting for them and us, and potentially result in better outcomes." Those better outcomes are healthier and happier animals.

At the University at Ghent in Belgium, researchers are using sound analysis to detect disease in pigs very early. "Most disease in pigs is respiratory. With some diseases you can detect signs just three hours after infection," Berkmanns said about the burgeoning technology. "The system detects a sick cough and sends an SMS message to the farmer, who can go out and decide if they need to call a vet. This kind of system reduces the use of antibiotics on a farm."

Another study by a multi-international team in Europe defined pig grunts succinctly: "There are clear differences in pig calls when we look at positive and negative situations" said Elodie Briefer. She co-led the study and is an Associate Professor of the University of Copenhagen's Department of Biology. "In the positive situations, the calls are far shorter, with minor fluctuations in amplitude. Grunts, more specifically, begin high and gradually go lower in frequency. By training an algorithm to recognize these sounds, we can classify 92% of the calls to the correct emotion," Briefer explained. The research team recorded 7,414 sounds from 411 pigs in different scenarios, from birth to death.

Sound and farm animals may go together like Oreos and milk. Farmers have been playing music to milk cows for some time now. Many swear by the results, and it appears research has backed them up. In the UK, the University of Leicester conducted a study that found cows prefer slow music, like Simon and Garfunkel's "Bridge Over Troubled Water" and Beethoven's "Pastoral Symphony" If milk cows have a low stress level, their milk production increases.

If they become stressed, like when listening to fast music (100 beats per minute or faster), their milk levels decrease.

How about music and crops? Studies have shown that house plants do indeed respond to music with more growth. Jazz and classical music with tones between 115 - 250 Hz a few hours a day seem to be optimum for plant health. Scientists think that frequency range is similar to the natural world, and in particular the sound of running water. This method may work in greenhouses, but blasting Charlie Parker's "Yardbird Suite" to acres and acres of crops isn't feasible for most farmers. Instead, they play sounds of birds.

There's no sound more frightening to a bird than that of a hawk dive-bombing toward them for the kill. That's what the makers of Bird Gard hope. The battle between farmers and birds has been long fought. Scarecrows, tin pans on stakes, netting, and other marginally effective solutions have been employed for years. But now farmers are strategically placing Auditory Deterrent Devices (ADD) around their fields that emit species-specific distress calls along with war cries of various birds of prey. Bird Guard can customize the units to a farmer's crop, industry, or problem bird. ADDs can also be used to deter deer from crops, seals from salmon farms, and bats from turbines. A propane canon, another ADD device, is also frequently used. These are very controversial because they let out a random thundering boom that scatters birds. They only work for so long, however. In time, birds seem to ignore the blasts. People however, don't.

And finally, noise pollution and exposure awareness are slowly making inroads to farms. A growing number of agriculture workers are using more hearing protection while operating large machinery and high-decibel tools. A large combine operated with the cabin closed can still generate sound levels equal to a typical gas-powered lawn mower. Sustained exposure over long periods is as damaging to hearing as short bursts of sounds like explosions. The Australian Parliament commissioned a report, "Extent and cause of hearing loss impairment in Australia" (2008-2010), that revealed the agricultural sector of farming has high levels of hearing loss. Australian farmers have 65% measurable hearing loss compared to 22-27 % of the general population. The data also found that young farmers have more hearing loss compared to the general population, and it occurs 10-15 years earlier.

All these recent developments just go to show you how tech-savvy and forward-thinking farmers are. New technology and methods are helping to create herds that are happy, crops that are content, and farmers that are fulfilled. The next frontier is psychology. Farmers must figure out how to get all those stress-free cows to counsel the pigs when they're blue.

IS THE WAX CYLINDER THE NEXT BIG THING?

If we look back over the last 140 years of sound recording, it seems that formats come and formats...come back. I've written many times about nearly dead technologies that seemingly get resurrected out of nowhere, such as the vinyl record, the cassette, and AM radio. The younger generations are partly responsible for breathing new life into these old formats, but most stand on their own merits.

Vinyl records have an aesthetic appeal. It can be held in your hand. If you look closely at the grooves, you can literally see the sound. Loud, busy sections are very compact, while slow, legato passages are spaced far apart. It's like stepping in close to a Rembrandt painting to see the brush marks. When you play a record, you take an active part in listening. You must clean the surface, place the needle in the groove, and turn the record over to hear the other side. The sound of a record played on a good audio system has a distinct purity to it. Apart from the scratches (which sometimes add character and flavor), the sound can be less harsh than a digital version. The continuous sound of the stylus' friction in the bottom of the groove brings warmth. Plus, records are like animals presumed to be extinct, roaming the earth until someone rediscovers their existence. There are thousands and thousands of recordings that never made the transition to a digital format. They're hiding in some basement, yard sale, or record bin just waiting to be found.

The new fascination with cassettes is a bit curious to me. This was a format born for convenience, not quality. As reel-to-reel recorders shrunk in the 1950s and 60s, the play time of an audio reel did too. For the home user, 5- and 7-inch reels became popular over the larger 10-inch reels. The diminutive 5-inch reel usually held 30-45 minutes per side (or 60-90 minutes if an ultra-slow speed was available), but most of these consumer-oriented units only recorded mono sound. They were great for documenting family events or to send "audio letters" across the country (see my article in this chapter "Audio Letters to Home" about families and GIs during the Vietnam War). But having to thread a fidgety tape onto a plastic reel just to listen to music was cumbersome.

The small compact cassette was the ideal replacement for open reels when it came along in the mid-1960s. It could be quickly loaded in a player and started. It held up to 90-minutes of stereo music (later 120-minutes with thinner tape), but the sound quality was inferior to reel-to-reel. No matter, consumers loved the portability and economics of cassettes. By the time cassette technology matured and the quality of recordings got better, they couldn't compete with the new kid on the block: the audio CD. This newfound interest in cassettes, especially by bands that release their music on them, has me flummoxed. There is only one manufacturer of cassette tape in the world, which leads enthusiasts on the hunt for NOS (new old stock), there are no high-quality recorders being made anymore, and nobody really loved the sound of cassettes when they were ubiquitous. We just accepted them as a convenient shuttle format to get from point A to point B. The only reasons I can come up with for their renewed popularity are: It can be held in the hand; It's a unique calling card; The "mixtape" is a hands-on love letter to music; And the discovery of NOS is intoxicating. If those are the only reasons, then I get it. But if it's for the sound...

More recent formats that may or may not be poised for a comeback someday are the audio CD and the mp3. Invented in the 1960s and brought to market in the 80s, the CD is currently on life support. I'm not sure it will have as large of a comeback as the LP, but it is a physical format that can be held in the hand. The mp3 file is a stubborn format that won't go away despite many superior alternatives. They are to a CD what cassettes were to reel-to-reels: convenient, compact, but woefully inferior. Maybe twenty-years from now it will be "cool" to "email" an mp3 to friends that have a "desktop" computer with *Windows 95* and "speakers" to hear it on.

As if we are downgrading our expectations even more, the latest format that is getting some new attention is the wax cylinder. Are you cringing at the thought of having to go find an Edison Gem phonograph player to hear the latest Billie Eilish single? Don't worry, most of the effort at raising the dead is for preservation, although there is one band that has released new music on wax cylinder. Nameless Dreamers is a collaboration between Equip and R23X. Their music is reminiscent of a video game, maybe because they're both game music composers. Even their website[136] is an homage to retro games. In 2021, they released two songs[137] on 4-minute wax cylinders. YouTube vintage audio guru Matt Taylor (a.k.a. Techmoan)[138] recently demonstrated an Edison Gem phonograph player by playing one of the songs.[139]

But Nameless Dreamers' tunes aren't the first to be released since the early 20th century. In 2013, Justin Martell and Benjamin Canady released 50 cylinders of Tiny Tim's 1979 performance of "Nobody Else Can Love Me (Like My Old Tomato Can)." The release fit right in with Tiny Tim's style of performing tunes from the early days of the phonograph. Others have been trying it as well, like this heavy metal band recording[140] in 2018 (shouldn't that be heavy wax?). If you want to release a new tune on wax, or buy century-old tunes re-recorded onto new wax cylinders, there are still a few companies providing this service. The Vulcan Cylinder Record Company[141] in Sheffield, England has a catalog of old recordings that you can impress your friends with on your renovated player.

Early phonograph recordings are the target for digital restoration by the New York Public Library. It had digitized only 6% of its 2,700 cylinder collection before it recently received the

---

[136] Nameless Dreamers: https://namelessdreamers.neocities.org/

[137] "The Yetee" on wax: https://theyetee.com/collections/nameless-dreamers

[138] Techmoan Channel on YouTube: https://www.youtube.com/channel/UC5I2hjZYiW9gZPVkvzM8_Cw

[139] Edison Gem: https://www.youtube.com/watch?v=HWtOAWWY010

[140] Heavy Metal on wax: https://www.youtube.com/watch?v=fR4BuM6dP44&t=59s

[141] Vulcan Cylinder Record Company: https://www.vulcanrecords.com/

Endpoint Audio Labs cylinder playback machine. Designed by Nicholas Bergh, the machine reads the grooves on the outside of the cylinder with a laser, rather than a traditional needle and modulator. The software smooths out the imperfections of the cylinder rotation that cause "wow," and cleans up surface noise and scratches. The usual erosion of the groove is avoided since no mechanical device actually touches the surface. You can hear a restored recording on this SoundCloud link.[142] Another option for historians is a modern phonograph player from Mechanical Concepts.[143] With an electric motor (instead of a hand-cranked spring motor on the original), it allows the use of a modern cartridge and stylus.

Why preserve these old recordings? Why not! These first recordings are a part of human history. We can hear the voices of important people, long-forgotten musical styles, and incredible performances. We can study the material to better understand how this new media influenced society, and how it helped shape future recordings. And you never know, we might discover a new recording star, a hundred years in the making!

SOFAR SO GOOD

As terrible as war is, it often brings scientific discoveries to the masses in peacetime. One such discovery from World War II is the Sound Fixing and Ranging channel, or SOFAR channel for short. It's not a TV channel, but an ocean channel. In 1944, geophysicist Maurice Ewing discovered a hidden horizontal oceanic layer about 1,000 meters (3,300 feet) deep under the ocean's surface. It's

---

[142] Endpoint Audio Labs cylinder playback machine:
https://soundcloud.com/user-99391671/frieda-hempels-evviva-la-
francia?utm_source=clipboard&utm_campaign=wtshare&utm_medium=widget
&utm_content=https%253A%252F%252Fsoundcloud.com%252Fuser-
99391671%252Ffrieda-hempels-evviva-la-francia

[143] Mechanical Concepts: https://www.mechconcepts.com/phonograph.html

sandwiched between warm, less salty and lighter upper waters, and cooler, more salty denser lower waters. What's unique about this layer is its ability to trap sound waves and channel them over vast distances.

The sounds that are trapped are very low frequencies (infrasound), mostly from explosions, eruptions, and earthquakes. These infrasounds travel very slowly along the channel, staying within the upper and lower boundaries, much like a boat cruising through a canal. Sounds are heard by dropping a hydrophone (a microphone that works under water) into this channel.

In the first tests of SOFAR in 1944, scientists clearly heard a controlled explosion more than 900 miles away. During the war and since, the SOFAR channel is used by navies to listen for submarines, by oceanographers to listen for whales, and by geologists to listen for volcanic eruptions and earthquakes. It's difficult to pinpoint the location of infrasound events because the SOFAR channel slows sound waves down, so data from several monitoring stations is used for triangulation.

Ewing also theorized that the atmosphere may have its own SOFAR channel. After the war, he headed up a top-secret mission named Project Mogul that was tasked with listening for Soviet nuclear weapon atmospheric tests. The search started in the tropopause, the boundary between the lower troposphere and upper stratosphere. The tropopause is about 10 to 20 kilometers above the earth's surface (33,000 and 65,000 feet). The tropopause is thought to behave similar to the ocean's SOFAR channel, trapping infrasounds within its boundaries.

Project Mogul was so secret, that records of its existence didn't materialize for 50 years after it's inception. The project was short-lived, but one of its experiments fueled one of the most famous conspiracy theories in human history – the Roswell UFO crash. In 1947, one of Project Mogul's balloons crashed near Roswell, New Mexico. What followed was a back-and-forth by the Army and government officials with the press, first admitting that a "flying disc" crashed, then denial. The news articles with the picture of an Army officer kneeling next to a shredded silver balloon carcass seem to back up what Project Mogul was all about – determining "the velocity and direction of winds at high altitude."

Now the search for an airborne SOFAR channel has been resurrected, in New Mexico of all places. Sarah Albert, a geophysicist at Sandia National Laboratories, uses solar-powered balloons with wireless telemetry that can float within the tropopause, listening for distant sounds. In April of 2021, Albert's team released a test balloon in Albuquerque, New Mexico and successfully captured the sound of the launch of Blue Origin's New Shepard rocket 250 miles away in Texas. It was the first verified instance of detecting distant infrasounds in the atmosphere while airborne.

They also heard a sound of unknown origin that repeated several times an hour. A later experiment with another rocket launch was unsuccessful. These inconsistent results have scientists theorizing that the SOFAR channel in the atmosphere is not always present. It may also be susceptible to drastic changes from winds, temperature variations, and the delicacy of the atmosphere. Fundamental principles of physics support this theory: Sound travels more efficiently through water and solids; Air, especially at 60,000 feet, is very thin and highly inefficient in carrying sounds.

Sarah Albert is convinced that the atmo-SOFAR channel exists, but is not as stable as the oceanic SOFAR channel. Experiments are ongoing to determine the best altitudes and conditions for using the atmo-SOFAR channel effectively. Another tool to detect and warn of a distant catastrophe can only benefit our planet. Who knows, the atmo-SOFAR channel may warn us of of an honest-to-goodness visit from a flying saucer.

PSSST!

During the American Revolution, patriot spies sent secret coded messages to each other through several means: newspaper advertisements, invisible ink or code words buried within innocent-looking letters, and even carefully arranged laundry on a clothesline. These messages that are in plain sight, but undetectable to the casual observer, are often mistakenly called subliminal messages. But they are in fact supraliminal messages - hidden in plain sight and detectable if one knows where to look.

There is a fine threshold between conscious and unconscious detection of stimuli. Subliminal stimuli is below the level of conscious detection, only affecting the subconscious. It can't be recognized, even when deliberately searching for it. Subliminal messaging is often intentionally directed at the subconscious to elicit a response or action that a person wouldn't normally do.

An example of subliminal stimuli can be found in my recording studios. We deliberately painted our walls a neutral gray so that any color would pop out. We carefully chose red chairs in our waiting area so that customers would immediately perceive a sense of energy and creativity.

The front lobby of Dynamix Productions. Ella Fitzgeraldine greets clients.

We then carried that theme to our control rooms with hanging red lamps over the producers' desks. In our recording booths, we lined the back walls with cool blue lights, which elicits a calming effect for the talent. Almost every person that walks into a booth for the first-time exhales contentedly and says "Wow," or some other pleasing remark. Supraliminal messages we employ are reel-to-reels, artwork, and other elements that outwardly suggest we are a creative business.

Studio A

Subliminal stimuli is also found in soundtracks: Choosing major or minor musical keys to manipulate mood, matching instruments with character personas, using drones to build tension, layering animal sounds with man-made ones to personify machines, the list goes on. Sound designers are usually trying to, frankly, manipulate the listener. We like to think the listener is a blank slate when they begin the experience of a movie or song. By controlling their mood with sounds, we can either lead the listener down a false path so that an upcoming event will have more impact (think of a surprise scare in a horror film), or leading the listener down a single emotional path (think new age music or ASMR).

Supraliminal messaging (not subliminal messaging) can be found in advertising, crowd control, etc. For instance, flashing a frame or two of a bucket of popcorn or soft drink during a movie to entice a purchase at the snack counter. Softly spoken suggestions to not steal merchandise under background music in a store is another tactic. What researchers have found is that supraliminal messaging can't necessarily jolt someone into doing something they aren't already considering, but it can influence an existing desire. A British experiment displayed German and French wines together that were similar in style and price. On alternating days, the supermarket played French music and German music. On days that German music played, those wines increased in sales, and vice versa for the French wines.

Advertising and business seem to be the most enthusiastic about using subliminal and supraliminal messaging. But it has found its way into music. A few examples are often referenced. The Beatles intentionally used backmasking (a recording is played backwards to reveal forward-playing sound, like speech or music) in 1968's "I'm So Tired" as a response to crazy fan theories that Paul McCartney died and had been replaced with a double. But Led Zeppelin fought off theories that "Stairway to Heaven," when played backwards, exalted Satan.

I would argue that messages found by playing records backwards aren't subliminal or supraliminal messages, they're really Easter eggs. Humans just aren't particularly good at deciphering backwards speech unless highly trained. This is true of any art form that one must actively decode in order to find any real or perceived messages that may or may not be hidden. When subjective interpretation is involved, like in "Stairway to Heaven," one's emotional state and cultural influences must also be taken into consideration. I'm guessing many of the bands that purposefully put vague, quasi-demonic messages in their music were probably having a big laugh and enjoying all the buzz about it.

Sometimes hidden messages cross art forms. The Silent Hill horror media franchise recently released a teaser trailer that included a message that can only be decoded by viewing its audio spectrogram. This clever blend of sound and visual art had fans buzzing once it was discovered by an eagle-eared observer.

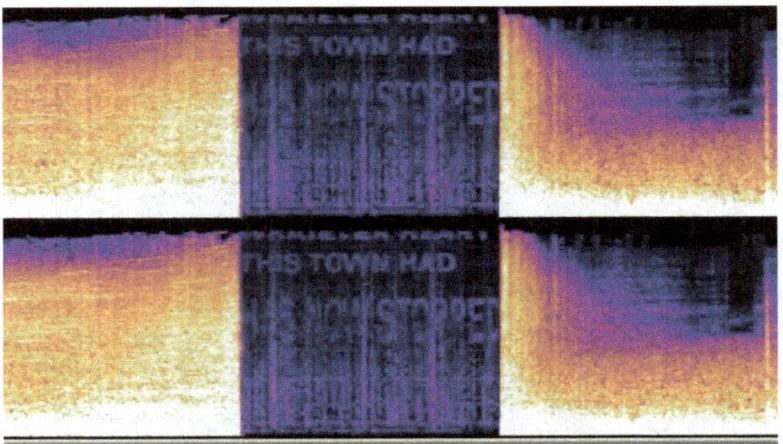

Keeping with spooky themes, I tried my own spectrogram message in Sonny Rollins' "Friday the 13th".

Artists, from filmmakers and painters, to writers, sculptors, architects, and musicians have been toying with us for eons.

- Michaelangelo hid the human brain in God's cloak in his Sistine Chapel masterpiece.
- Leonardo Da Vinci painted his initials in Mona Lisa's right eye.
- Film director David Fincher placed Starbucks coffee cups in every *Fight Club* scene, and used the name Tyler Durden, Brad Pitt's character from that movie, in *The Social Network*.
- Steven Spielberg hid *Star Wars'* R2-D2 and C-3PO as hieroglyphs in *Raiders of the Lost Ark*.

- One World Trade Center in New York is exactly 1,776 feet tall to the top mast (referencing the American Revolution), with the height of the building itself being 1,362 feet, the measurements of the original twin towers.
- The World War II memorial in Washington, D.C. has "Kilroy was here" graffiti, popular during the war, in two places.
- Washington, D.C. designer Pierre Charles L'Enfant placed the Capitol building exactly in the center of our capital.

For as long as there is art, there will be secret, subliminal, and supraliminal messages hidden within. The same can be said for business and advertising. Outside of direct manipulation, like online and social media companies do with our personal data, eliciting a response from a listener/viewer is always the goal. And when a secret door is found, it seems to bring a whole new meaning to that song, painting, poem, film, or building. I say, "Gyihmuck tihpeek!" (That's "Keep it coming!" backwards.)

REQUIEM OF THE BELLS

"Ding-dong, ding-dong
Ding-dong, ding-dong
Hark how the bells
Sweet silver bells
All seem to say
Throw cares away"

Peter Wilhousky / Mykola Leontovich

The month of December can be joyous, especially for holiday music lovers. Christmas tunes flow out of stores and TV sets, and holiday concerts fill December's weekends. But with Christmas being so commercialized these days, you can get pretty sick of the constant yule soundtrack. However, I have a few favorites that I never tire of: "It's the Most Wonderful Time of the Year" by Andy Williams, "Good King Wenceslas," and "Carol of the Bells." It's a little telling that two of my top picks are ancient by pop song standards. The melody of "Good King Wenceslas" was based on the 13th century Finnish carol "Tempus adest floridum" ("Eastertime has come"), and the lyrics were changed in 1853 by John Mason Neale to tell the story of the real-life 10th century Bohemian King Wenceslas.

The melody of "Carol of the Bells" is based on the very old Ukrainian New Year's folk song "Shchedryk," which means "bountiful evening." In 1914, Ukrainian composer Mykola Leontovych took the first 4 notes of "Shchedryk" that we're all so familiar with, and wrote a Christmas carol for the Ukrainian Republic Chorus. The first public performance was by students at Kiev University in 1916, but when the Soviet Union soon gained control of Ukraine, it fell out of public awareness. When the Ukrainian National Chorus toured Europe and the Americas in 1919, it became very popular with western audiences.

In the 1930s, American composer Peter J. Wilhousky, who is of Ukrainian descent, penned new lyrics for the carol. Wilhousky, who was an arranger for NBC's Symphony Orchestra, said he started off the lyrics with "Hark! How the bells" because the melody reminded him of hand bells. The carol would be heard during the Depression by millions on NBC's vast radio network. In the 1940s when several artists started to record the carol, it gained even more popularity. In 1947, Minna Louis Hohman wrote a variation based on the nativity called "Ring, Christmas Bells." Two other versions of lyrics were written in the following decades. In the 1970s, an acapella version of "Carol of the Bells" by the French vocal group The Swingle Singers was used in an André champagne television commercial. This was a very popular commercial, and I remember it well when it played every Christmas season for several years.

Now to address the white elephant in the room. The first four notes of "Carol of the Bells" are also the first four notes of Dies Irae, The Day of Wrath. Doom and gloom. The text is based on a medieval Latin poem about Judgment Day – you know, when God either delivers the saved to Heaven or casts the unsaved into Hell. That dates back to at least the 13th century, perhaps as far back as the 7th century. It was later set to Gregorian Chant, which is a simple single tone (and later polyphonic) melody. This was mostly used for Roman Catholic funeral masses.

You know the song, but you probably don't realize it. Since the 1600s, composers have been either blatantly using the melody, or sneaking parts of it into works by altering the rhythm, order of notes, or key. It's in the Dorian mode (only the white piano keys) and in 4/4. The first measure, the most famous (or infamous), comprises eight simple eighth notes. Let's sing along carolers:

G-F-G-E-F-D-E-E

'Di-es i-rae di-es il-la."

Oh no, what did you just chant?! Did you just raise the dead from the grave? Will God's wrath rain down on us?! Don't worry, you just said "Day of wrath! O day of mourning!" You can go ahead and try the melody with the English words for fun. It's quite the catchy tune, if you're into death and doom and gloom. Classical composers like Haydn snatched the melody to signal impending doom or death. In the later Romantic period, Berlioz, Liszt, Mussorgsky, Brahms, Tchaikovsky, Rachmaninoff, Mahler, and Holtz incorporated the deadly notes into their works.

When serious films began playing to audiences in the early 1900s, live music was often played to audiences before talkies came along. Contemporary music was too atonal and out of reach for most audiences, so composers fell back onto music from the Romantic era (ca. 1825-1900) for inspiration. Often highly emotive and sweeping, it seemed to easily connect the film to the audience. When talkies came along in the late 1920s and became established during the Depression, film composers like Erich Korngold looked back to greats such as Richard Wagner and his "Ring" operas for thematic melodies and leitmotifs (a recurring music phrase for a character, place or idea). Bernard Hermann followed suit and used Dies irae in the main theme for *Citizen Kane* (1941), Gerald Fried scores it in the opening theme of *Dracula Returns* (1958), Wendy Carlos and Rachel Elkind start *The Shining* (1980) with the full eight notes, and Jerry Goldsmith uses it in *Poltergeist* (1982), just to name a very few of the hundreds and hundreds of instances of its use in movies, television, theater, and games.

John Williams would look back to Korngold and Wagner when crafting his epic movie scores for *Star Wars* (1977), *Jaws* (1975),

Raiders of the Lost Ark (1981), *Home Alone* (1990), *Jurassic Park* (1993), and many others. Williams was a prolific borrower of the Dies irae theme, even incorporating it into the main theme of *Star Wars*. The shark music in *Jaws* is based on Dies irae (it starts on the second note-F-G-E-G). and in *Home Alone*, "Carol of the Bells" is being sung by a choir in church when he marvelously blends it into the "Old Man Marley" leitmotif that relies heavily on Dies irae. The notes didn't change, only the sinister accompaniment. So even John Williams heard the chilling death tune in "Carol of the Bells."

Is the old Ukrainian folk song a warning? An omen? A call for judgment day? The original "Shchedryk" was sang to welcome in a new year. But several hundred years ago in the Ukraine, the new year started in April. It can be thought of as a "rebirth," much like death and ascension into heaven. When Christianity and the Julian calendar came to the Ukraine, the new year moved to January and the song became associated with the Feast of Epiphany, a Christian celebration of the revelation. It's possible that someone carried the tune from a Roman Catholic region of Europe into the Ukraine where it was assimilated into the culture. But my guess is that it's just a big cowinkiedink. There are only 12 notes in western music, so stumbling onto the same sequence – albeit with a different rhythm – was bound to happen. I hope that when the composer had that eureka moment, they toasted everyone around them with a glass of André champagne and exclaimed, "It's a song for drinking champagne and ringing bells!

POTS AND PANS: COOKING UP STEREO

Most of us are fortunate to have two working ears. When they work together, we hear our world in stereo. From a purely scientific view, they can detect the direction a sound is coming from. Your two ears are useful for locating sounds of danger - like when your pot of soup is about to boil over as you're dicing the potatoes. But they're also useful for pleasure - like listening to a great music recording with spatial depth.

The quest for a natural sounding stereo recording is almost as old as electronic sound itself. Two-channel sound had its start in 1881 but was not really accessible to the masses. By the 1930s, Alan Blumlein at EMI had patented stereo records, film sound, and surround sound. As with most technology that's created in the lab, it's usually another decade or so before it hits the mainstream market. Stereo LPs landed in the record shops in the 1950s, and FM stereo radio rocked the 60s.

But as enticing as these new stereo delights were, they were treats only cherished by audiophiles. AM radio was how most people heard music, albeit in mono, and it drove pop record sales until the 1970s. So, it's not surprising that when records were mixed, the mono version got all the attention. The stereo version, if it even existed, was an afterthought. After all, mono sound coming from a box was normal. Most people hadn't even heard a stereo recording until the Eisenhower years (his two ears sure stood out, by the way).

How was stereo being created back then? Most stereo records being released in the 50s were often organic. That is, they were recorded with two microphones in front of the performers, usually in a concert hall or large studio. In the smaller studio, it was much easier to record straight to full-track mono because the musicians were not set up in a line like they would be on a concert stage. During studio sessions, two- and three-channel reel-to-reel recorders were sometimes used as back-ups. For instance, an engineer might place all vocals and leads on the left, and all rhythm instruments on the right. These back-ups were only there to remix the mono version if something went wrong.

In 1957, Blue Note Records wanted to start releasing studio-recorded albums in stereo. They couldn't go back into their catalog of mono recordings and just magically make them stereo, so they had to think forward. Recording technology created challenges, however. Creating a stereo master and then dubbing that down to mono created several problems, mostly generation loss and excessive tape hiss (this was before any effective noise reduction technology existed). But legendary recording engineer Rudy Van

Gelder, who recorded a wealth of their albums, came up with an efficient way to produce a stereo and mono mix at the same time.

In those days, the majority of mixing consoles that were stereo-capable only allowed the engineer to assign a channel to left, center, or right with a switch. Pan pots ("panoramic potentiometers" that were rotary knobs allowing a mono signal to be swept across the stereo field) weren't commonplace until the 1970s. So, instruments got panned hard left, hard right, or smack down the middle.

During the tracking/mixing session, Van Gelder used two recording machines and monitored in mono (he only had one speaker in the control room). The primary recorder was full-track mono. On the second, a two-track, Van Gelder assigned instruments to either left, center, or right. Since mono was king, the engineer, producer, and musicians worked on perfecting the mono version. It's important to note that in this era, Van Gelder and other engineers were recording AND mixing the sessions down to final masters on the fly!

The positioning of instruments hard-left and hard-right is a little jolting to us today. This was the mono era, so this stereo mix that's odd to us now was novel back then. It was new and different, and each instrument could be heard more discretely. But converting an entire audience to a new way of listening wasn't going to happen overnight. Even Van Gelder admits that little attention was given to the stereo field. After some experimentation, he settled on the following stereo assignment for a typical jazz quintet:

Left: trumpet < **Center**: bass, piano > **Right**: drums, sax

In the 60s, rock musicians like the Beach Boys, the Beatles, and Jimmy Hendrix started experimenting with manufactured stereo. Meanwhile, the transistor allowed mixing boards to shrink in size and the pan pot became commonplace. Engineers could now place, or "fly" sounds throughout the stereo field more easily. They could create a stereoscape that was both natural and unreal. Now they were cooking with gas! (And pan pots)

22 BAZILLION ● 2 GAZILLION

1.0, 2.0, 4.0, 5.1, 7.1, 10.2, 11.1, 22.2 – the numbers get bigger and bigger, like monsters stomping toward us. Oh no, we're surrounded! And it's a good thing!

Ever since recordings progressed from one channel (mono) into two (stereo), audio producers have been trying to create the ultimate immersive sound experience. The natural way is to add more channels, hence more speakers. But that usually comes at a cost, usually on the listener's end. If you have a surround system in your house, do you remember how much more expensive it was than a traditional stereo? Sure, you can go to a theater or theme park with a bazillion speakers for your listening pleasure. To get that same exhilarating experience at home you'll have to pay up.

Most television surround broadcasts are in 5.1, which is really six channels: a front stereo pair, a center dialog channel, a back stereo pair, and a subwoofer (the "point one" in 5.1). DVDs, Blue rays, games, and some music releases use this format. Speaker placement is somewhat critical, but I've heard systems with haphazardly placed rear speakers that are still effective. In the early days of surround, engineers mostly used the rear channels for precisely located content, like sound effects and ambience. Now, engineers try to evenly spread environmental sounds and music around the four primary speakers to immerse the listener. It's not perfect because the rear speakers are usually smaller, have reduced fidelity, and there are pronounced gaps between front and rear speakers.

OK, let's add a couple of more speakers, space them more evenly around us, and call it 7.1 surround. Most movie theaters, Blue rays, and some games are now in 7.1. Engineers are able to immerse the listener better with fewer gaps than in 5.1. Most new home theater systems come in this variety.

So far, all the speakers are line-of-sight...err...line-of-ears What about height? 10.2 surround adds four more front speakers, two of which are over the others at a 45-degree angle. One more rear channel and subwoofer are added. The 11.1 and 11.2 systems are similar in that they create height by adding overhead speakers.

These formats were designed for cinemas and are now creeping into high-end home theaters.

And then we have this new beast – 22.2. Like Godzilla, this monster surround system hails from Japan. NHK, Japan's public broadcasting network, unleashed the new system in the 2000s and have incorporated it into their new Ultra HD Television broadcast standard (UHDT transmits 4K and 8K video). What exactly is 22.2? It's three layers of sound utilizing front, side, back, and overhead speakers. With 22.2, engineers will have to learn how to place sounds in a three-dimensional space. Researchers have noted that early programs are using the three distinct layers similarly to the earliest days of stereo and 5.1, by placing specific sounds in specific locations:

Upper layer

Reverberation and ambience

Sound localized above, such as loudspeakers in gymnasiums, airplanes, and fireworks shows

Middle layer
The anchor layer of the basic sound field, including surround environments

Lower layer

Sounds of water such as the sea, rivers, and drops of water

Sound on the ground in scenes with bird's-eye views

Though still in its infancy, it will probably become the next standard because as of 2016, 6 million 4K TV sets have been sold, and there are already more than forty 4K TV channels worldwide. Is 22.2 surround sound just a fanciful idea? Apparently not, as major heavy weight broadcasting organizations around the world are testing and standardizing its incorporation into their new UHDT schemes.

The big question though, is "Will I ever have one in my home?" Probably not, unless I hit the lottery. I don't think the average home theater will for some time either because sound systems are really just another piece of furniture. Correctly installing a surround system is already a big commitment, I can't imagine having to deal with 24 speakers. Besides, I've rearranged my living room a few times in the last five years, and I'm not about to also move 24 speakers. My guess is that the format will just filter cinema movies down to those lucky enough to have 22.4 in their home. Remember how excited we were that DVDs would have multi-angle camera views, soundtracks in twenty-two languages, and multiple story lines? Didn't happen. Too much work. Like moving furniture.

INDEX

PHOTO CREDITS

All photos courtesy of the author, unless noted below:

Photo 1. Photo by Ingo Schulz, Unsplash

Photo 2. Frans Dobbelaar and Peter Lankhaar

Photo 3, 4. Photo by Post Time Productions, Lexington, KY.

Photo 5. Photo by Erol Ahmed, Unsplash, modified by the author.

Photo 6. Public domain

Photo 7. Olli Niemitalo

Photo 8. Library of Congress's Prints and Photographs division, public domain

Photo 9. Library of Congress, public domain

Photo 10. TV Guide, public domain

Photo 11. Creative Commons, public domain

Photo 12. Library of Congress, public domain

Photo 13. William E. Garity, John N. A. Hawkins, Journal of the Society of Motion Pictures Engineers, public domain

Photo 14. Creative Commons license: ttps://commons.wikimedia.org/wiki/File:35mm_film_audio_macro.jpg

Photos 15, 16. Public domain

ACKNOWLEDGEMENTS

There are so many mentors, co-workers, family members, teachers, and students who have helped shape who I am, both personally and professionally. I've probably left a few people out, and for that I'm sorry. However, a few people have been instrumental in helping me finish this book. First of all my daughter Mara who has shouldered the load of keeping my business going, reading my essays, correcting my mistakes, and giving me encouragement.

I also have to thank Kathie Stamps, a Jill of all trades when it comes to creativity. Her expertise in writing coupled with audio engineering, producing, announcing, and directing gives her a rare insight into our world. She has continually encouraged me to keep going and finish this gargantuan task.

Dane Dickmann and I first met when he was a student at the University of Kentucky. He interned with me and then worked in my studios for several years. What he accomplished as a student is stunning: recording, editing, designing and mixing a full-length movie; writing a business plan; playing gigs in a band; working in my studio; and earning his degree. He then went on to help me build our studios that include two voice-over and control rooms, custom furniture, nearly 80 custom acoustic panels, and completely new floors and paint. I tend to overexplain things, so Dane helped me chisel down and focus my teaching skills. His encouragement has been priceless.

John Campbell helped me get my job at Host Communications. I barely knew him, but he was a connection at Host that I called on to get introductions. Although we only worked together there for a few months, we continue to collaborate thirty-plus years later. John's a world-class writer and narrator, and he's also been a world-class friend. His support and cheerleading along the way has kept me on my path to success.

I also have to give thanks to two friends and colleagues that are no longer with us, Greg King and Michael Kilbourne. Greg was a great author and screenwriter, and had the voice of God. He also had my ear because he had owned businesses, including an advertising agency, for many years. Greg was an immense help when I started my business, including having my logo professionally designed. He would never take any money for that act of kindness. Greg also taught me to not worry about what other people thought of me ("F*** 'em!" as he would say). Our last project together, an audiobook for children, will always be one of my most rewarding and treasured moments in my career. Michael "Killer" Kilbourne ran the radio networks division at Host Communications before I started working there. He struck out on his own to produce videos, broadcast TV/radio commercials, and programs. He also had the voice of God. Killer used to record and produce all his own soundtracks in our studios until we went all-digital. Because he was unwilling to learn the new systems, I became the only engineer he would work with. When I revealed that I was starting my own business and had set up recording gear in my basement, he was eager to be my first customer. He continued to give me encouragement for the rest of his life.

My mother was one of the great unsung heroes of society – a teacher. Not just in the classroom, but at home, work – anywhere really. She wasn't pretentious about it, just delighted to share a little bit of knowledge or help guide someone to a new understanding. That seems to have been passed on to me. She taught me how to teach, leading by example and showing me the ropes.

My father imposed weekly teaching sessions with me. I felt special that he would take time out of his weekends just to teach me how to be self-sufficient. He would start off a Saturday morning with, "Today you're going to learn how to…" His lessons in carpentry were no doubt instrumental in allowing me to build studios.

I've been fortunate to have had many, many great students. I appreciate being pushed beyond the limits of my knowledge with great questions. If I don't know the answer, I see it as an opportunity to learn. I usually respond with, "I don't know, but let's learn together." No teacher knows everything, nor can we explain something in one way that everybody understands. I've found that if you have ten students, then you'd better have ten ways to teach something.

I've had many mentors along the way that have directly or indirectly prepared me for my career. Like Art Ferguson, the managing editor at my hometown newspaper who taught me how to be punctual. Sue Green, my high school English teacher who seriously taught me how to write. Jim Andy Caudill, my jazz instructor in college who taught me how to play music while someone is screaming in my ear. Bob Davis, an engineering wizard who taught me how to wire a studio. Ed Commons, my first real boss in this business who taught me creative nuance. Graeme Hart, an audio and video producer and voice-over artist who taught me how to produce the hell out of a radio spot. Brad Wills, a stage and voice actor who taught me how to really edit an audiobook. And my parents who taught me how to laugh at any situation, no matter how absurd.

ABOUT THE AUTHOR

Neil Kesterson has been a sound designer for film, video, television, radio, audiobooks, theatre, games, web, and multimedia since 1985. His very first sound design job was to recreate the Bell X-1 rocket plane breaking the sound barrier, of which pilot and aviation legend Chuck Yeager said was the most realistic depiction of the historic event he had ever heard.

His work has been heard on most major television and radio networks, in theaters, streaming, and in arenas. Some projects of note include the television shows *Treme* and *White Lotus* on HBO; *Mad Dogs* on Amazon; *Valley of the Boom* on NatGeo; *Chicago Fire* and *Law & Order: SVU* on NBC; *Girl from Plainville* on Hulu; and *Mind Games* and *The Crossing* on ABC.

Documentaries include *A&E Biography: The Monkees; The Lincolns in Kentucky; Nick Nolte: No Exit*; and *The Johnny Cash Anthology*, and the self-produced documentary *The Beat of a Different Drummer: The Story of America's Last All-Female Military Band*.

Motion pictures include *War for the Planet of the Apes; Uncle Frank; 8-Bit Christmas; Diary of a Wimpy Kid: Dog Days; Strange Wilderness*; and *Hide and Seek*.

Other projects of note include sound for "The Dick Vitale Alarm Clock"; comedy albums for Greg Warren and Mike Macrae; and live radio broadcast work for the NCAA, The Triple Crown Radio Network, and NPR.

Awards include those from the International Broadcasting Awards, Telly Awards, Silver Microphone Awards, the American Advertising Federation (including a lifetime achievement award), and an Emmy nomination.

Neil Kesterson was born in Ironton, Ohio. His father was the city finance director and served in Europe during WWII, and later in the Army Reserves and National Guard. His mother was a high school and university teacher, and later a university administrator and grant writer. During high school and the early days of college, Neil worked as a photojournalist for daily and school newspapers while also working as an event photographer. He continues his passion for photography today by collecting and restoring vintage cameras and selling prints. Neil went to Pikeville College (Pikeville, KY), Ohio University Southern, and the University of Kentucky, majoring in music education.

His first job in the audio industry was as a part-time announcer at WBKY-FM (now WUKY) at the University of Kentucky in 1983. In 1985 he started part-time, then later full-time at House of Commons Films in Lexington, KY. From 1989 until 2003 he managed the audio production studios at Host Communications, Inc. in Lexington. In 2003 he started his own business, Dynamix Productions, Inc., which is still in operation today.

Neil has taught, volunteered, or given lectures and crash courses at several schools including Fayette County Schools Technical School in Lexington; The University of Kentucky School of Journalism; Elkhorn Crossing School's Media Arts village in Georgetown, KY; Asbury University's Media Communications Department in Asbury, KY; and the Film Studies program at Kentucky Community and Technical College System in Lexington.

His daughter Mara Kesterson is operations manager and an audio producer at Dynamix Productions. His sister Abbe is a microbiologist.

www.neilkesterson.com/book

www.ingramcontent.com/pod-product-compliance
Lightning Source LLC
Chambersburg PA
CBHW060756120626
46557CB00001B/1